air

A HISTORY OF THE FUTURE

A HISTORY OF THE FUTURE

G. Willow Wilson Writer

M. K. Perker Artist

Chris Chuckry Colorist

Jared K. Fletcher Letterer

AIR created by Wilson and Perker

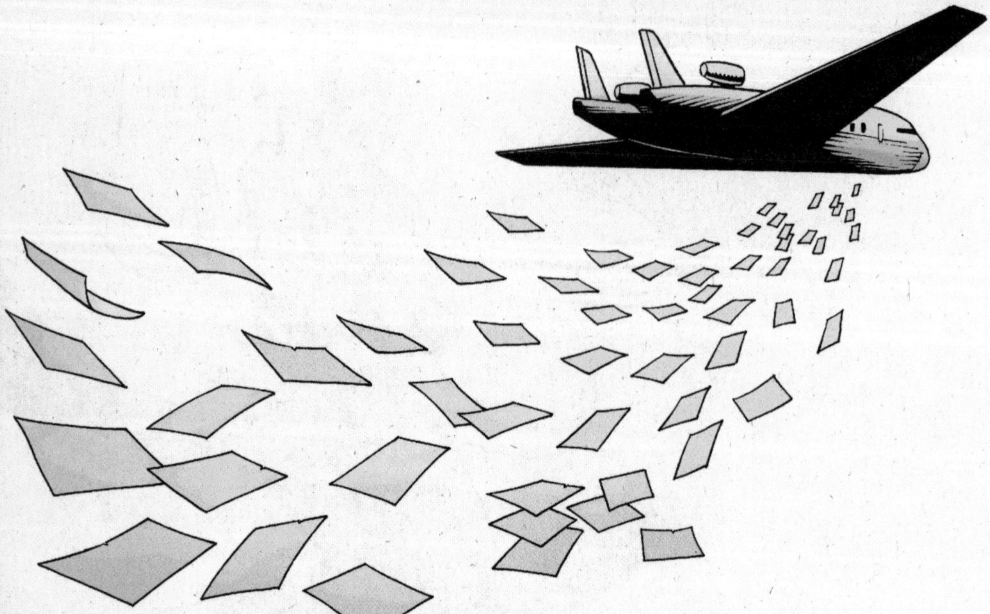

Karen Berger SVP-Executive Editor & Editor-original series
Sarah Litt Assistant Editor-original series
Bob Harras Group Editor-Collected Editions & Editor
Robbin Brosterman Design Director-Books
Louis Prandi Art Director

DC COMICS
Diane Nelson President
Dan DiDio and Jim Lee Co-Publishers
Geoff Johns Chief Creative Officer
Patrick Caldon EVP-Finance and Administration
John Rood EVP-Sales, Marketing and Business Development
Amy Genkins SVP-Business and Legal Affairs
Steve Rotterdam SVP-Sales and Marketing
John Cunningham VP-Marketing
Terri Cunningham VP-Managing Editor
Alison Gill VP-Manufacturing
David Hyde VP-Publicity
Sue Pohja VP-Book Trade Sales
Alysse Soll VP-Advertising and Custom Publishing
Bob Wayne VP-Sales
Mark Chiarello Art Director

AIR: A HISTORY OF THE FUTURE

DC Comics, 1700 Broadway, New York, NY 10019
A Warner Bros. Entertainment Company
Printed in USA. First Printing.
ISBN:978-1-4012-2983-2

SFI CERTIFIED SOURCING
Fiber used in this product line meets the sourcing requirements of the SFI program.
www.sfiprogram.org
PWC-SFICOC-260

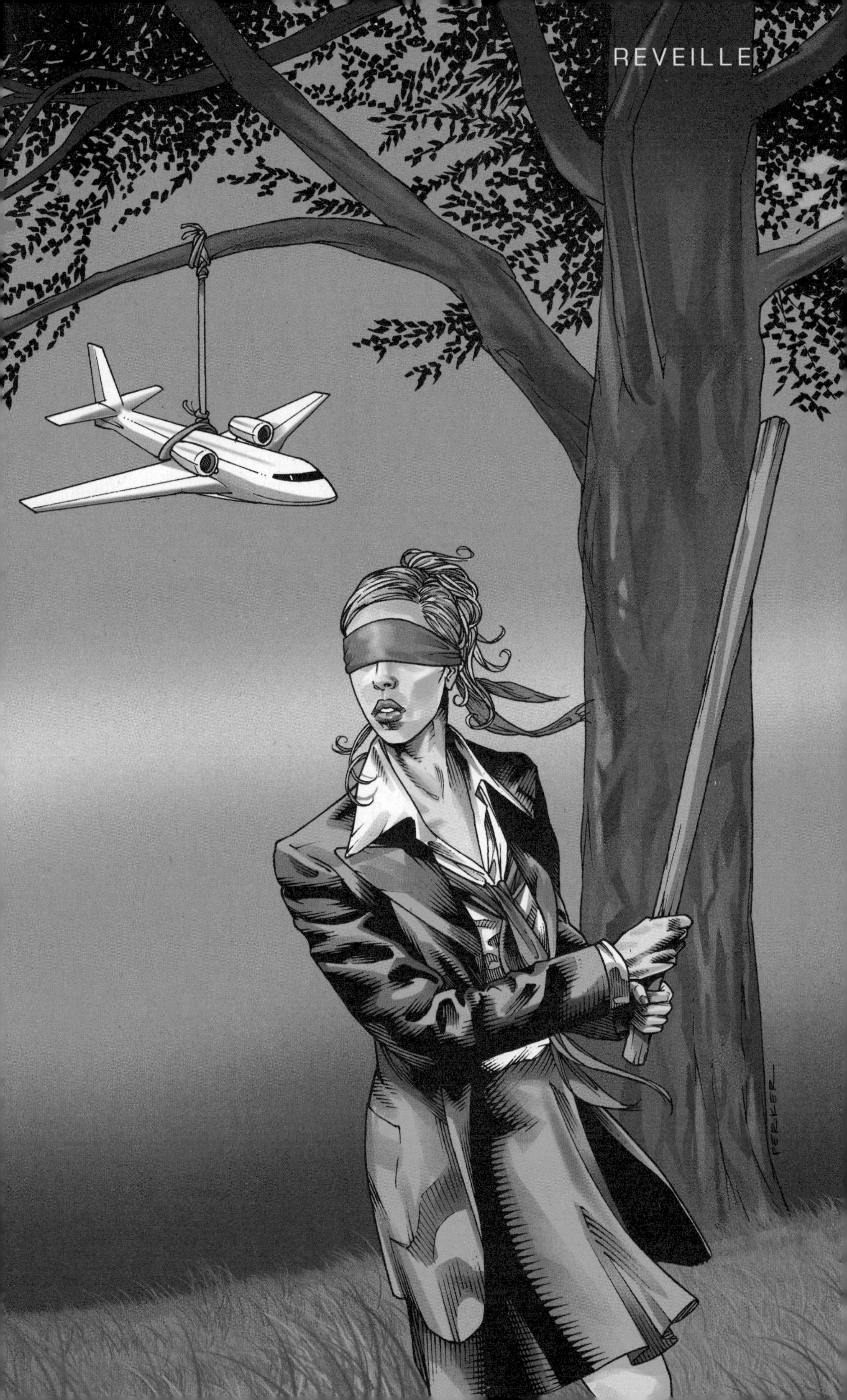
REVEILLE
PERKER

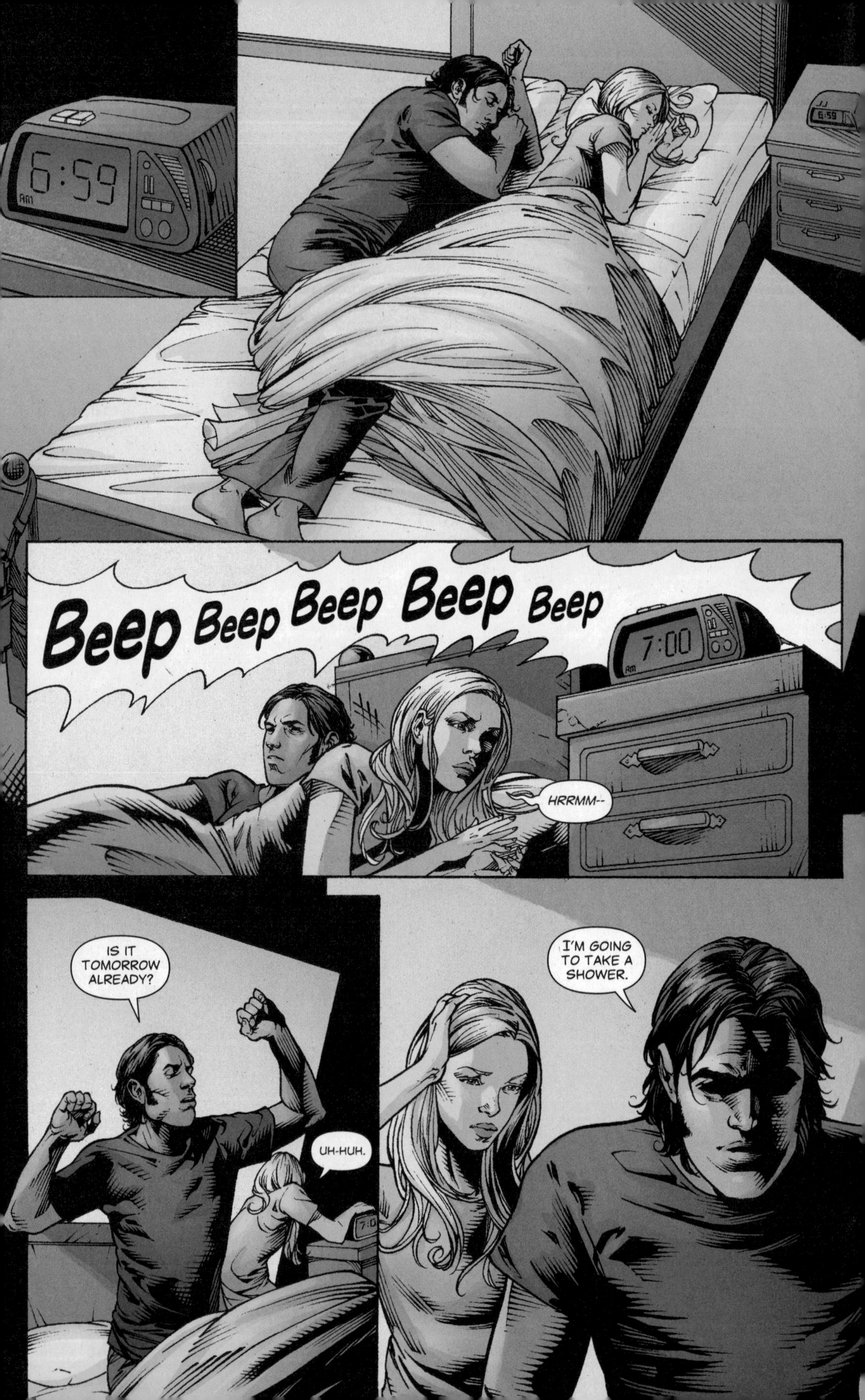
6:59
AM
6:59
Beep Beep Beep Beep Beep
7:00
AM
HRRMM--
IS IT TOMORROW ALREADY?
UH-HUH.
I'M GOING TO TAKE A SHOWER.

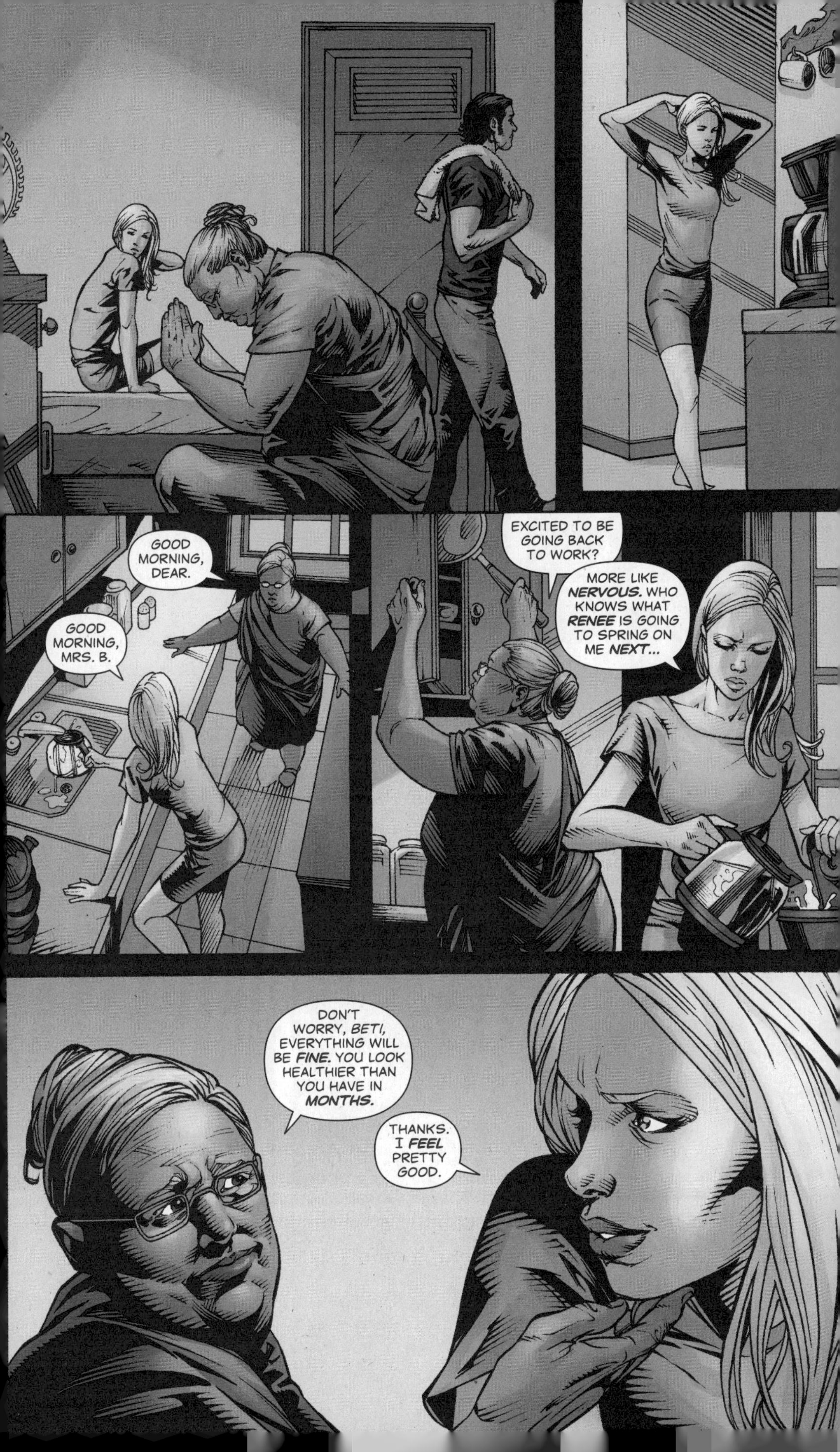
GOOD MORNING, DEAR.
GOOD MORNING, MRS. B.
EXCITED TO BE GOING BACK TO WORK?
MORE LIKE **NERVOUS.** WHO KNOWS WHAT **RENEE** IS GOING TO SPRING ON ME **NEXT...**
DON'T WORRY, *BETI*, EVERYTHING WILL BE **FINE.** YOU LOOK HEALTHIER THAN YOU HAVE IN **MONTHS.**
THANKS. I **FEEL** PRETTY GOOD.

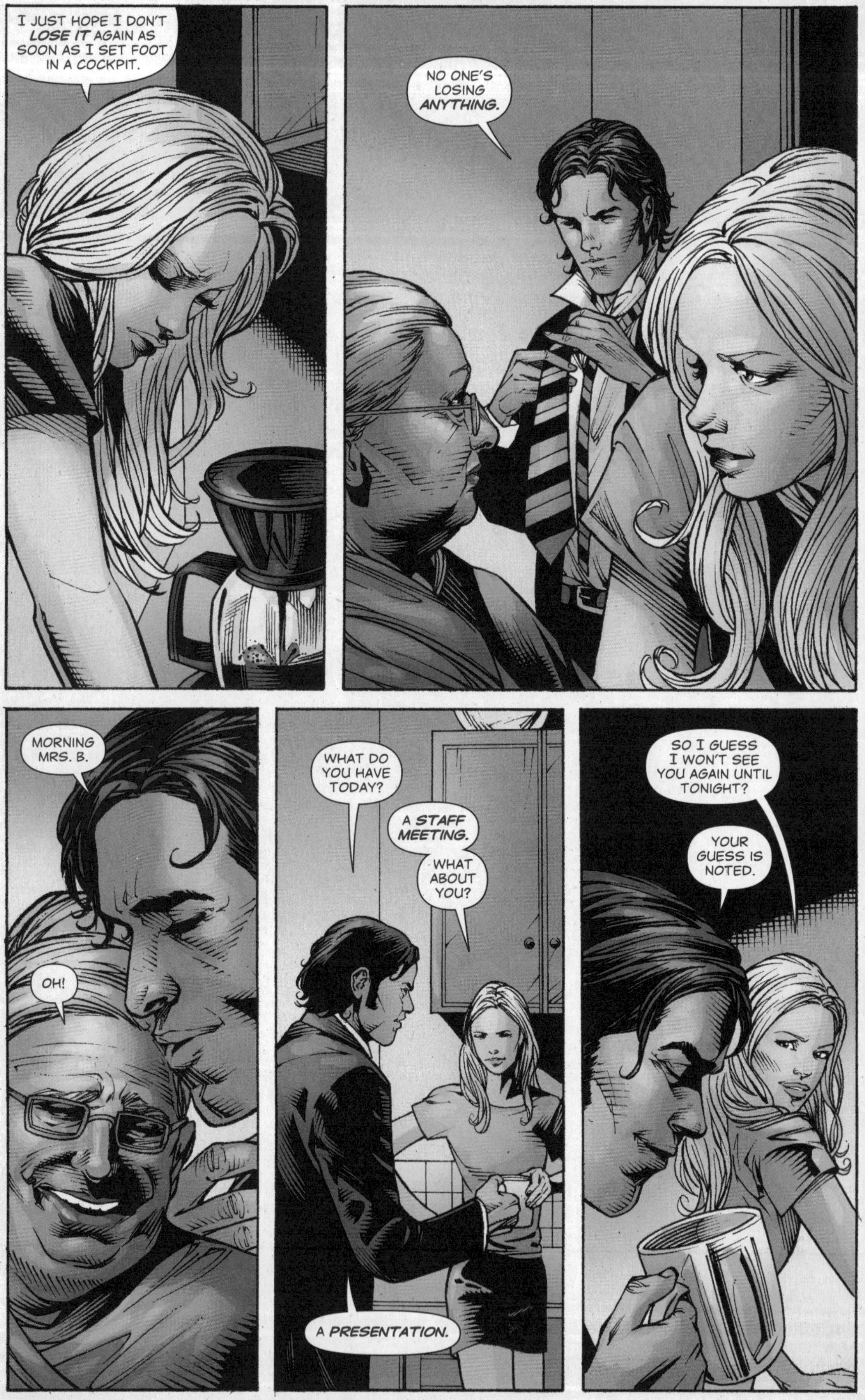
I JUST HOPE I DON'T LOSE IT AGAIN AS SOON AS I SET FOOT IN A COCKPIT.
NO ONE'S LOSING ANYTHING.
MORNING MRS. B.
OH!
WHAT DO YOU HAVE TODAY?
A STAFF MEETING.
WHAT ABOUT YOU?
A PRESENTATION.
SO I GUESS I WON'T SEE YOU AGAIN UNTIL TONIGHT?
YOUR GUESS IS NOTED.

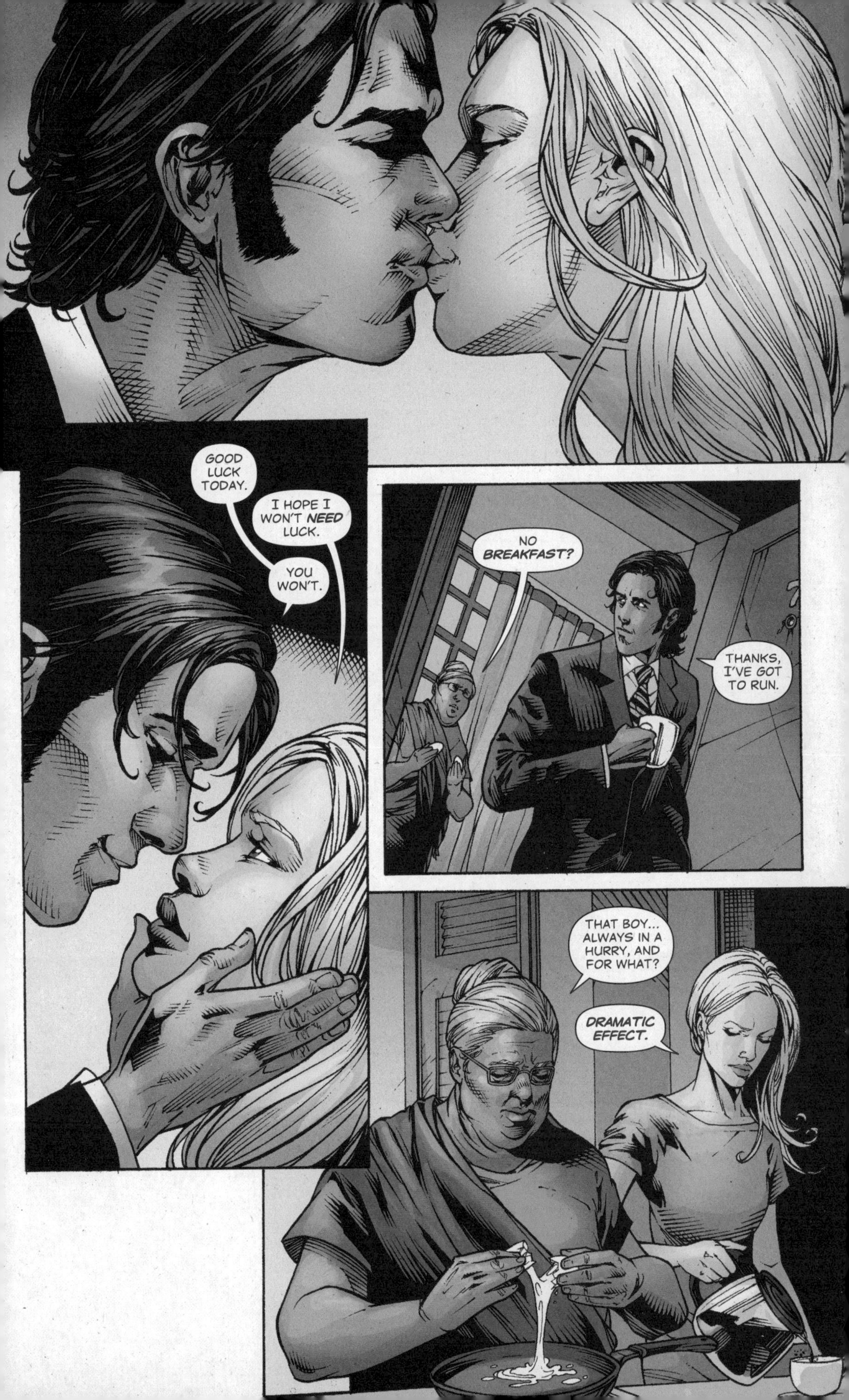
GOOD LUCK TODAY.
I HOPE I WON'T NEED LUCK.
YOU WON'T.
NO BREAKFAST?
THANKS, I'VE GOT TO RUN.
THAT BOY... ALWAYS IN A HURRY, AND FOR WHAT?
DRAMATIC EFFECT.

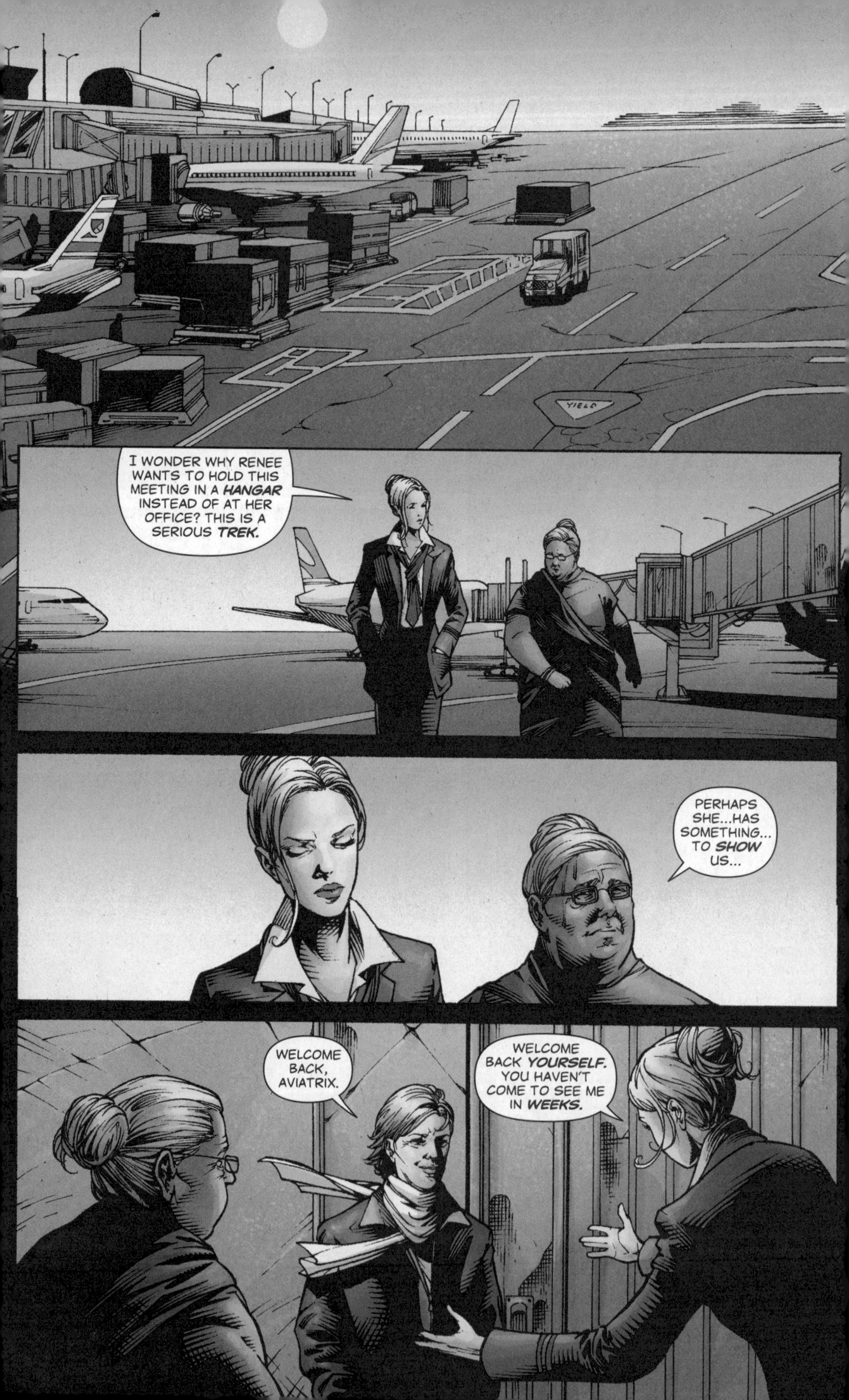
YIELD
I WONDER WHY RENEE WANTS TO HOLD THIS MEETING IN A **HANGAR** INSTEAD OF AT HER OFFICE? THIS IS A SERIOUS **TREK.**
PERHAPS SHE...HAS SOMETHING... TO **SHOW** US...
WELCOME BACK, AVIATRIX.
WELCOME BACK **YOURSELF.** YOU HAVEN'T COME TO SEE ME IN **WEEKS.**

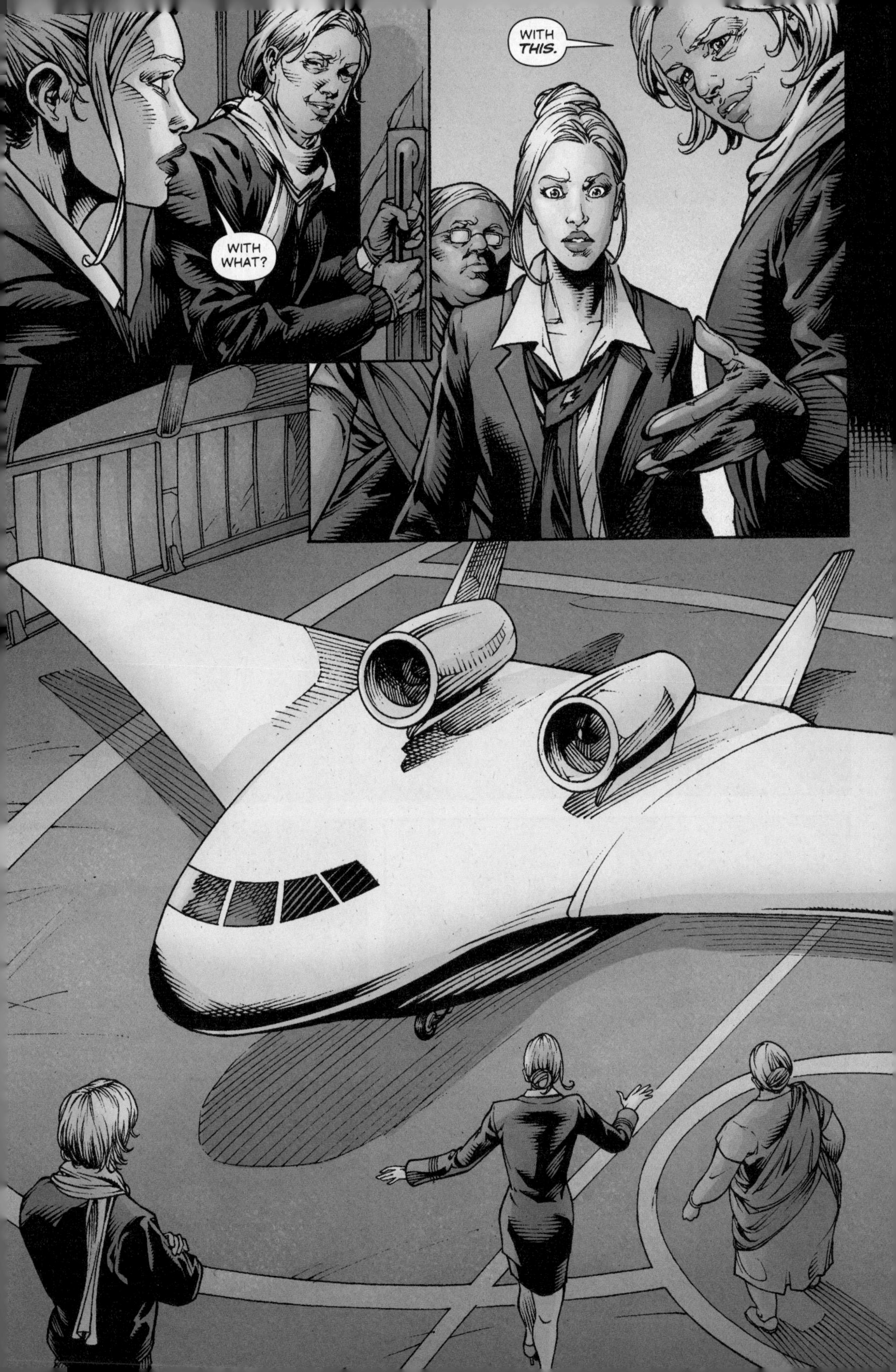
WITH WHAT?
WITH THIS.

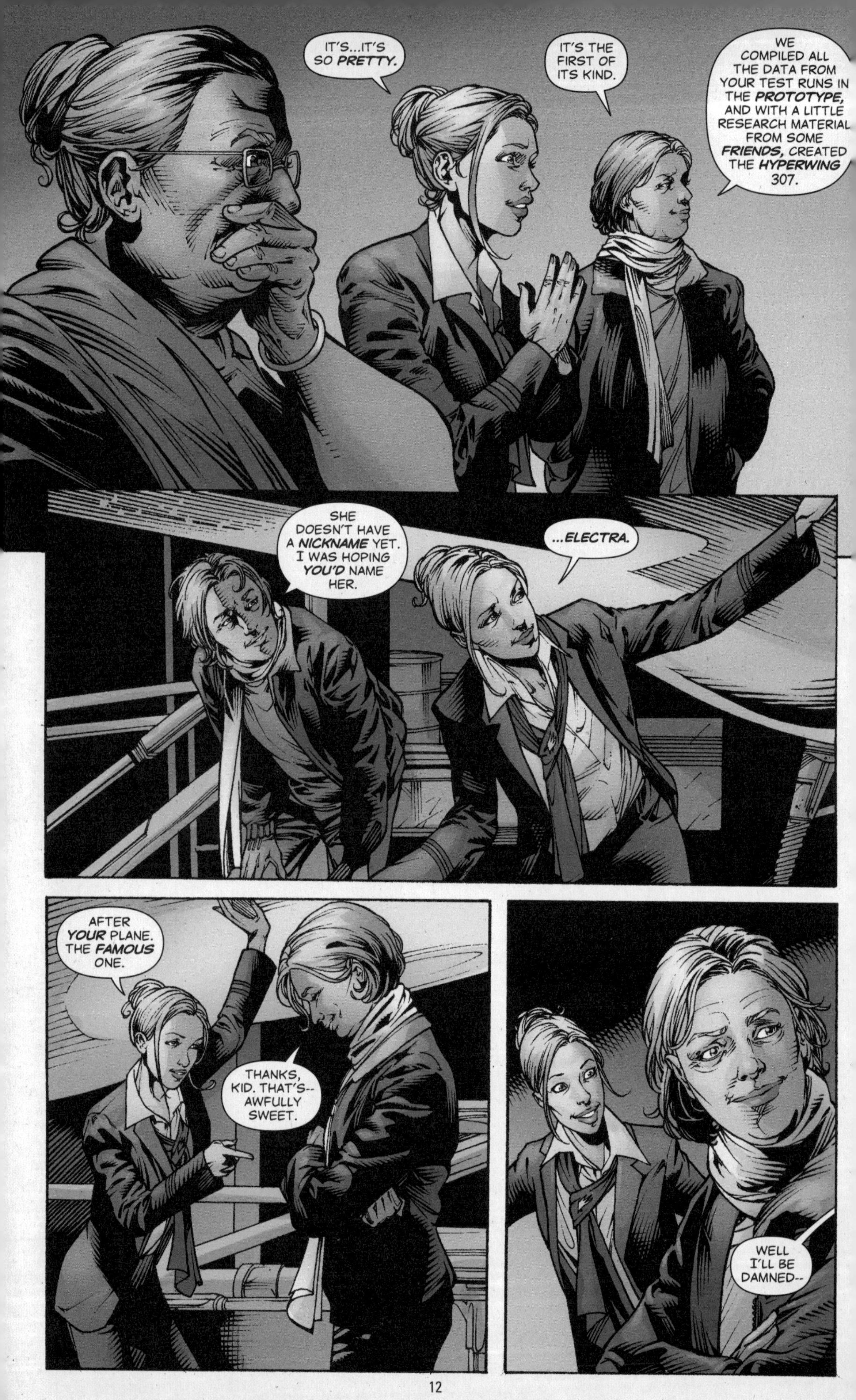
IT'S...IT'S SO PRETTY.
IT'S THE FIRST OF ITS KIND.
WE COMPILED ALL THE DATA FROM YOUR TEST RUNS IN THE PROTOTYPE, AND WITH A LITTLE RESEARCH MATERIAL FROM SOME FRIENDS, CREATED THE HYPERWING 307.
SHE DOESN'T HAVE A NICKNAME YET. I WAS HOPING YOU'D NAME HER.
...ELECTRA.
AFTER YOUR PLANE. THE FAMOUS ONE.
THANKS, KID. THAT'S-- AWFULLY SWEET.
WELL I'LL BE DAMNED--

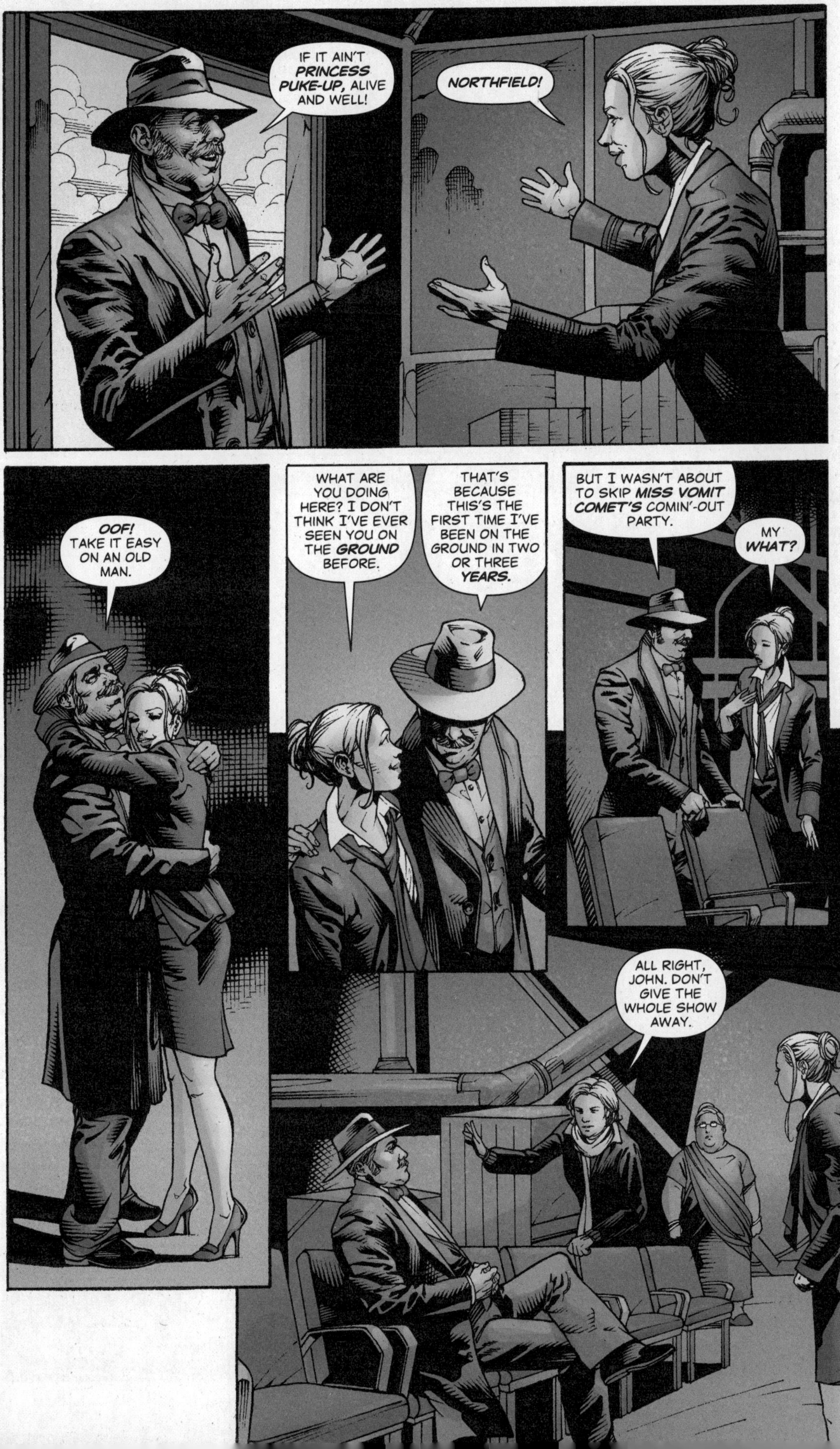
IF IT AIN'T **PRINCESS PUKE-UP,** ALIVE AND WELL!
NORTHFIELD!
OOF! TAKE IT EASY ON AN OLD MAN.
WHAT ARE YOU DOING HERE? I DON'T THINK I'VE EVER SEEN YOU ON THE **GROUND** BEFORE.
THAT'S BECAUSE THIS'S THE FIRST TIME I'VE BEEN ON THE GROUND IN TWO OR THREE **YEARS.**
BUT I WASN'T ABOUT TO SKIP **MISS VOMIT COMET'S** COMIN'-OUT PARTY.
MY **WHAT?**
ALL RIGHT, JOHN. DON'T GIVE THE WHOLE SHOW AWAY.

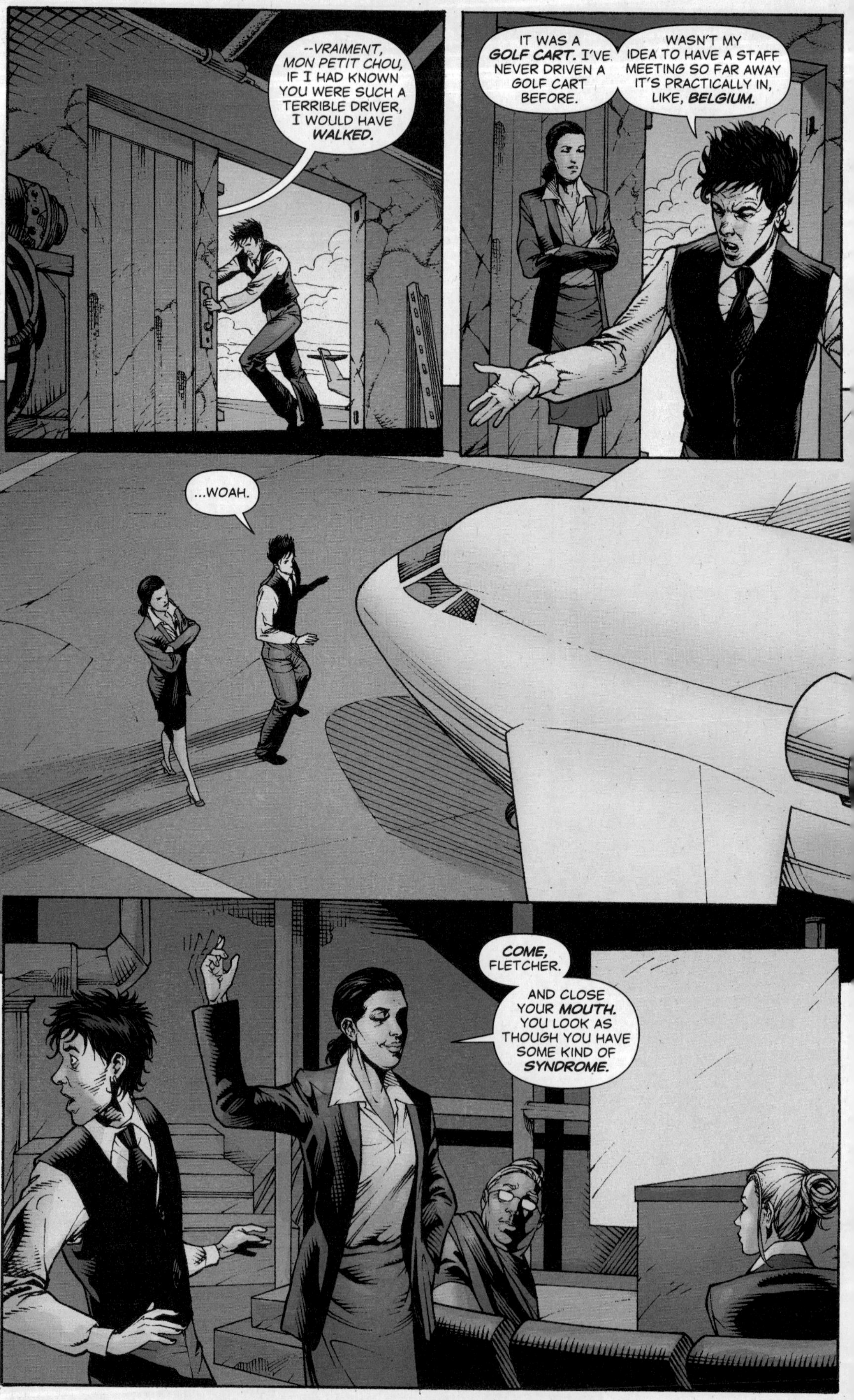
--VRAIMENT, MON PETIT CHOU, IF I HAD KNOWN YOU WERE SUCH A TERRIBLE DRIVER, I WOULD HAVE WALKED.
IT WAS A GOLF CART. I'VE NEVER DRIVEN A GOLF CART BEFORE.
WASN'T MY IDEA TO HAVE A STAFF MEETING SO FAR AWAY IT'S PRACTICALLY IN, LIKE, BELGIUM.
...WOAH.
COME, FLETCHER.
AND CLOSE YOUR MOUTH. YOU LOOK AS THOUGH YOU HAVE SOME KIND OF SYNDROME.

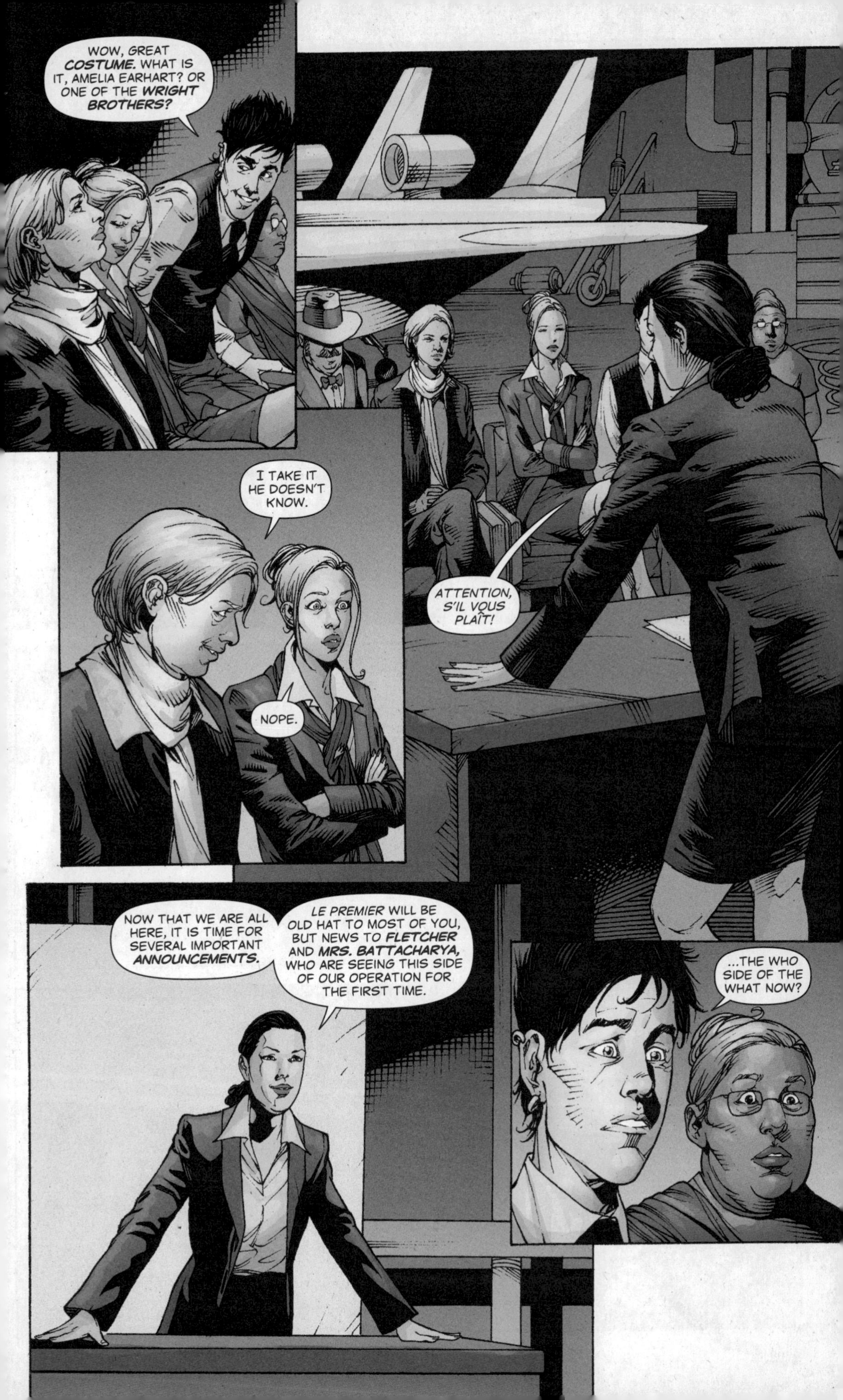
WOW, GREAT COSTUME. WHAT IS IT, AMELIA EARHART? OR ONE OF THE WRIGHT BROTHERS?
ATTENTION, S'IL VOUS PLAÎT!
I TAKE IT HE DOESN'T KNOW.
NOPE.
NOW THAT WE ARE ALL HERE, IT IS TIME FOR SEVERAL IMPORTANT ANNOUNCEMENTS.
LE PREMIER WILL BE OLD HAT TO MOST OF YOU, BUT NEWS TO FLETCHER AND MRS. BATTACHARYA, WHO ARE SEEING THIS SIDE OF OUR OPERATION FOR THE FIRST TIME.
...THE WHO SIDE OF THE WHAT NOW?

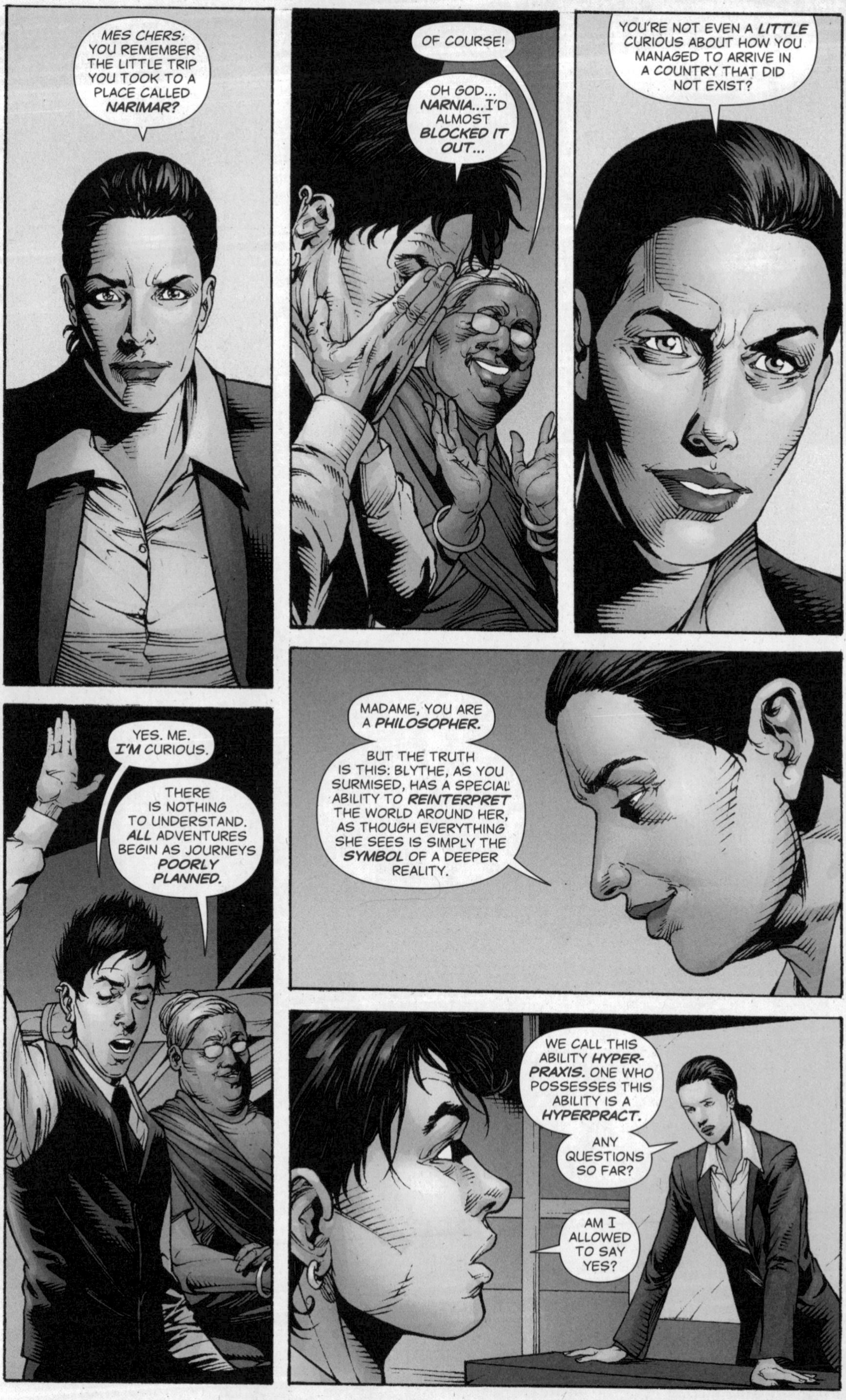
MES CHERS: YOU REMEMBER THE LITTLE TRIP YOU TOOK TO A PLACE CALLED NARIMAR?
OF COURSE!
OH GOD... NARNIA...I'D ALMOST BLOCKED IT OUT...
YOU'RE NOT EVEN A LITTLE CURIOUS ABOUT HOW YOU MANAGED TO ARRIVE IN A COUNTRY THAT DID NOT EXIST?
YES. ME. I'M CURIOUS.
THERE IS NOTHING TO UNDERSTAND. ALL ADVENTURES BEGIN AS JOURNEYS POORLY PLANNED.
MADAME, YOU ARE A PHILOSOPHER.
BUT THE TRUTH IS THIS: BLYTHE, AS YOU SURMISED, HAS A SPECIAL ABILITY TO REINTERPRET THE WORLD AROUND HER, AS THOUGH EVERYTHING SHE SEES IS SIMPLY THE SYMBOL OF A DEEPER REALITY.
WE CALL THIS ABILITY HYPER-PRAXIS. ONE WHO POSSESSES THIS ABILITY IS A HYPERPRACT.
ANY QUESTIONS SO FAR?
AM I ALLOWED TO SAY YES?

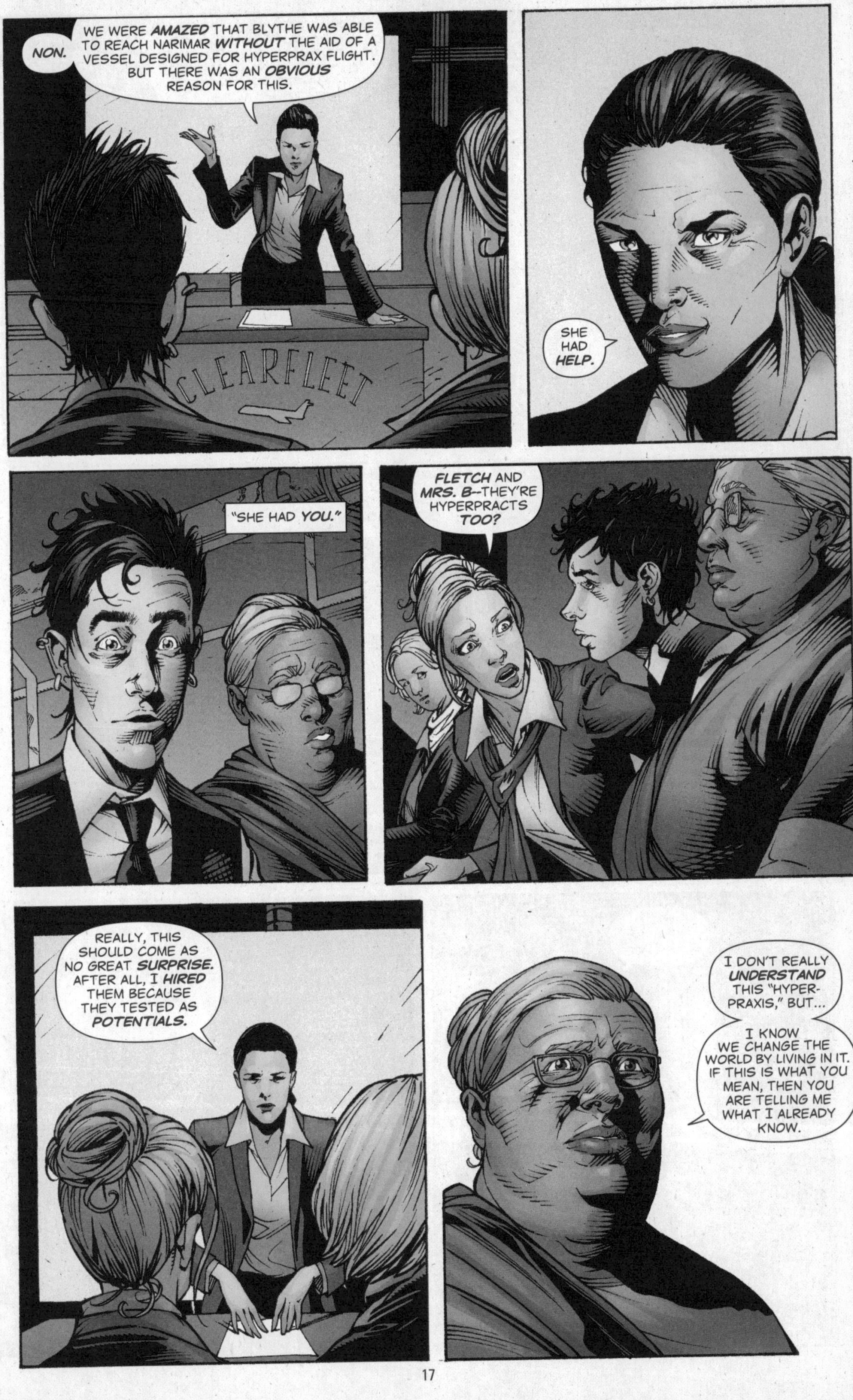
NON.
WE WERE AMAZED THAT BLYTHE WAS ABLE TO REACH NARIMAR WITHOUT THE AID OF A VESSEL DESIGNED FOR HYPERPRAX FLIGHT. BUT THERE WAS AN OBVIOUS REASON FOR THIS.
CLEARFLEET
SHE HAD HELP.
"SHE HAD YOU."
FLETCH AND MRS. B--THEY'RE HYPERPRACTS TOO?
REALLY, THIS SHOULD COME AS NO GREAT SURPRISE. AFTER ALL, I HIRED THEM BECAUSE THEY TESTED AS POTENTIALS.
I DON'T REALLY UNDERSTAND THIS "HYPER-PRAXIS," BUT...
I KNOW WE CHANGE THE WORLD BY LIVING IN IT. IF THIS IS WHAT YOU MEAN, THEN YOU ARE TELLING ME WHAT I ALREADY KNOW.

WAIT, WAIT. ARE YOU SAYING WE HAVE, LIKE, *SUPERPOWERS?*

MORE LIKE *SUPRAPOWERS.*

IN DAY-TO-DAY LIFE, YOU ARE OBVIOUSLY QUITE *ORDINARY.* BUT WITH TRAINING, YOU COULD LEARN TO PILOT A PLANE OUTFITTED WITH A HYPERPRAX ENGINE BY *THOUGHT* ALONE.

LIKE *BLYTHE.*

THOUGH IN MY CASE, THINGS TEND TO GO FUNKY EVEN WHEN I'M *NOT* IN THE COCKPIT.

BIEN. MOVING ALONG.

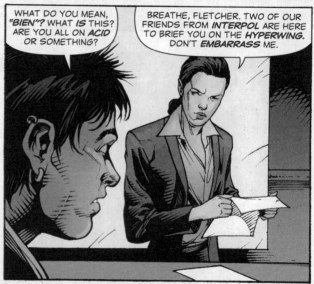

WHAT DO YOU MEAN, *"BIEN"?* WHAT *IS* THIS? ARE YOU ALL ON *ACID* OR SOMETHING?

BREATHE, FLETCHER. TWO OF OUR FRIENDS FROM *INTERPOL* ARE HERE TO BRIEF YOU ON THE *HYPERWING.* DON'T *EMBARRASS* ME.

GOOD MORNING, CLEARFLEET.

SAURAV!

MANUEL?

ZAYN.

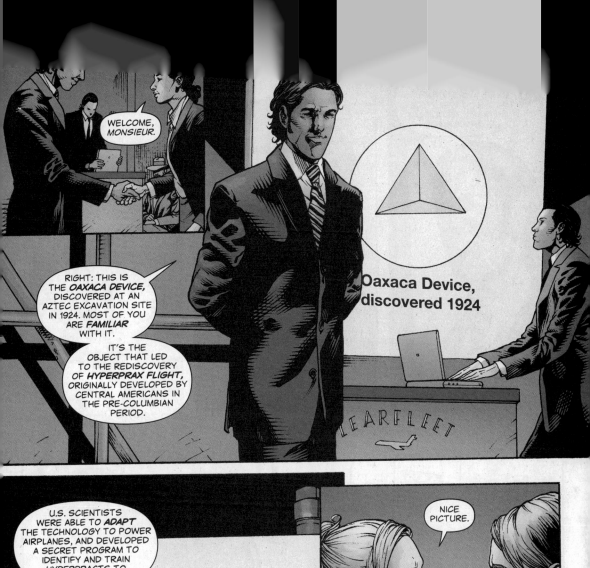

WELCOME, MONSIEUR.

RIGHT: THIS IS THE *OAXACA DEVICE*, DISCOVERED AT AN AZTEC EXCAVATION SITE IN 1924. MOST OF YOU ARE *FAMILIAR* WITH IT.

IT'S THE OBJECT THAT LED TO THE REDISCOVERY OF *HYPERPRAX FLIGHT*, ORIGINALLY DEVELOPED BY CENTRAL AMERICANS IN THE PRE-COLUMBIAN PERIOD.

Oaxaca Device, discovered 1924

EARFLEET

U.S. SCIENTISTS WERE ABLE TO *ADAPT* THE TECHNOLOGY TO POWER AIRPLANES, AND DEVELOPED A SECRET PROGRAM TO IDENTIFY AND TRAIN HYPERPRACTS TO FLY THEM.

INCLUDING *AMELIA EARHART.*

NICE PICTURE.

THANKS.

A *SECOND* DEVICE WAS FOUND LAST YEAR ON A DIG NEAR MEXICO CITY. NATURALLY, A LOT OF PEOPLE WERE EAGER TO GET THEIR HANDS ON IT.

THIS DEVICE WAS THOUGHT TO BE *NEWER* THAN THE OAXACA ARTIFACT--PRODUCED AT THE *HEIGHT* OF AZTEC CIVILIZATION.

New Device, discovered 2008

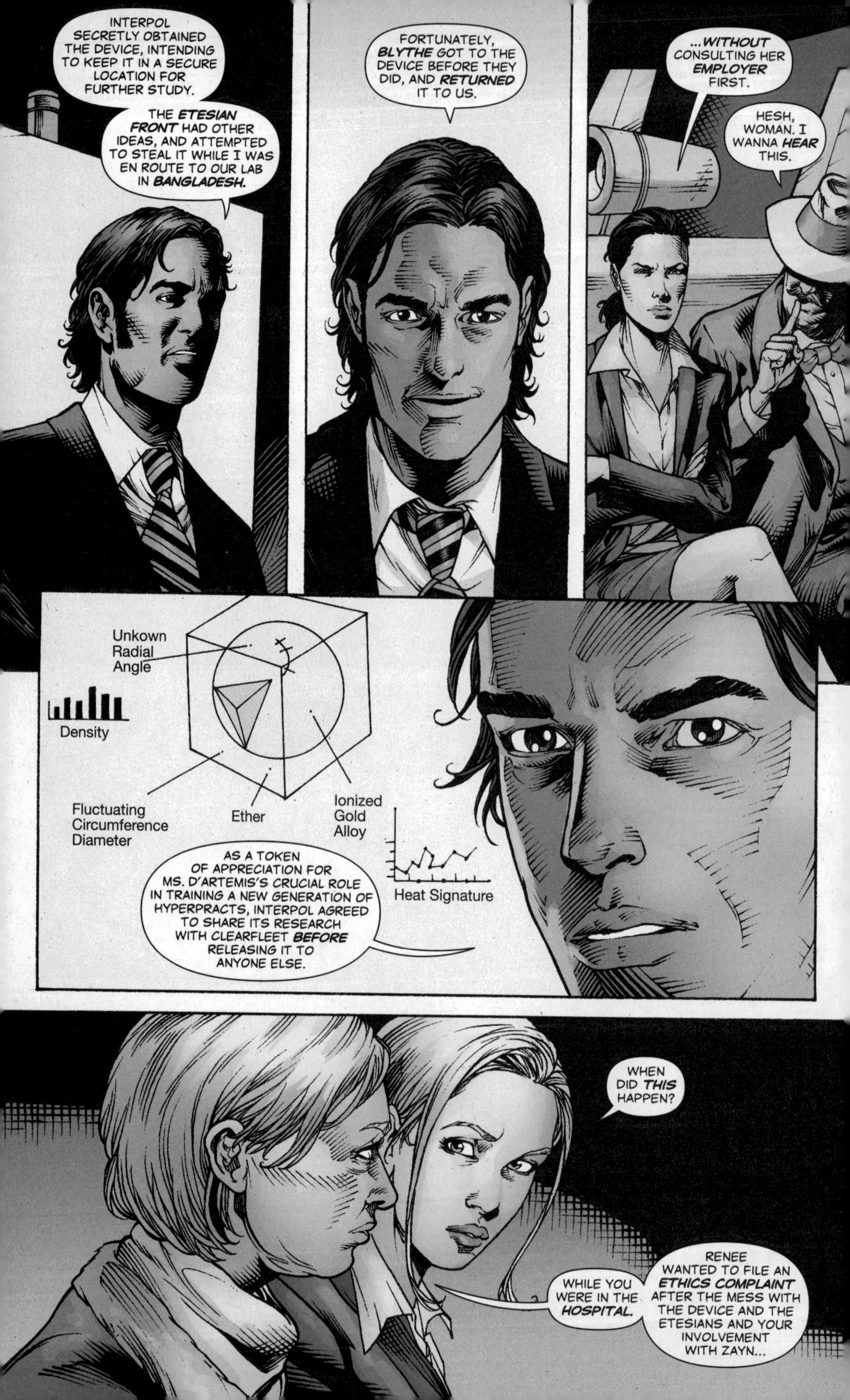
INTERPOL SECRETLY OBTAINED THE DEVICE, INTENDING TO KEEP IT IN A SECURE LOCATION FOR FURTHER STUDY.
THE ETESIAN FRONT HAD OTHER IDEAS, AND ATTEMPTED TO STEAL IT WHILE I WAS EN ROUTE TO OUR LAB IN BANGLADESH.
FORTUNATELY, BLYTHE GOT TO THE DEVICE BEFORE THEY DID, AND RETURNED IT TO US.
...WITHOUT CONSULTING HER EMPLOYER FIRST.
HESH, WOMAN. I WANNA HEAR THIS.
Unkown Radial Angle
Density
Fluctuating Circumference Diameter
Ether
Ionized Gold Alloy
Heat Signature
AS A TOKEN OF APPRECIATION FOR MS. D'ARTEMIS'S CRUCIAL ROLE IN TRAINING A NEW GENERATION OF HYPERPRACTS, INTERPOL AGREED TO SHARE ITS RESEARCH WITH CLEARFLEET BEFORE RELEASING IT TO ANYONE ELSE.
WHEN DID THIS HAPPEN?
WHILE YOU WERE IN THE HOSPITAL.
RENEE WANTED TO FILE AN ETHICS COMPLAINT AFTER THE MESS WITH THE DEVICE AND THE ETESIANS AND YOUR INVOLVEMENT WITH ZAYN...

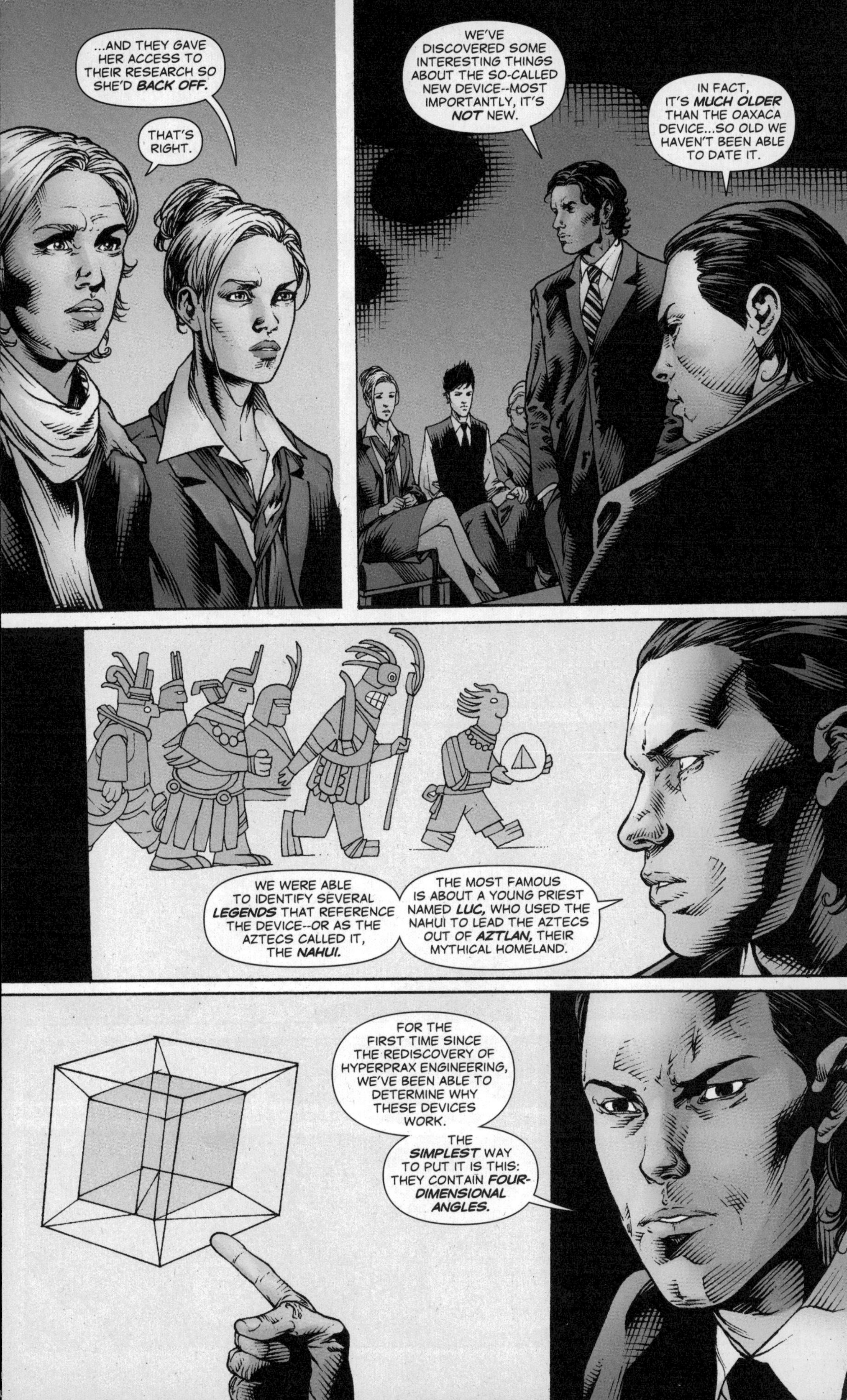
...AND THEY GAVE HER ACCESS TO THEIR RESEARCH SO SHE'D BACK OFF.
THAT'S RIGHT.
WE'VE DISCOVERED SOME INTERESTING THINGS ABOUT THE SO-CALLED NEW DEVICE--MOST IMPORTANTLY, IT'S NOT NEW.
IN FACT, IT'S MUCH OLDER THAN THE OAXACA DEVICE...SO OLD WE HAVEN'T BEEN ABLE TO DATE IT.
WE WERE ABLE TO IDENTIFY SEVERAL LEGENDS THAT REFERENCE THE DEVICE--OR AS THE AZTECS CALLED IT, THE NAHUI.
THE MOST FAMOUS IS ABOUT A YOUNG PRIEST NAMED LUC, WHO USED THE NAHUI TO LEAD THE AZTECS OUT OF AZTLAN, THEIR MYTHICAL HOMELAND.
FOR THE FIRST TIME SINCE THE REDISCOVERY OF HYPERPRAX ENGINEERING, WE'VE BEEN ABLE TO DETERMINE WHY THESE DEVICES WORK.
THE SIMPLEST WAY TO PUT IT IS THIS: THEY CONTAIN FOUR-DIMENSIONAL ANGLES.

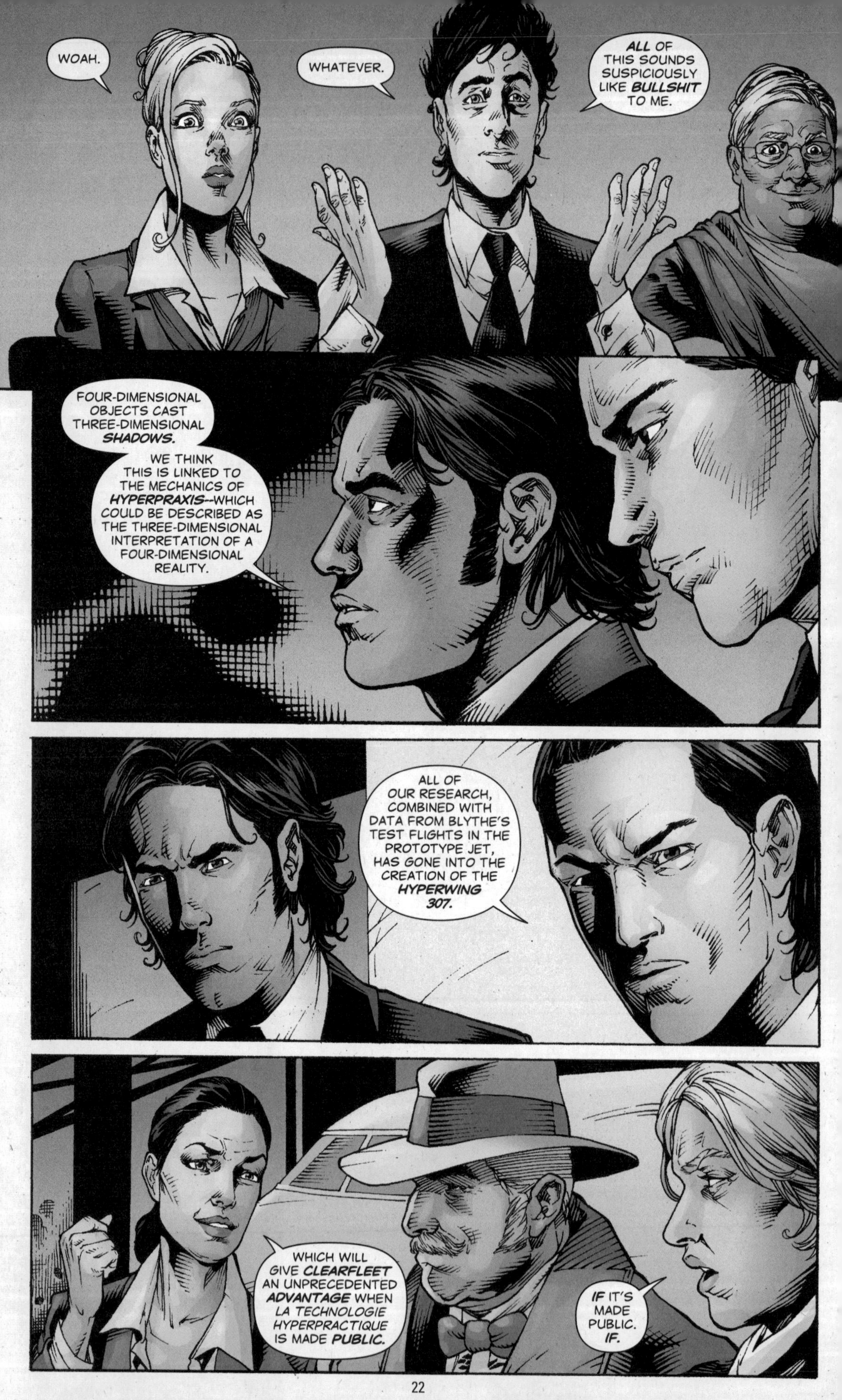
WOAH.
WHATEVER.
ALL OF THIS SOUNDS SUSPICIOUSLY LIKE BULLSHIT TO ME.
FOUR-DIMENSIONAL OBJECTS CAST THREE-DIMENSIONAL SHADOWS.
WE THINK THIS IS LINKED TO THE MECHANICS OF HYPERPRAXIS--WHICH COULD BE DESCRIBED AS THE THREE-DIMENSIONAL INTERPRETATION OF A FOUR-DIMENSIONAL REALITY.
ALL OF OUR RESEARCH, COMBINED WITH DATA FROM BLYTHE'S TEST FLIGHTS IN THE PROTOTYPE JET, HAS GONE INTO THE CREATION OF THE HYPERWING 307.
WHICH WILL GIVE CLEARFLEET AN UNPRECEDENTED ADVANTAGE WHEN LA TECHNOLOGIE HYPERPRACTIQUE IS MADE PUBLIC.
IF IT'S MADE PUBLIC. IF.

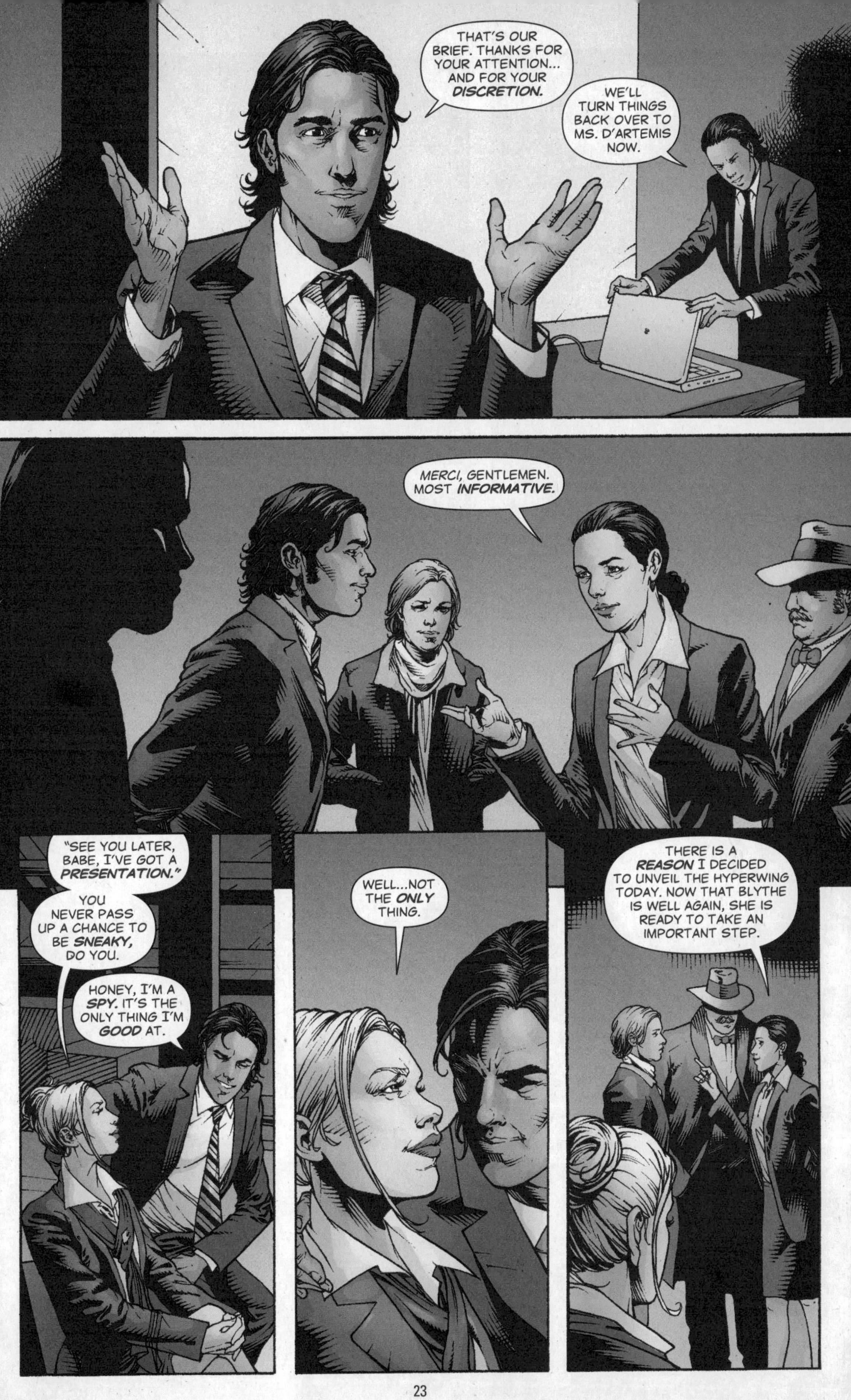
THAT'S OUR BRIEF. THANKS FOR YOUR ATTENTION... AND FOR YOUR **DISCRETION.**
WE'LL TURN THINGS BACK OVER TO MS. D'ARTEMIS NOW.
MERCI, GENTLEMEN. MOST ***INFORMATIVE.***
"SEE YOU LATER, BABE, I'VE GOT A ***PRESENTATION.***"
YOU NEVER PASS UP A CHANCE TO BE ***SNEAKY,*** DO YOU.
HONEY, I'M A ***SPY.*** IT'S THE ONLY THING I'M ***GOOD*** AT.
WELL...NOT THE ***ONLY*** THING.
THERE IS A ***REASON*** I DECIDED TO UNVEIL THE HYPERWING TODAY. NOW THAT BLYTHE IS WELL AGAIN, SHE IS READY TO TAKE AN IMPORTANT STEP.

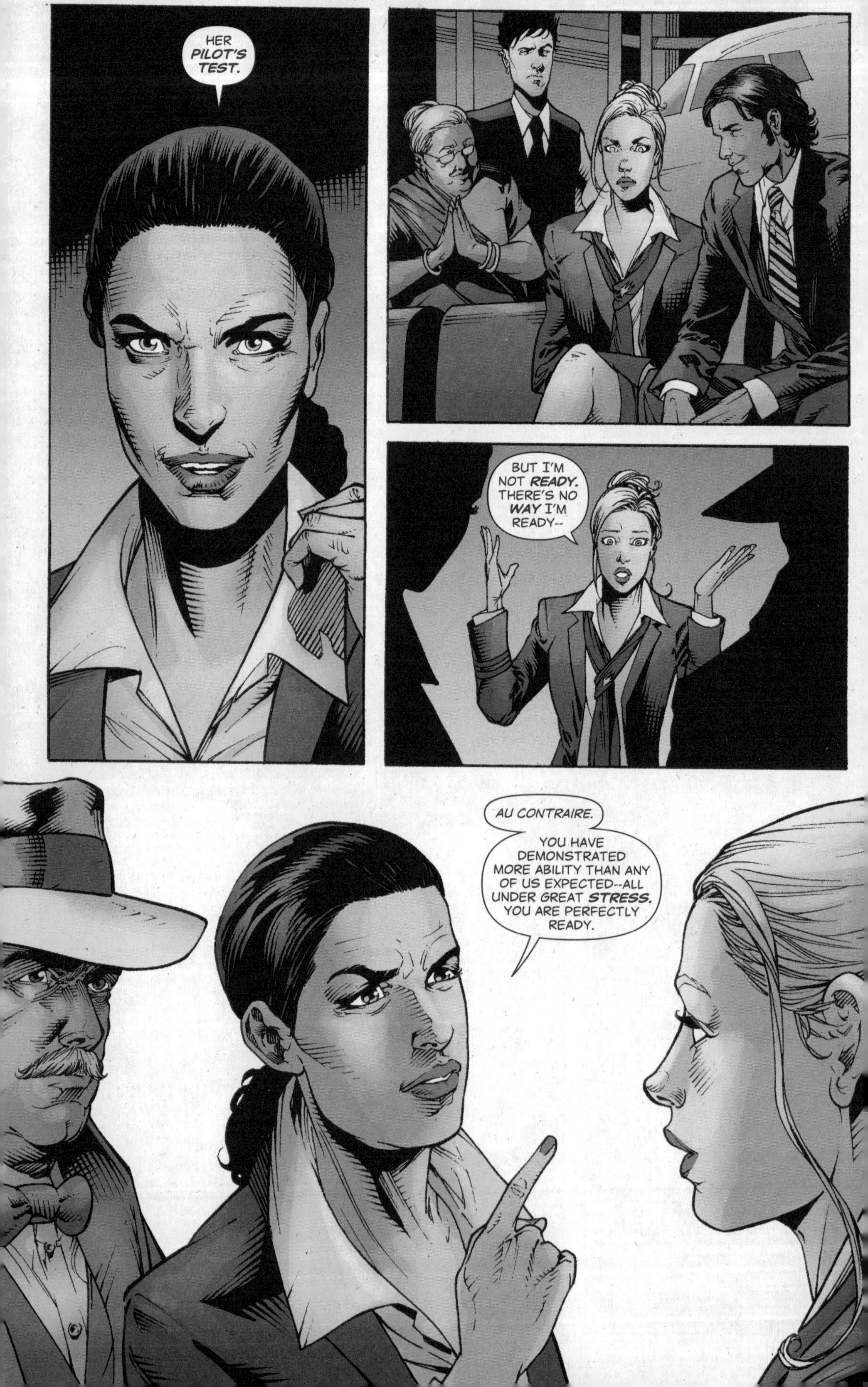
HER PILOT'S TEST.
BUT I'M NOT READY. THERE'S NO WAY I'M READY--
AU CONTRAIRE.
YOU HAVE DEMONSTRATED MORE ABILITY THAN ANY OF US EXPECTED--ALL UNDER GREAT STRESS. YOU ARE PERFECTLY READY.

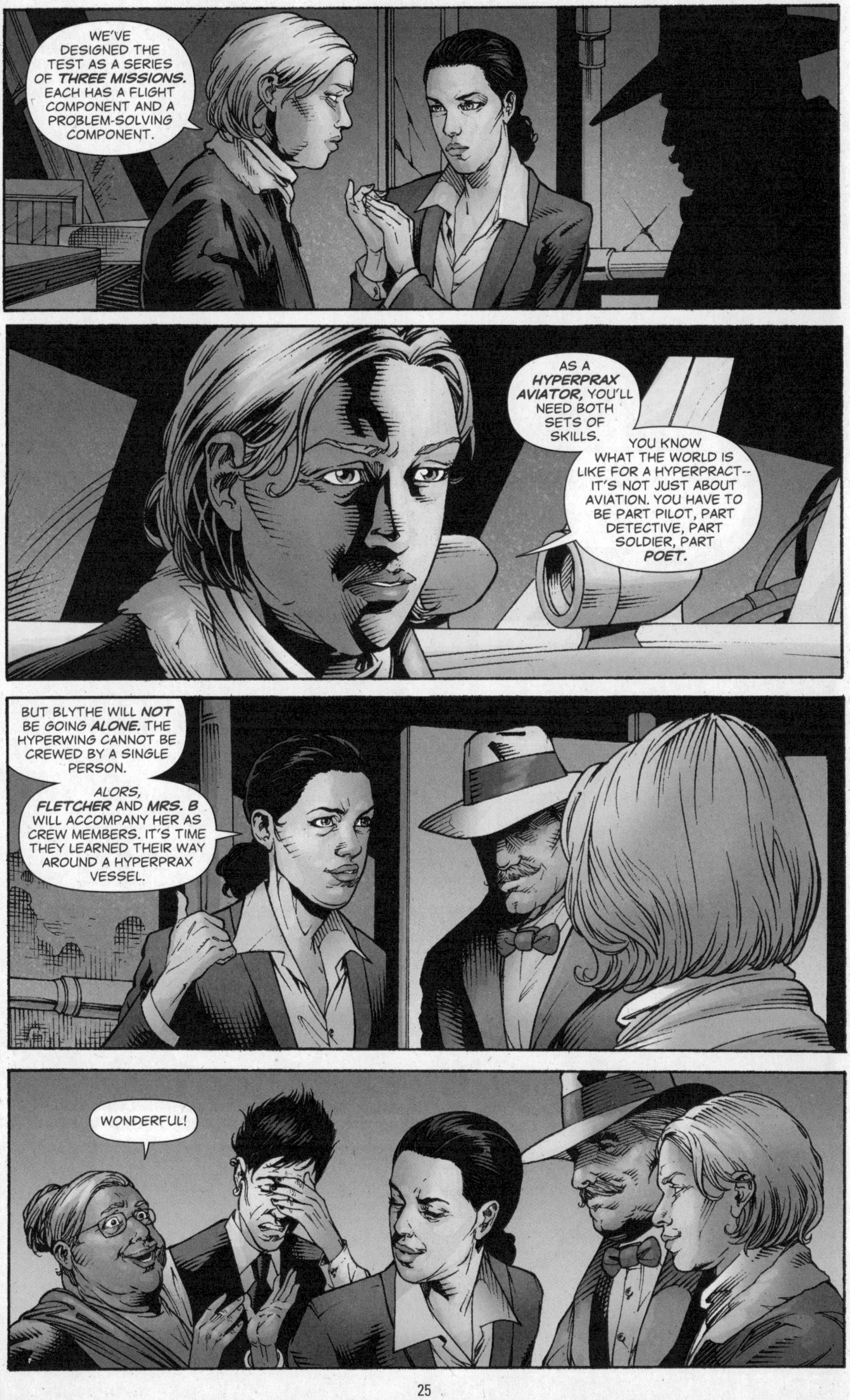

WE'VE DESIGNED THE TEST AS A SERIES OF THREE MISSIONS. EACH HAS A FLIGHT COMPONENT AND A PROBLEM-SOLVING COMPONENT.
AS A HYPERPRAX AVIATOR, YOU'LL NEED BOTH SETS OF SKILLS.
YOU KNOW WHAT THE WORLD IS LIKE FOR A HYPERPRACT-- IT'S NOT JUST ABOUT AVIATION. YOU HAVE TO BE PART PILOT, PART DETECTIVE, PART SOLDIER, PART POET.
BUT BLYTHE WILL NOT BE GOING ALONE. THE HYPERWING CANNOT BE CREWED BY A SINGLE PERSON.
ALORS, FLETCHER AND MRS. B WILL ACCOMPANY HER AS CREW MEMBERS. IT'S TIME THEY LEARNED THEIR WAY AROUND A HYPERPRAX VESSEL.
WONDERFUL!

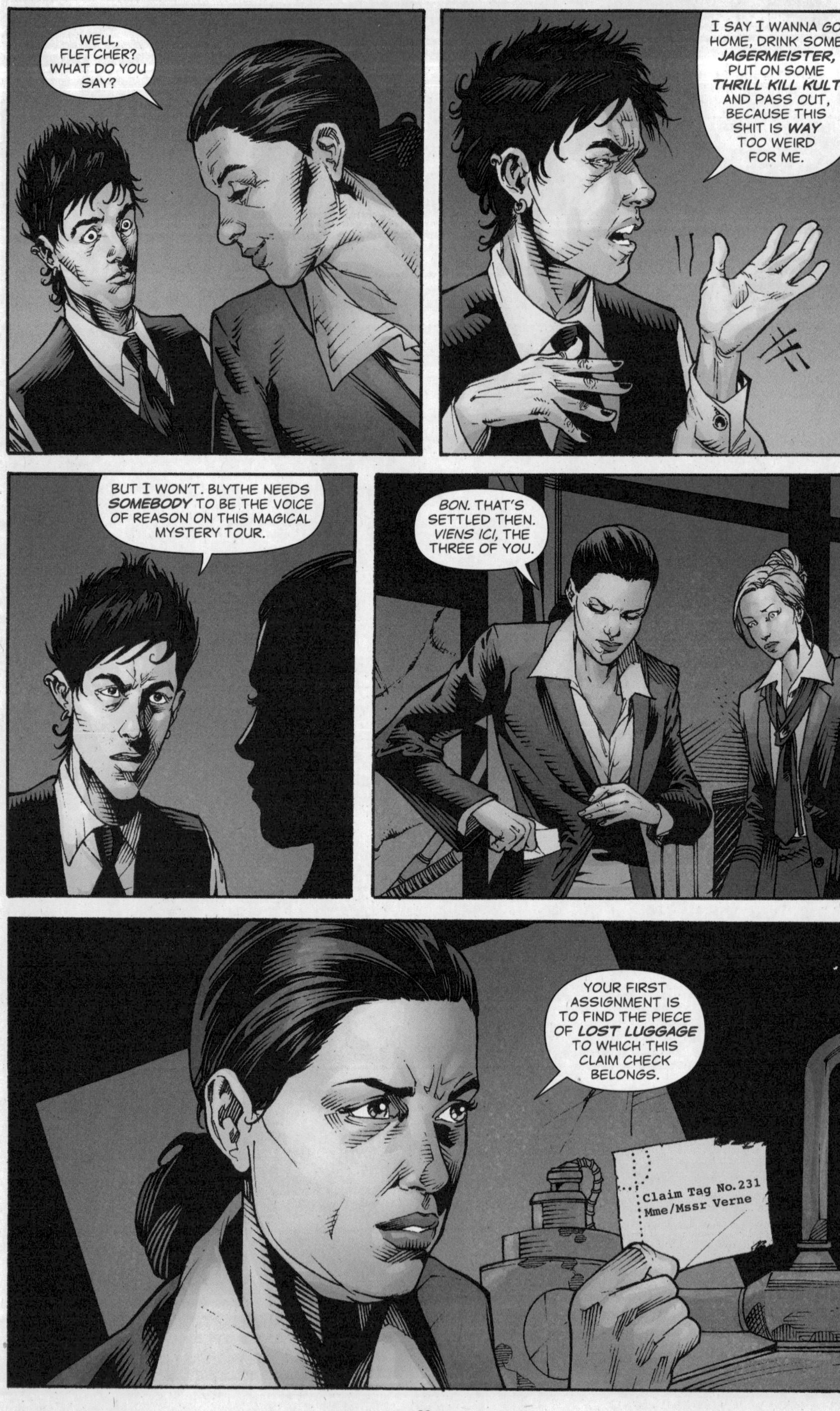
WELL, FLETCHER? WHAT DO YOU SAY?
I SAY I WANNA GO HOME, DRINK SOME JAGERMEISTER, PUT ON SOME THRILL KILL KULT AND PASS OUT, BECAUSE THIS SHIT IS WAY TOO WEIRD FOR ME.
BUT I WON'T. BLYTHE NEEDS SOMEBODY TO BE THE VOICE OF REASON ON THIS MAGICAL MYSTERY TOUR.
BON. THAT'S SETTLED THEN. VIENS ICI, THE THREE OF YOU.
YOUR FIRST ASSIGNMENT IS TO FIND THE PIECE OF LOST LUGGAGE TO WHICH THIS CLAIM CHECK BELONGS.
Claim Tag No.231
Mme/Mssr Verne

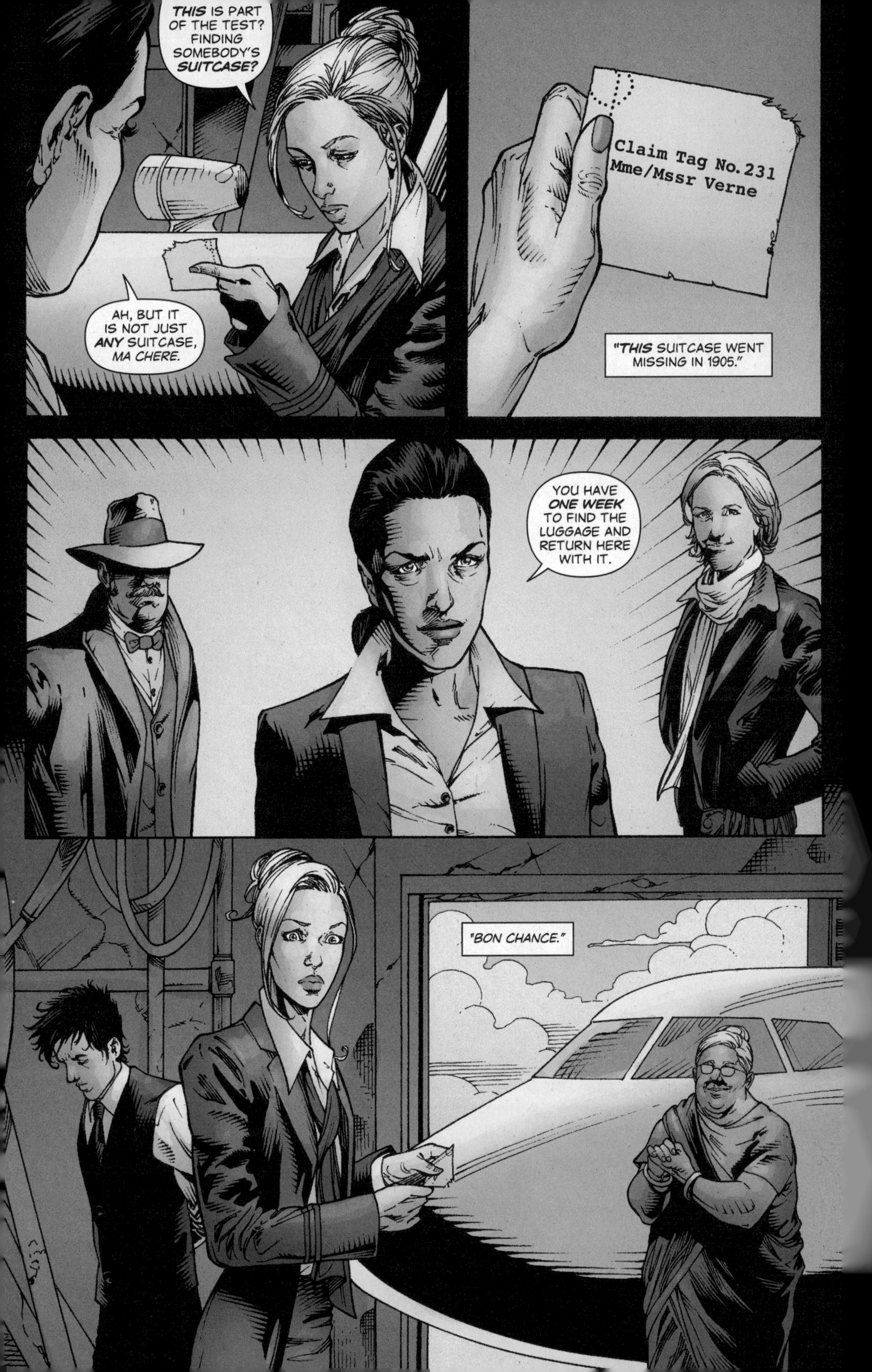
THIS IS PART OF THE TEST? FINDING SOMEBODY'S SUITCASE?
AH, BUT IT IS NOT JUST ANY SUITCASE, MA CHERE.
Claim Tag No.231
Mme/Mssr Verne
"THIS SUITCASE WENT MISSING IN 1905."
YOU HAVE ONE WEEK TO FIND THE LUGGAGE AND RETURN HERE WITH IT.
"BON CHANCE."

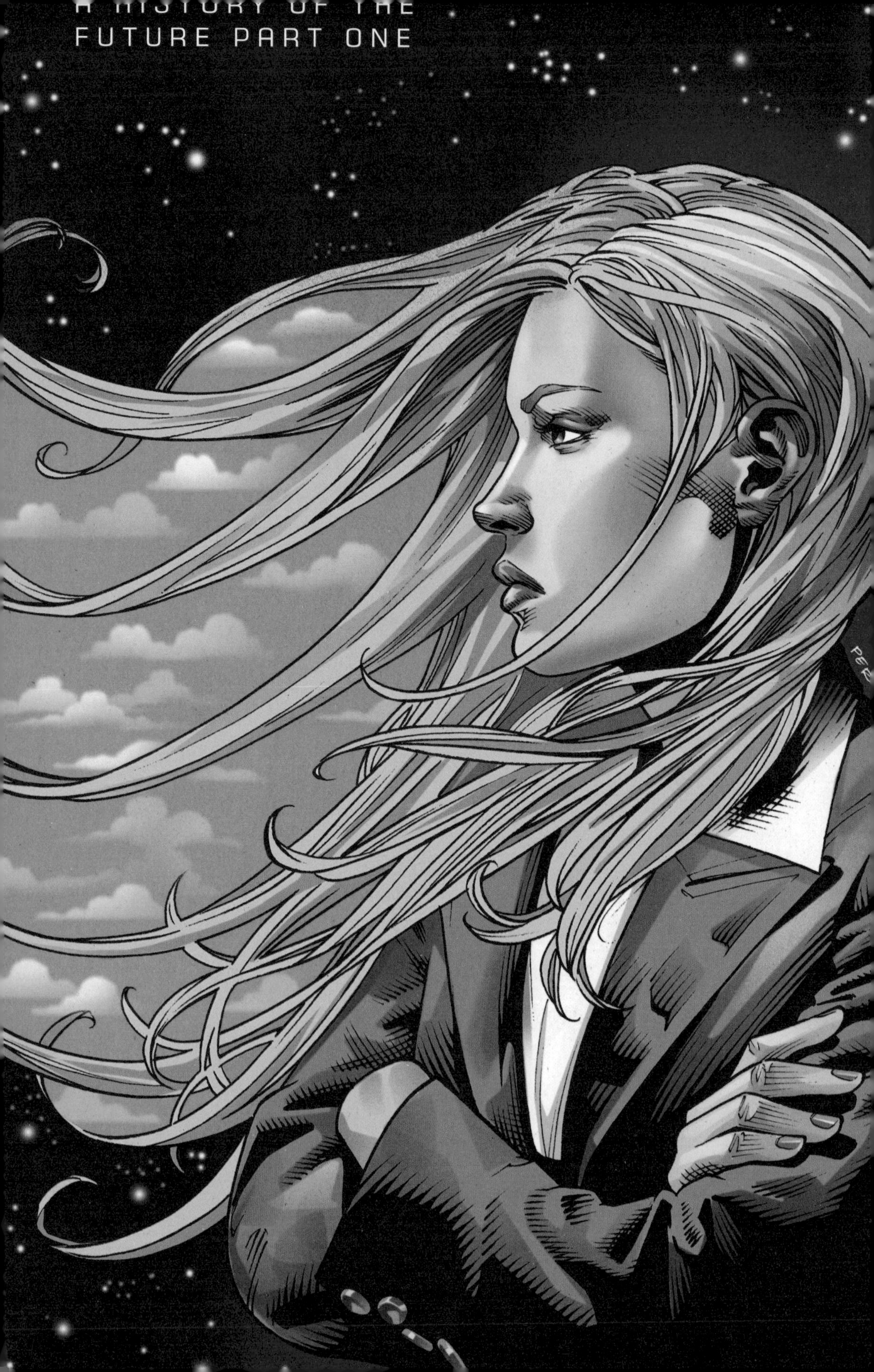
A HISTORY OF THE
FUTURE PART ONE

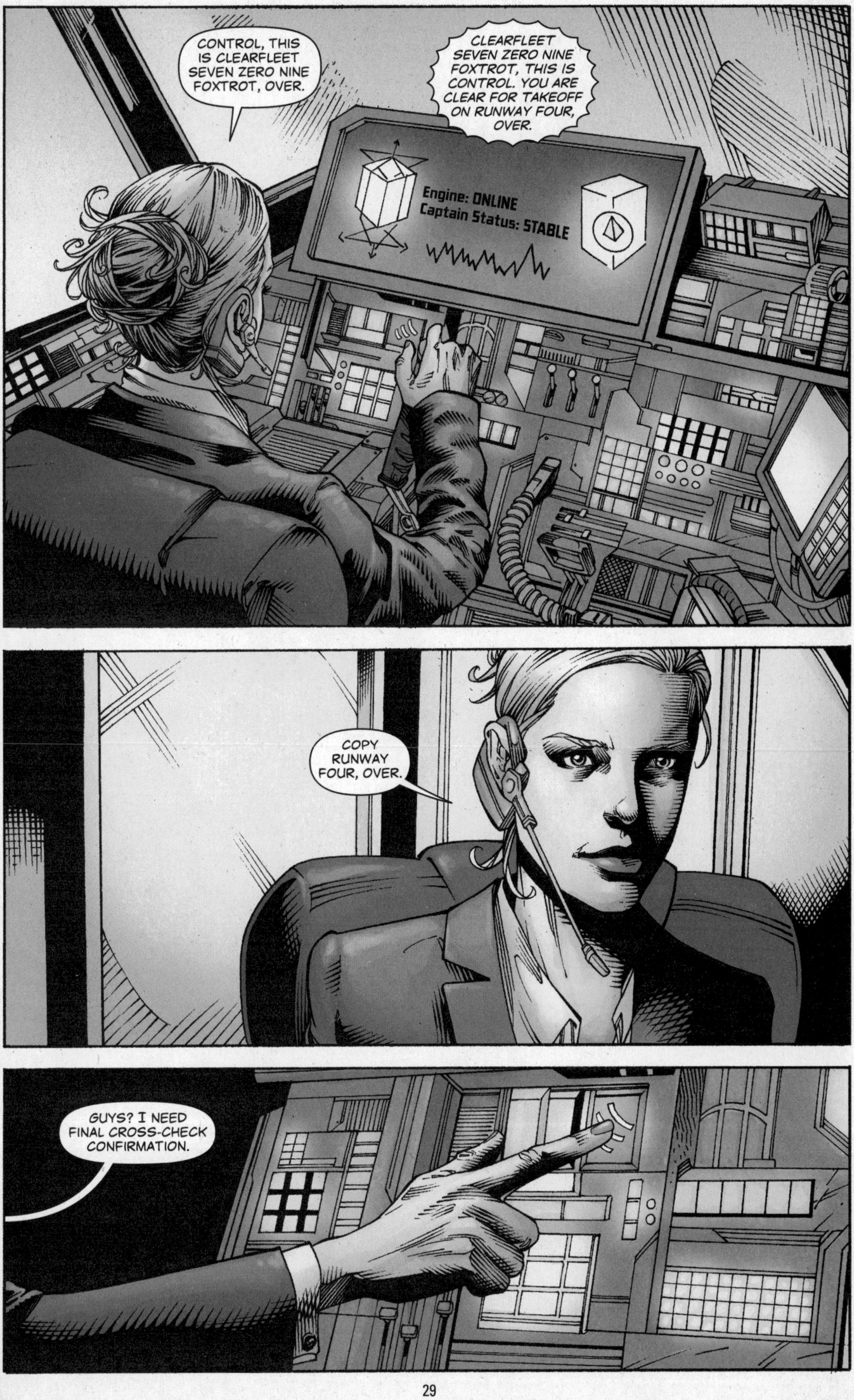
CONTROL, THIS IS CLEARFLEET SEVEN ZERO NINE FOXTROT, OVER.
CLEARFLEET SEVEN ZERO NINE FOXTROT, THIS IS CONTROL. YOU ARE CLEAR FOR TAKEOFF ON RUNWAY FOUR, OVER.
Engine: ONLINE
Captain Status: STABLE
COPY RUNWAY FOUR, OVER.
GUYS? I NEED FINAL CROSS-CHECK CONFIRMATION.

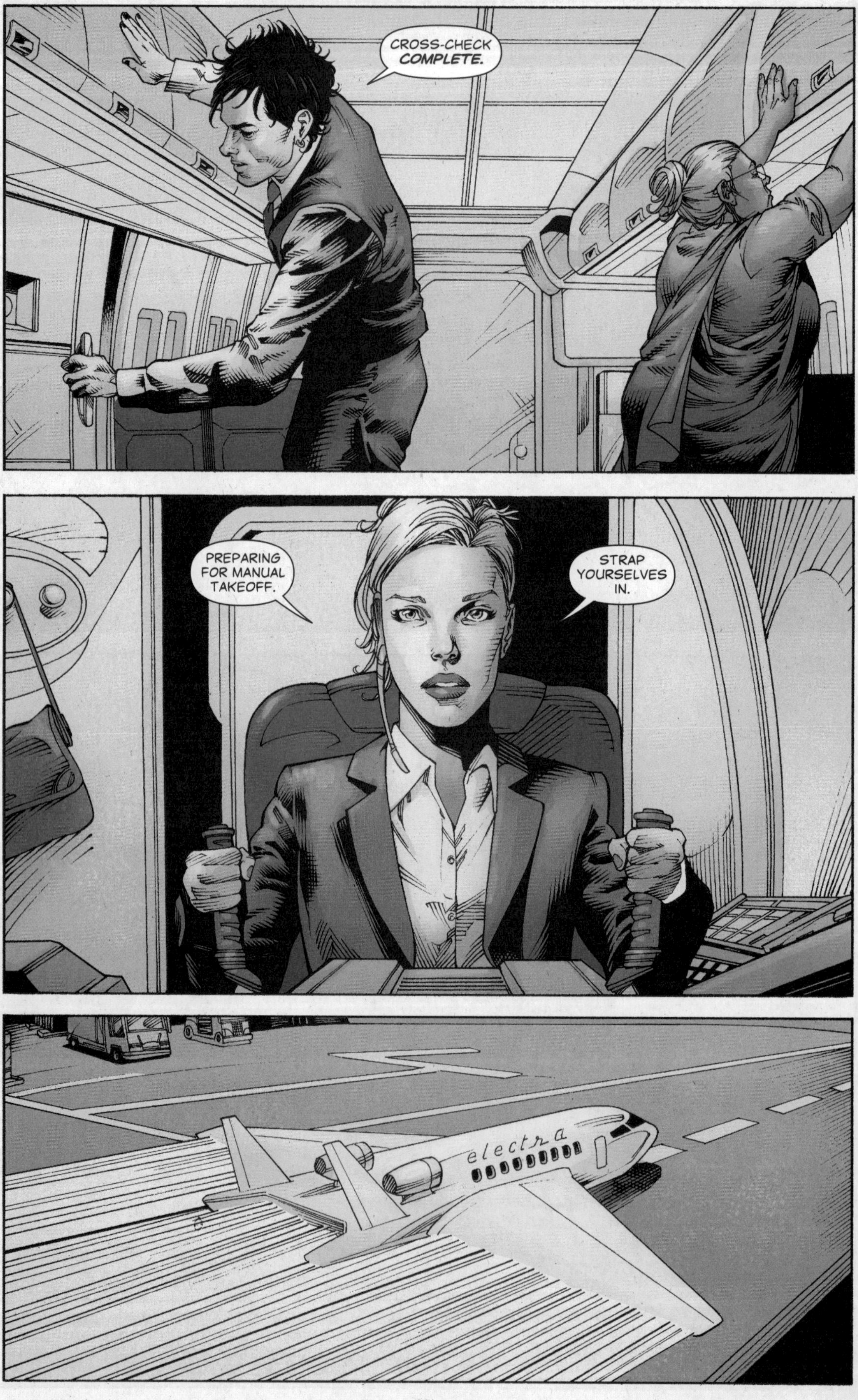
CROSS-CHECK COMPLETE.
PREPARING FOR MANUAL TAKEOFF.
STRAP YOURSELVES IN.
electra

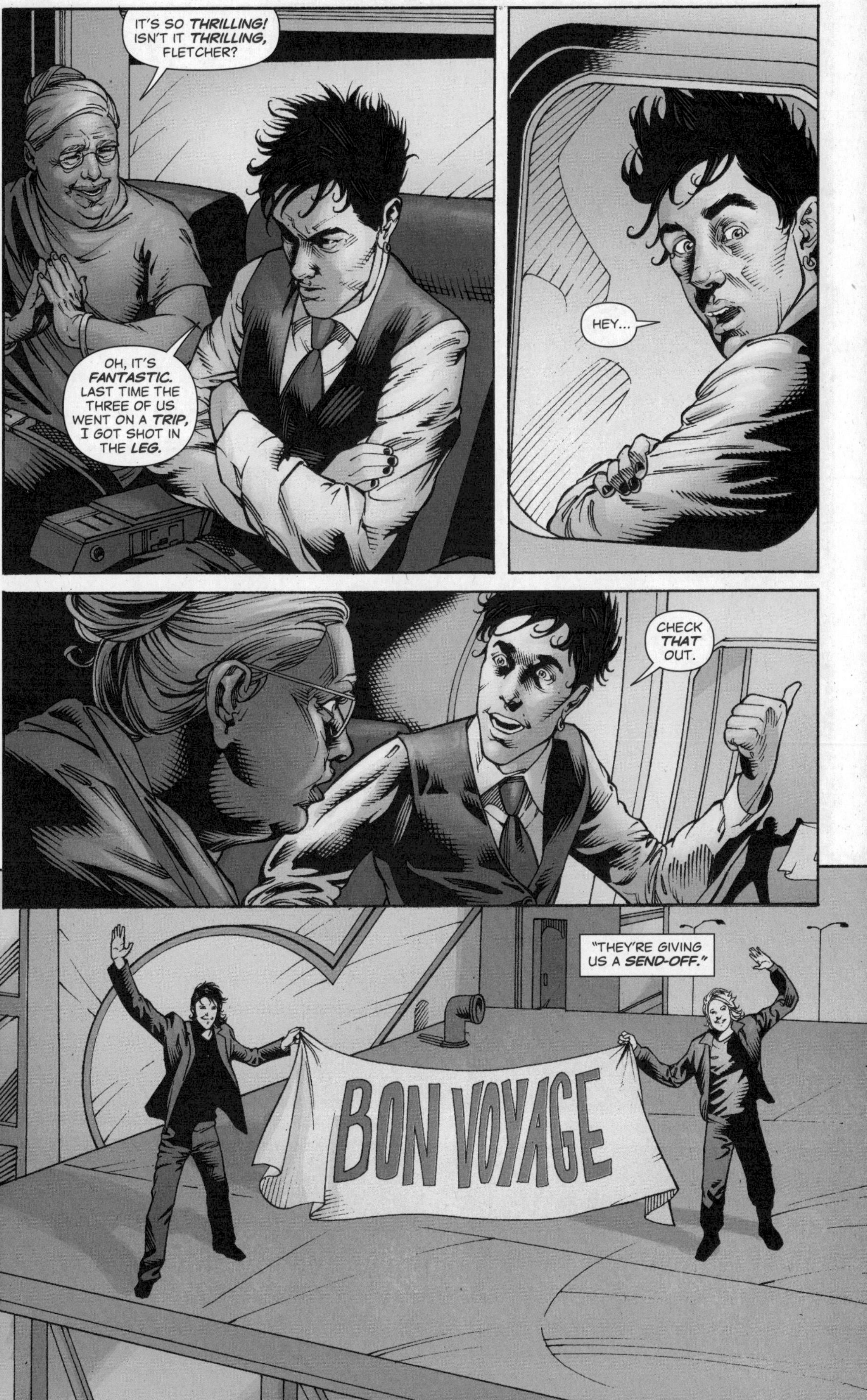
IT'S SO THRILLING! ISN'T IT THRILLING, FLETCHER?
OH, IT'S FANTASTIC. LAST TIME THE THREE OF US WENT ON A TRIP, I GOT SHOT IN THE LEG.
HEY...
CHECK THAT OUT.
"THEY'RE GIVING US A SEND-OFF."
BON VOYAGE

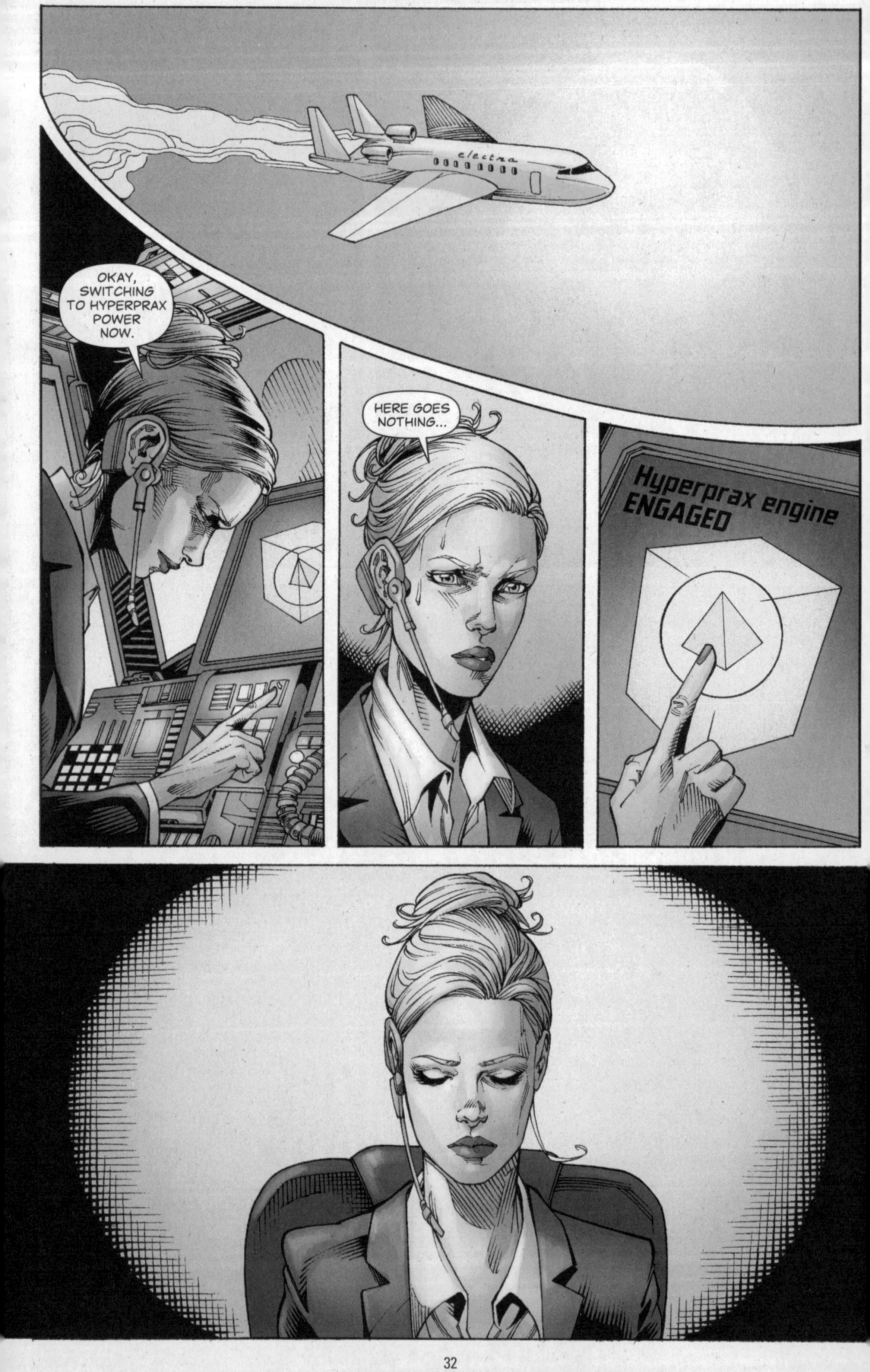

electra
OKAY, SWITCHING TO HYPERPRAX POWER NOW.
HERE GOES NOTHING...
Hyperprax engine ENGAGED

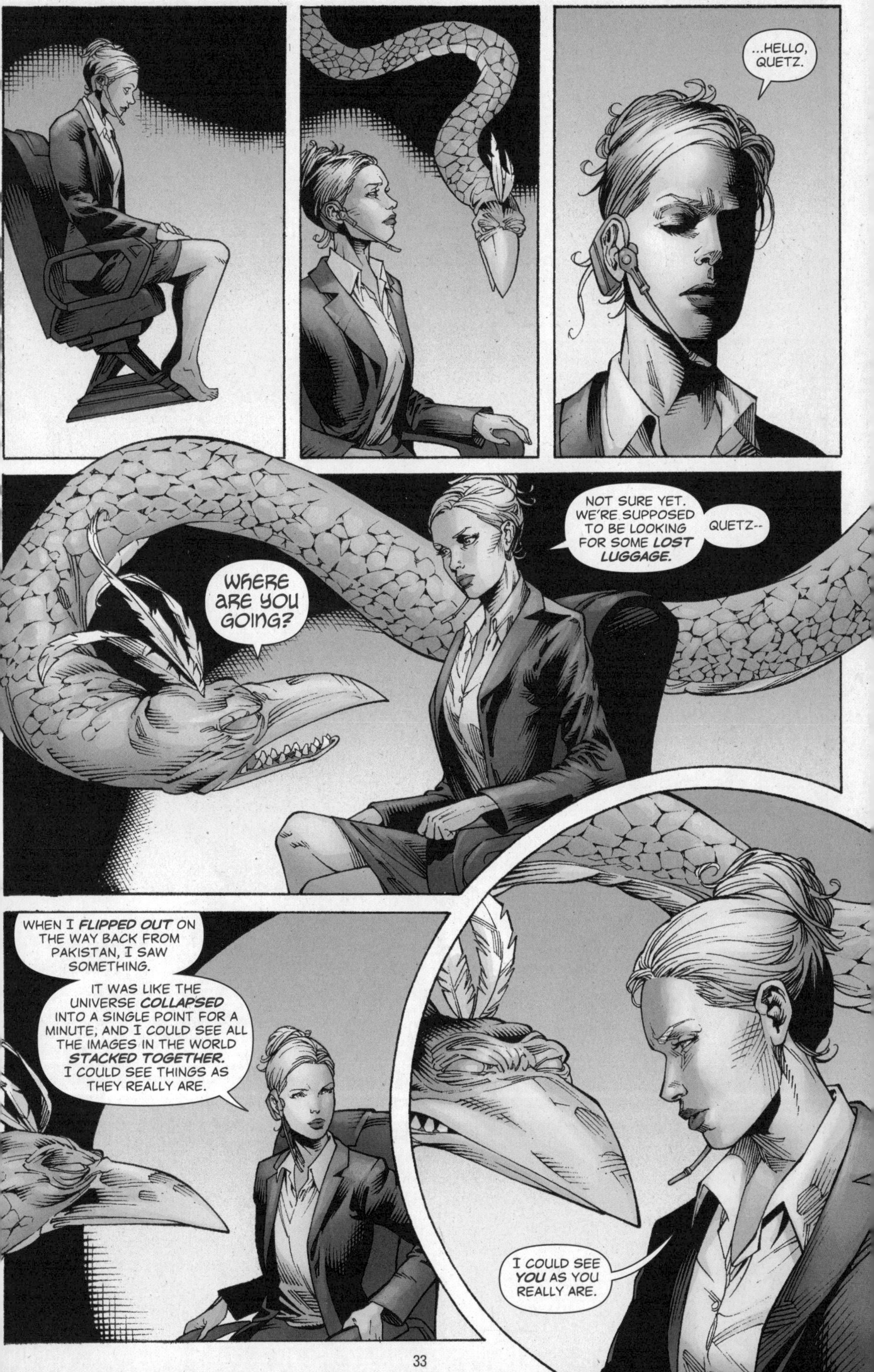
...HELLO, QUETZ.
WHERE ARE YOU GOING?
NOT SURE YET. WE'RE SUPPOSED TO BE LOOKING FOR SOME LOST LUGGAGE.
QUETZ--
WHEN I FLIPPED OUT ON THE WAY BACK FROM PAKISTAN, I SAW SOMETHING.
IT WAS LIKE THE UNIVERSE COLLAPSED INTO A SINGLE POINT FOR A MINUTE, AND I COULD SEE ALL THE IMAGES IN THE WORLD STACKED TOGETHER. I COULD SEE THINGS AS THEY REALLY ARE.
I COULD SEE YOU AS YOU REALLY ARE.

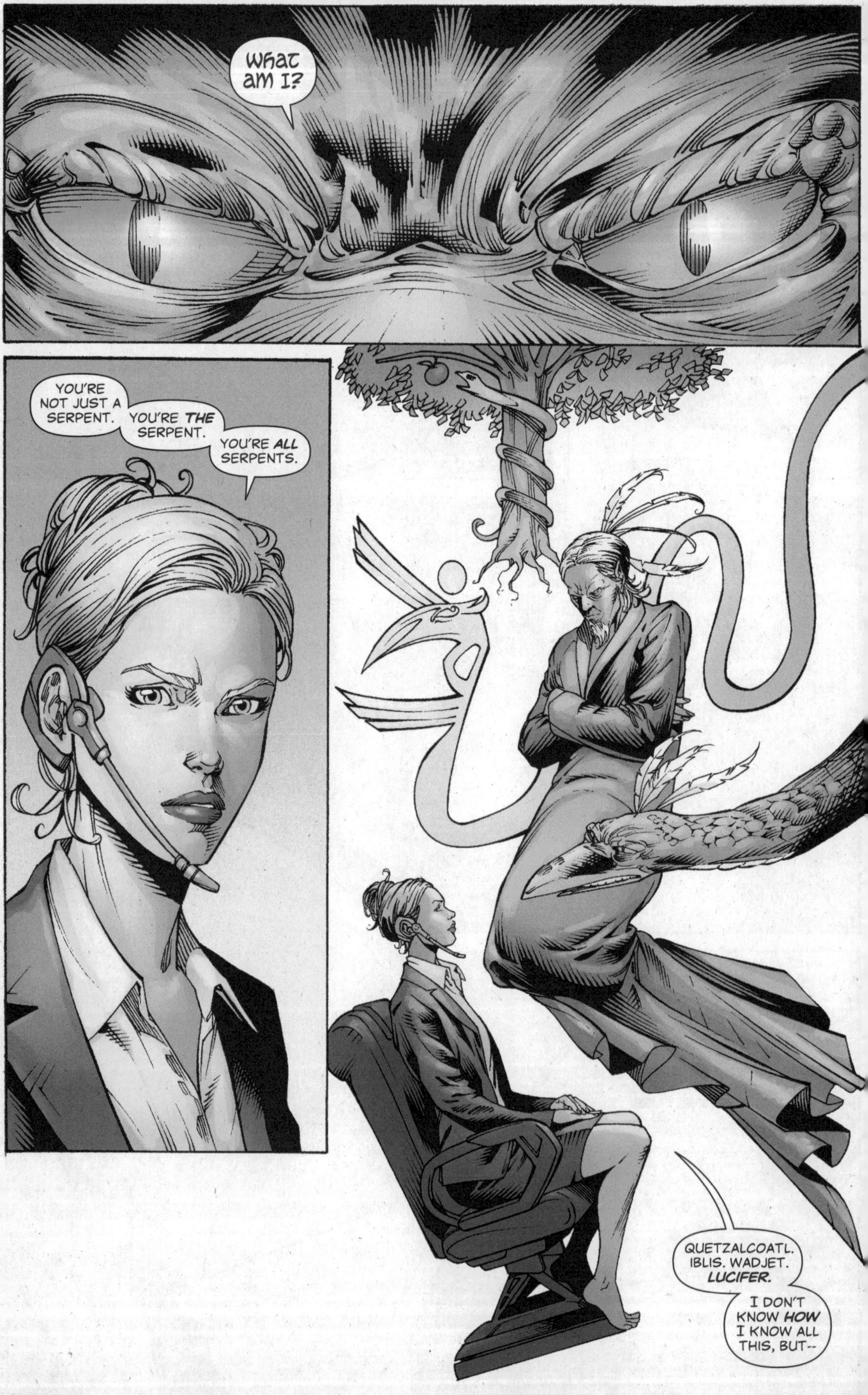
WHAT AM I?
YOU'RE NOT JUST A SERPENT.
YOU'RE *THE* SERPENT.
YOU'RE *ALL* SERPENTS.
QUETZALCOATL. IBLIS. WADJET. *LUCIFER.*
I DON'T KNOW *HOW* I KNOW ALL THIS, BUT--

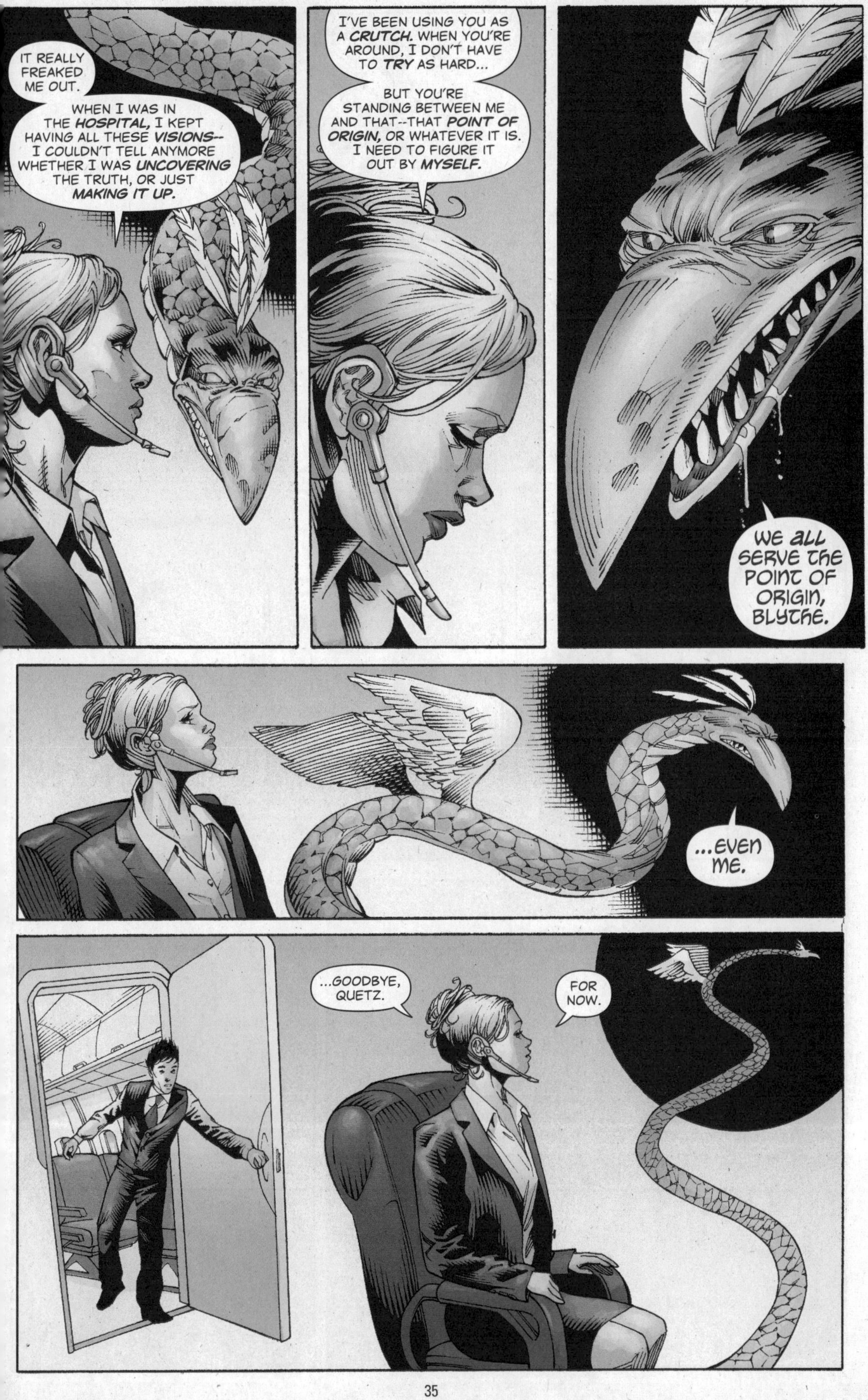
IT REALLY FREAKED ME OUT.
WHEN I WAS IN THE HOSPITAL, I KEPT HAVING ALL THESE VISIONS-- I COULDN'T TELL ANYMORE WHETHER I WAS UNCOVERING THE TRUTH, OR JUST MAKING IT UP.
I'VE BEEN USING YOU AS A CRUTCH. WHEN YOU'RE AROUND, I DON'T HAVE TO TRY AS HARD...
BUT YOU'RE STANDING BETWEEN ME AND THAT--THAT POINT OF ORIGIN, OR WHATEVER IT IS. I NEED TO FIGURE IT OUT BY MYSELF.
WE ALL SERVE THE POINT OF ORIGIN, BLYTHE.
...EVEN ME.
...GOODBYE, QUETZ.
FOR NOW.

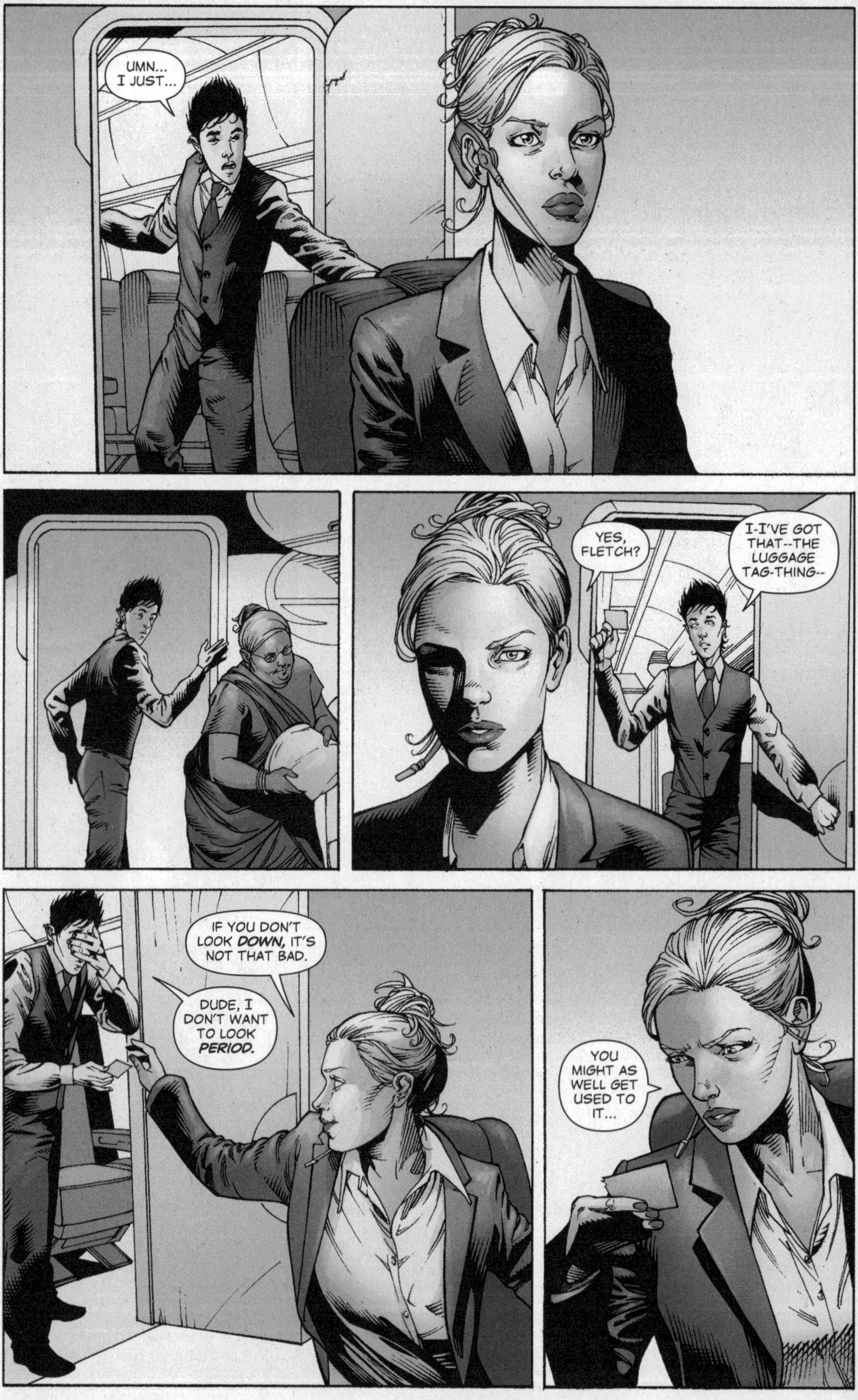
UMN... I JUST...
YES, FLETCH?
I-I'VE GOT THAT--THE LUGGAGE TAG-THING--
IF YOU DON'T LOOK *DOWN*, IT'S NOT THAT BAD.
DUDE, I DON'T WANT TO LOOK *PERIOD.*
YOU MIGHT AS WELL GET USED TO IT...

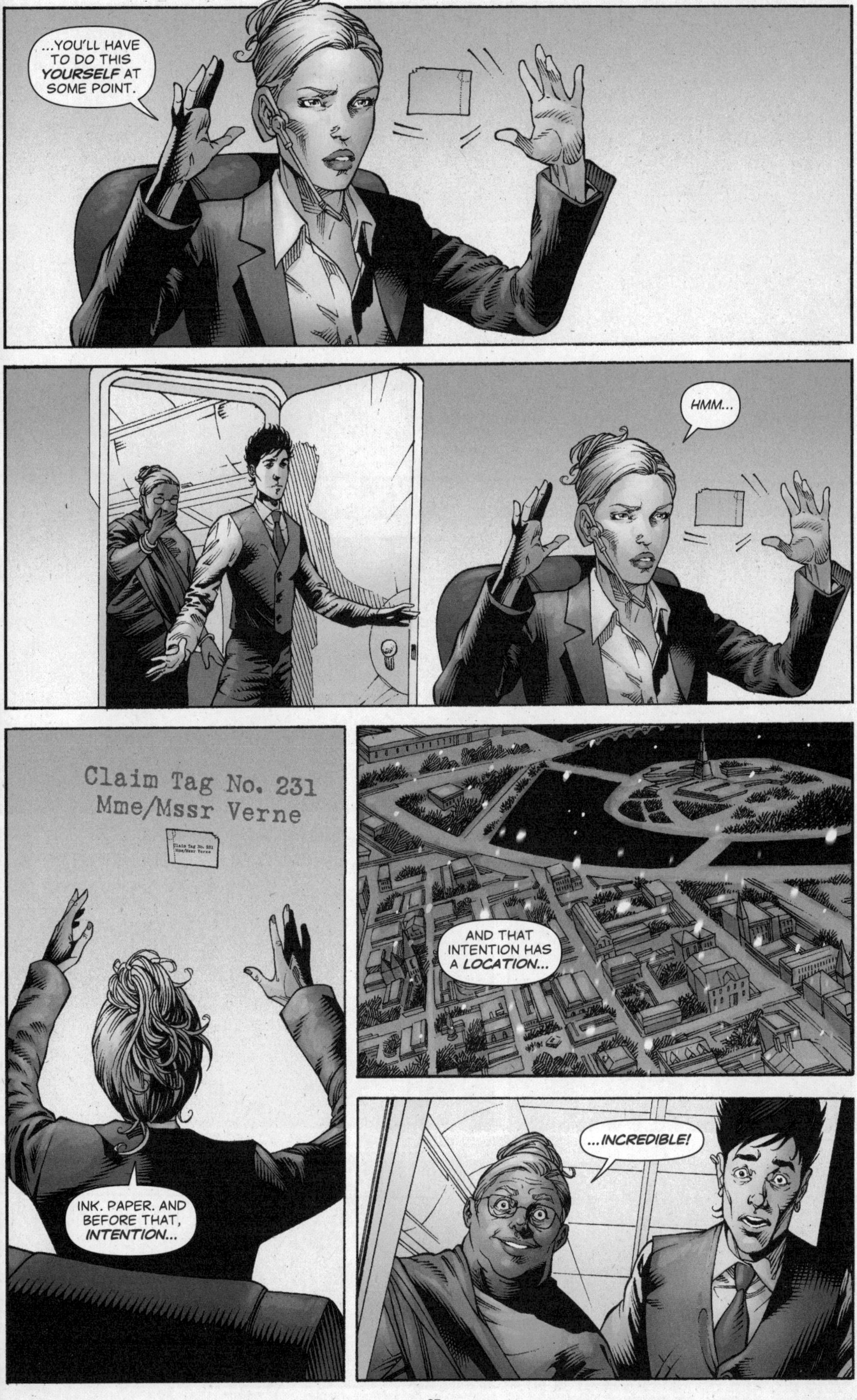
...YOU'LL HAVE TO DO THIS YOURSELF AT SOME POINT.
HMM...
Claim Tag No. 231
Mme/Mssr Verne
INK. PAPER. AND BEFORE THAT, INTENTION...
AND THAT INTENTION HAS A LOCATION...
...INCREDIBLE!

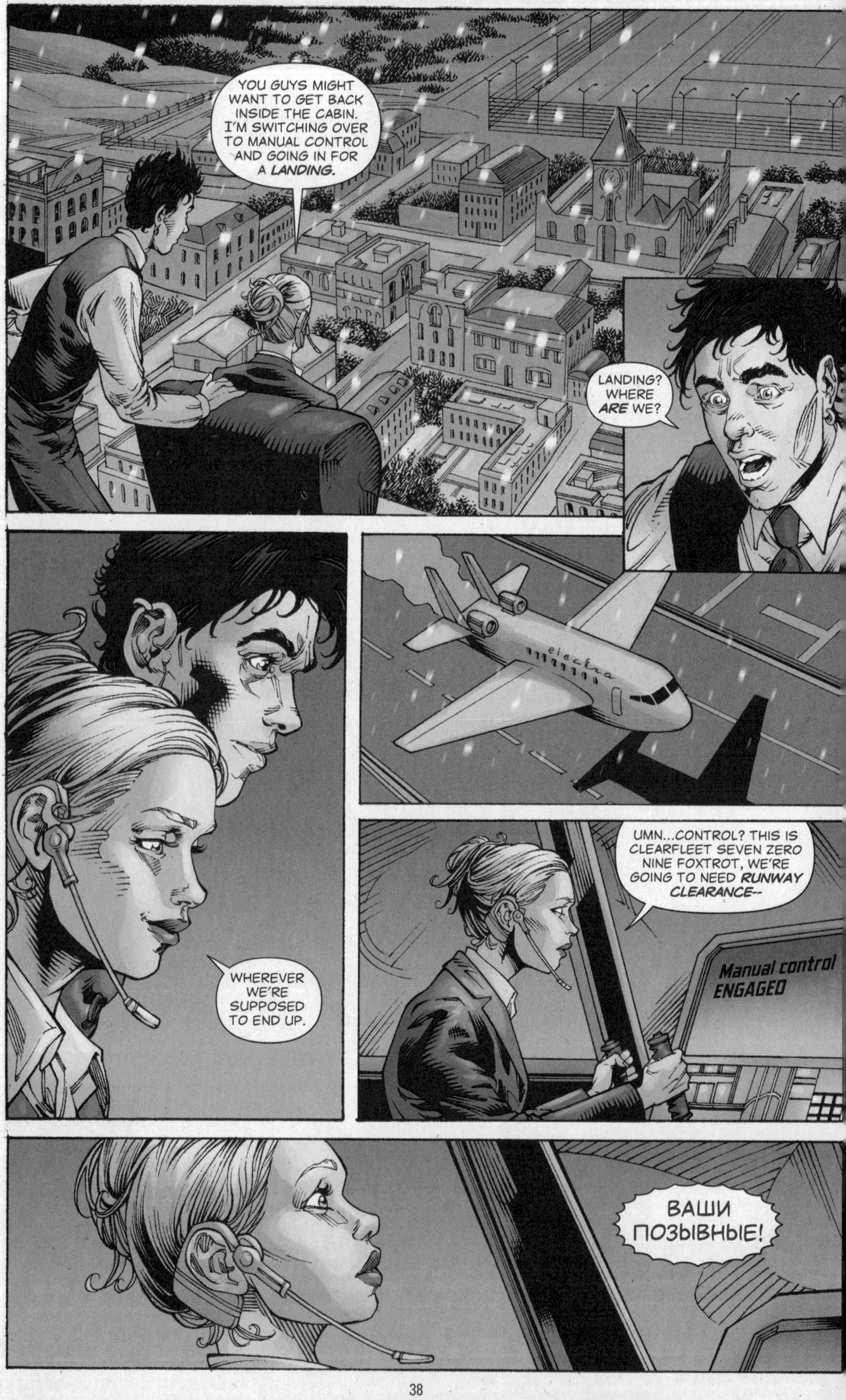
YOU GUYS MIGHT WANT TO GET BACK INSIDE THE CABIN. I'M SWITCHING OVER TO MANUAL CONTROL AND GOING IN FOR A LANDING.
LANDING? WHERE ARE WE?
WHEREVER WE'RE SUPPOSED TO END UP.
electra
UMN...CONTROL? THIS IS CLEARFLEET SEVEN ZERO NINE FOXTROT, WE'RE GOING TO NEED RUNWAY CLEARANCE--
Manual control ENGAGED
ВАШИ ПОЗЫВНЫЕ!

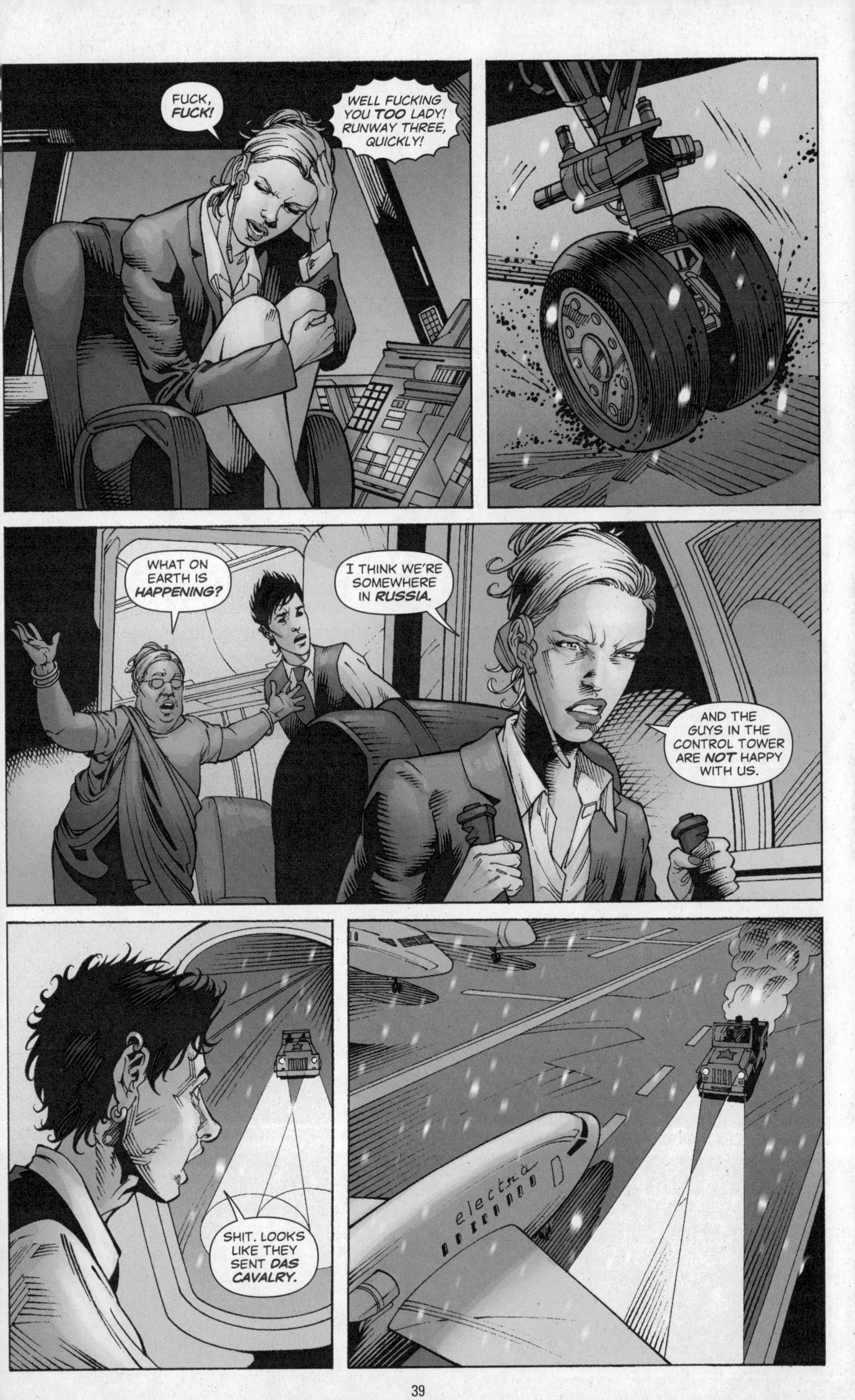
FUCK, FUCK!
WELL FUCKING YOU TOO LADY! RUNWAY THREE, QUICKLY!
WHAT ON EARTH IS HAPPENING?
I THINK WE'RE SOMEWHERE IN RUSSIA.
AND THE GUYS IN THE CONTROL TOWER ARE NOT HAPPY WITH US.
SHIT. LOOKS LIKE THEY SENT DAS CAVALRY.
electra

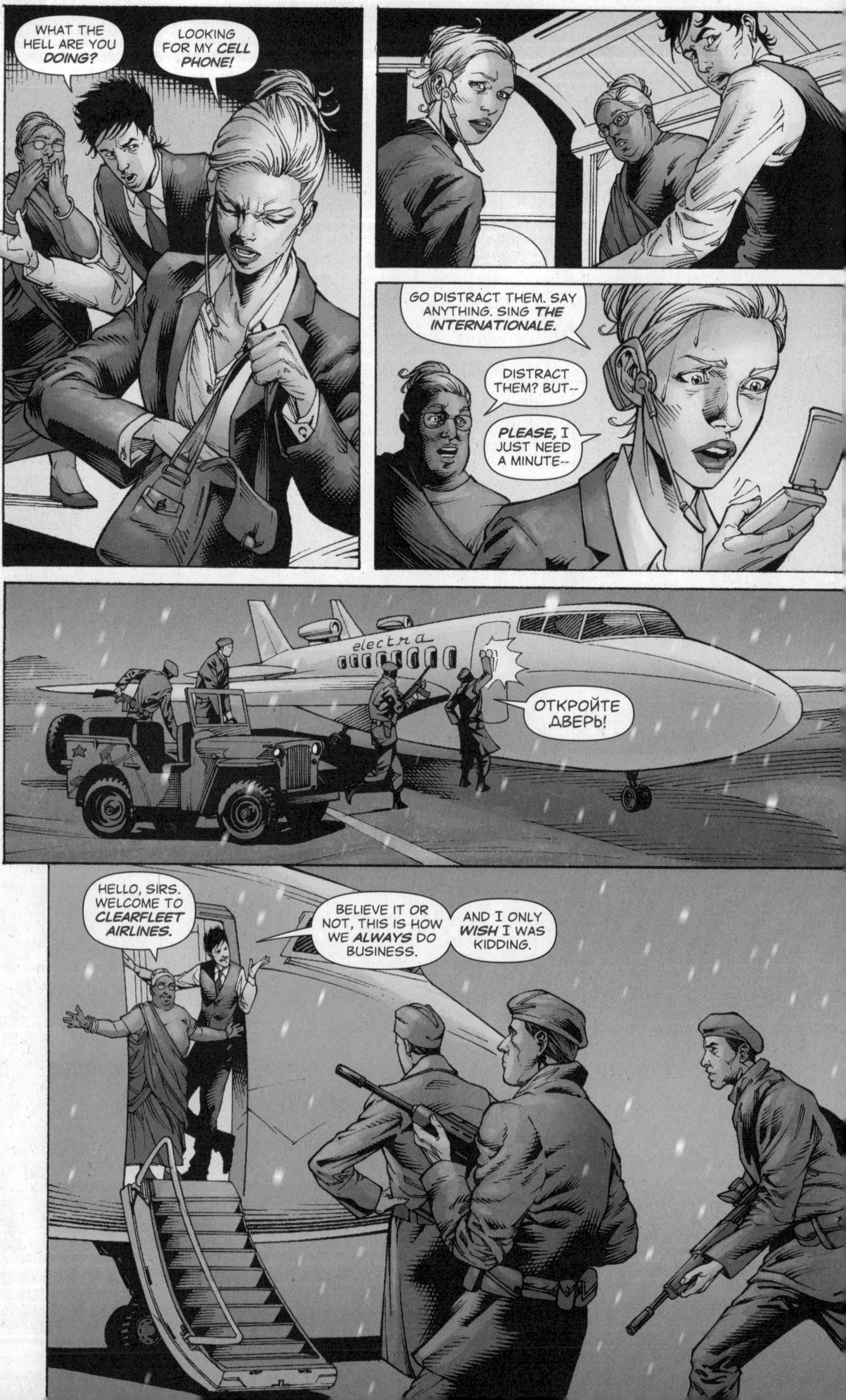
WHAT THE HELL ARE YOU DOING?
LOOKING FOR MY CELL PHONE!
GO DISTRACT THEM. SAY ANYTHING. SING THE INTERNATIONALE.
DISTRACT THEM? BUT--
PLEASE, I JUST NEED A MINUTE--
electra
ОТКРОЙТЕ ДВЕРЬ!
HELLO, SIRS. WELCOME TO CLEARFLEET AIRLINES.
BELIEVE IT OR NOT, THIS IS HOW WE ALWAYS DO BUSINESS.
AND I ONLY WISH I WAS KIDDING.

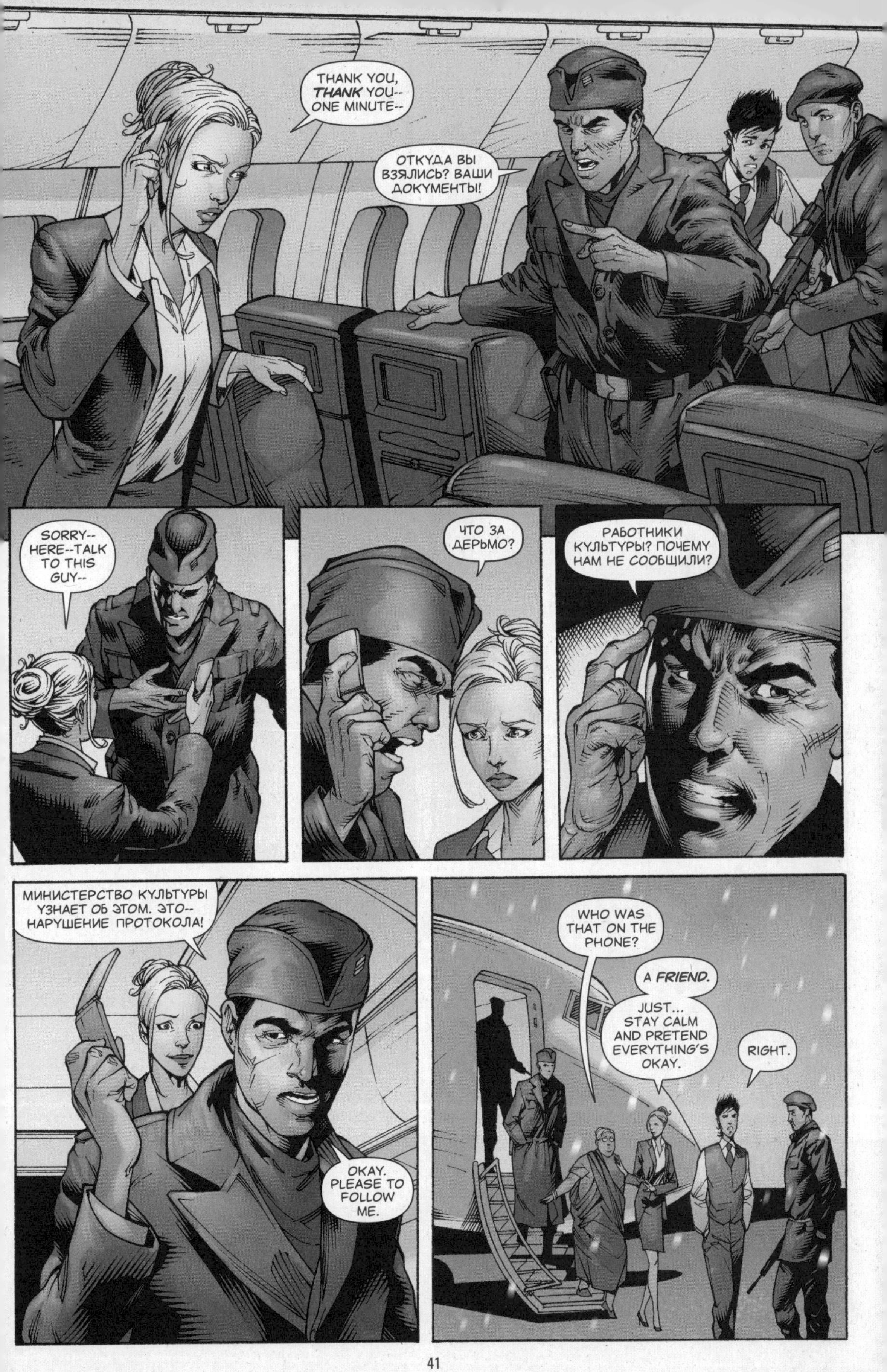
THANK YOU, THANK YOU-- ONE MINUTE--
ОТКУДА ВЫ ВЗЯЛИСЬ? ВАШИ ДОКУМЕНТЫ!
SORRY-- HERE--TALK TO THIS GUY--
ЧТО ЗА ДЕРЬМО?
РАБОТНИКИ КУЛЬТУРЫ? ПОЧЕМУ НАМ НЕ СООБЩИЛИ?
МИНИСТЕРСТВО КУЛЬТУРЫ УЗНАЕТ ОБ ЭТОМ. ЭТО-- НАРУШЕНИЕ ПРОТОКОЛА!
OKAY. PLEASE TO FOLLOW ME.
WHO WAS THAT ON THE PHONE?
A FRIEND.
JUST... STAY CALM AND PRETEND EVERYTHING'S OKAY.
RIGHT.

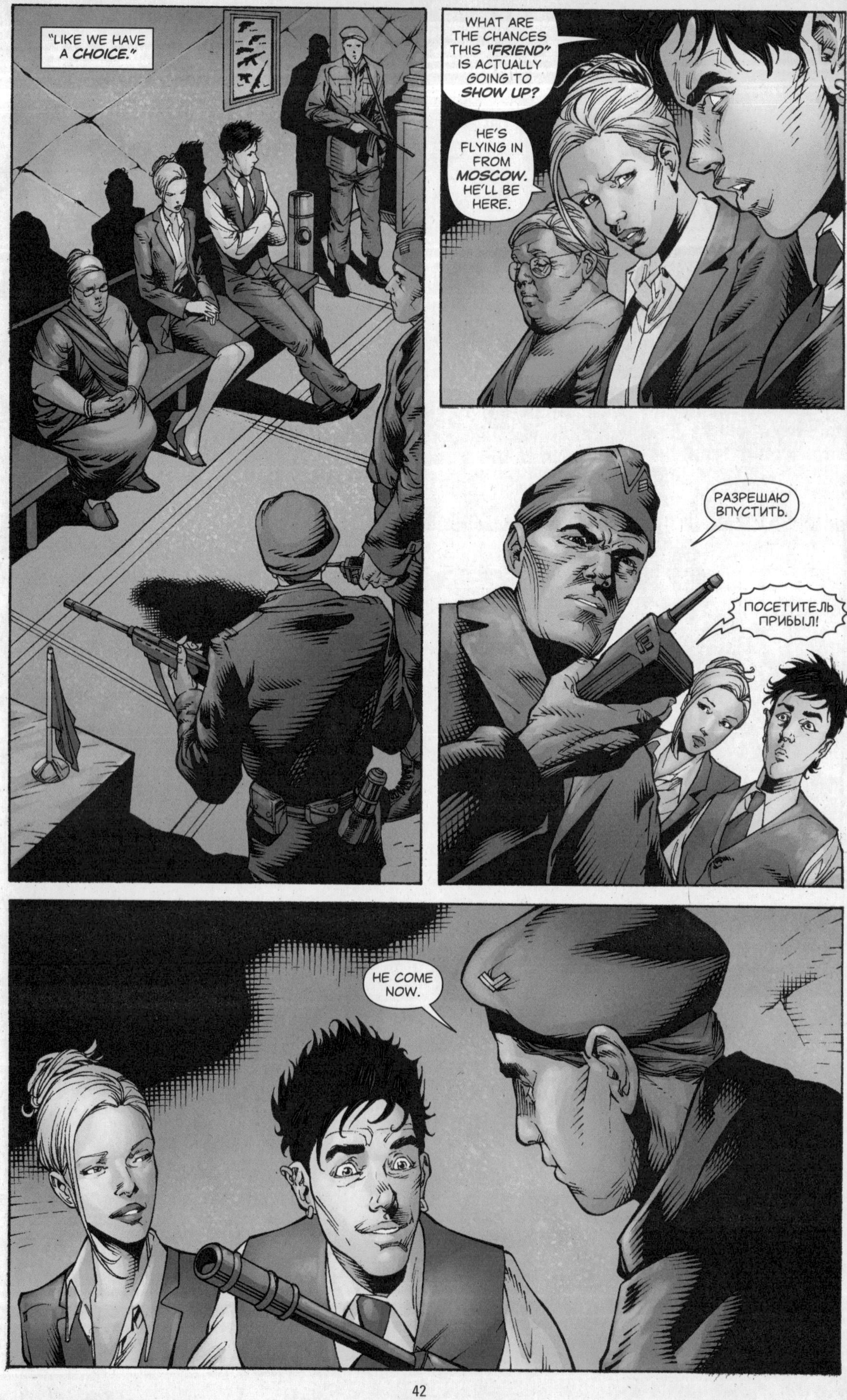
"LIKE WE HAVE A *CHOICE*."
WHAT ARE THE CHANCES THIS *"FRIEND"* IS ACTUALLY GOING TO *SHOW UP?*
HE'S FLYING IN FROM *MOSCOW*. HE'LL BE HERE.
РАЗРЕШАЮ ВПУСТИТЬ.
ПОСЕТИТЕЛЬ ПРИБЫЛ!
HE COME NOW.

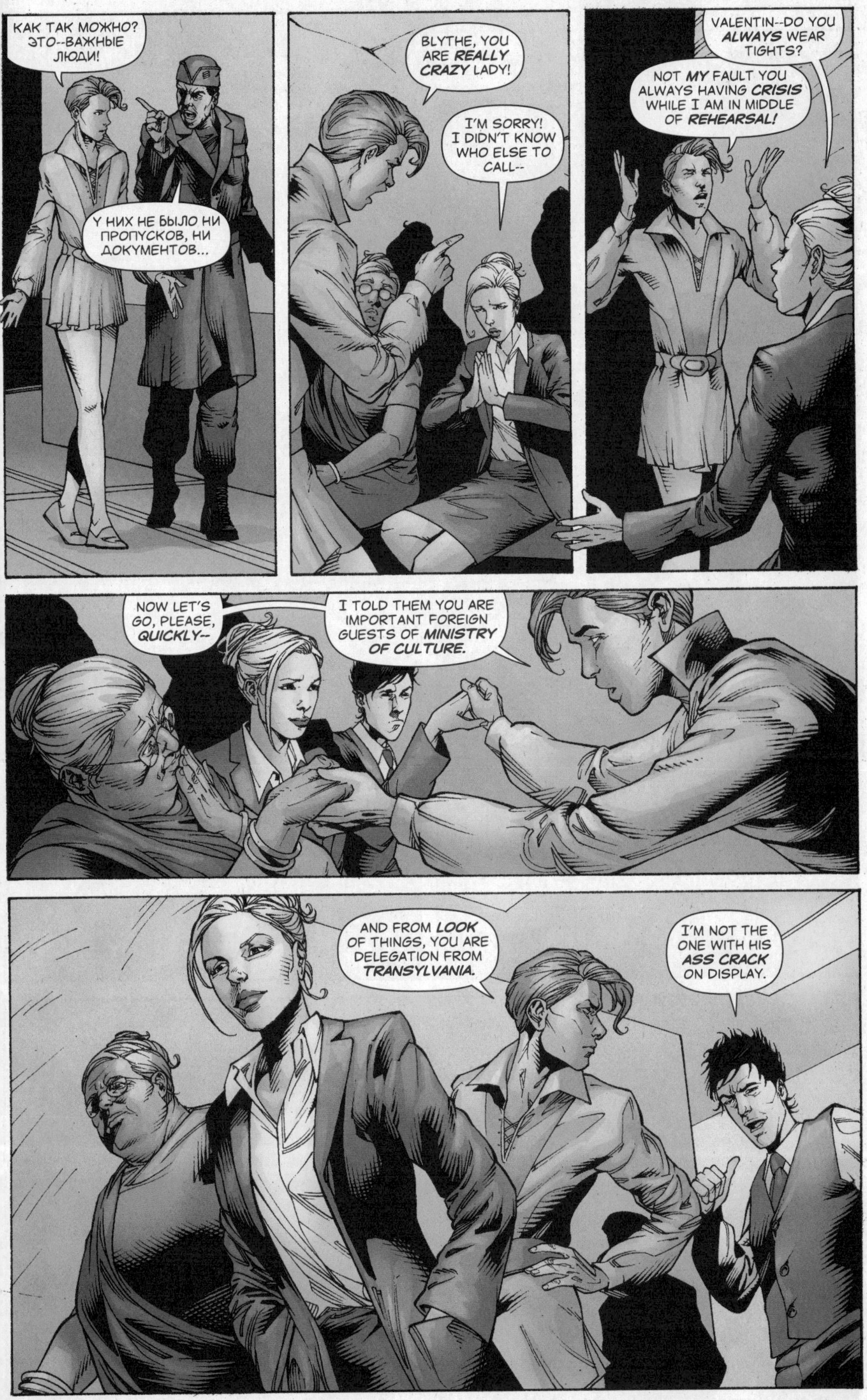
КАК ТАК МОЖНО? ЭТО--ВАЖНЫЕ ЛЮДИ!
У НИХ НЕ БЫЛО НИ ПРОПУСКОВ, НИ ДОКУМЕНТОВ...
BLYTHE, YOU ARE REALLY CRAZY LADY!
I'M SORRY! I DIDN'T KNOW WHO ELSE TO CALL--
VALENTIN--DO YOU ALWAYS WEAR TIGHTS?
NOT MY FAULT YOU ALWAYS HAVING CRISIS WHILE I AM IN MIDDLE OF REHEARSAL!
NOW LET'S GO, PLEASE, QUICKLY--
I TOLD THEM YOU ARE IMPORTANT FOREIGN GUESTS OF MINISTRY OF CULTURE.
AND FROM LOOK OF THINGS, YOU ARE DELEGATION FROM TRANSYLVANIA.
I'M NOT THE ONE WITH HIS ASS CRACK ON DISPLAY.

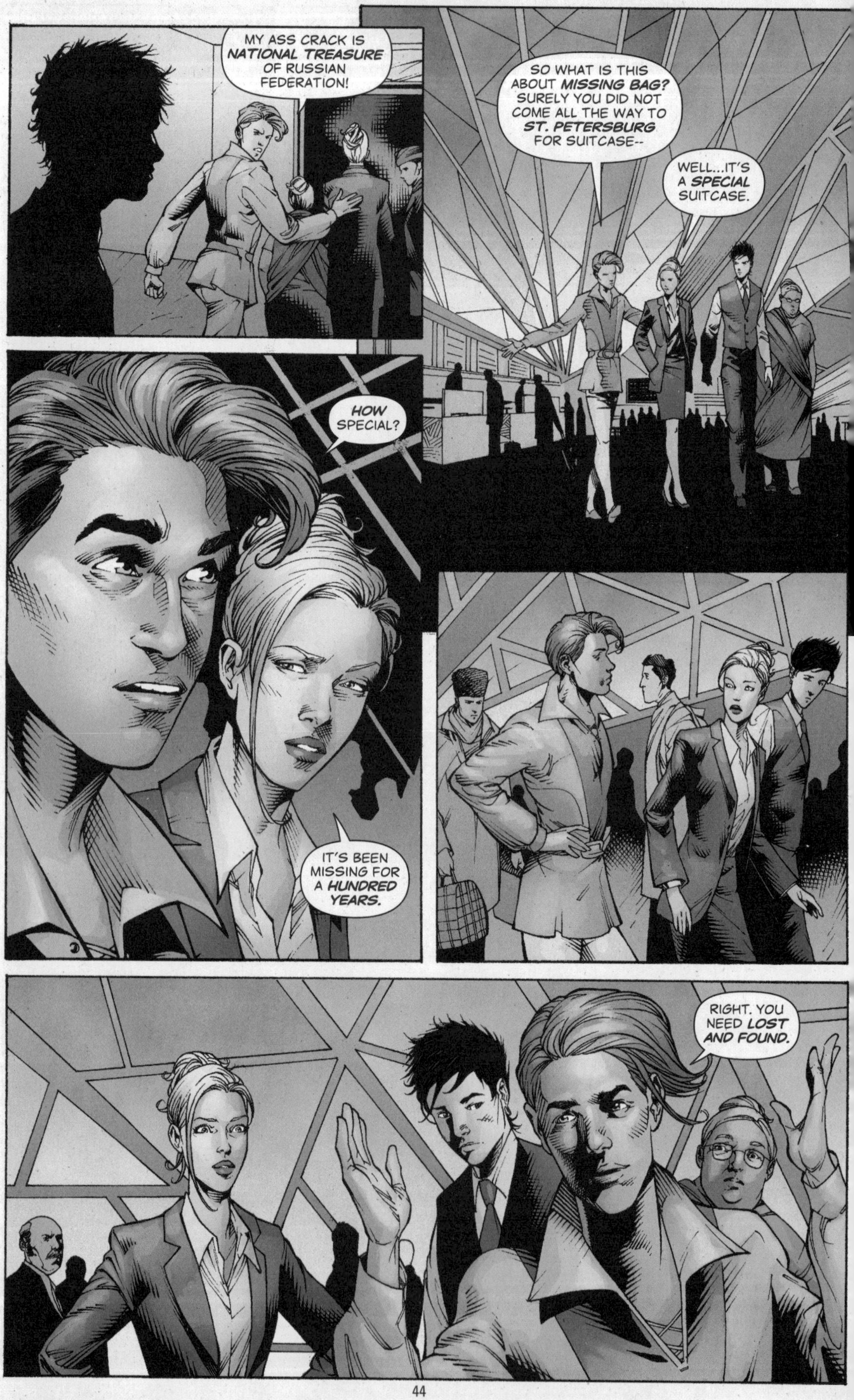
MY ASS CRACK IS NATIONAL TREASURE OF RUSSIAN FEDERATION!
SO WHAT IS THIS ABOUT MISSING BAG? SURELY YOU DID NOT COME ALL THE WAY TO ST. PETERSBURG FOR SUITCASE--
WELL...IT'S A SPECIAL SUITCASE.
HOW SPECIAL?
IT'S BEEN MISSING FOR A HUNDRED YEARS.
RIGHT. YOU NEED LOST AND FOUND.

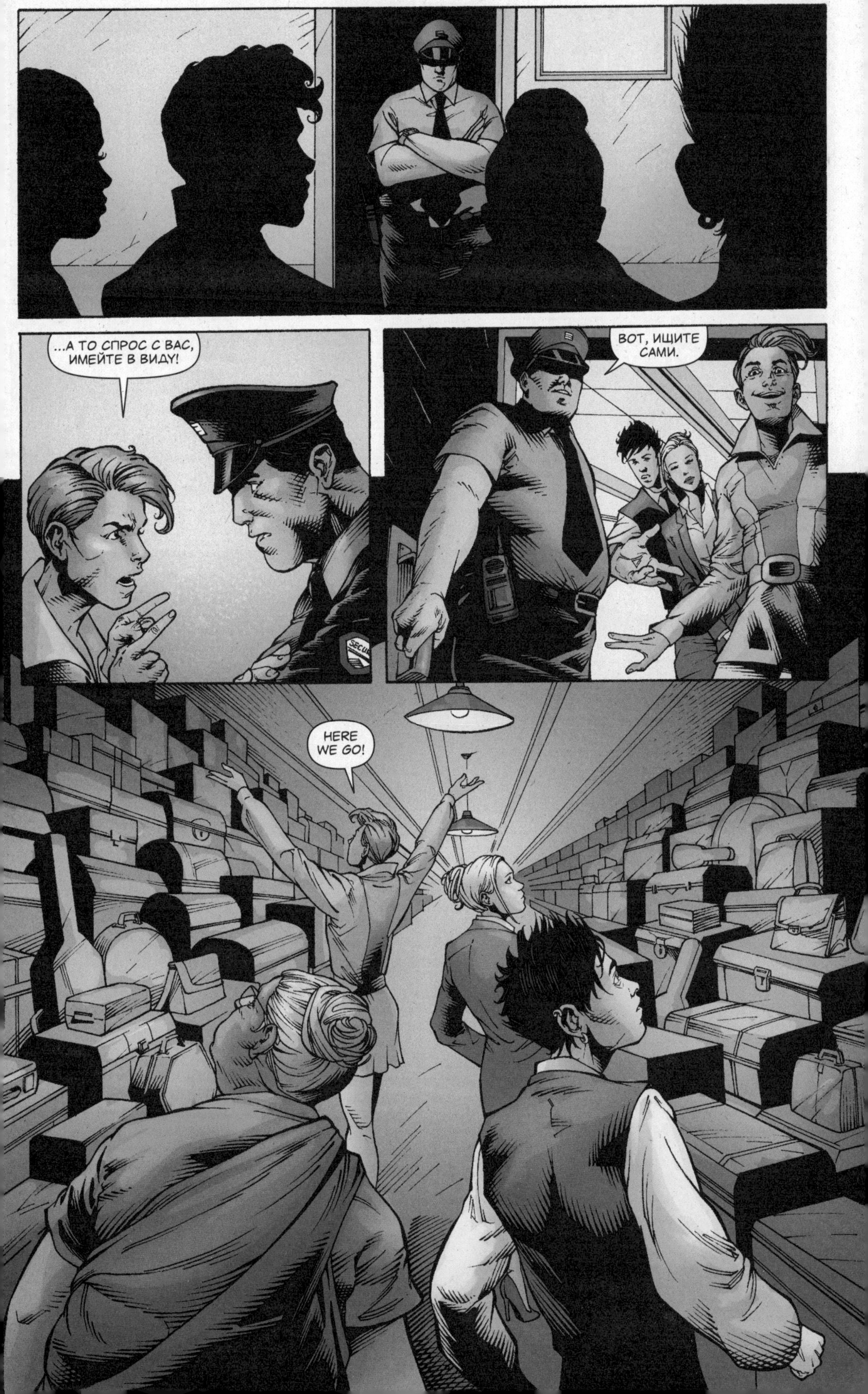
...А ТО СПРОС С ВАС, ИМЕЙТЕ В ВИДУ!
ВОТ, ИЩИТЕ САМИ.
HERE WE GO!

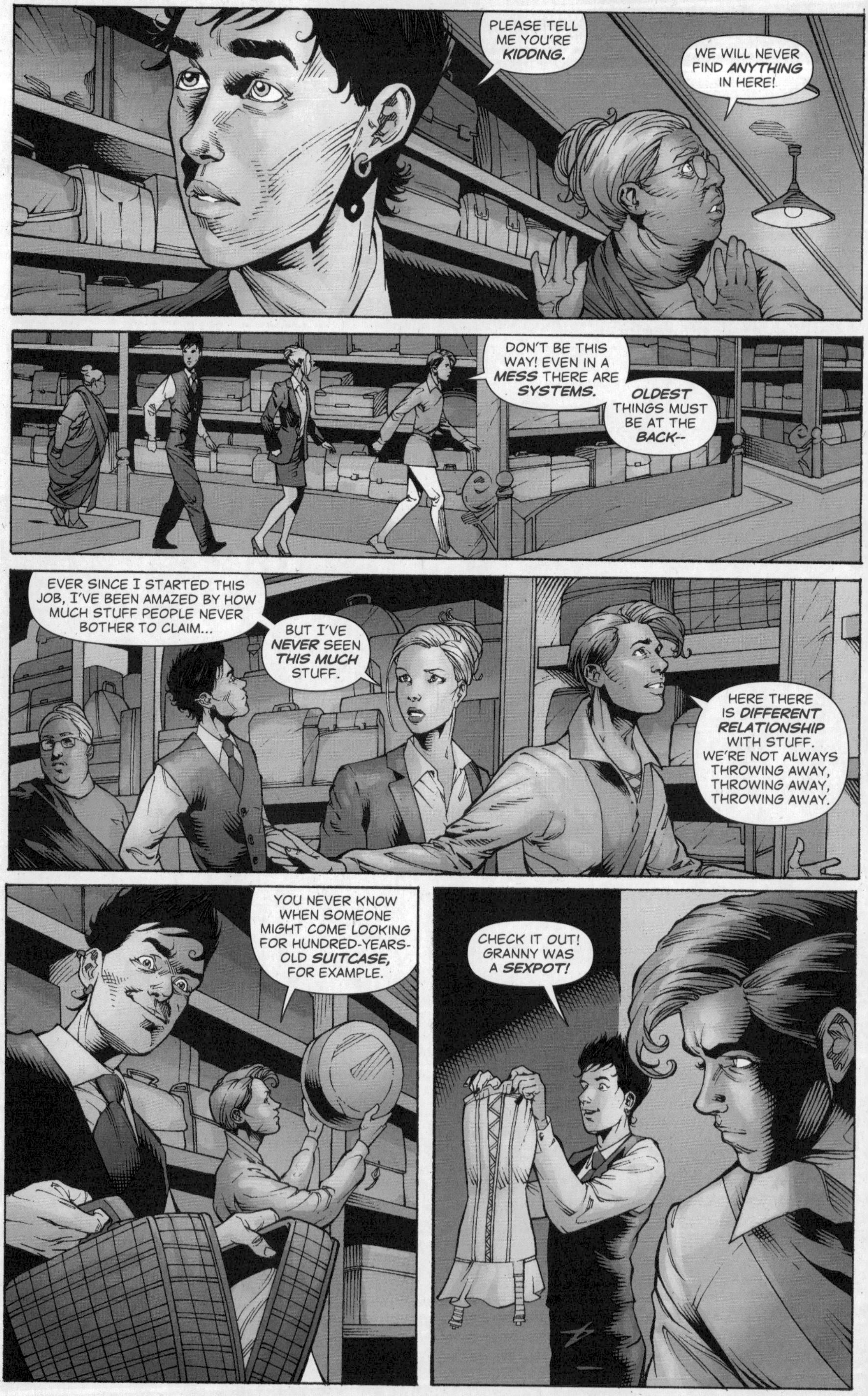
PLEASE TELL ME YOU'RE *KIDDING.*
WE WILL NEVER FIND *ANYTHING* IN HERE!
DON'T BE THIS WAY! EVEN IN A *MESS* THERE ARE *SYSTEMS.*
OLDEST THINGS MUST BE AT THE *BACK--*
EVER SINCE I STARTED THIS JOB, I'VE BEEN AMAZED BY HOW MUCH STUFF PEOPLE NEVER BOTHER TO CLAIM...
BUT I'VE *NEVER* SEEN *THIS MUCH* STUFF.
HERE THERE IS *DIFFERENT RELATIONSHIP* WITH STUFF. WE'RE NOT ALWAYS THROWING AWAY, THROWING AWAY, THROWING AWAY.
YOU NEVER KNOW WHEN SOMEONE MIGHT COME LOOKING FOR HUNDRED-YEARS-OLD *SUITCASE,* FOR EXAMPLE.
CHECK IT OUT! GRANNY WAS A *SEXPOT!*

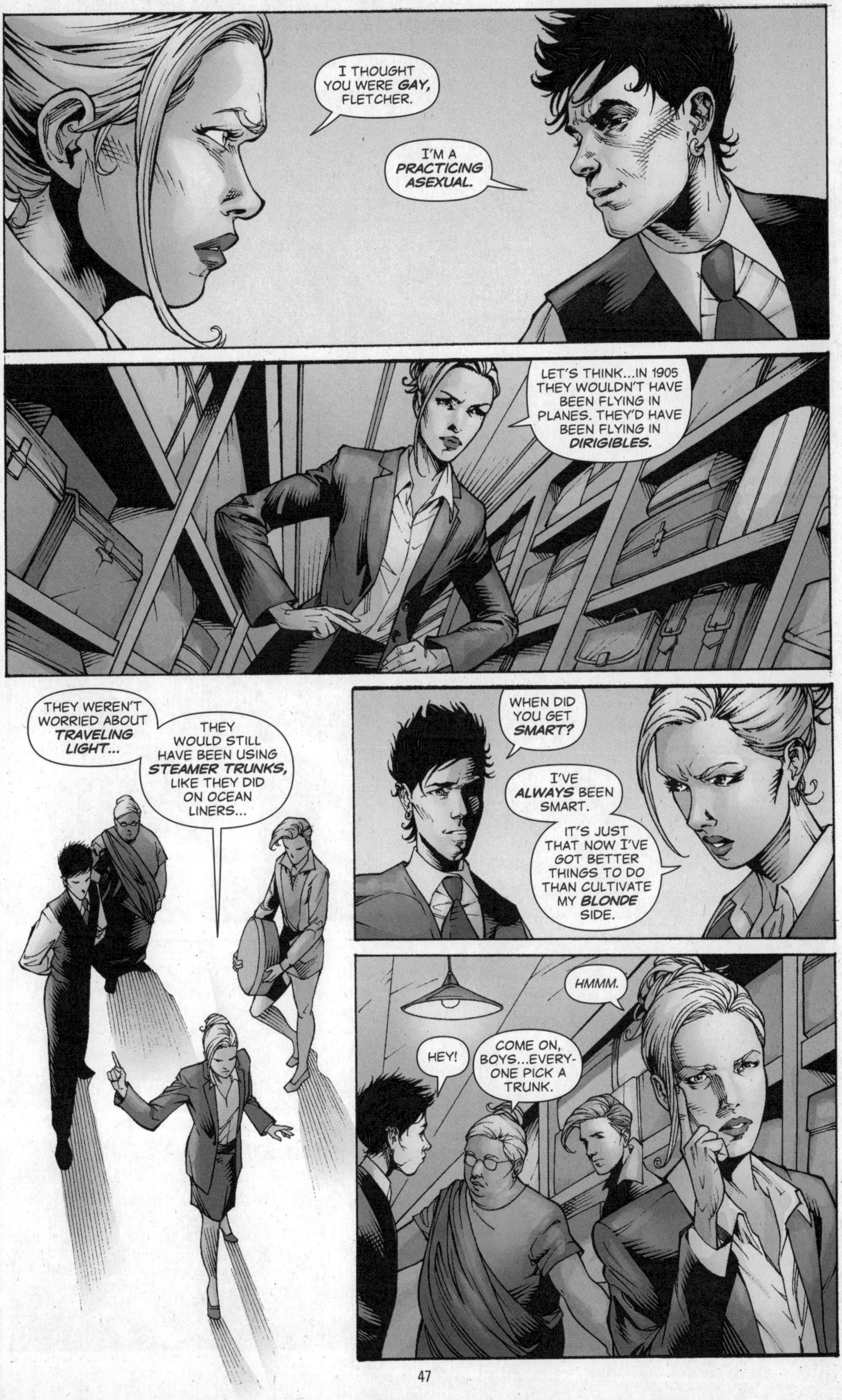
I THOUGHT YOU WERE GAY, FLETCHER.
I'M A PRACTICING ASEXUAL.
LET'S THINK...IN 1905 THEY WOULDN'T HAVE BEEN FLYING IN PLANES. THEY'D HAVE BEEN FLYING IN DIRIGIBLES.
THEY WEREN'T WORRIED ABOUT TRAVELING LIGHT...
THEY WOULD STILL HAVE BEEN USING STEAMER TRUNKS, LIKE THEY DID ON OCEAN LINERS...
WHEN DID YOU GET SMART?
I'VE ALWAYS BEEN SMART.
IT'S JUST THAT NOW I'VE GOT BETTER THINGS TO DO THAN CULTIVATE MY BLONDE SIDE.
HMMM.
HEY!
COME ON, BOYS...EVERY-ONE PICK A TRUNK.

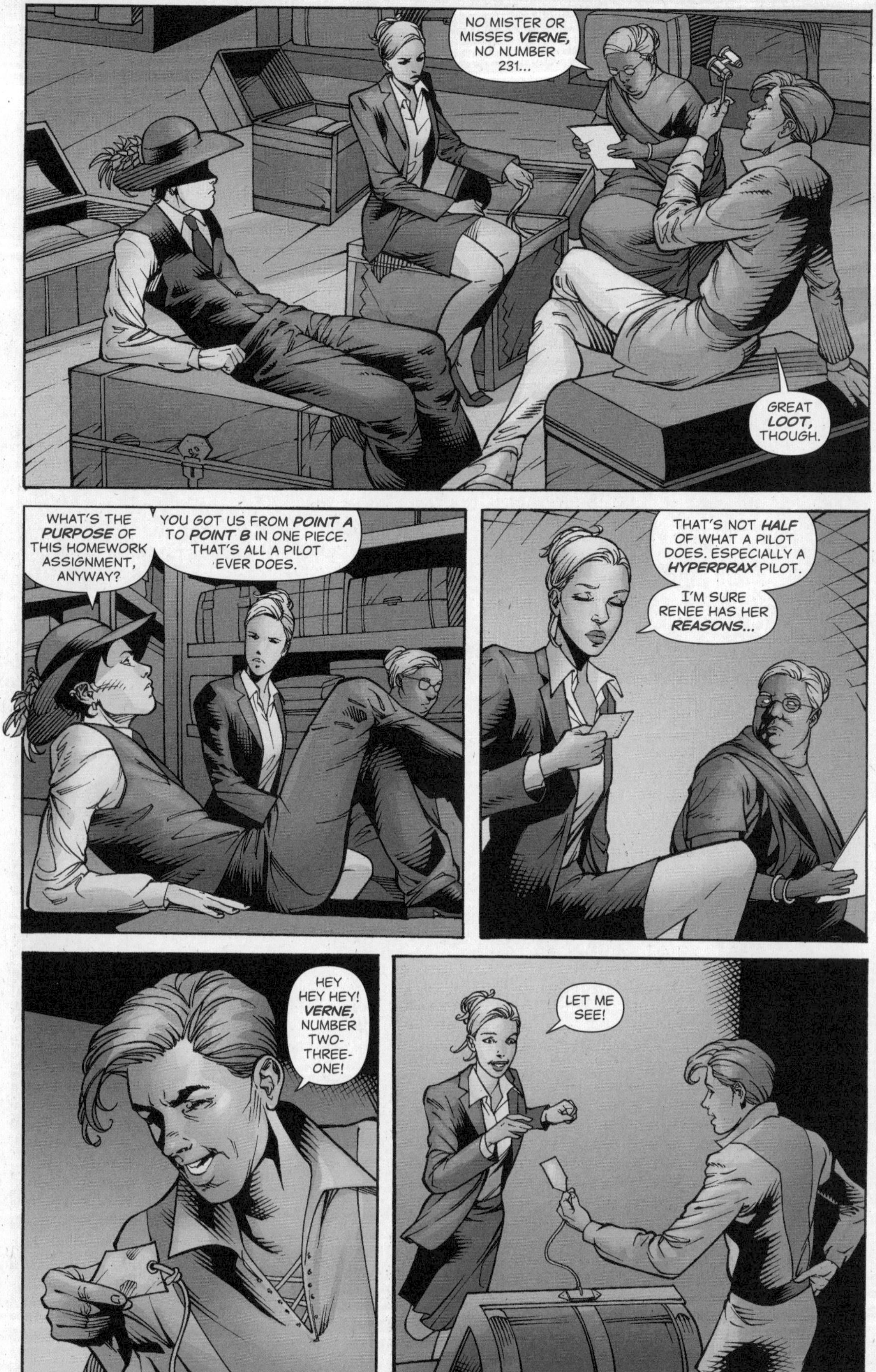
NO MISTER OR MISSES VERNE, NO NUMBER 231...
GREAT LOOT, THOUGH.
WHAT'S THE PURPOSE OF THIS HOMEWORK ASSIGNMENT, ANYWAY?
YOU GOT US FROM POINT A TO POINT B IN ONE PIECE. THAT'S ALL A PILOT EVER DOES.
THAT'S NOT HALF OF WHAT A PILOT DOES. ESPECIALLY A HYPERPRAX PILOT.
I'M SURE RENEE HAS HER REASONS...
HEY HEY HEY! VERNE, NUMBER TWO-THREE-ONE!
LET ME SEE!

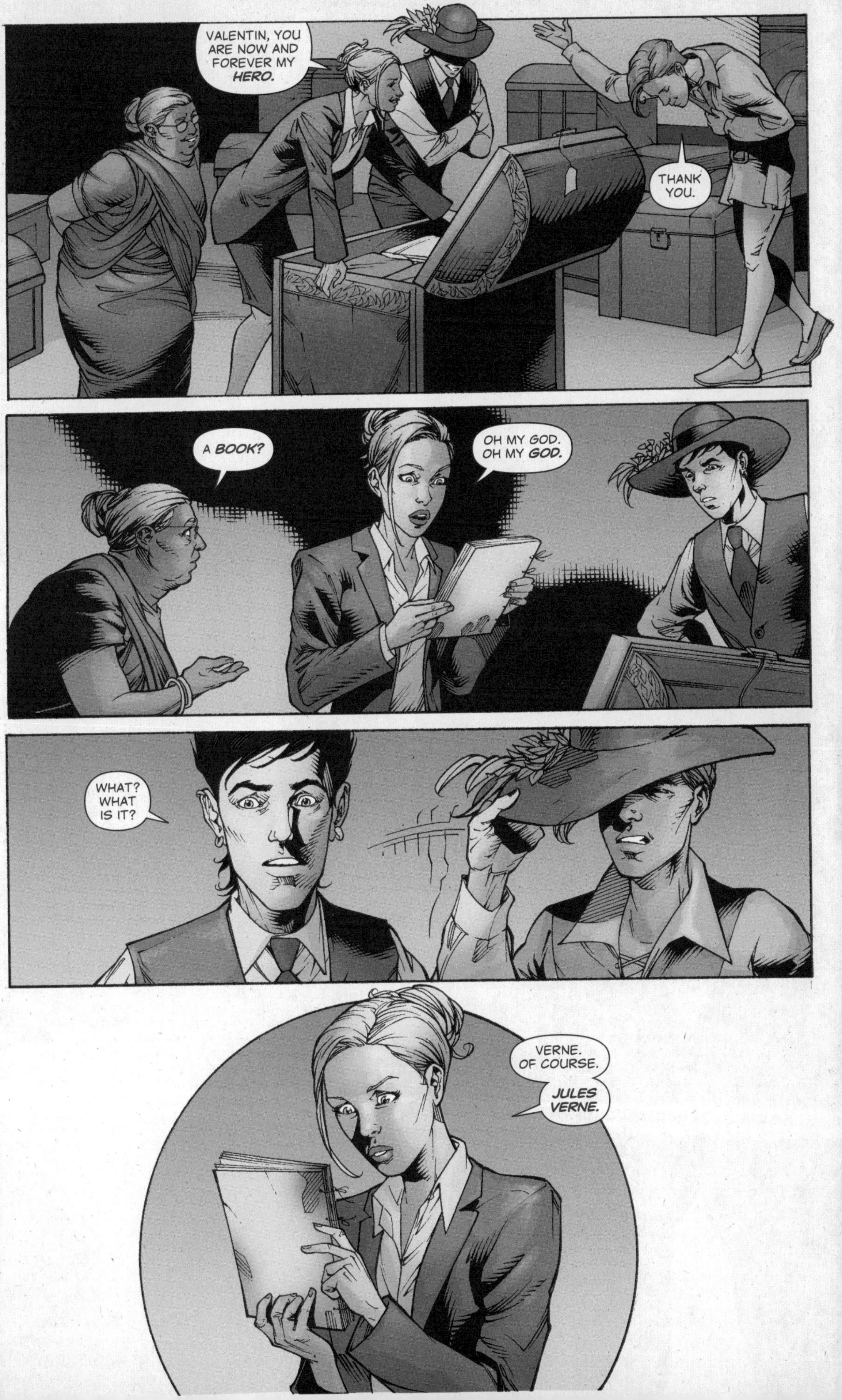
VALENTIN, YOU ARE NOW AND FOREVER MY HERO.
THANK YOU.
A BOOK?
OH MY GOD. OH MY GOD.
WHAT? WHAT IS IT?
VERNE. OF COURSE.
JULES VERNE.

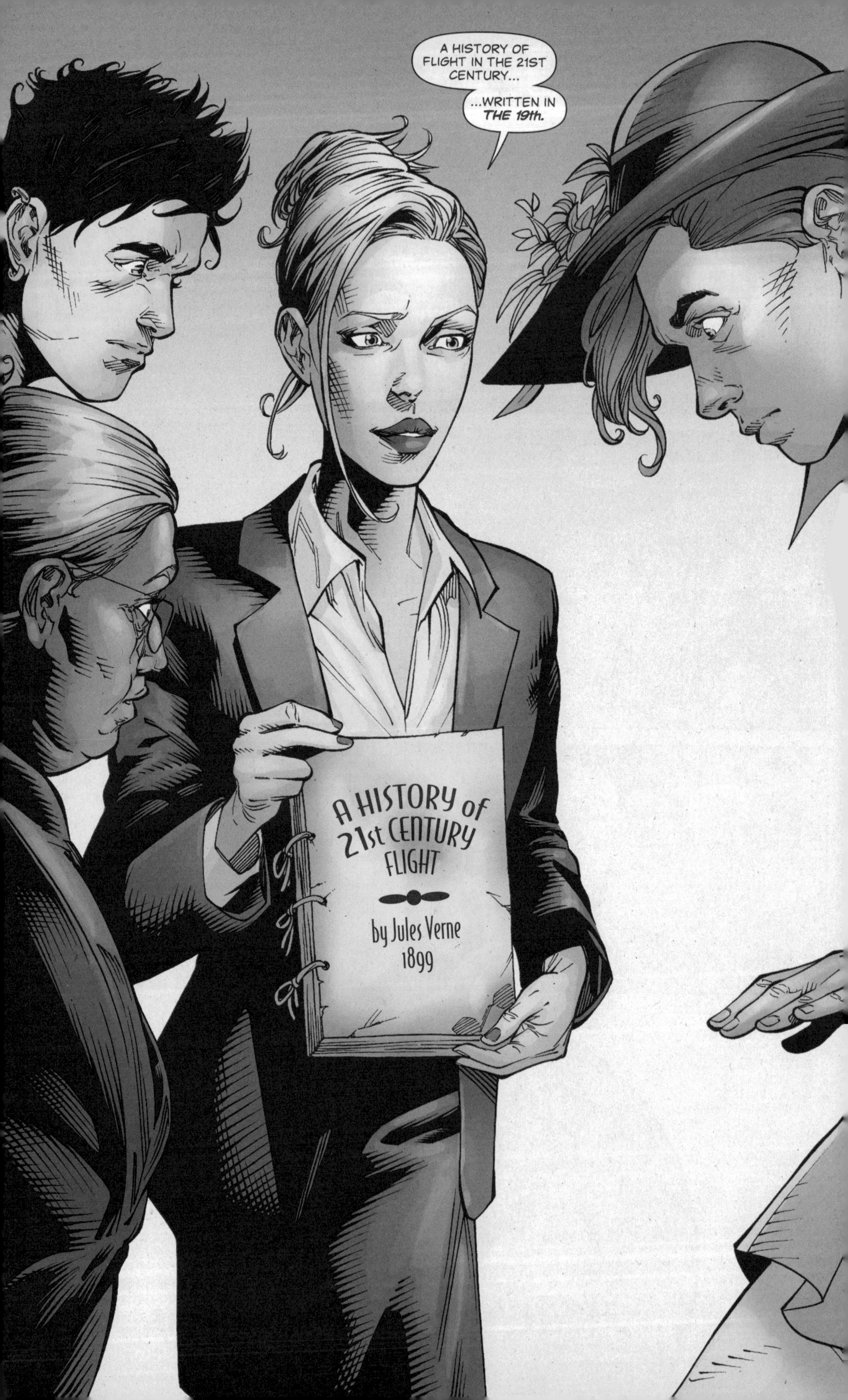
A HISTORY OF FLIGHT IN THE 21ST CENTURY...
...WRITTEN IN *THE 19th.*
A HISTORY of 21st CENTURY FLIGHT
by Jules Verne
1899

A HISTORY OF THE FUTURE
PART TWO

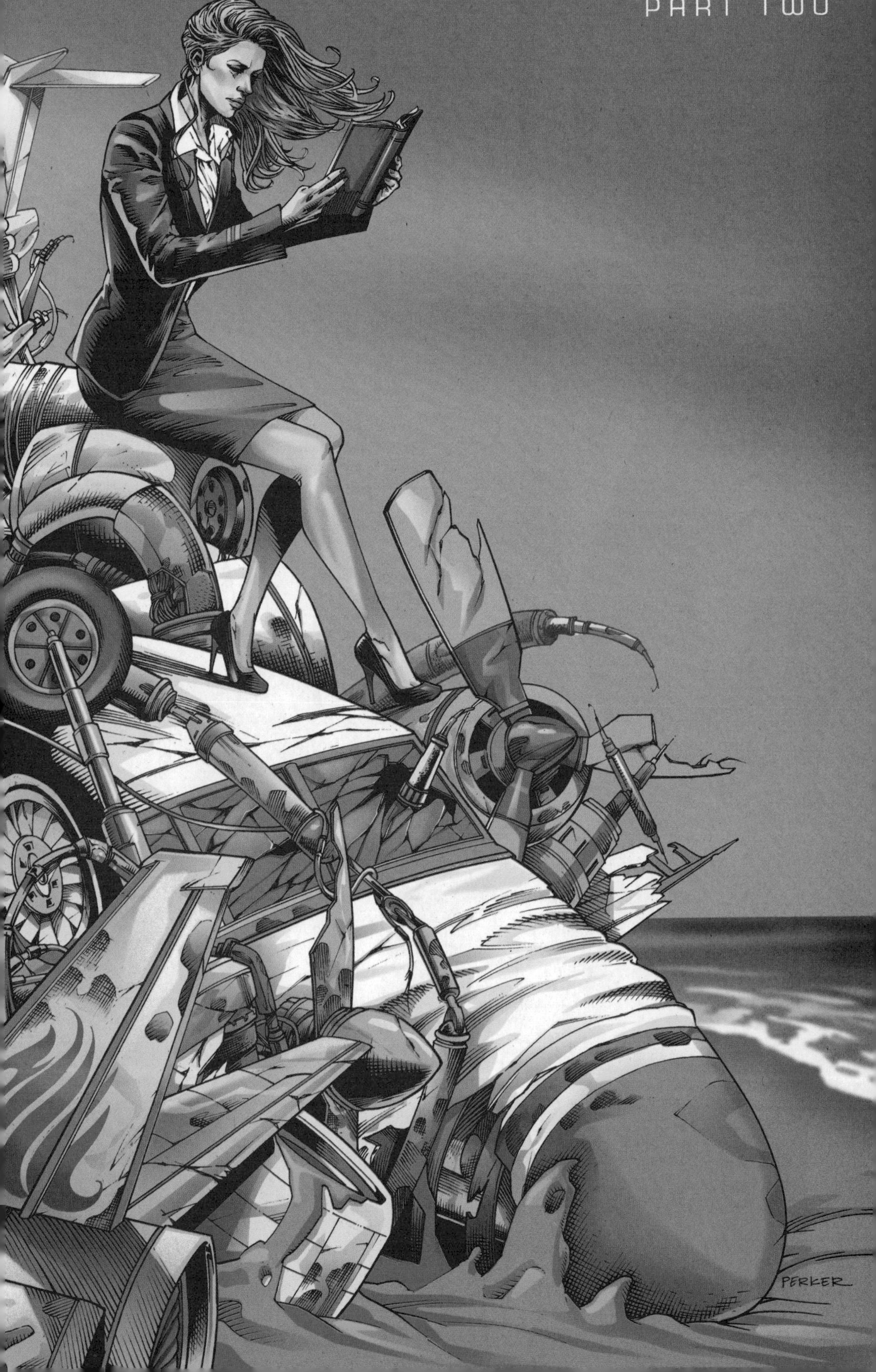
PERKER

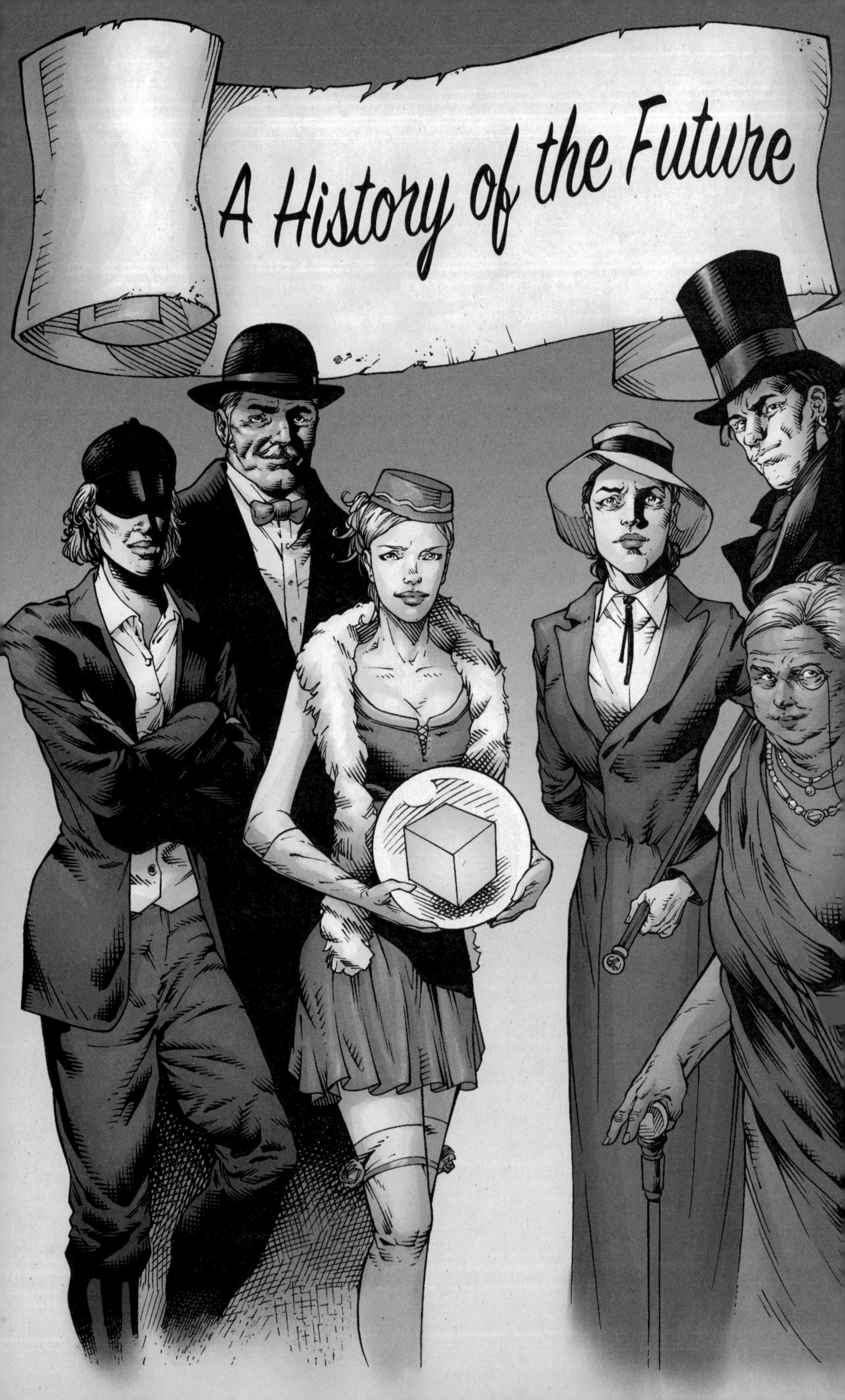
A History of the Future

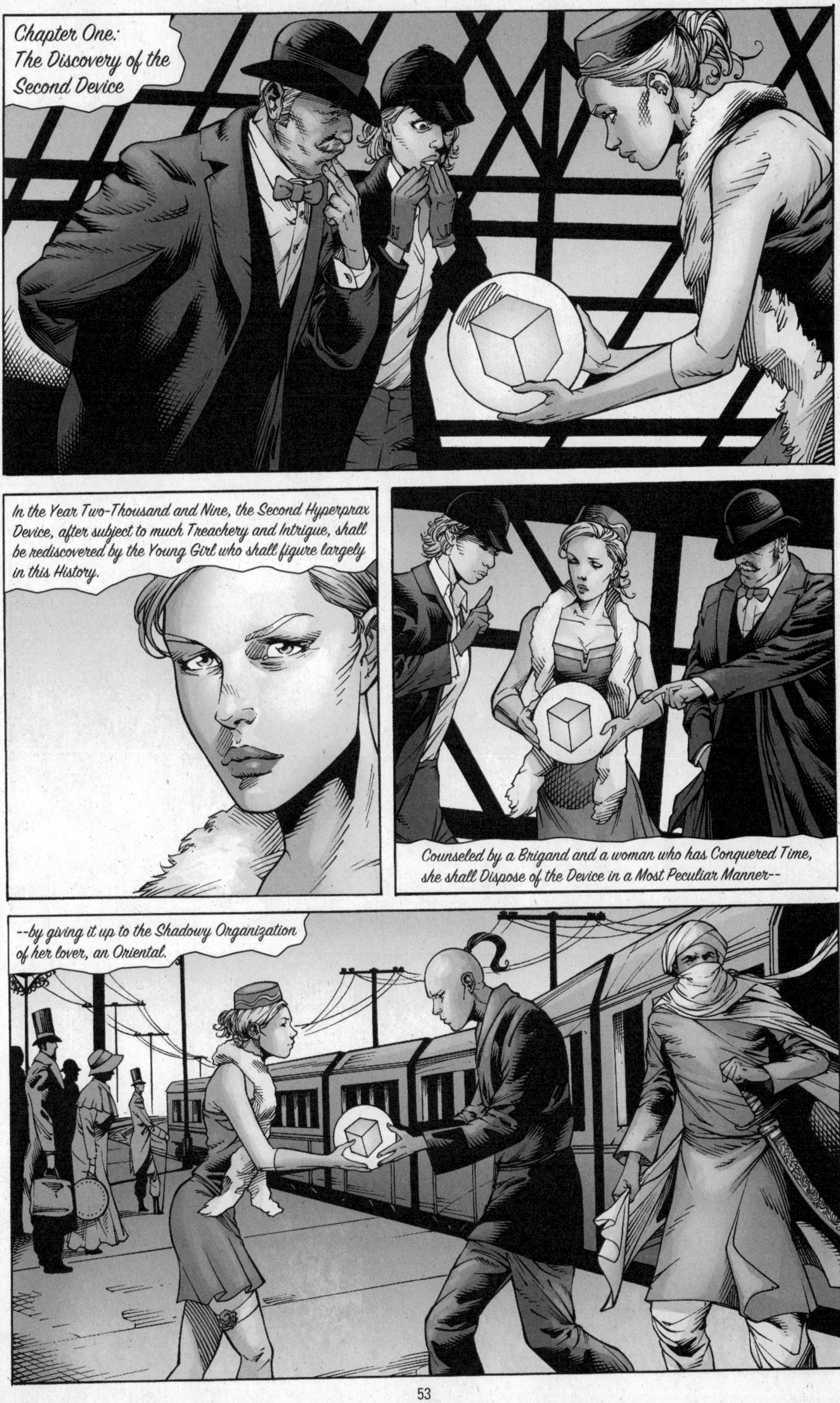
Chapter One: The Discovery of the Second Device
In the Year Two-Thousand and Nine, the Second Hyperprax Device, after subject to much Treachery and Intrigue, shall be rediscovered by the Young Girl who shall figure largely in this History.
Counseled by a Brigand and a woman who has Conquered Time, she shall Dispose of the Device in a Most Peculiar Manner--
--by giving it up to the Shadowy Organization of her lover, an Oriental.

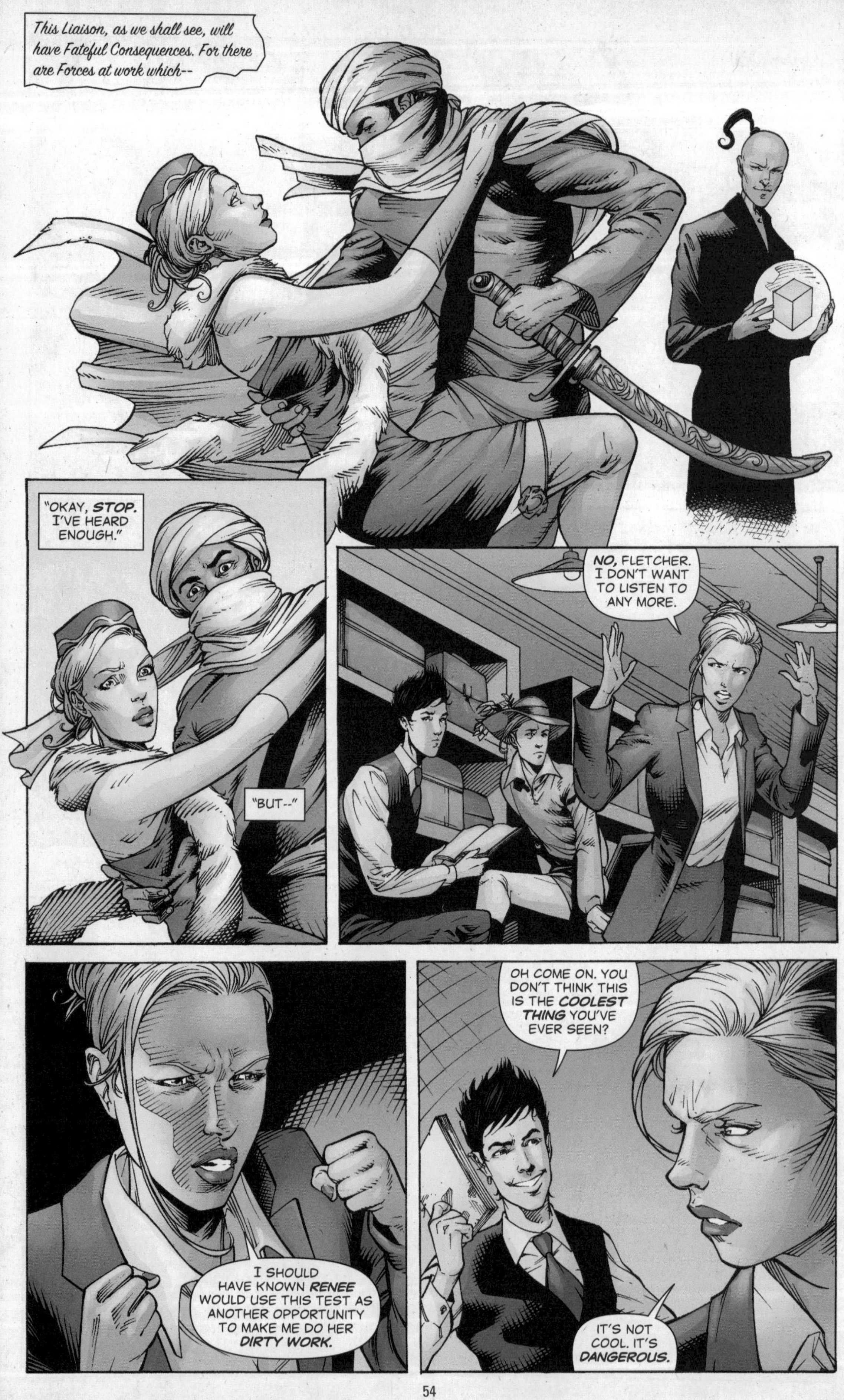
This Liaison, as we shall see, will have Fateful Consequences. For there are Forces at work which--
"OKAY, STOP. I'VE HEARD ENOUGH."
"BUT--"
NO, FLETCHER. I DON'T WANT TO LISTEN TO ANY MORE.
I SHOULD HAVE KNOWN RENEE WOULD USE THIS TEST AS ANOTHER OPPORTUNITY TO MAKE ME DO HER DIRTY WORK.
OH COME ON. YOU DON'T THINK THIS IS THE COOLEST THING YOU'VE EVER SEEN?
IT'S NOT COOL. IT'S DANGEROUS.

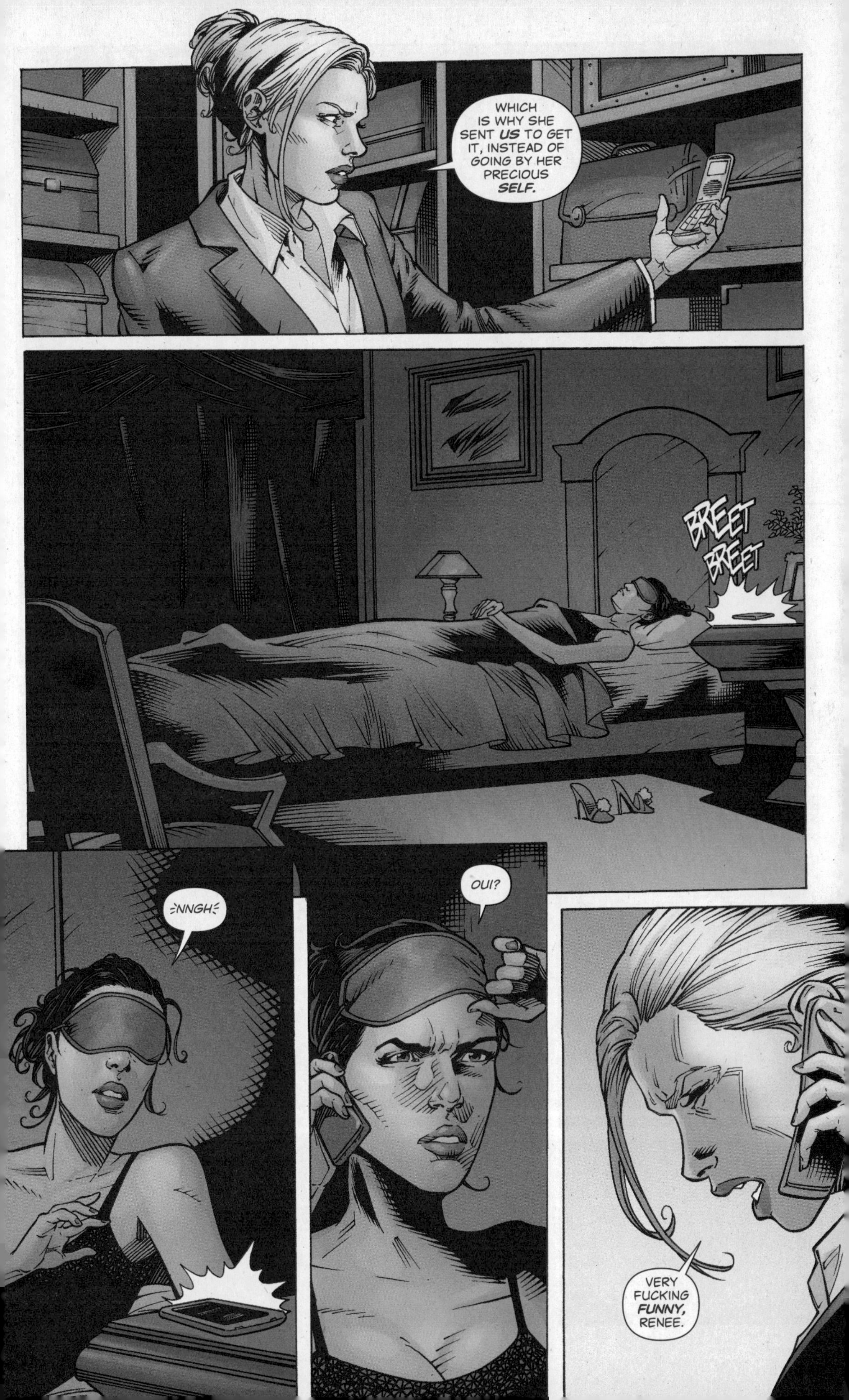
WHICH IS WHY SHE SENT US TO GET IT, INSTEAD OF GOING BY HER PRECIOUS SELF.
BREET BREET
NNGH
OUI?
VERY FUCKING FUNNY, RENEE.

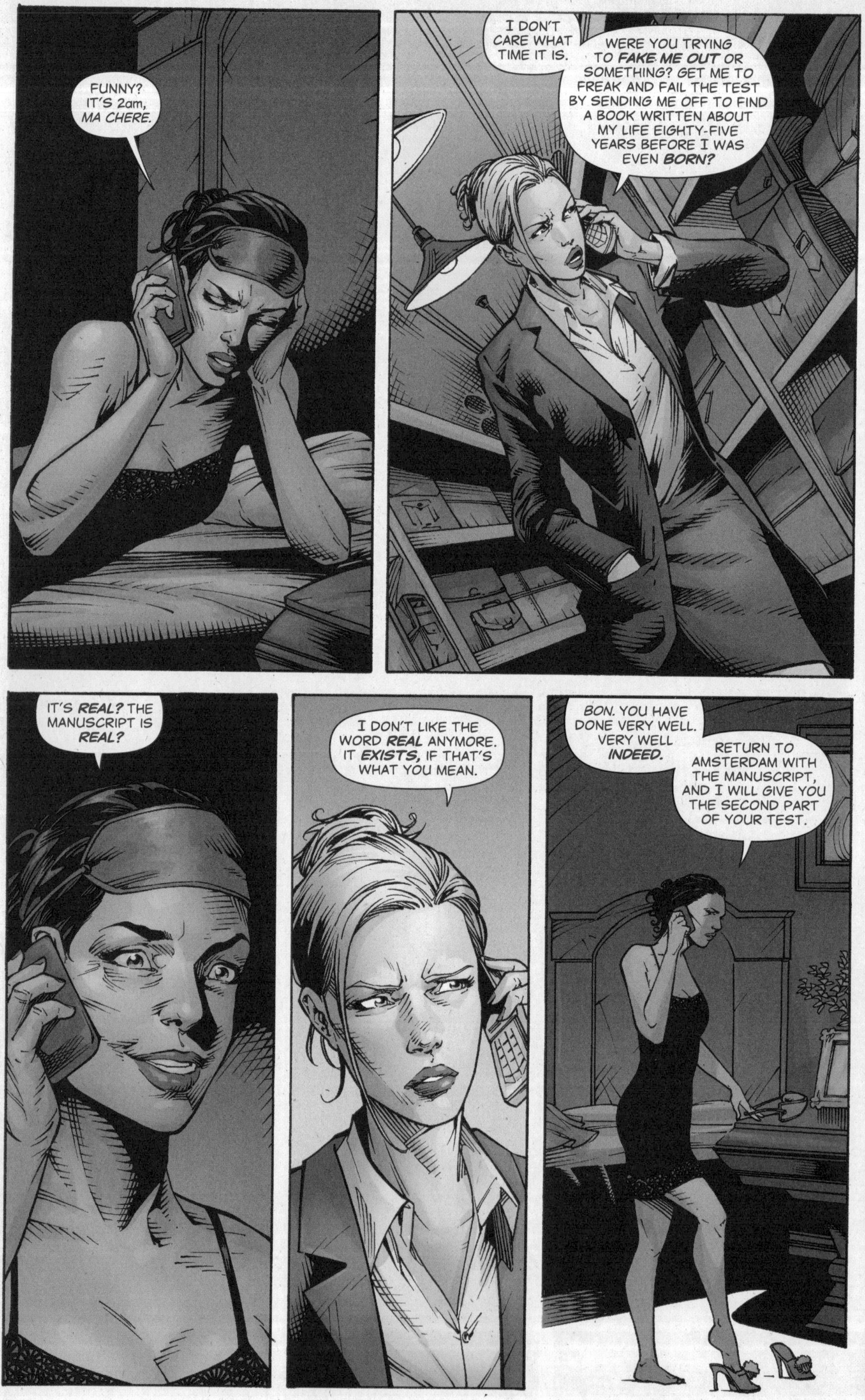
FUNNY? IT'S 2am, MA CHERE.
I DON'T CARE WHAT TIME IT IS.
WERE YOU TRYING TO FAKE ME OUT OR SOMETHING? GET ME TO FREAK AND FAIL THE TEST BY SENDING ME OFF TO FIND A BOOK WRITTEN ABOUT MY LIFE EIGHTY-FIVE YEARS BEFORE I WAS EVEN BORN?
IT'S REAL? THE MANUSCRIPT IS REAL?
I DON'T LIKE THE WORD REAL ANYMORE. IT EXISTS, IF THAT'S WHAT YOU MEAN.
BON. YOU HAVE DONE VERY WELL. VERY WELL INDEED.
RETURN TO AMSTERDAM WITH THE MANUSCRIPT, AND I WILL GIVE YOU THE SECOND PART OF YOUR TEST.

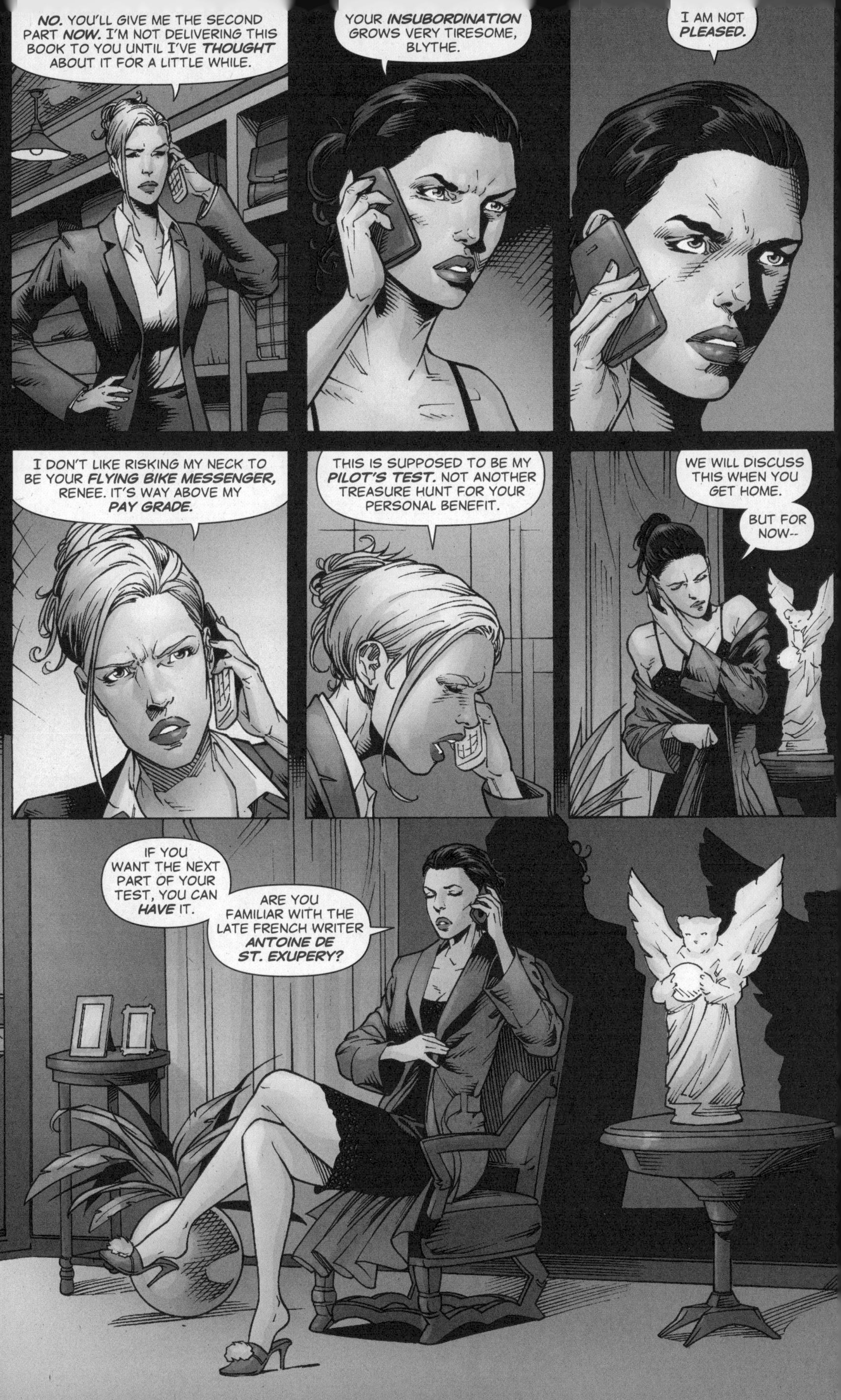
NO. YOU'LL GIVE ME THE SECOND PART NOW. I'M NOT DELIVERING THIS BOOK TO YOU UNTIL I'VE THOUGHT ABOUT IT FOR A LITTLE WHILE.
YOUR INSUBORDINATION GROWS VERY TIRESOME, BLYTHE.
I AM NOT PLEASED.
I DON'T LIKE RISKING MY NECK TO BE YOUR FLYING BIKE MESSENGER, RENEE. IT'S WAY ABOVE MY PAY GRADE.
THIS IS SUPPOSED TO BE MY PILOT'S TEST. NOT ANOTHER TREASURE HUNT FOR YOUR PERSONAL BENEFIT.
WE WILL DISCUSS THIS WHEN YOU GET HOME.
BUT FOR NOW--
IF YOU WANT THE NEXT PART OF YOUR TEST, YOU CAN HAVE IT.
ARE YOU FAMILIAR WITH THE LATE FRENCH WRITER ANTOINE DE ST. EXUPERY?

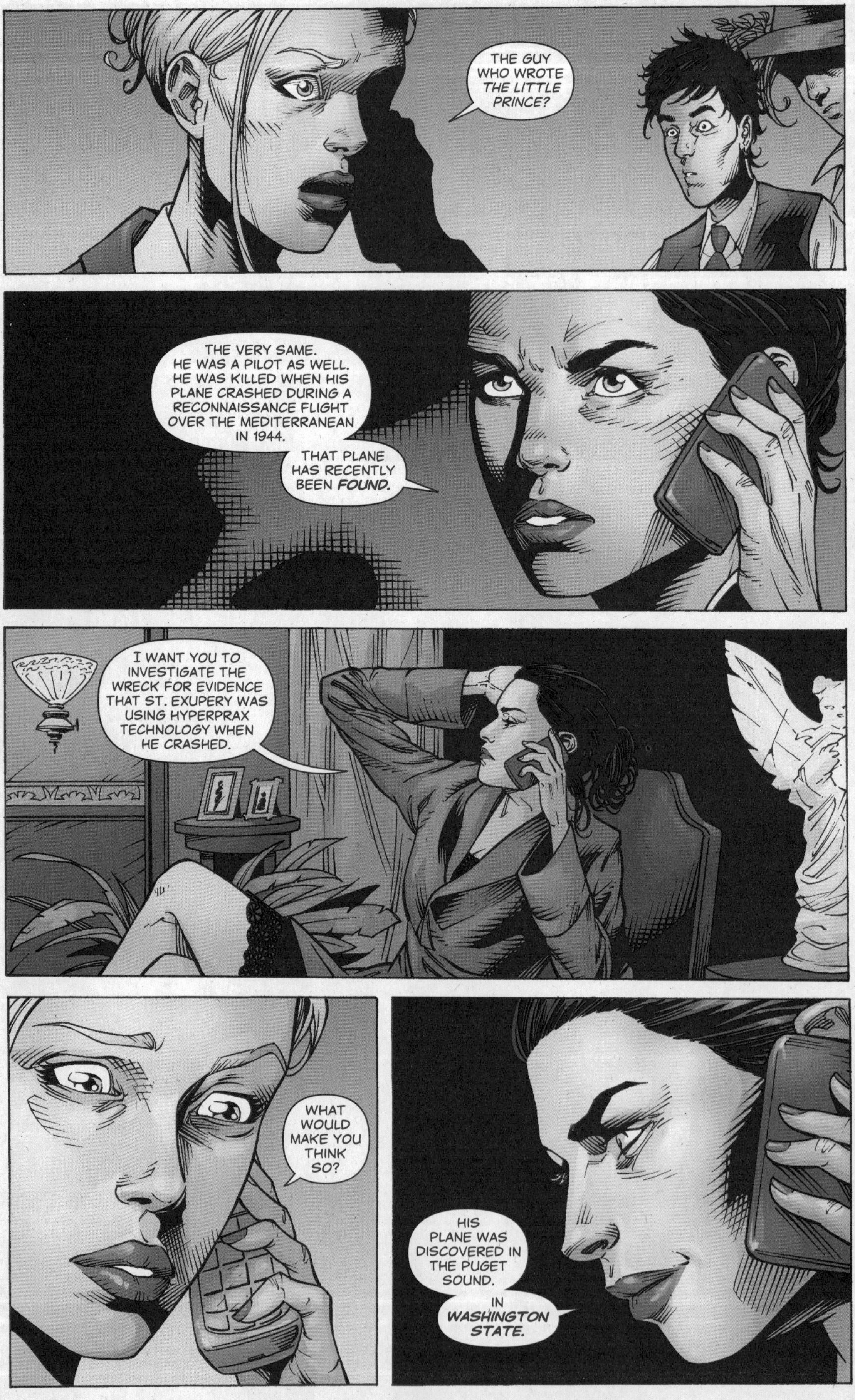
THE GUY WHO WROTE THE LITTLE PRINCE?
THE VERY SAME. HE WAS A PILOT AS WELL. HE WAS KILLED WHEN HIS PLANE CRASHED DURING A RECONNAISSANCE FLIGHT OVER THE MEDITERRANEAN IN 1944.
THAT PLANE HAS RECENTLY BEEN FOUND.
I WANT YOU TO INVESTIGATE THE WRECK FOR EVIDENCE THAT ST. EXUPERY WAS USING HYPERPRAX TECHNOLOGY WHEN HE CRASHED.
WHAT WOULD MAKE YOU THINK SO?
HIS PLANE WAS DISCOVERED IN THE PUGET SOUND.
IN WASHINGTON STATE.

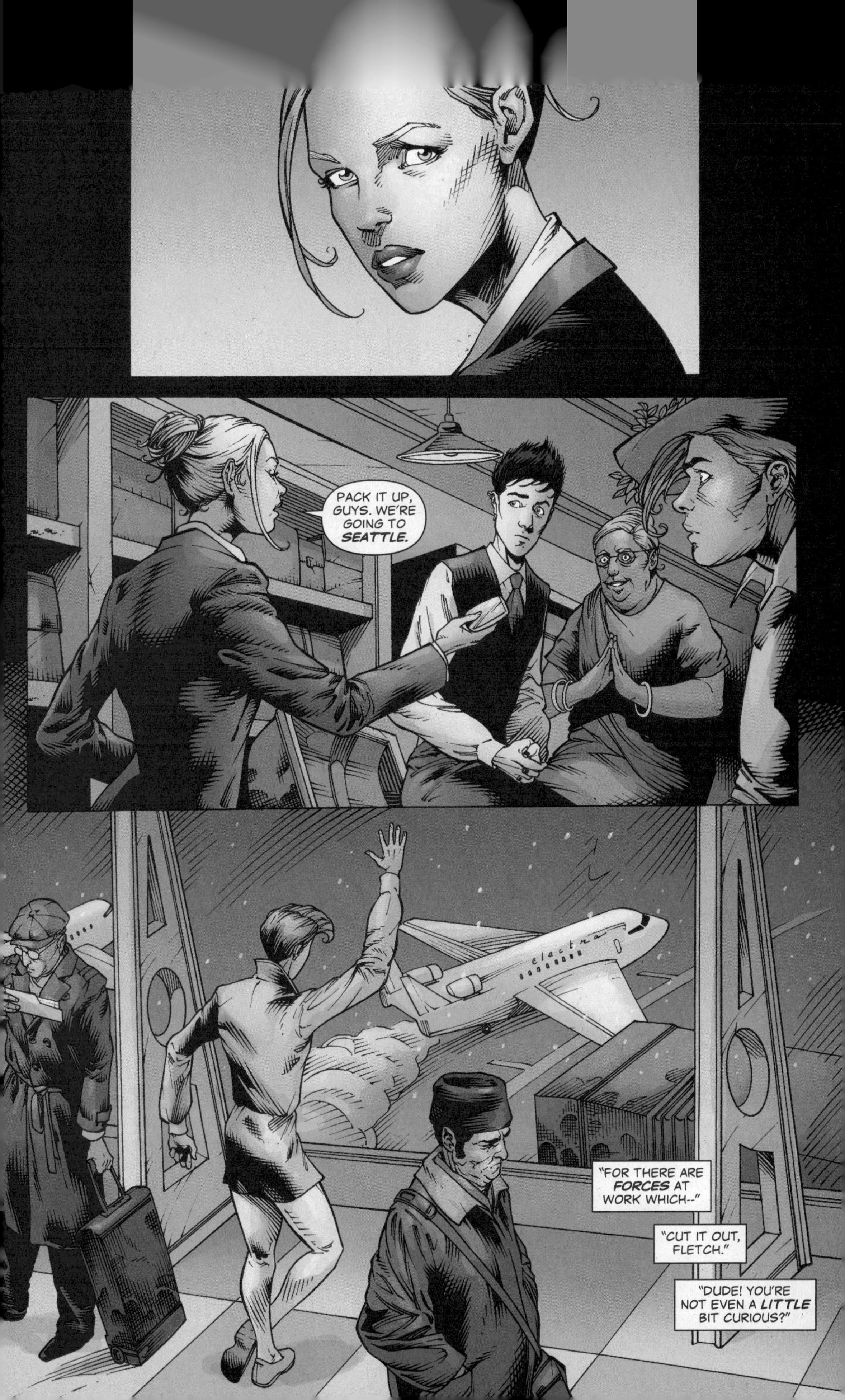
PACK IT UP, GUYS. WE'RE GOING TO SEATTLE.
"FOR THERE ARE FORCES AT WORK WHICH--"
"CUT IT OUT, FLETCH."
"DUDE! YOU'RE NOT EVEN A LITTLE BIT CURIOUS?"

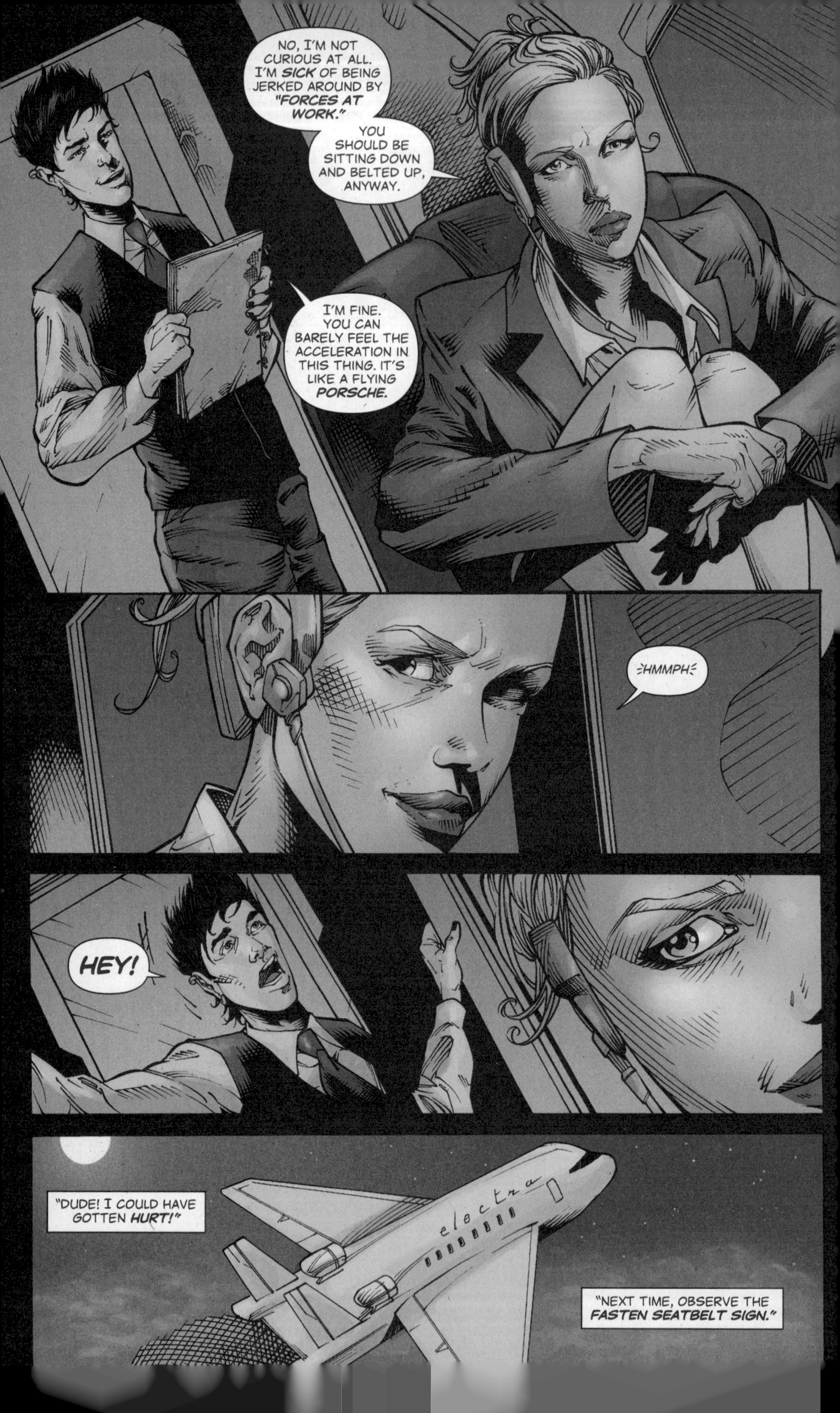
NO, I'M NOT CURIOUS AT ALL. I'M SICK OF BEING JERKED AROUND BY "FORCES AT WORK."
YOU SHOULD BE SITTING DOWN AND BELTED UP, ANYWAY.
I'M FINE. YOU CAN BARELY FEEL THE ACCELERATION IN THIS THING. IT'S LIKE A FLYING PORSCHE.
HMMPH
HEY!
"DUDE! I COULD HAVE GOTTEN HURT!"
electra
"NEXT TIME, OBSERVE THE FASTEN SEATBELT SIGN."

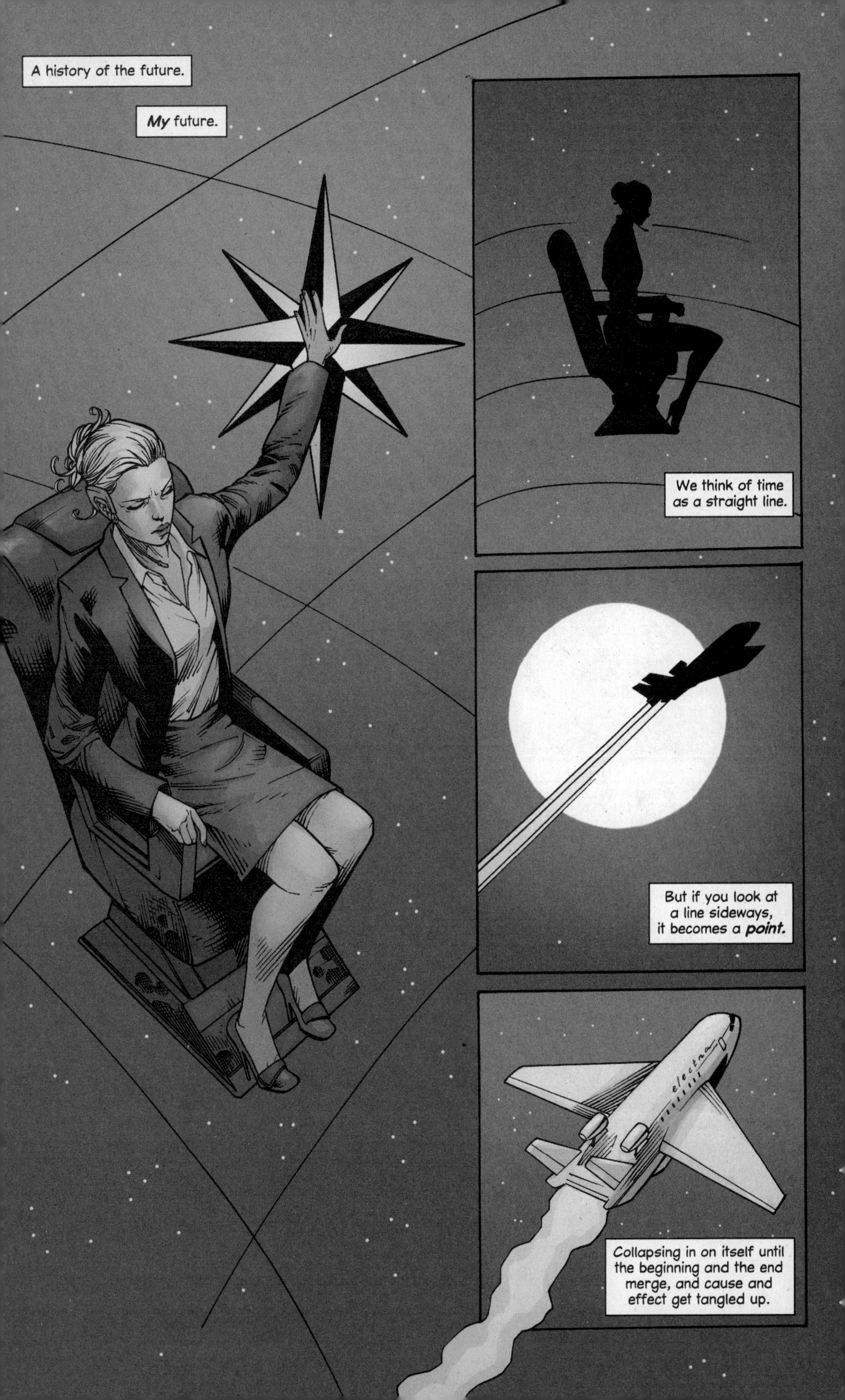
A history of the future.
My future.
We think of time as a straight line.
But if you look at a line sideways, it becomes a ***point.***
electra
Collapsing in on itself until the beginning and the end merge, and cause and effect get tangled up.

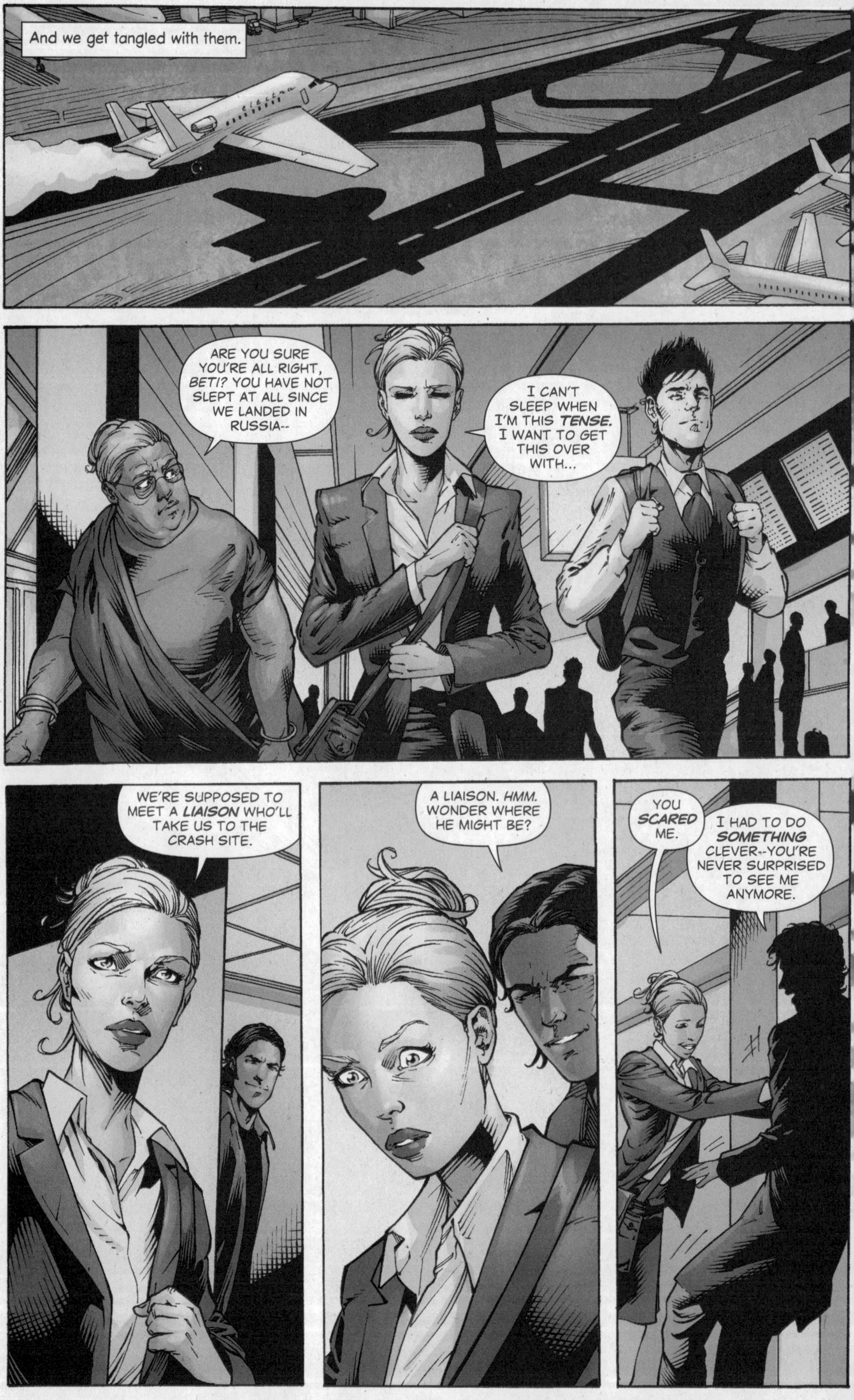
And we get tangled with them.
ARE YOU SURE YOU'RE ALL RIGHT, BETI? YOU HAVE NOT SLEPT AT ALL SINCE WE LANDED IN RUSSIA--
I CAN'T SLEEP WHEN I'M THIS *TENSE.* I WANT TO GET THIS OVER WITH...
WE'RE SUPPOSED TO MEET A *LIAISON* WHO'LL TAKE US TO THE CRASH SITE.
A LIAISON. *HMM.* WONDER WHERE HE MIGHT BE?
YOU *SCARED* ME.
I HAD TO DO *SOMETHING* CLEVER--YOU'RE NEVER SURPRISED TO SEE ME ANYMORE.

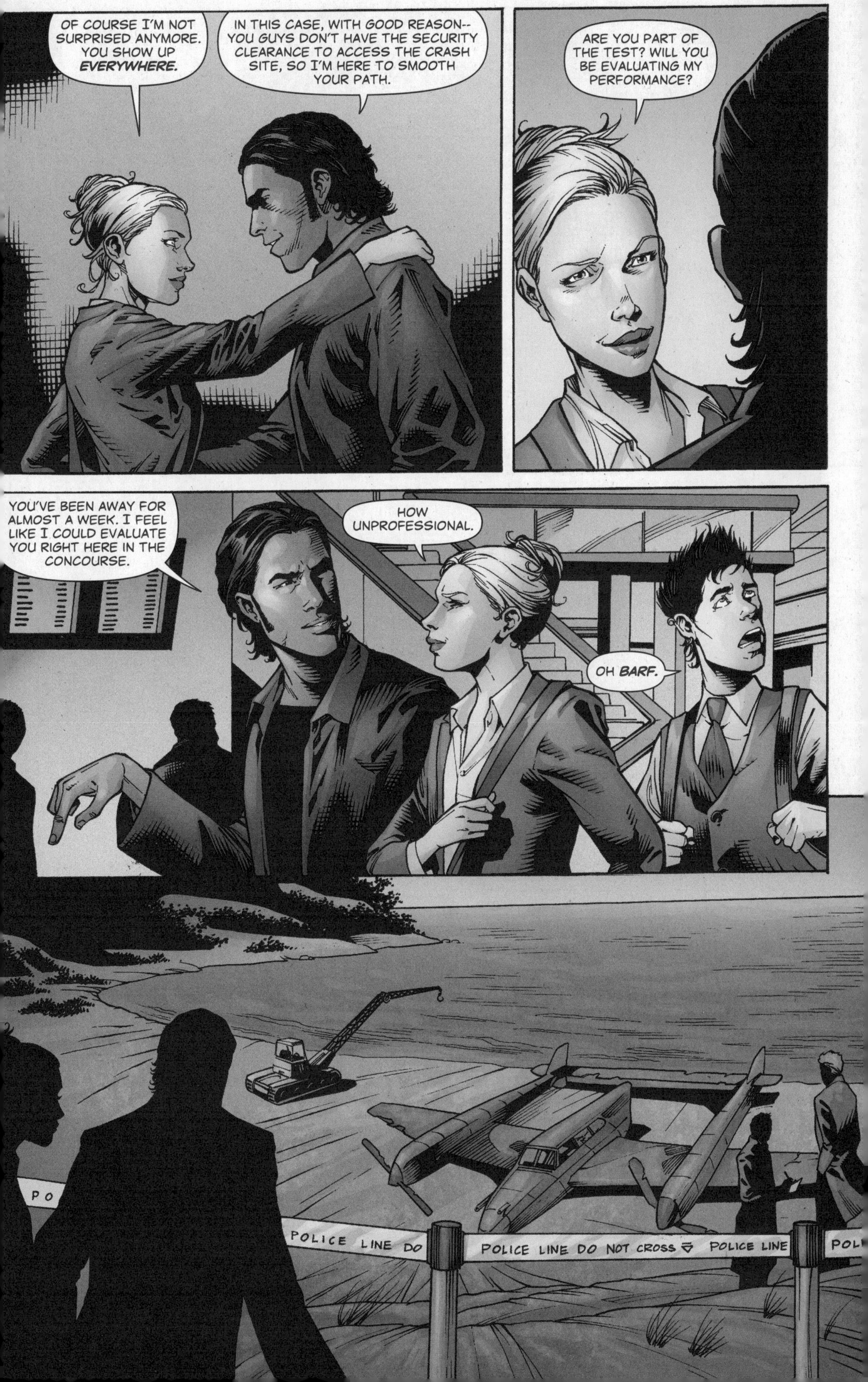
OF COURSE I'M NOT SURPRISED ANYMORE. YOU SHOW UP *EVERYWHERE.*
IN THIS CASE, WITH GOOD REASON-- YOU GUYS DON'T HAVE THE SECURITY CLEARANCE TO ACCESS THE CRASH SITE, SO I'M HERE TO SMOOTH YOUR PATH.
ARE YOU PART OF THE TEST? WILL YOU BE EVALUATING MY PERFORMANCE?
YOU'VE BEEN AWAY FOR ALMOST A WEEK. I FEEL LIKE I COULD EVALUATE YOU RIGHT HERE IN THE CONCOURSE.
HOW UNPROFESSIONAL.
OH *BARF.*
PO
POLICE LINE DO
POLICE LINE DO NOT CROSS
POLICE LINE
POL

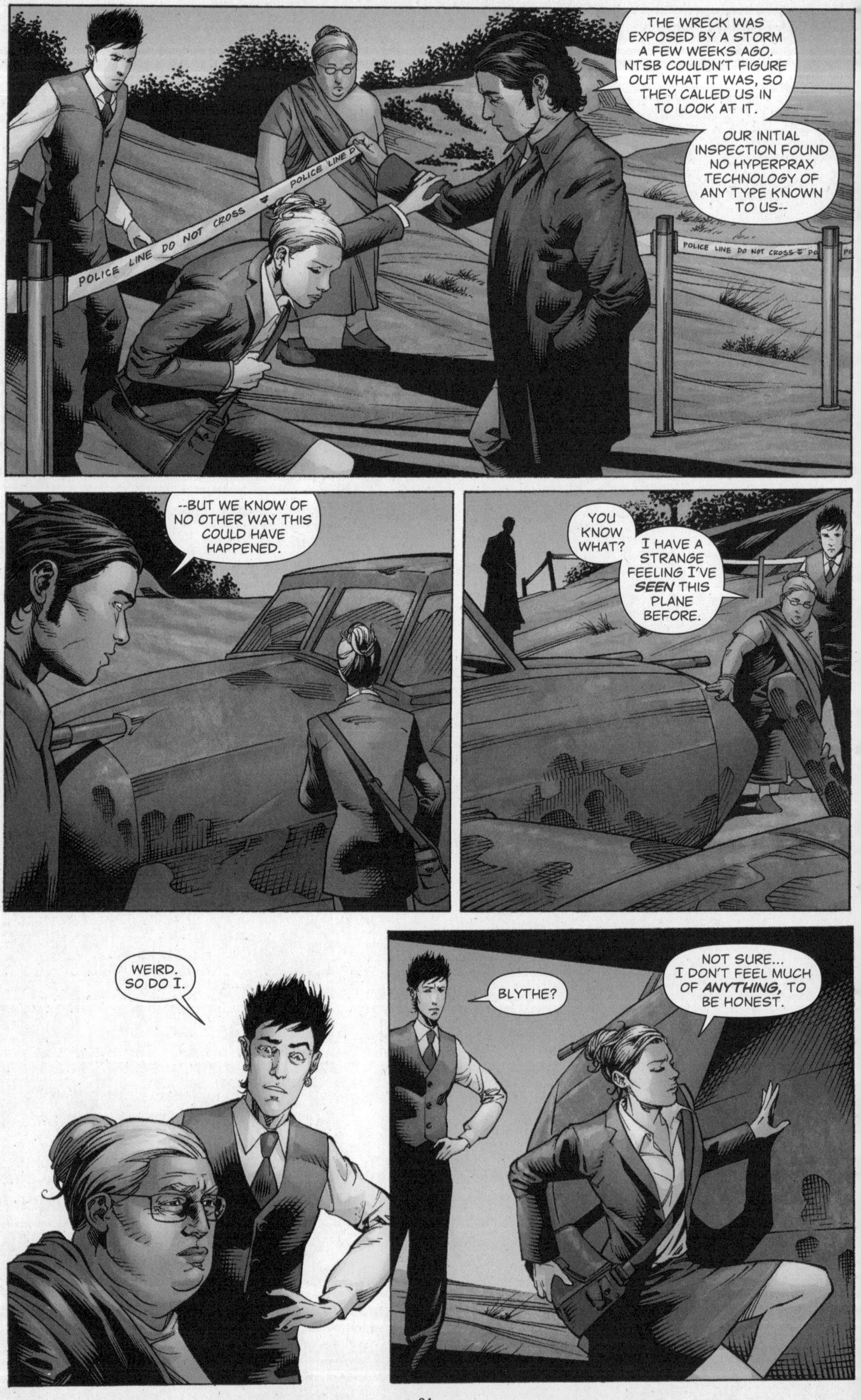
THE WRECK WAS EXPOSED BY A STORM A FEW WEEKS AGO. NTSB COULDN'T FIGURE OUT WHAT IT WAS, SO THEY CALLED US IN TO LOOK AT IT.
OUR INITIAL INSPECTION FOUND NO HYPERPRAX TECHNOLOGY OF ANY TYPE KNOWN TO US--
POLICE LINE DO NOT CROSS
POLICE LINE DO NOT CROSS
--BUT WE KNOW OF NO OTHER WAY THIS COULD HAVE HAPPENED.
YOU KNOW WHAT?
I HAVE A STRANGE FEELING I'VE *SEEN* THIS PLANE BEFORE.
WEIRD. SO DO I.
BLYTHE?
NOT SURE... I DON'T FEEL MUCH OF *ANYTHING,* TO BE HONEST.

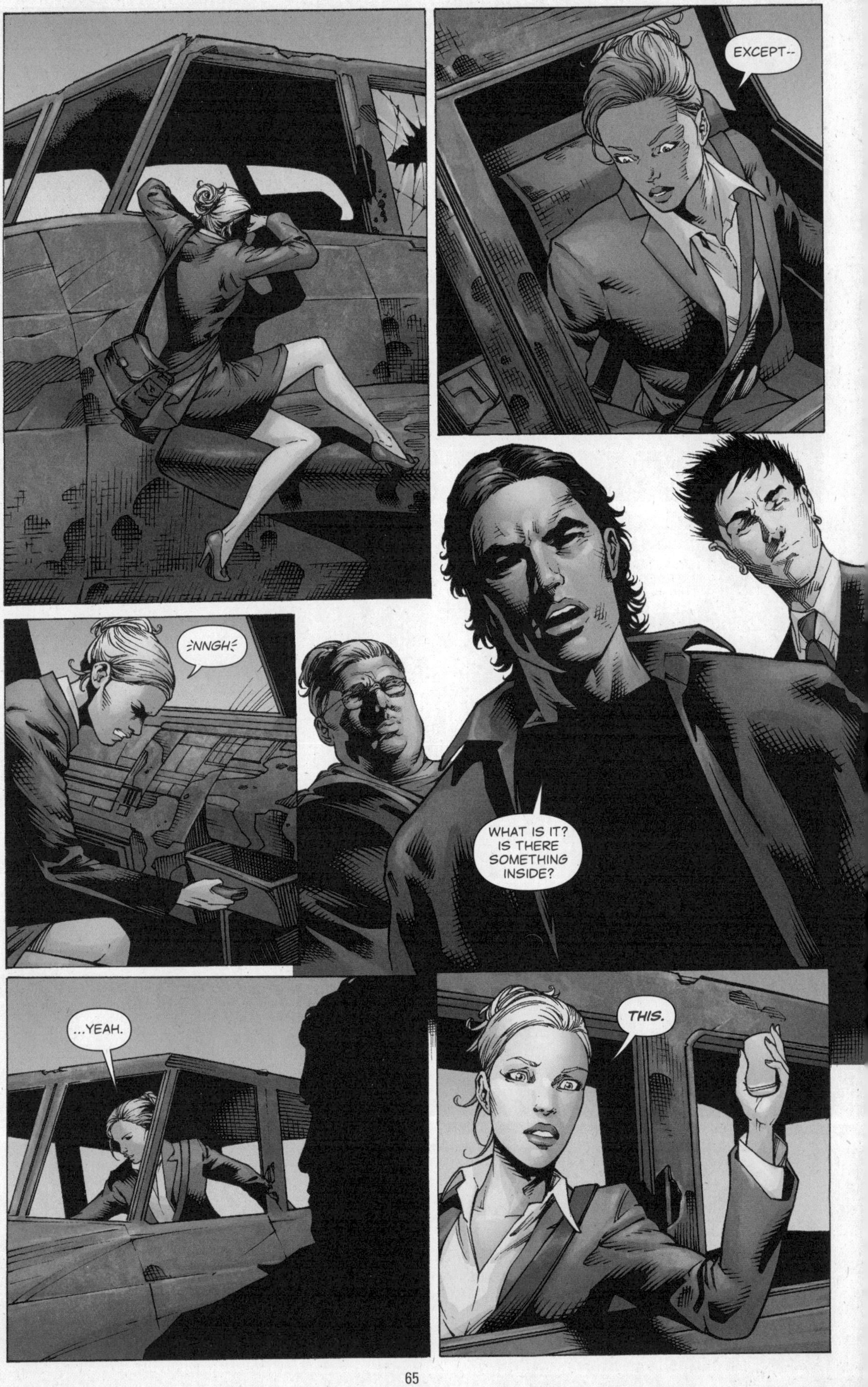
EXCEPT--
NNGH
WHAT IS IT? IS THERE SOMETHING INSIDE?
...YEAH.
THIS.

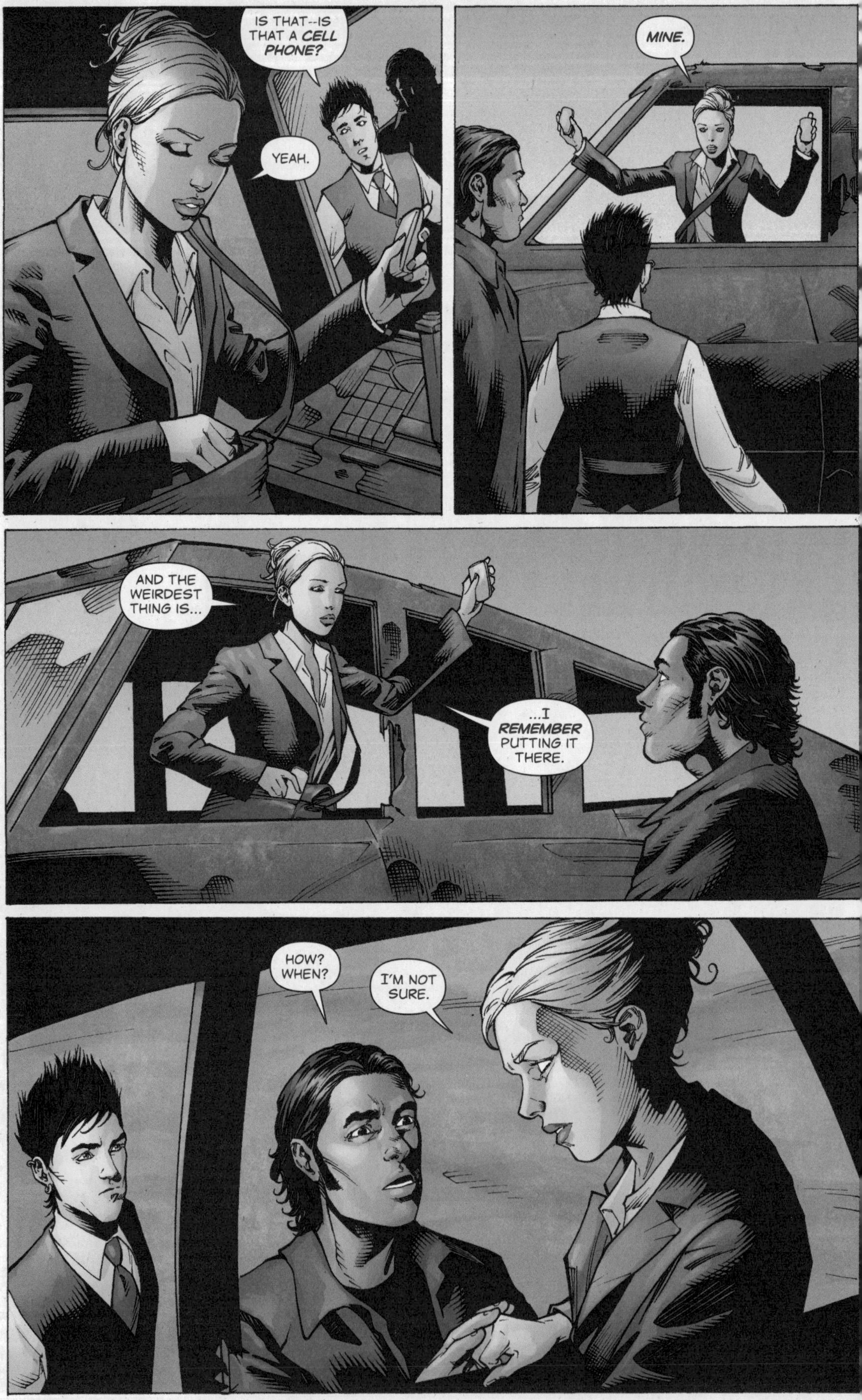
IS THAT--IS THAT A *CELL PHONE?*
YEAH.
MINE.
AND THE WEIRDEST THING IS...
...I *REMEMBER* PUTTING IT THERE.
HOW? WHEN?
I'M NOT SURE.

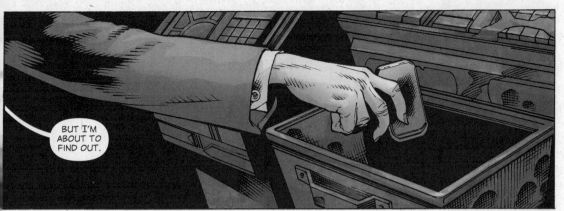

BUT I'M ABOUT TO FIND OUT.

SORRY ABOUT THIS.

ABOUT WHAT, BETI?

THE TEN MINUTES OF *LOST TIME* YOU'RE ABOUT TO EXPERIENCE.

I think about what I did in *Pakistan,* using the engine of the prototype from a distance...

I reach out for the Hyperwing. I try to remember that it's always there.

The Engine.

Waiting for me to tell it where we're going. When we're going. What we're going.

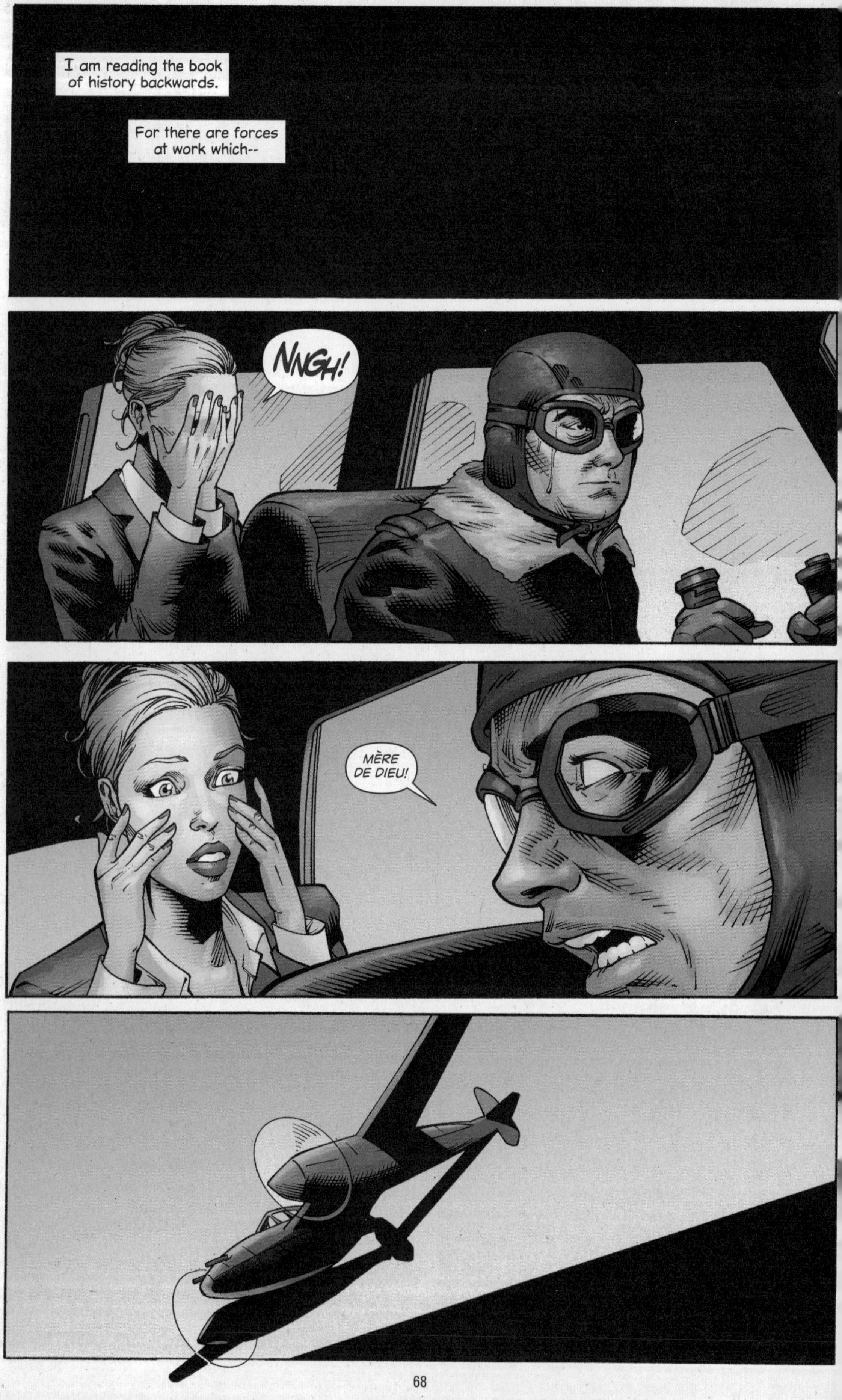
I am reading the book of history backwards.
For there are forces at work which--
NNGH!
MÈRE DE DIEU!

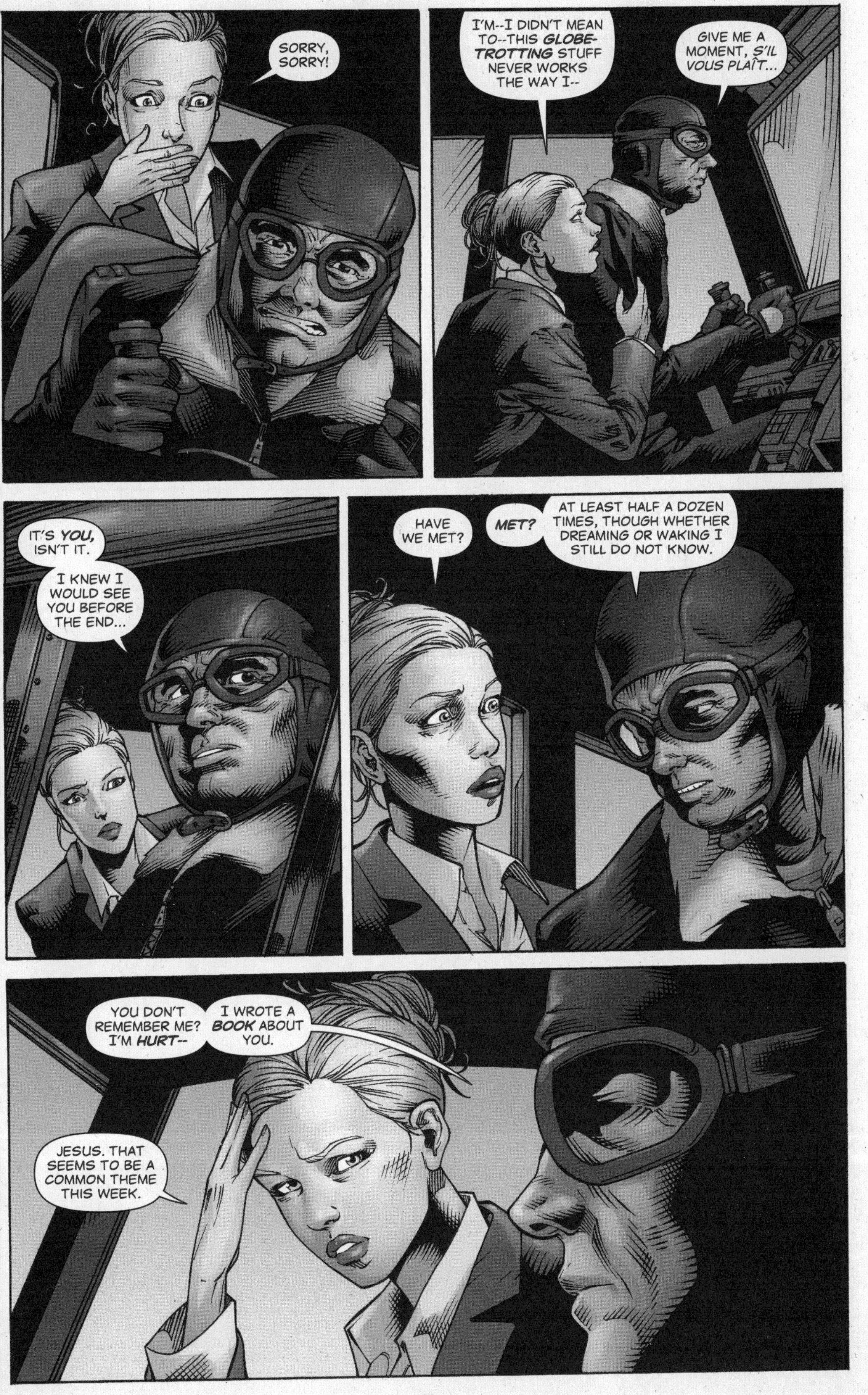
SORRY, SORRY!
I'M--I DIDN'T MEAN TO--THIS GLOBE-TROTTING STUFF NEVER WORKS THE WAY I--
GIVE ME A MOMENT, S'IL VOUS PLAÎT...
IT'S YOU, ISN'T IT.
I KNEW I WOULD SEE YOU BEFORE THE END...
HAVE WE MET?
MET?
AT LEAST HALF A DOZEN TIMES, THOUGH WHETHER DREAMING OR WAKING I STILL DO NOT KNOW.
YOU DON'T REMEMBER ME? I'M HURT--
I WROTE A BOOK ABOUT YOU.
JESUS. THAT SEEMS TO BE A COMMON THEME THIS WEEK.

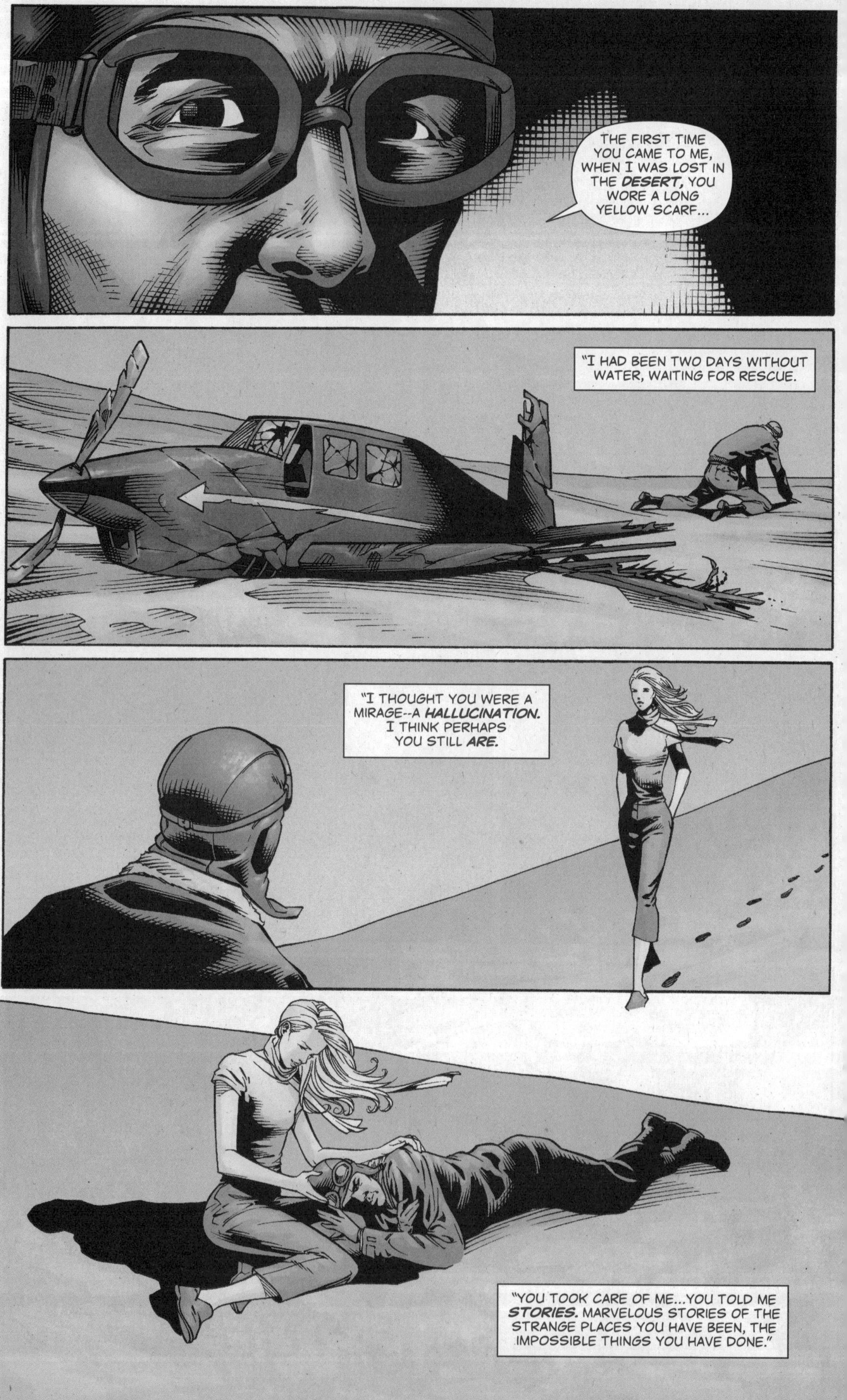
THE FIRST TIME YOU CAME TO ME, WHEN I WAS LOST IN THE DESERT, YOU WORE A LONG YELLOW SCARF...
"I HAD BEEN TWO DAYS WITHOUT WATER, WAITING FOR RESCUE.
"I THOUGHT YOU WERE A MIRAGE--A HALLUCINATION. I THINK PERHAPS YOU STILL ARE.
"YOU TOOK CARE OF ME...YOU TOLD ME STORIES. MARVELOUS STORIES OF THE STRANGE PLACES YOU HAVE BEEN, THE IMPOSSIBLE THINGS YOU HAVE DONE."

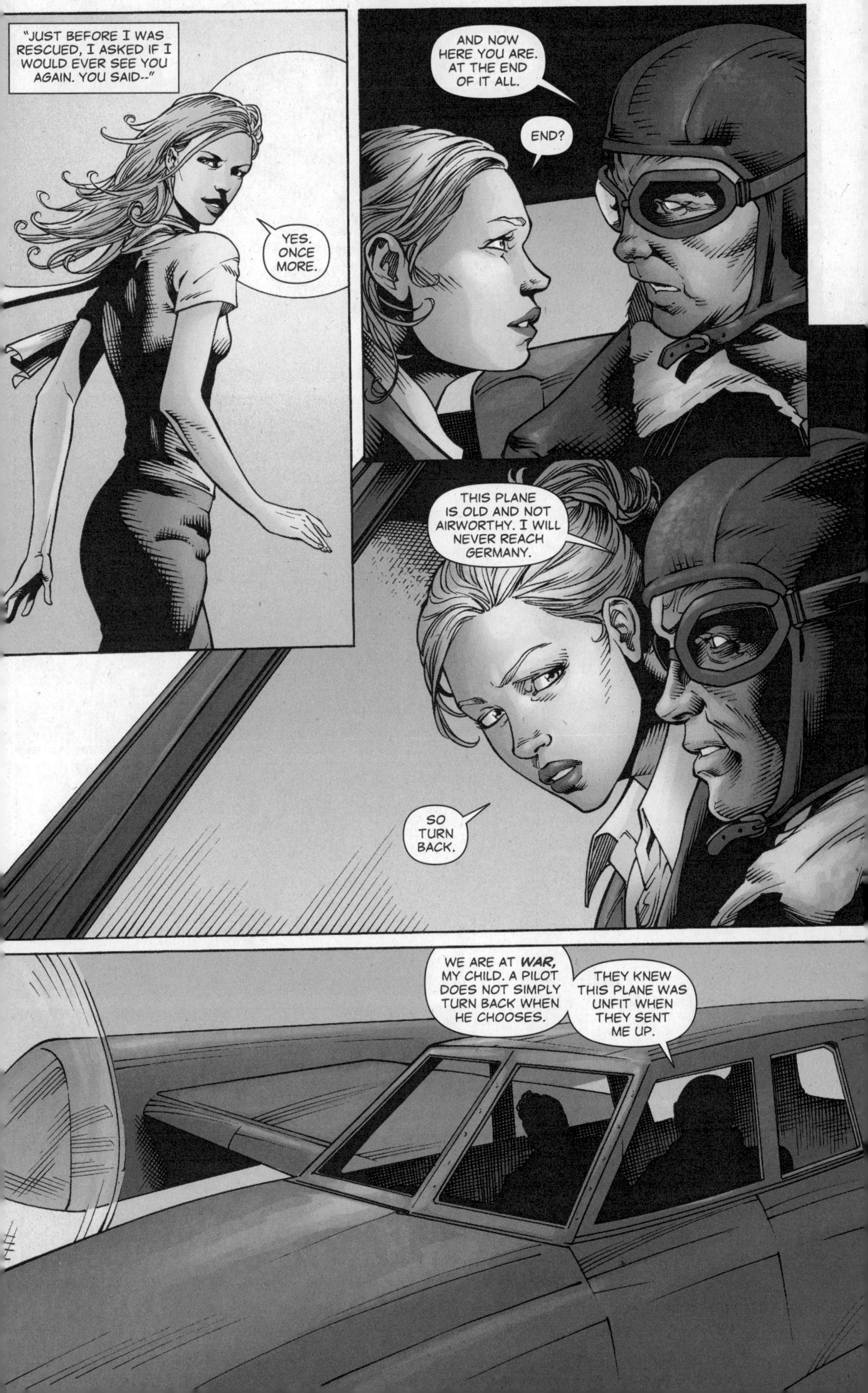
"JUST BEFORE I WAS RESCUED, I ASKED IF I WOULD EVER SEE YOU AGAIN. YOU SAID--"
YES. ONCE MORE.
AND NOW HERE YOU ARE. AT THE END OF IT ALL.
END?
THIS PLANE IS OLD AND NOT AIRWORTHY. I WILL NEVER REACH GERMANY.
SO TURN BACK.
WE ARE AT *WAR,* MY CHILD. A PILOT DOES NOT SIMPLY TURN BACK WHEN HE CHOOSES.
THEY KNEW THIS PLANE WAS UNFIT WHEN THEY SENT ME UP.

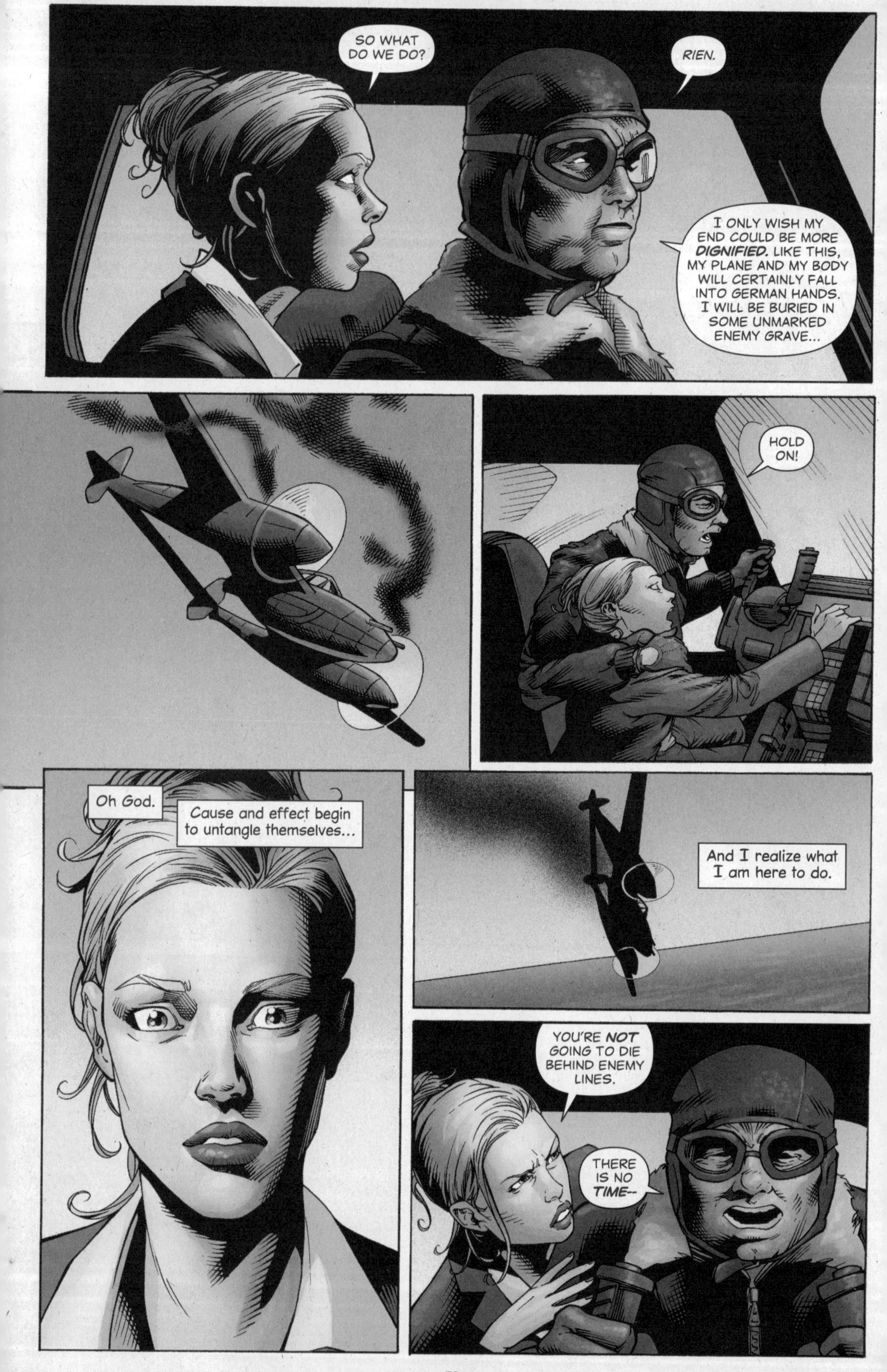
SO WHAT DO WE DO?
RIEN.
I ONLY WISH MY END COULD BE MORE DIGNIFIED. LIKE THIS, MY PLANE AND MY BODY WILL CERTAINLY FALL INTO GERMAN HANDS. I WILL BE BURIED IN SOME UNMARKED ENEMY GRAVE...
HOLD ON!
Oh God.
Cause and effect begin to untangle themselves...
And I realize what I am here to do.
YOU'RE NOT GOING TO DIE BEHIND ENEMY LINES.
THERE IS NO TIME--

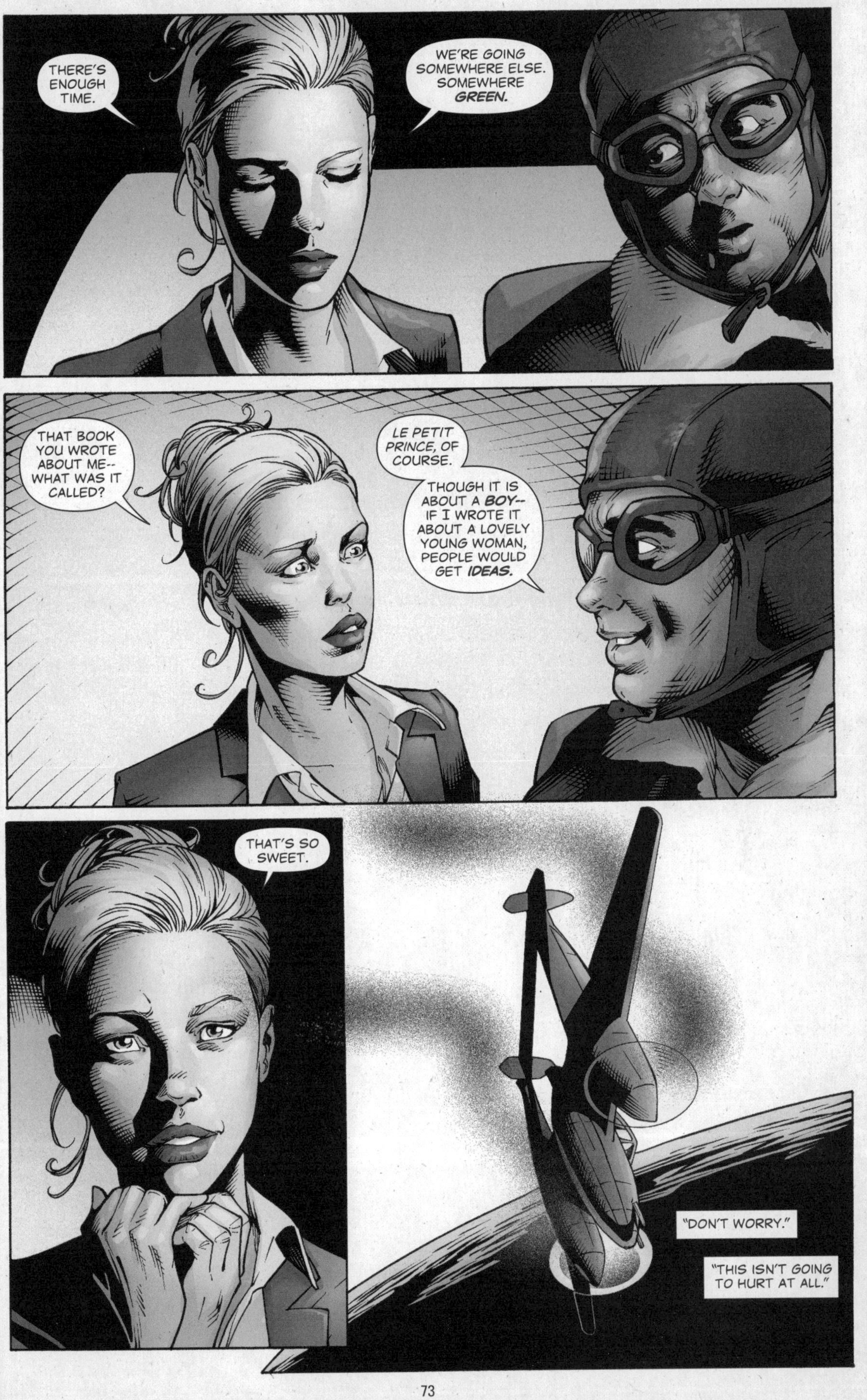
THERE'S ENOUGH TIME.
WE'RE GOING SOMEWHERE ELSE. SOMEWHERE **GREEN.**
THAT BOOK YOU WROTE ABOUT ME-- WHAT WAS IT CALLED?
LE PETIT PRINCE, OF COURSE.
THOUGH IT IS ABOUT A **BOY--** IF I WROTE IT ABOUT A LOVELY YOUNG WOMAN, PEOPLE WOULD GET **IDEAS.**
THAT'S SO SWEET.
"DON'T WORRY."
"THIS ISN'T GOING TO HURT AT ALL."

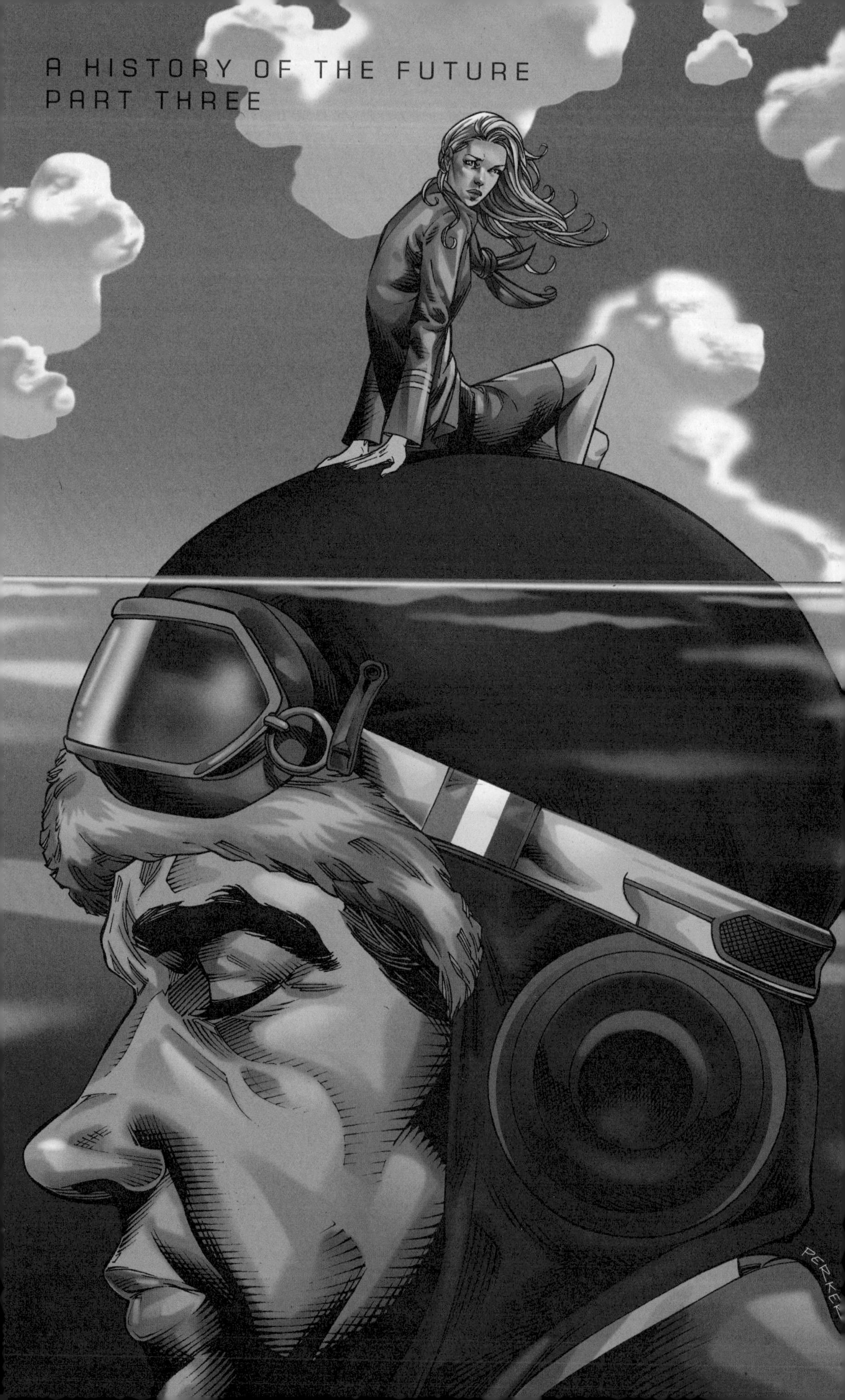
A HISTORY OF THE FUTURE
PART THREE
PERKER

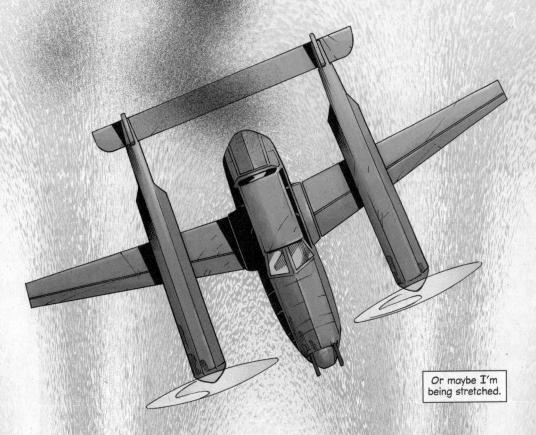

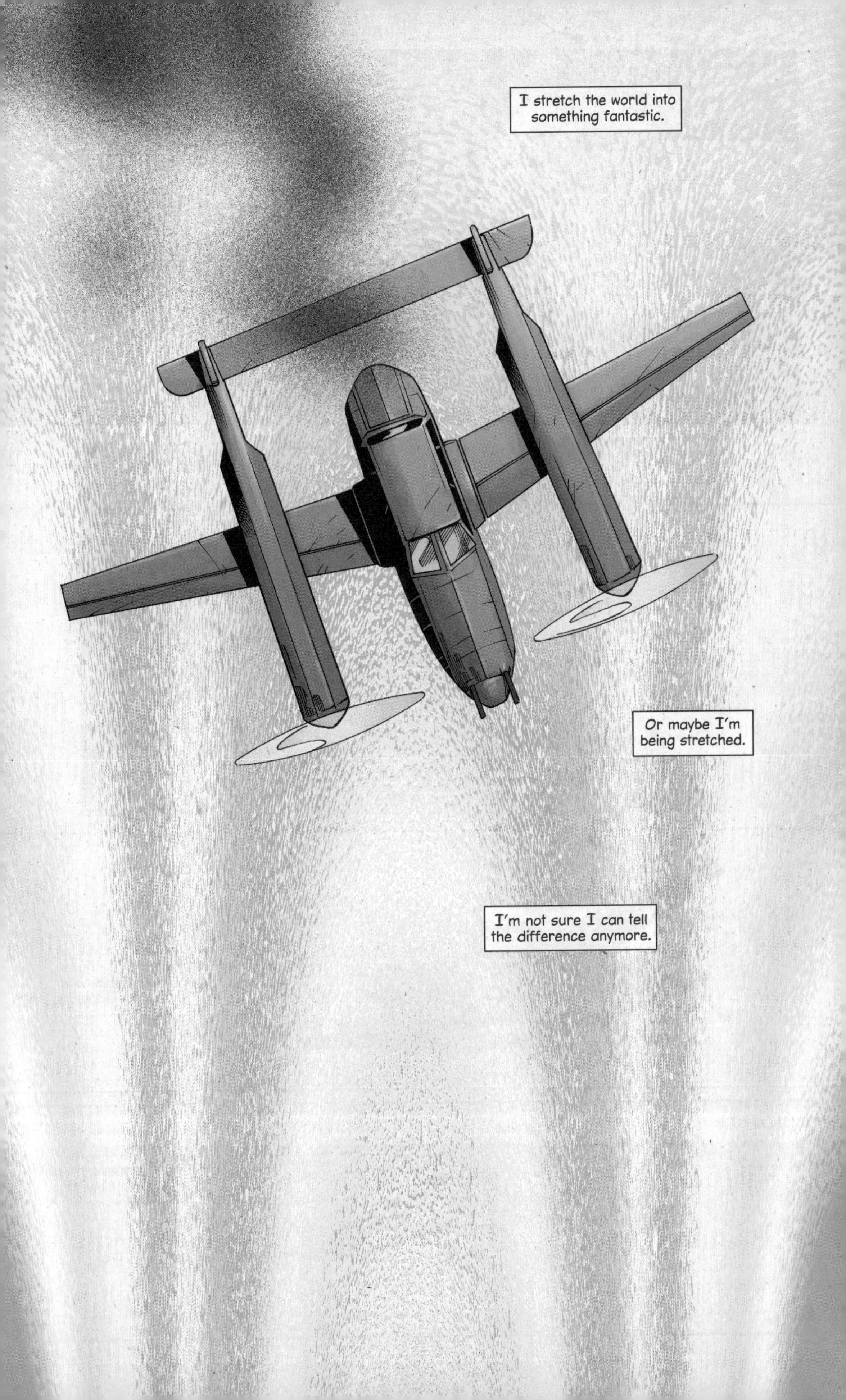

I stretch the world into something fantastic.

Or maybe I'm being stretched.

I'm not sure I can tell the difference anymore.

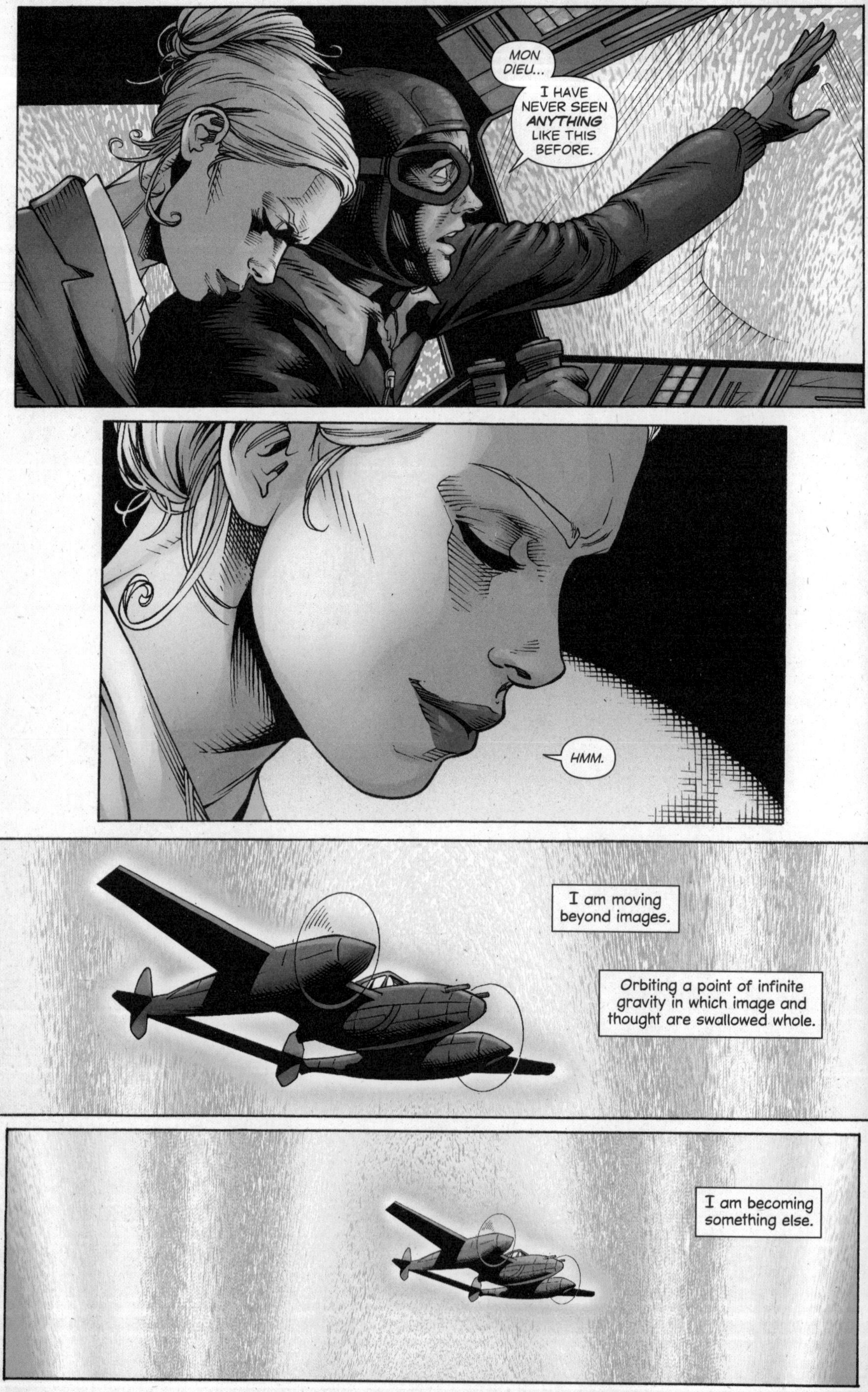
MON DIEU...
I HAVE NEVER SEEN ANYTHING LIKE THIS BEFORE.
HMM.
I am moving beyond images.
Orbiting a point of infinite gravity in which image and thought are swallowed whole.
I am becoming something else.

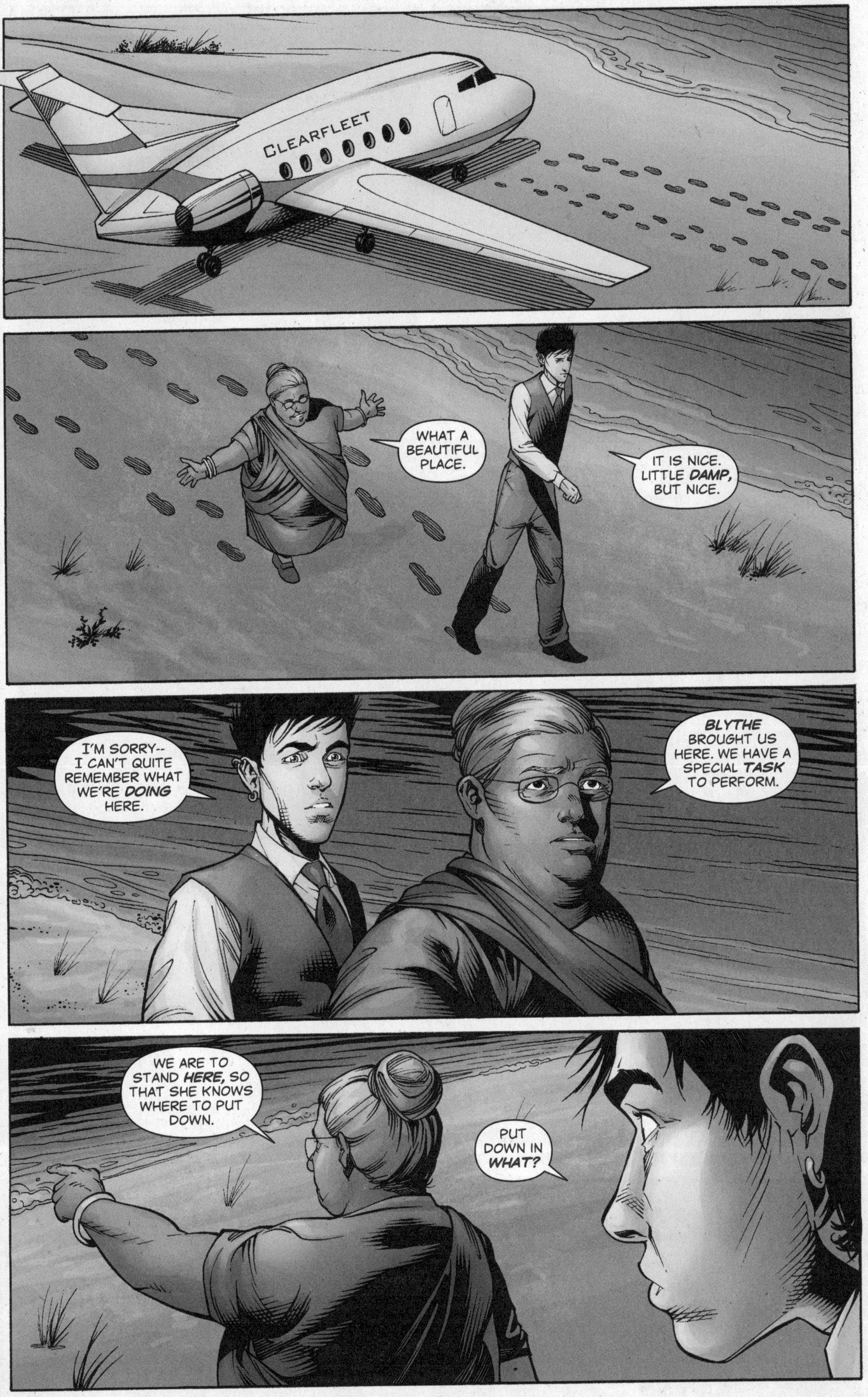
CLEARFLEET
WHAT A BEAUTIFUL PLACE.
IT IS NICE. LITTLE *DAMP,* BUT NICE.
I'M SORRY-- I CAN'T QUITE REMEMBER WHAT WE'RE *DOING* HERE.
BLYTHE BROUGHT US HERE. WE HAVE A SPECIAL *TASK* TO PERFORM.
WE ARE TO STAND *HERE,* SO THAT SHE KNOWS WHERE TO PUT DOWN.
PUT DOWN IN *WHAT?*

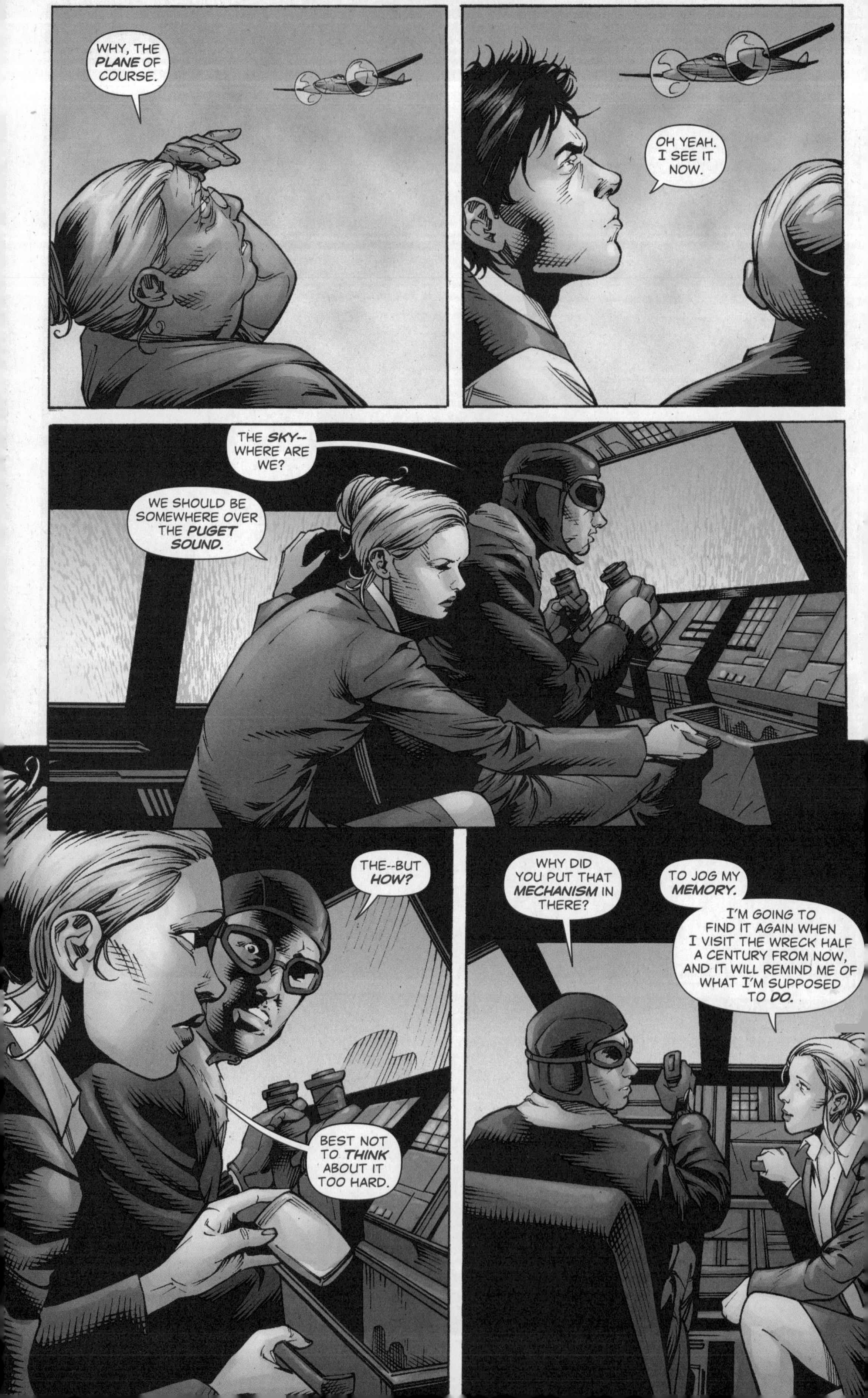
WHY, THE PLANE OF COURSE.
OH YEAH. I SEE IT NOW.
THE SKY-- WHERE ARE WE?
WE SHOULD BE SOMEWHERE OVER THE PUGET SOUND.
THE--BUT HOW?
BEST NOT TO THINK ABOUT IT TOO HARD.
WHY DID YOU PUT THAT MECHANISM IN THERE?
TO JOG MY MEMORY.
I'M GOING TO FIND IT AGAIN WHEN I VISIT THE WRECK HALF A CENTURY FROM NOW, AND IT WILL REMIND ME OF WHAT I'M SUPPOSED TO DO.

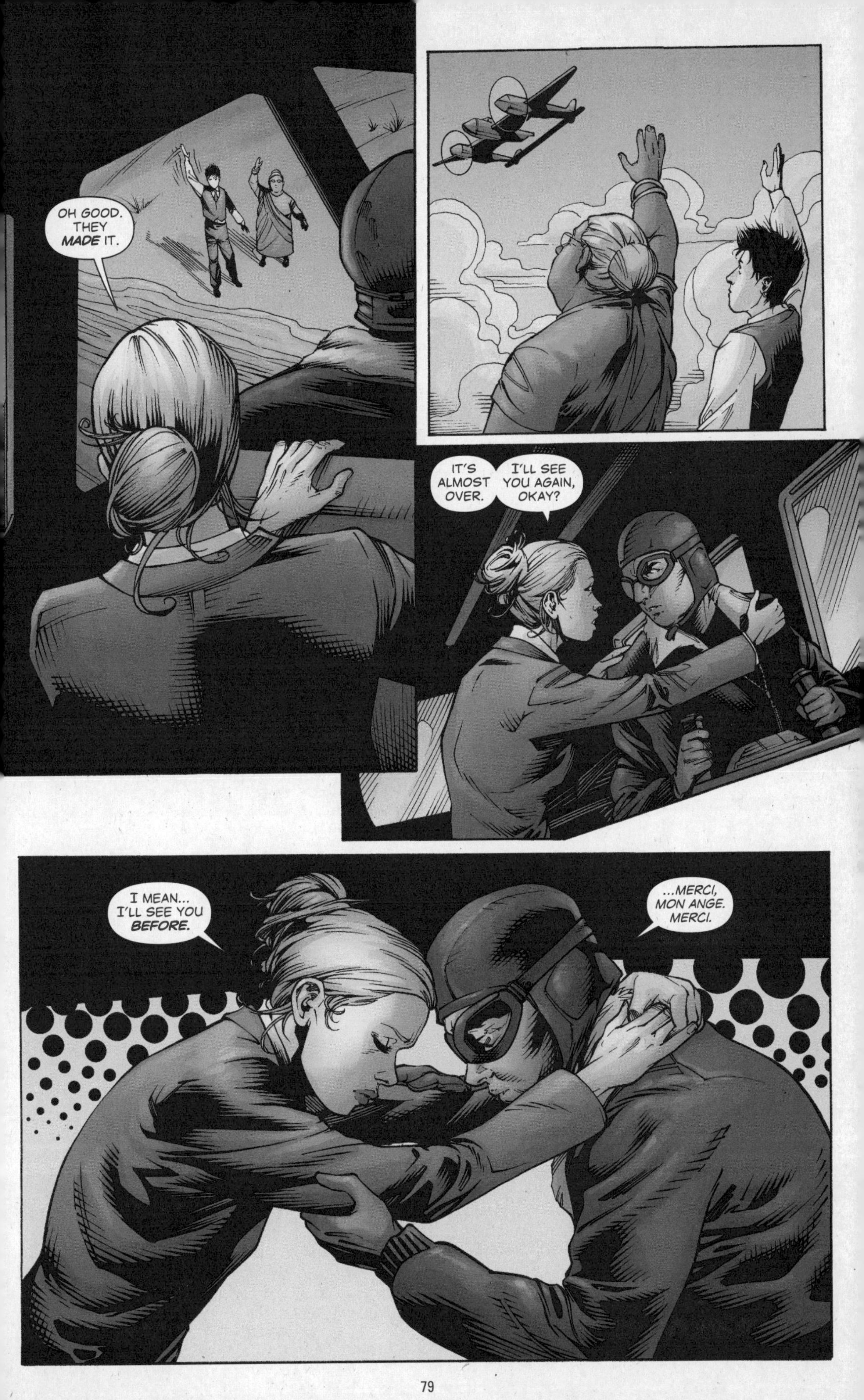
OH GOOD. THEY MADE IT.
IT'S ALMOST OVER.
I'LL SEE YOU AGAIN, OKAY?
I MEAN... I'LL SEE YOU BEFORE.
...MERCI, MON ANGE. MERCI.

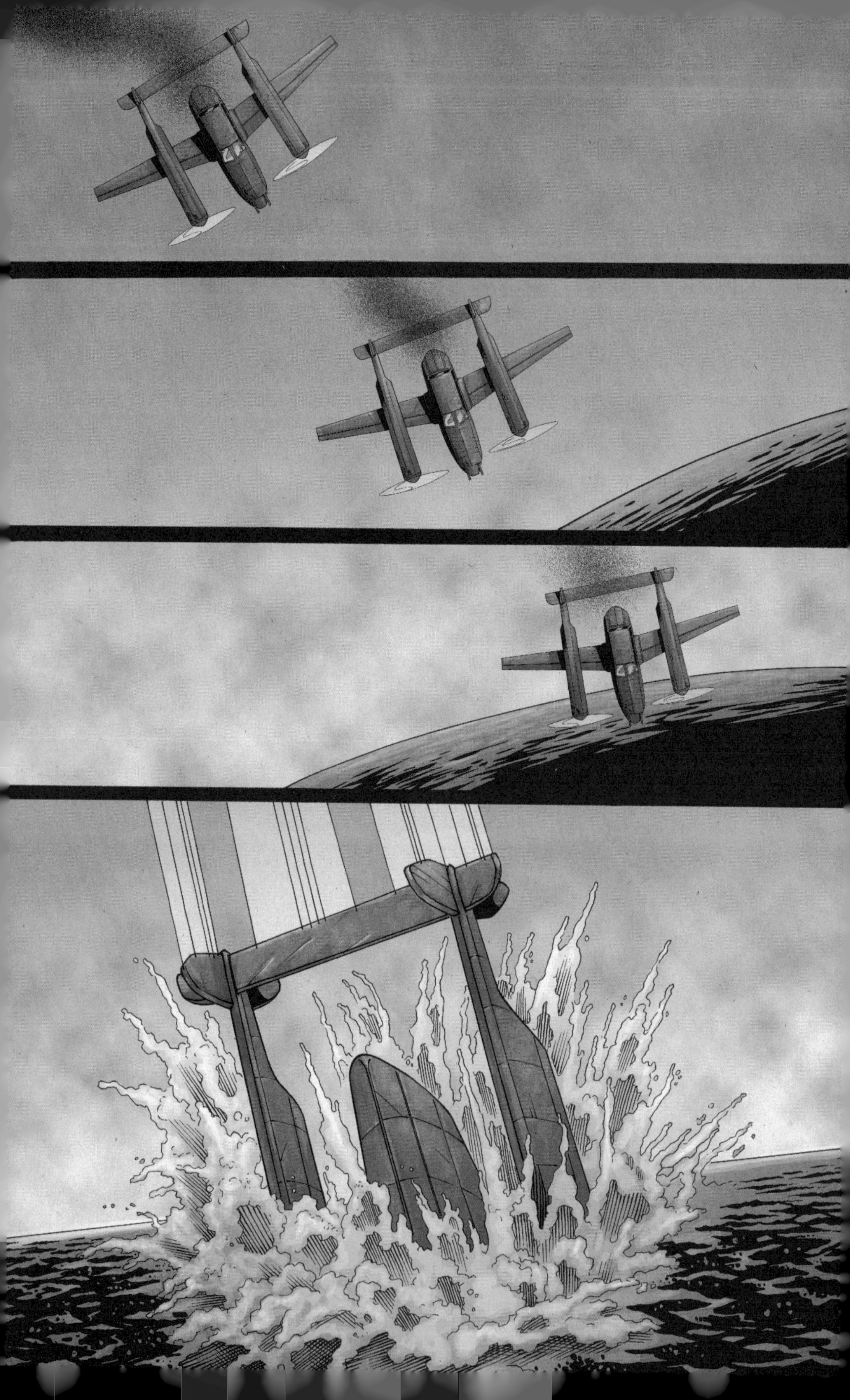

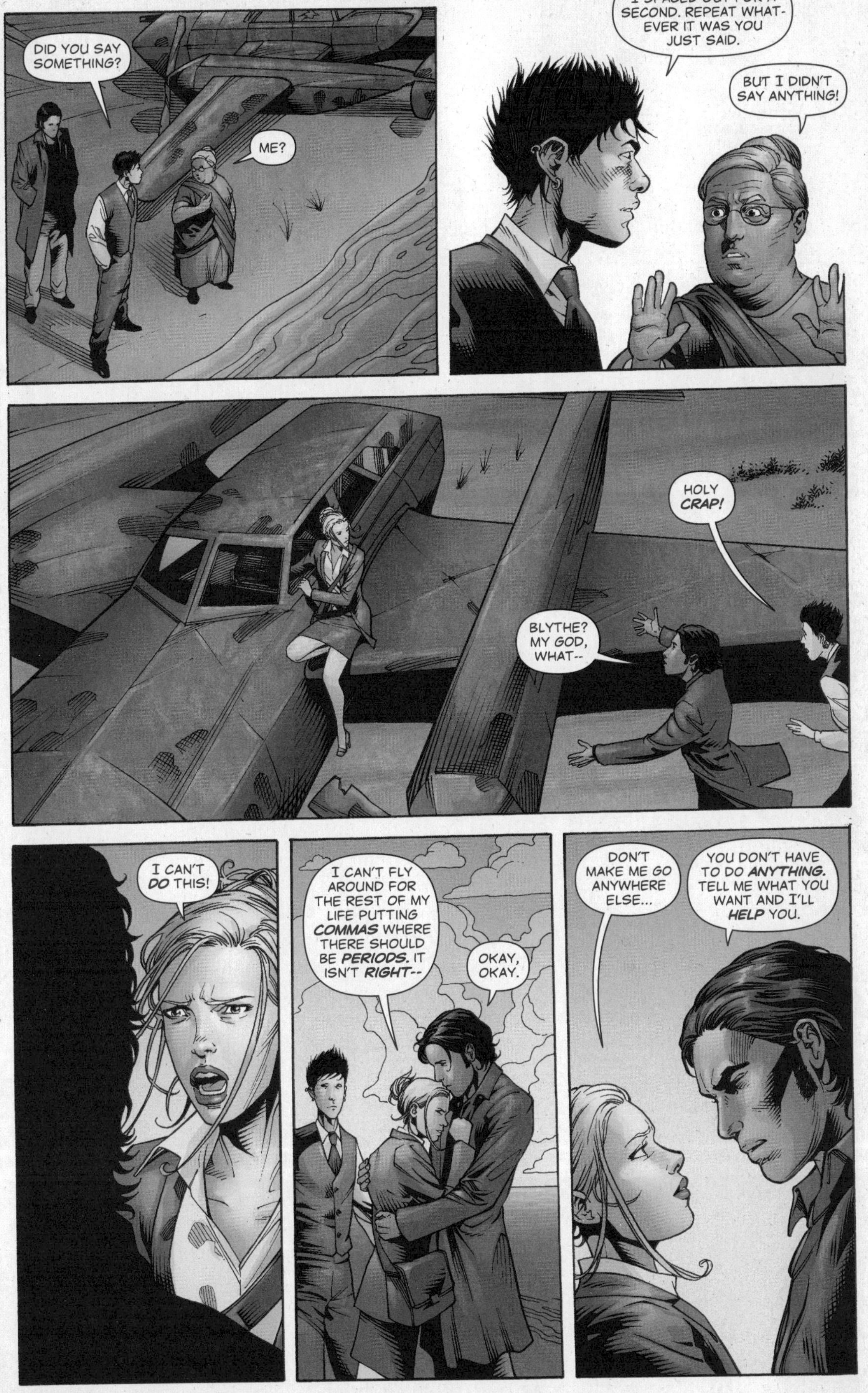

DID YOU SAY SOMETHING?
ME?
I'M SORRY, I SPACED OUT FOR A SECOND. REPEAT WHAT-EVER IT WAS YOU JUST SAID.
BUT I DIDN'T SAY ANYTHING!
HOLY CRAP!
BLYTHE? MY GOD, WHAT--
I CAN'T DO THIS!
I CAN'T FLY AROUND FOR THE REST OF MY LIFE PUTTING COMMAS WHERE THERE SHOULD BE PERIODS. IT ISN'T RIGHT--
OKAY, OKAY.
DON'T MAKE ME GO ANYWHERE ELSE...
YOU DON'T HAVE TO DO ANYTHING. TELL ME WHAT YOU WANT AND I'LL HELP YOU.

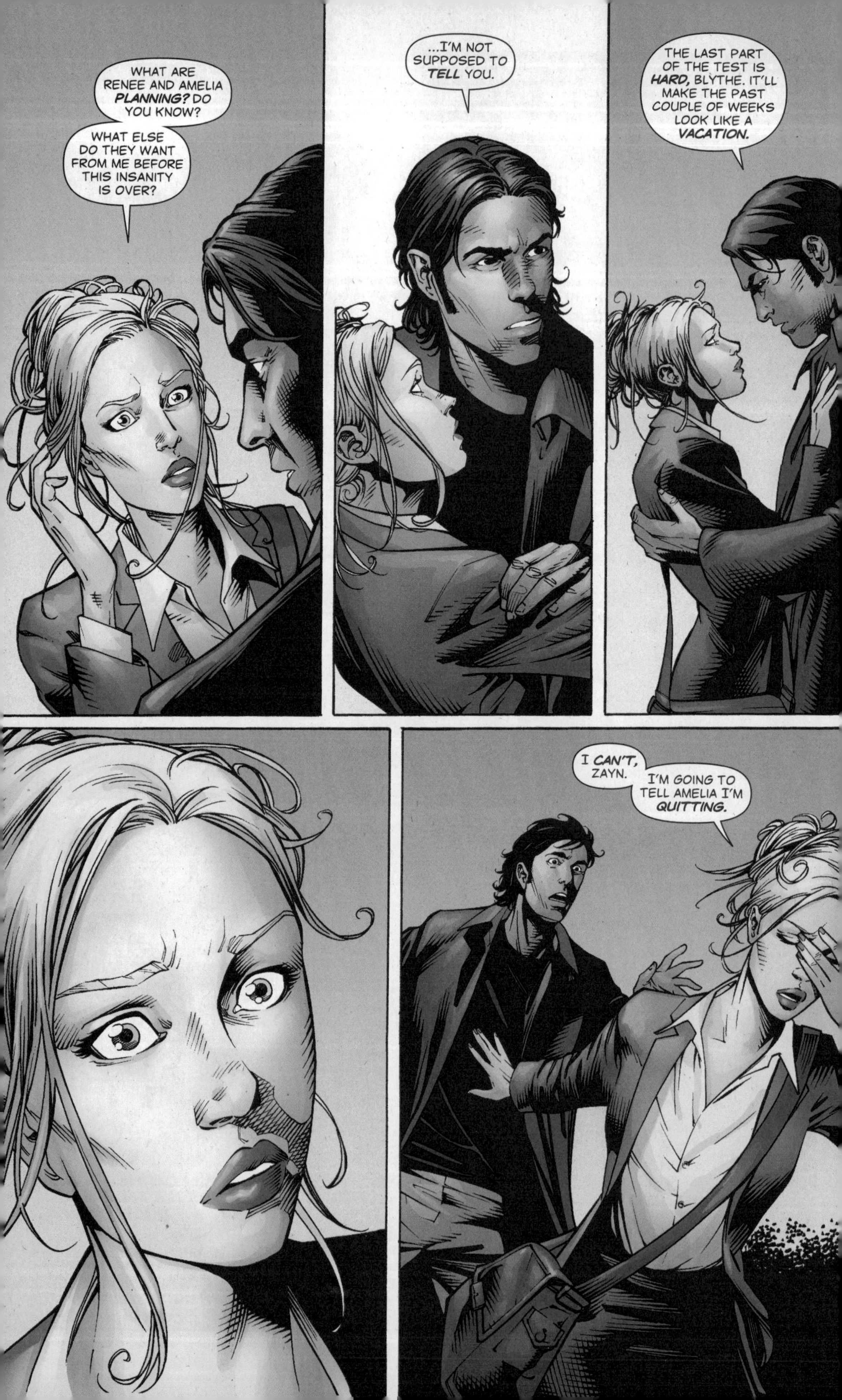
WHAT ARE RENEE AND AMELIA PLANNING? DO YOU KNOW?
WHAT ELSE DO THEY WANT FROM ME BEFORE THIS INSANITY IS OVER?
...I'M NOT SUPPOSED TO TELL YOU.
THE LAST PART OF THE TEST IS HARD, BLYTHE. IT'LL MAKE THE PAST COUPLE OF WEEKS LOOK LIKE A VACATION.
I CAN'T, ZAYN.
I'M GOING TO TELL AMELIA I'M QUITTING.

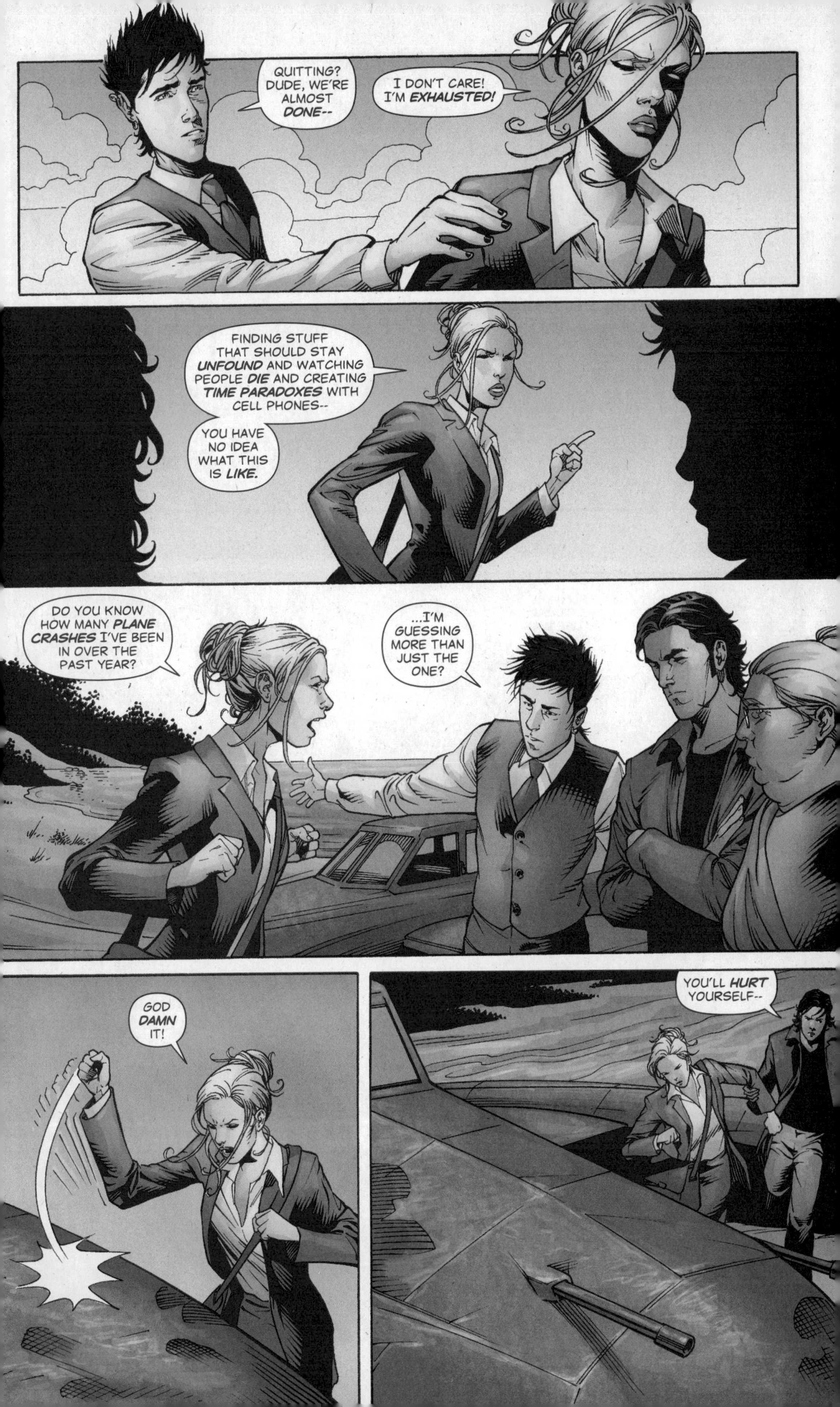
QUITTING? DUDE, WE'RE ALMOST DONE--
I DON'T CARE! I'M EXHAUSTED!
FINDING STUFF THAT SHOULD STAY UNFOUND AND WATCHING PEOPLE DIE AND CREATING TIME PARADOXES WITH CELL PHONES--
YOU HAVE NO IDEA WHAT THIS IS LIKE.
DO YOU KNOW HOW MANY PLANE CRASHES I'VE BEEN IN OVER THE PAST YEAR?
...I'M GUESSING MORE THAN JUST THE ONE?
GOD DAMN IT!
YOU'LL HURT YOURSELF--

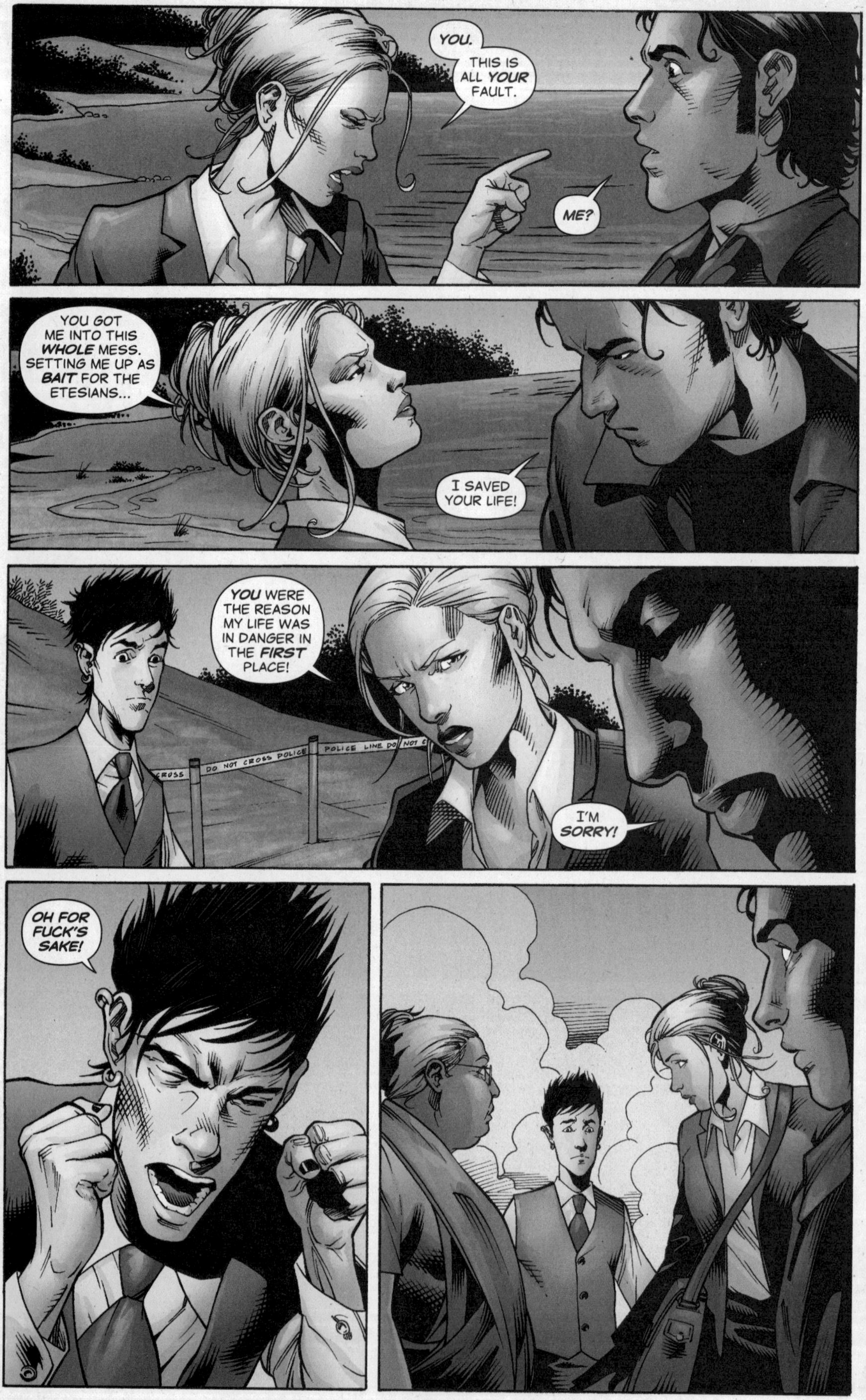

YOU.
THIS IS ALL YOUR FAULT.
ME?
YOU GOT ME INTO THIS WHOLE MESS. SETTING ME UP AS BAIT FOR THE ETESIANS...
I SAVED YOUR LIFE!
YOU WERE THE REASON MY LIFE WAS IN DANGER IN THE FIRST PLACE!
I'M SORRY!
DO NOT CROSS POLICE
POLICE LINE DO NOT C
OH FOR FUCK'S SAKE!

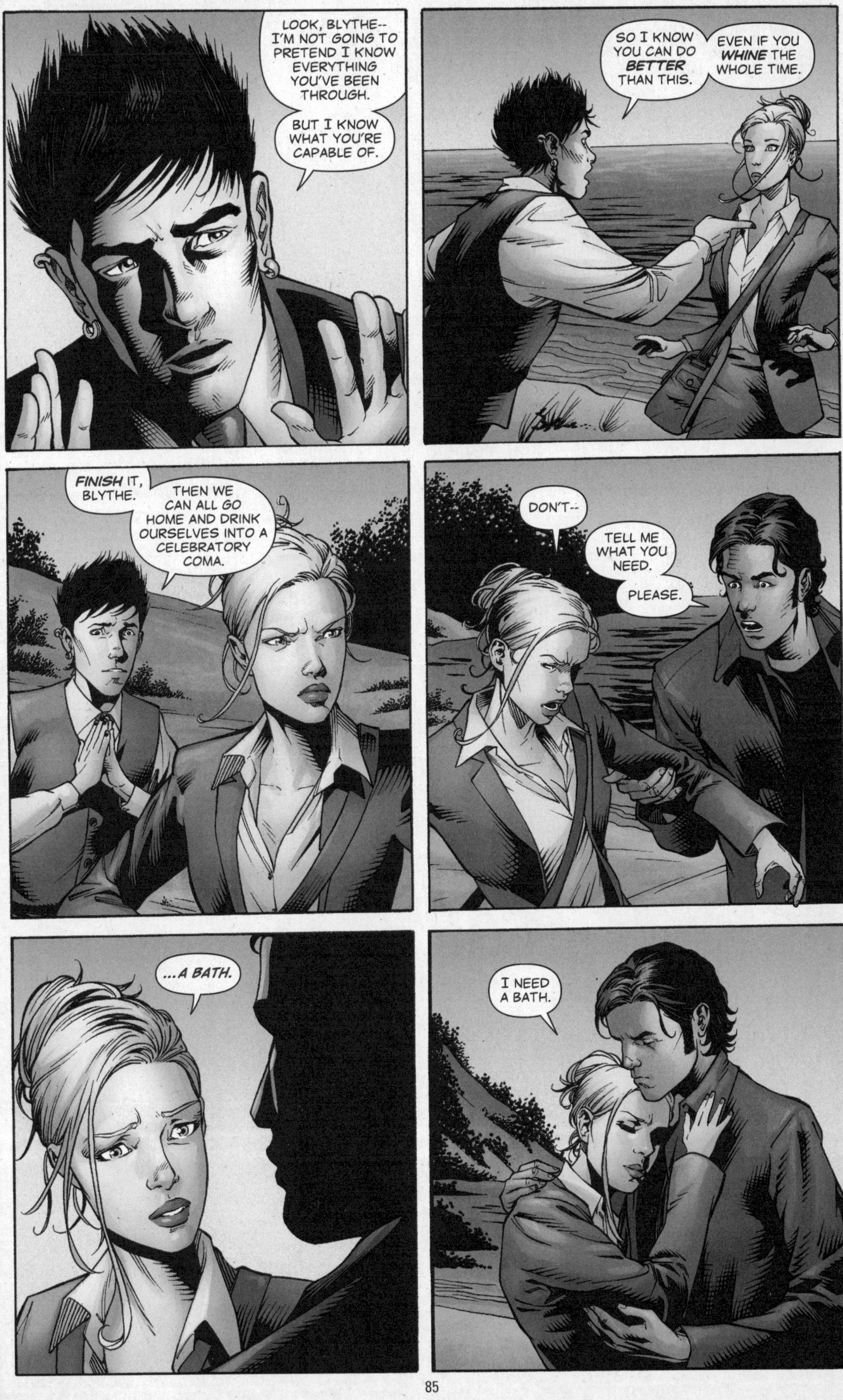
LOOK, BLYTHE-- I'M NOT GOING TO PRETEND I KNOW EVERYTHING YOU'VE BEEN THROUGH.
BUT I KNOW WHAT YOU'RE CAPABLE OF.
SO I KNOW YOU CAN DO BETTER THAN THIS.
EVEN IF YOU WHINE THE WHOLE TIME.
FINISH IT, BLYTHE.
THEN WE CAN ALL GO HOME AND DRINK OURSELVES INTO A CELEBRATORY COMA.
DON'T--
TELL ME WHAT YOU NEED.
PLEASE.
...A BATH.
I NEED A BATH.

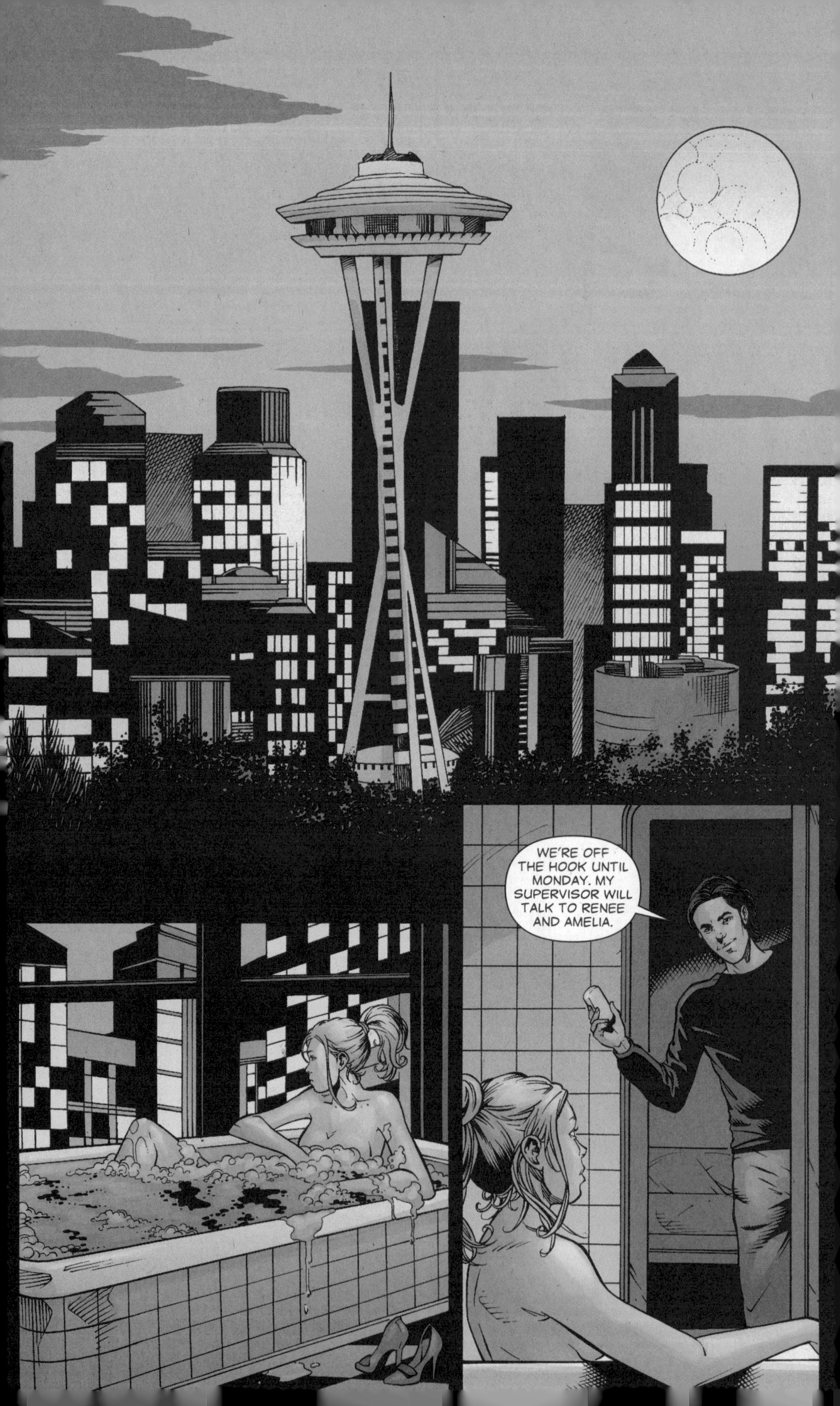
WE'RE OFF THE HOOK UNTIL MONDAY. MY SUPERVISOR WILL TALK TO RENEE AND AMELIA.

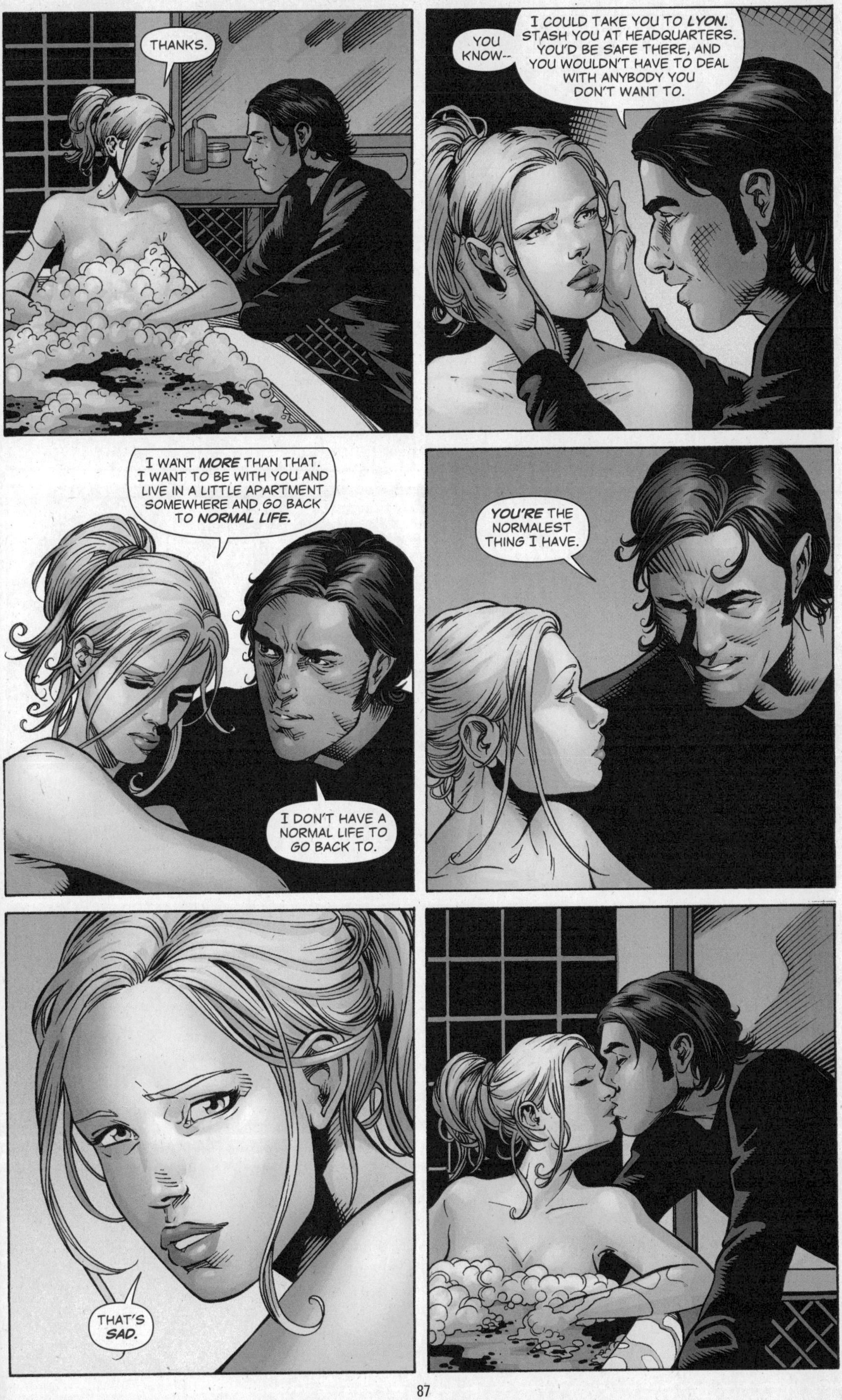
THANKS.
YOU KNOW--
I COULD TAKE YOU TO LYON. STASH YOU AT HEADQUARTERS. YOU'D BE SAFE THERE, AND YOU WOULDN'T HAVE TO DEAL WITH ANYBODY YOU DON'T WANT TO.
I WANT MORE THAN THAT. I WANT TO BE WITH YOU AND LIVE IN A LITTLE APARTMENT SOMEWHERE AND GO BACK TO NORMAL LIFE.
I DON'T HAVE A NORMAL LIFE TO GO BACK TO.
YOU'RE THE NORMALEST THING I HAVE.
THAT'S SAD.

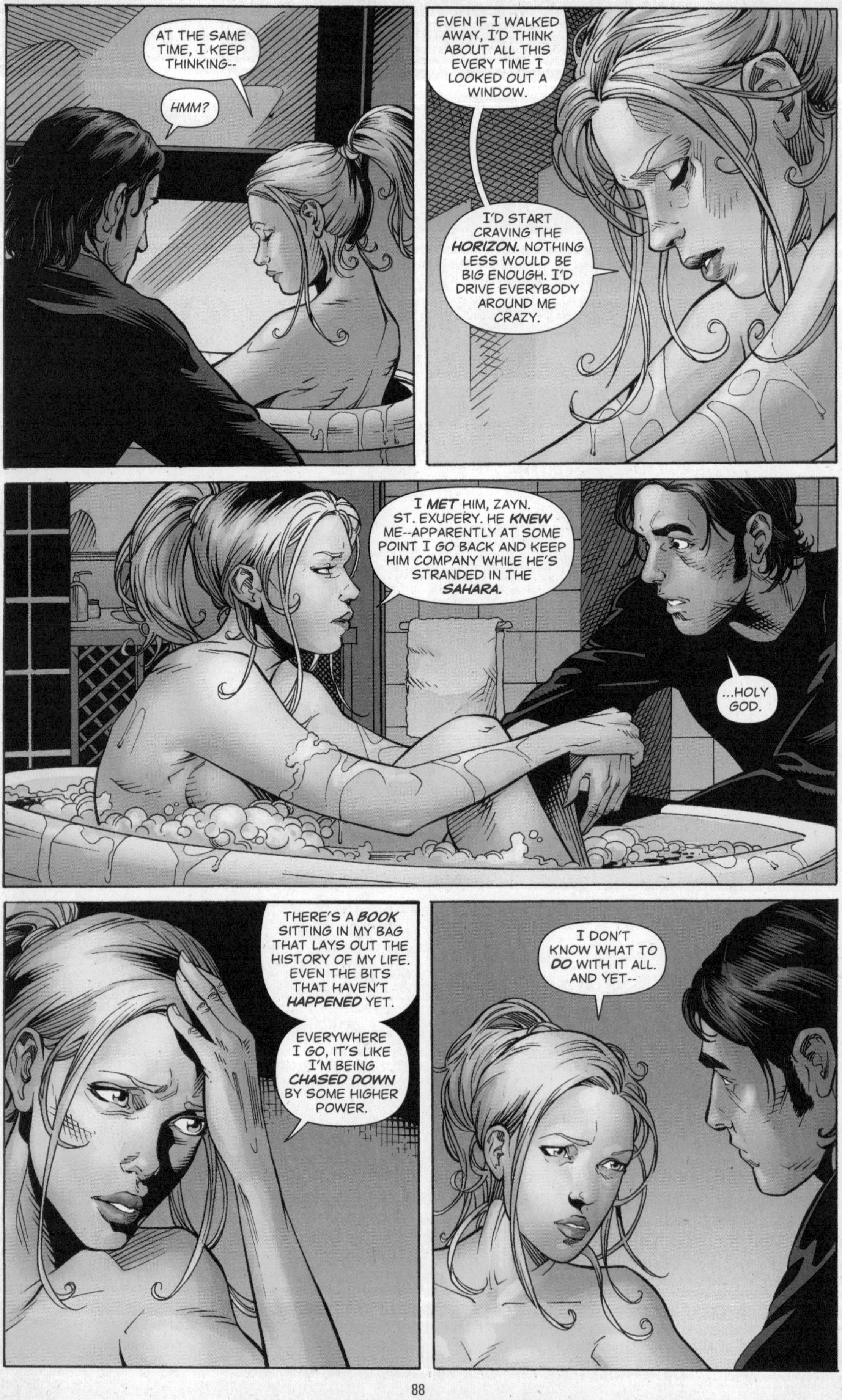
AT THE SAME TIME, I KEEP THINKING--
HMM?
EVEN IF I WALKED AWAY, I'D THINK ABOUT ALL THIS EVERY TIME I LOOKED OUT A WINDOW.
I'D START CRAVING THE **HORIZON.** NOTHING LESS WOULD BE BIG ENOUGH. I'D DRIVE EVERYBODY AROUND ME CRAZY.
I **MET** HIM, ZAYN. ST. EXUPERY. HE **KNEW** ME--APPARENTLY AT SOME POINT I GO BACK AND KEEP HIM COMPANY WHILE HE'S STRANDED IN THE **SAHARA.**
...HOLY GOD.
THERE'S A **BOOK** SITTING IN MY BAG THAT LAYS OUT THE HISTORY OF MY LIFE. EVEN THE BITS THAT HAVEN'T **HAPPENED** YET.
EVERYWHERE I GO, IT'S LIKE I'M BEING **CHASED DOWN** BY SOME HIGHER POWER.
I DON'T KNOW WHAT TO **DO** WITH IT ALL. AND YET--

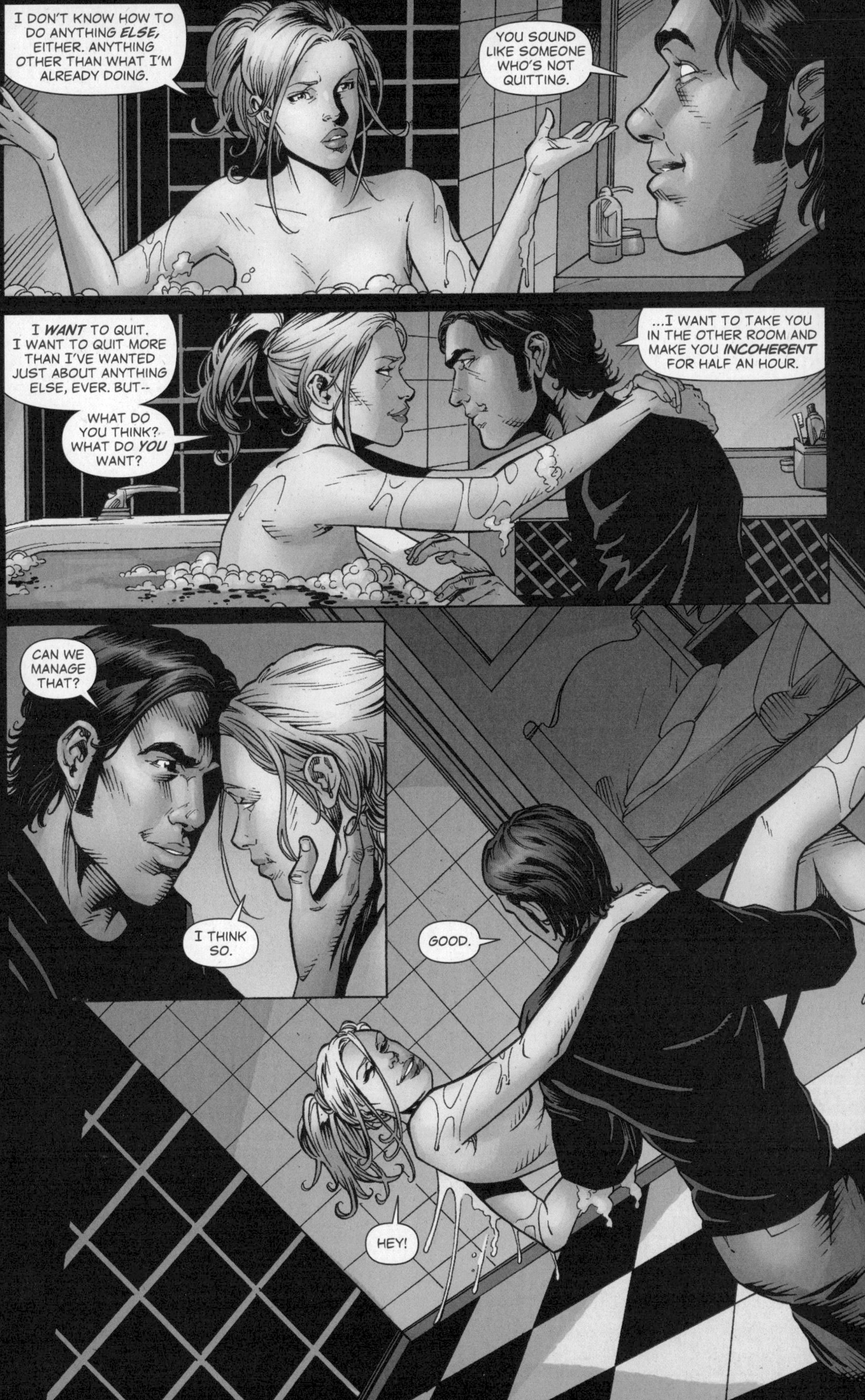
I DON'T KNOW HOW TO DO ANYTHING ELSE, EITHER. ANYTHING OTHER THAN WHAT I'M ALREADY DOING.
YOU SOUND LIKE SOMEONE WHO'S NOT QUITTING.
I WANT TO QUIT. I WANT TO QUIT MORE THAN I'VE WANTED JUST ABOUT ANYTHING ELSE, EVER. BUT--
WHAT DO YOU THINK? WHAT DO YOU WANT?
...I WANT TO TAKE YOU IN THE OTHER ROOM AND MAKE YOU INCOHERENT FOR HALF AN HOUR.
CAN WE MANAGE THAT?
I THINK SO.
GOOD.
HEY!

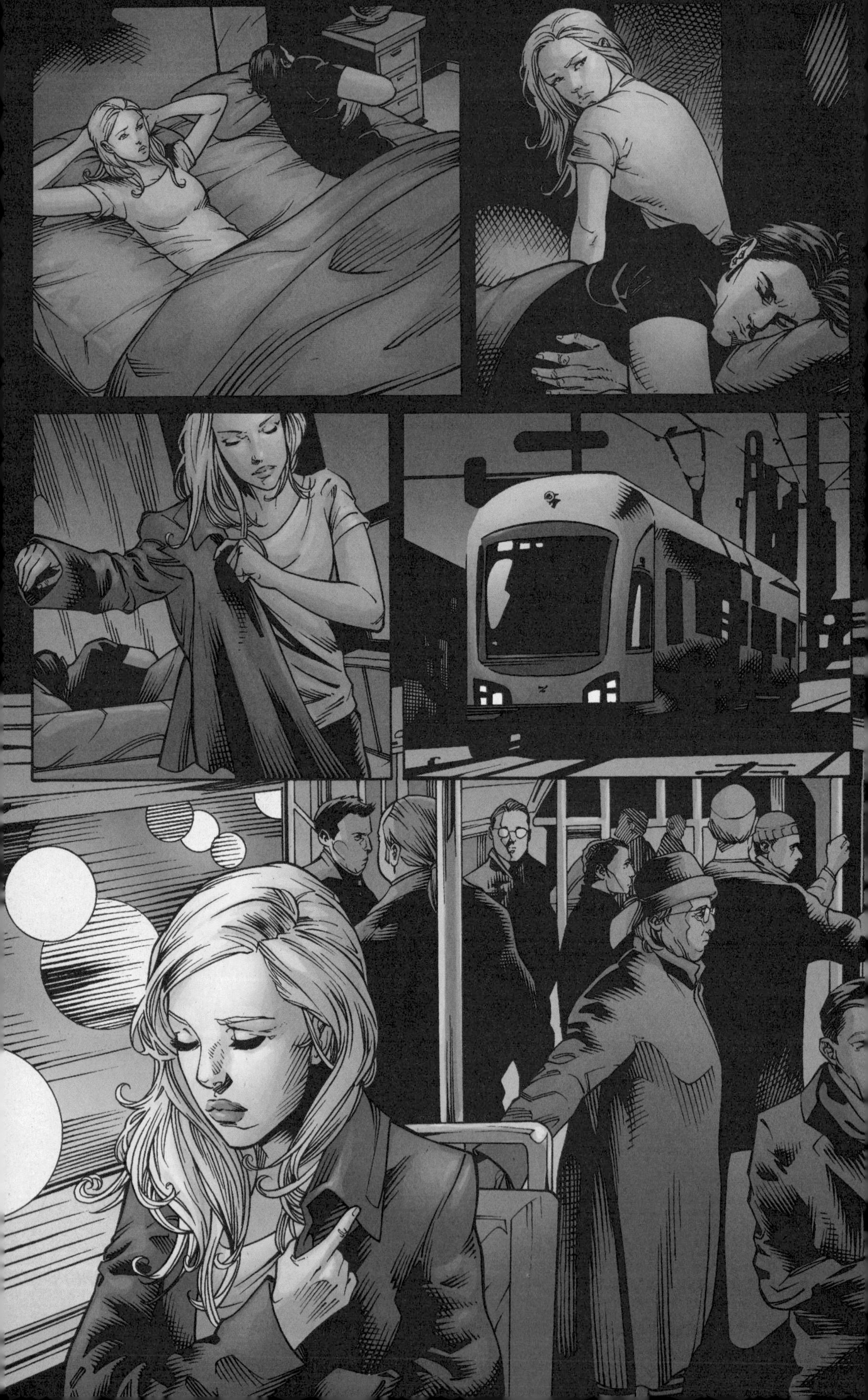

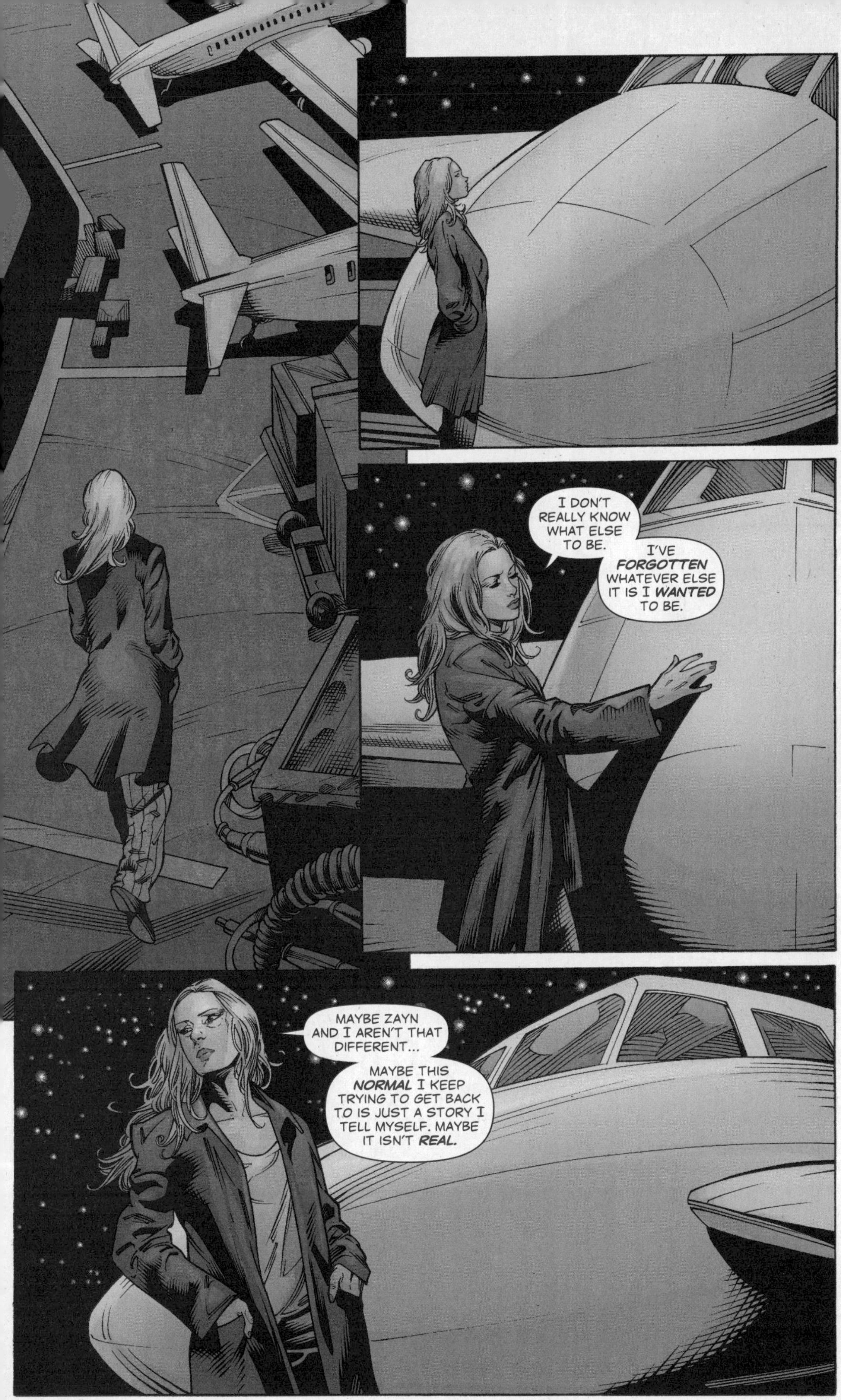
I DON'T REALLY KNOW WHAT ELSE TO BE.
I'VE FORGOTTEN WHATEVER ELSE IT IS I WANTED TO BE.
MAYBE ZAYN AND I AREN'T THAT DIFFERENT...
MAYBE THIS NORMAL I KEEP TRYING TO GET BACK TO IS JUST A STORY I TELL MYSELF. MAYBE IT ISN'T REAL.

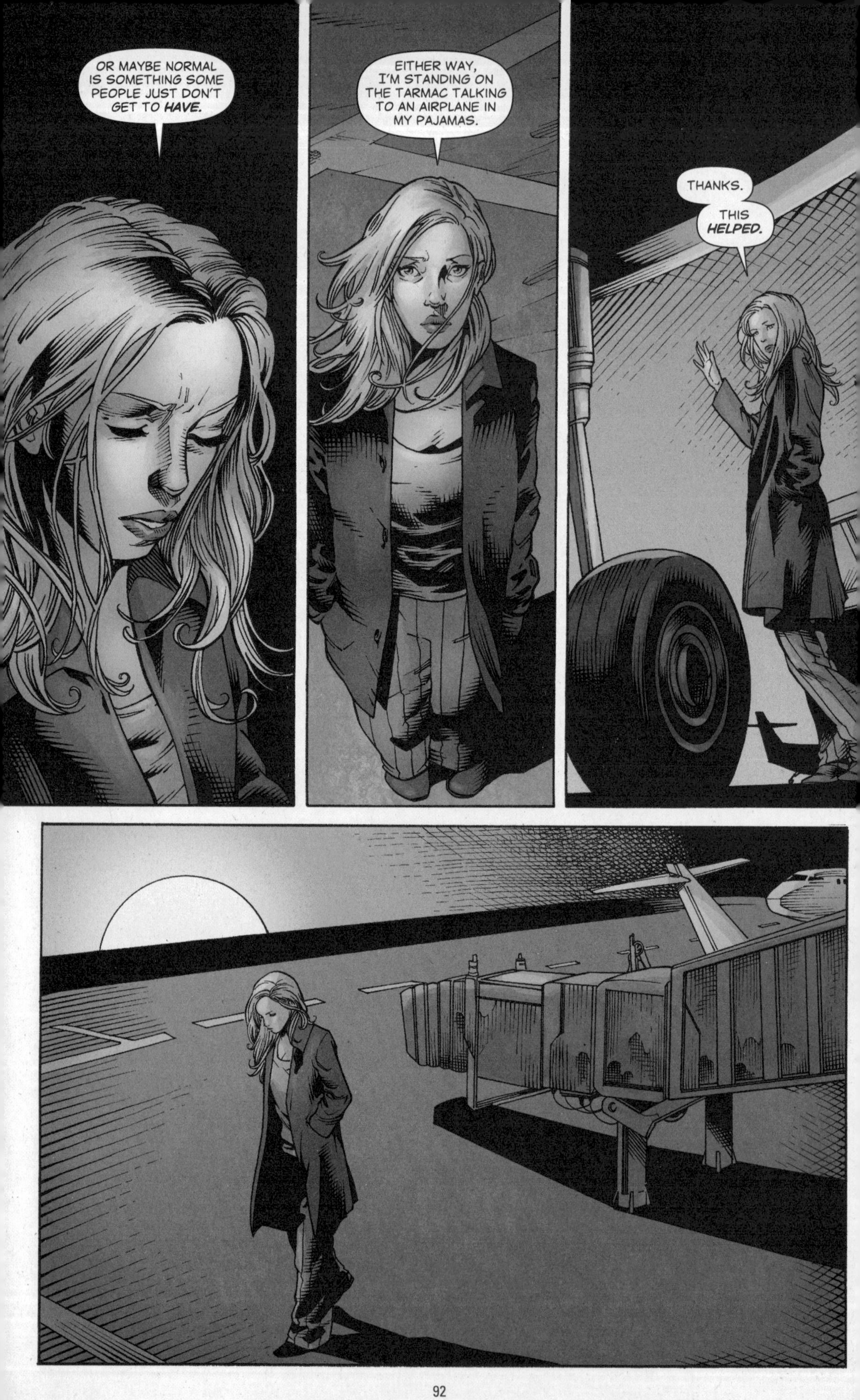
OR MAYBE NORMAL IS SOMETHING SOME PEOPLE JUST DON'T GET TO *HAVE.*
EITHER WAY, I'M STANDING ON THE TARMAC TALKING TO AN AIRPLANE IN MY PAJAMAS.
THANKS.
THIS *HELPED.*

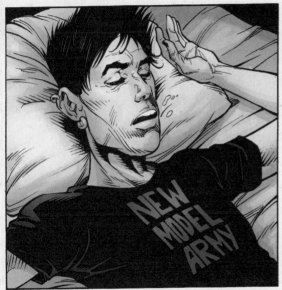

NNGH!

GET UP.

WHAT IS *WRONG* WITH YOU?

WE'RE LEAVING AT OH-NINE-HUNDRED.

LIKE HELL WE'RE--

OR YOU CAN FLY *COACH* BACK TO AMSTERDAM AND SIT NEXT TO SOMEBODY WITH SWINE FLU AND A CRYING BABY.

THIS IS WHAT I GET FOR GIVING *PEP TALKS*.

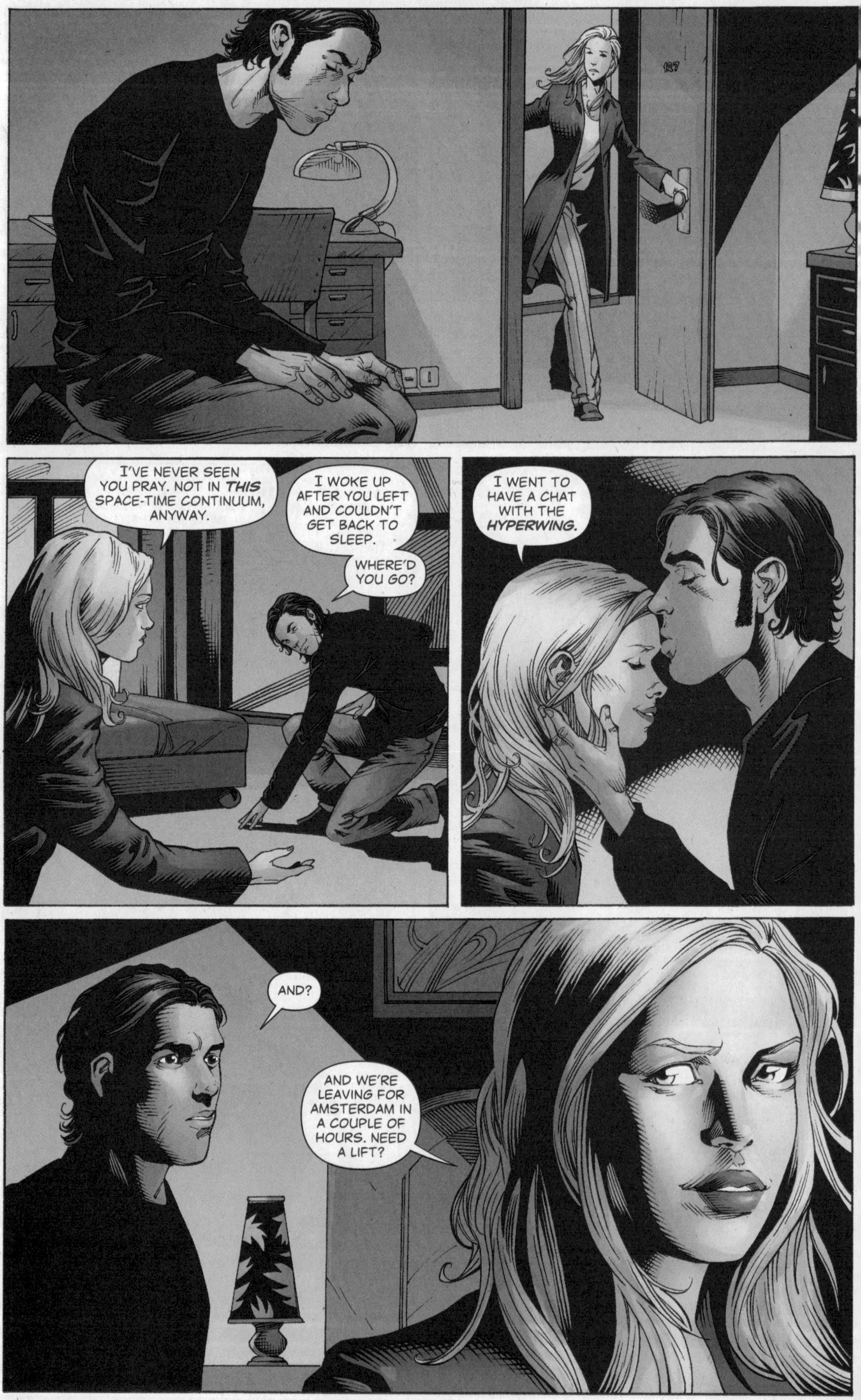
I'VE NEVER SEEN YOU PRAY. NOT IN THIS SPACE-TIME CONTINUUM, ANYWAY.
I WOKE UP AFTER YOU LEFT AND COULDN'T GET BACK TO SLEEP.
WHERE'D YOU GO?
I WENT TO HAVE A CHAT WITH THE HYPERWING.
AND?
AND WE'RE LEAVING FOR AMSTERDAM IN A COUPLE OF HOURS. NEED A LIFT?

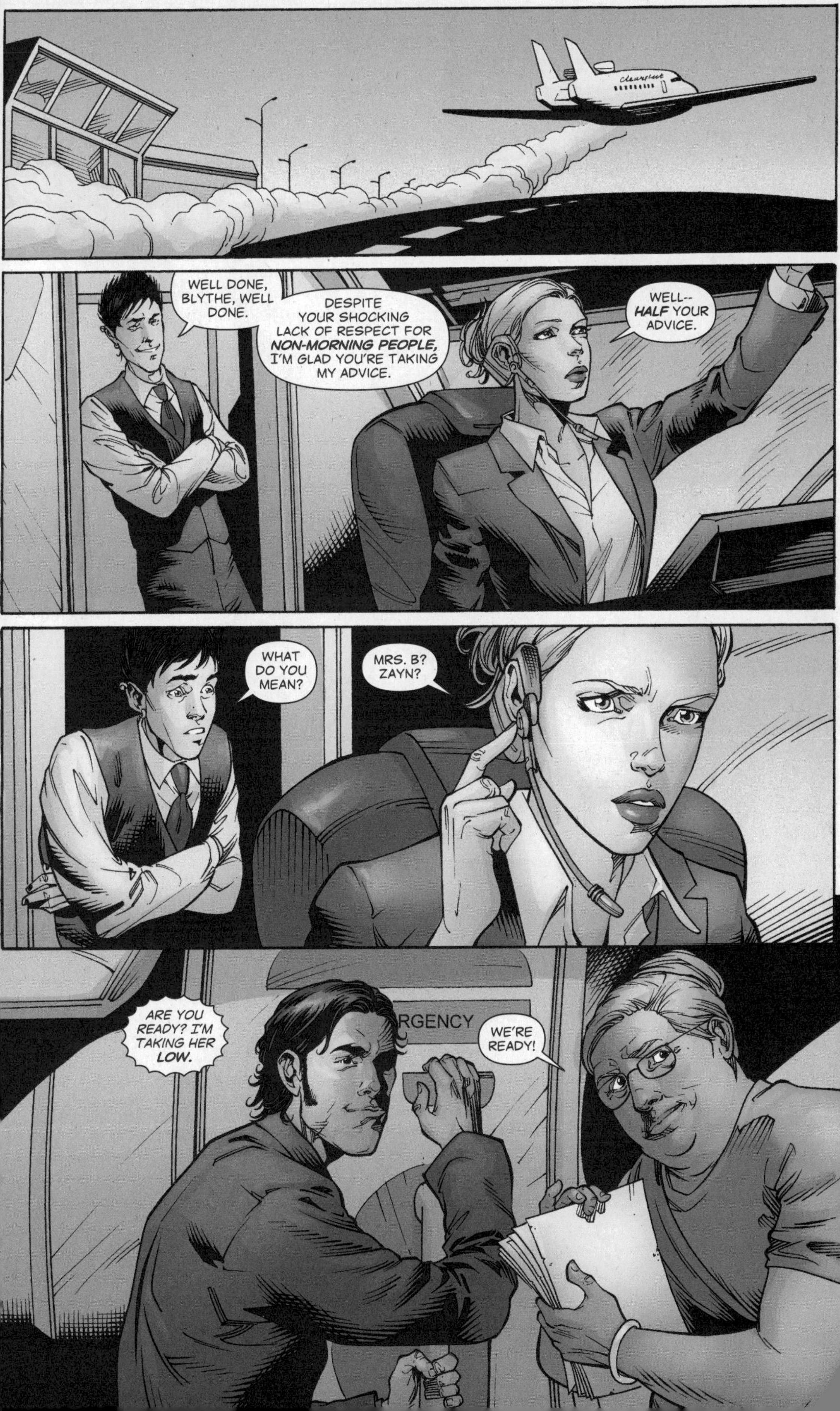
WELL DONE, BLYTHE, WELL DONE.
DESPITE YOUR SHOCKING LACK OF RESPECT FOR NON-MORNING PEOPLE, I'M GLAD YOU'RE TAKING MY ADVICE.
WELL-- HALF YOUR ADVICE.
WHAT DO YOU MEAN?
MRS. B? ZAYN?
ARE YOU READY? I'M TAKING HER LOW.
RGENCY
WE'RE READY!

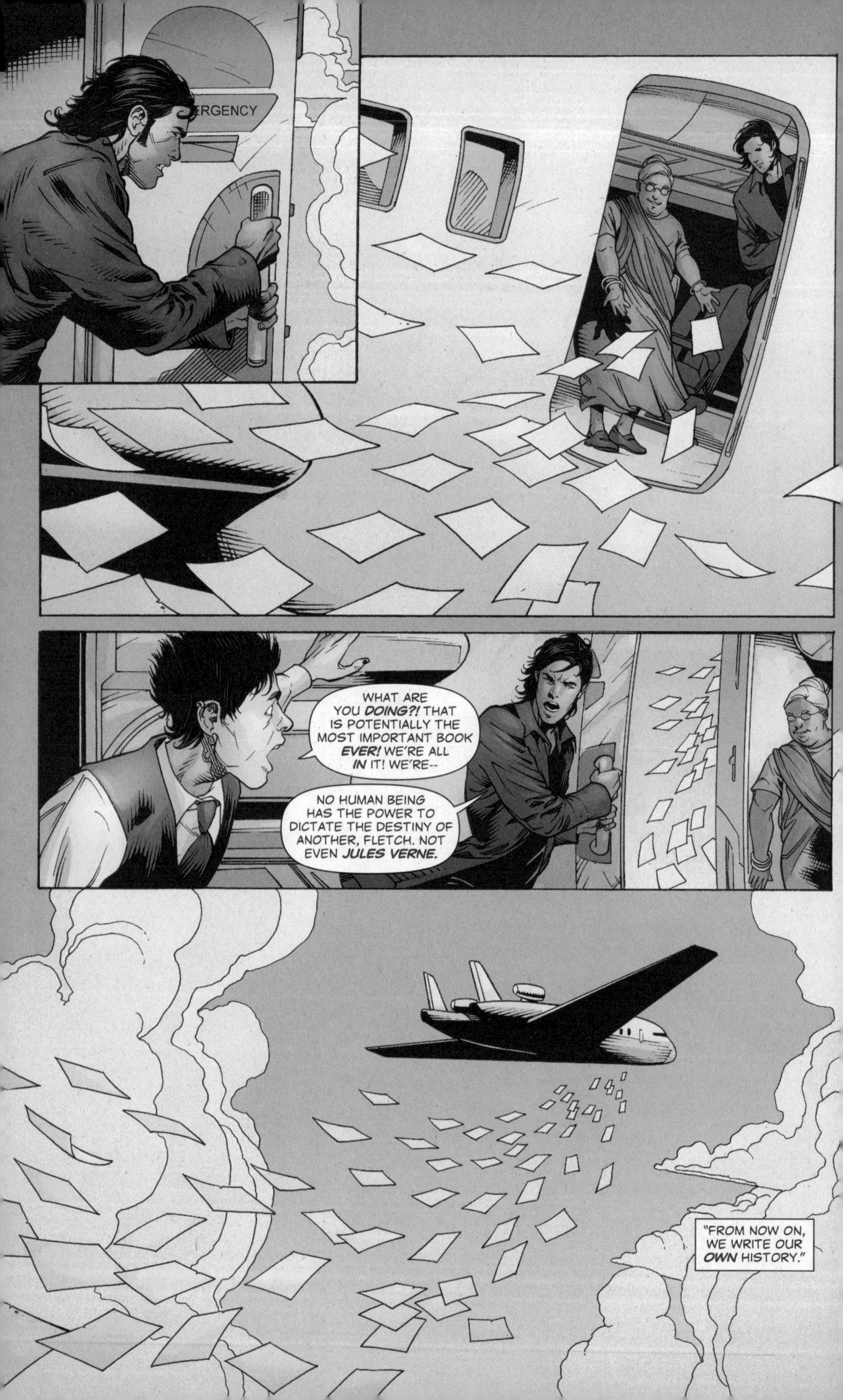

ERGENCY
WHAT ARE YOU DOING?! THAT IS POTENTIALLY THE MOST IMPORTANT BOOK EVER! WE'RE ALL IN IT! WE'RE--
NO HUMAN BEING HAS THE POWER TO DICTATE THE DESTINY OF ANOTHER, FLETCH. NOT EVEN JULES VERNE.
"FROM NOW ON, WE WRITE OUR OWN HISTORY."

WILD BLUE YONDER

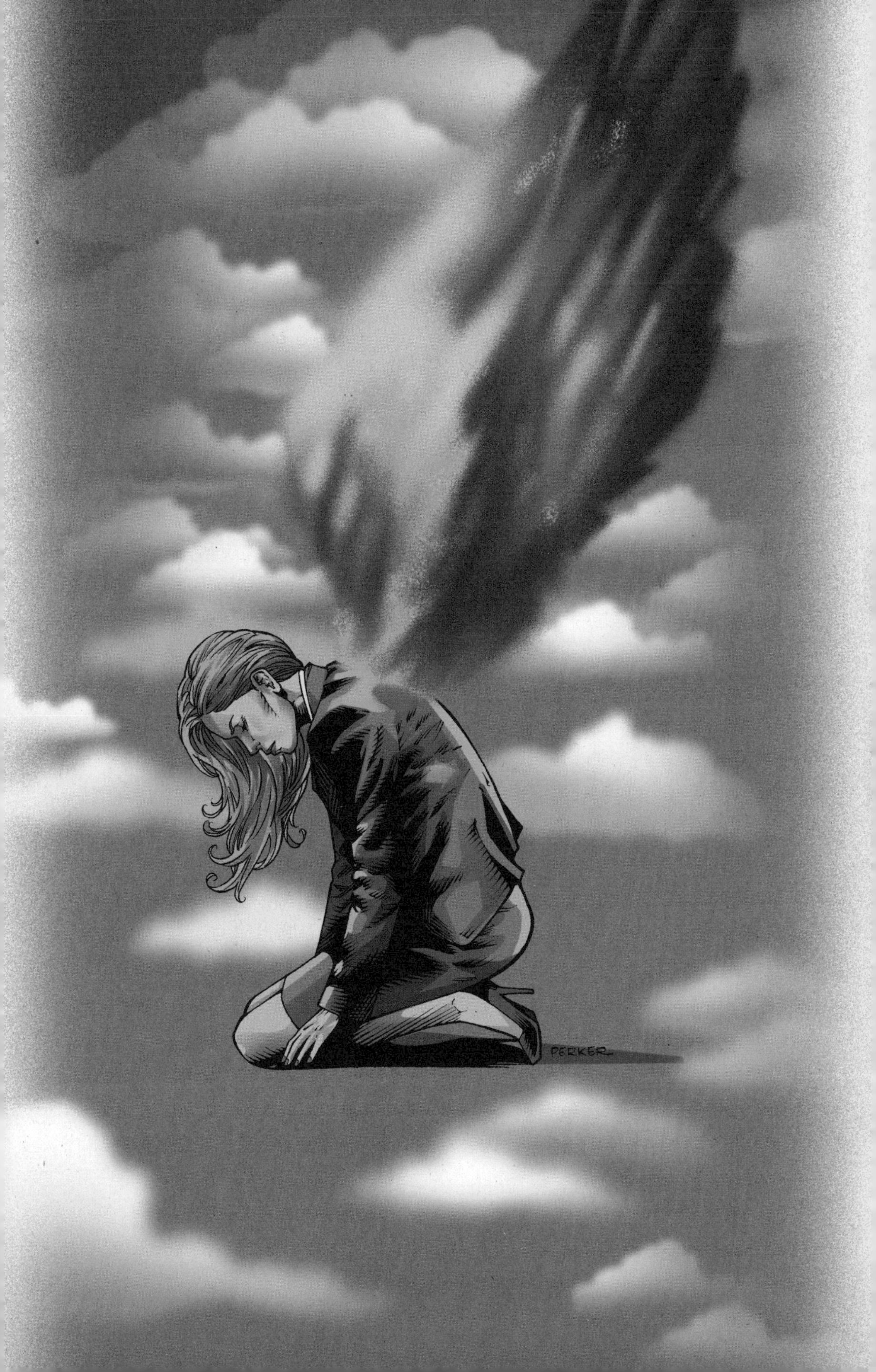
PERKER

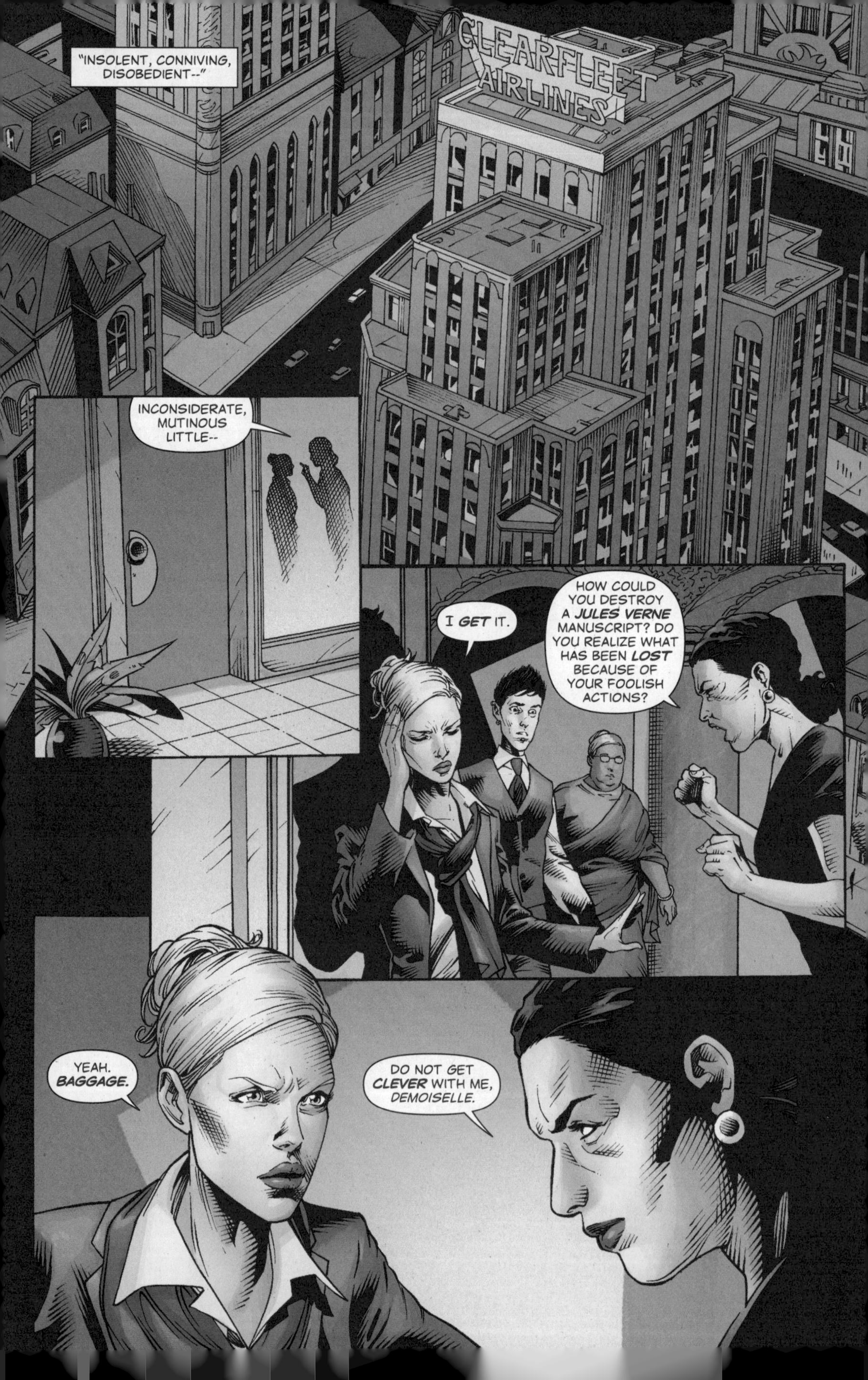
"INSOLENT, CONNIVING, DISOBEDIENT--"
CLEARFLEET AIRLINES
INCONSIDERATE, MUTINOUS LITTLE--
I GET IT.
HOW COULD YOU DESTROY A JULES VERNE MANUSCRIPT? DO YOU REALIZE WHAT HAS BEEN LOST BECAUSE OF YOUR FOOLISH ACTIONS?
YEAH. BAGGAGE.
DO NOT GET CLEVER WITH ME, DEMOISELLE.

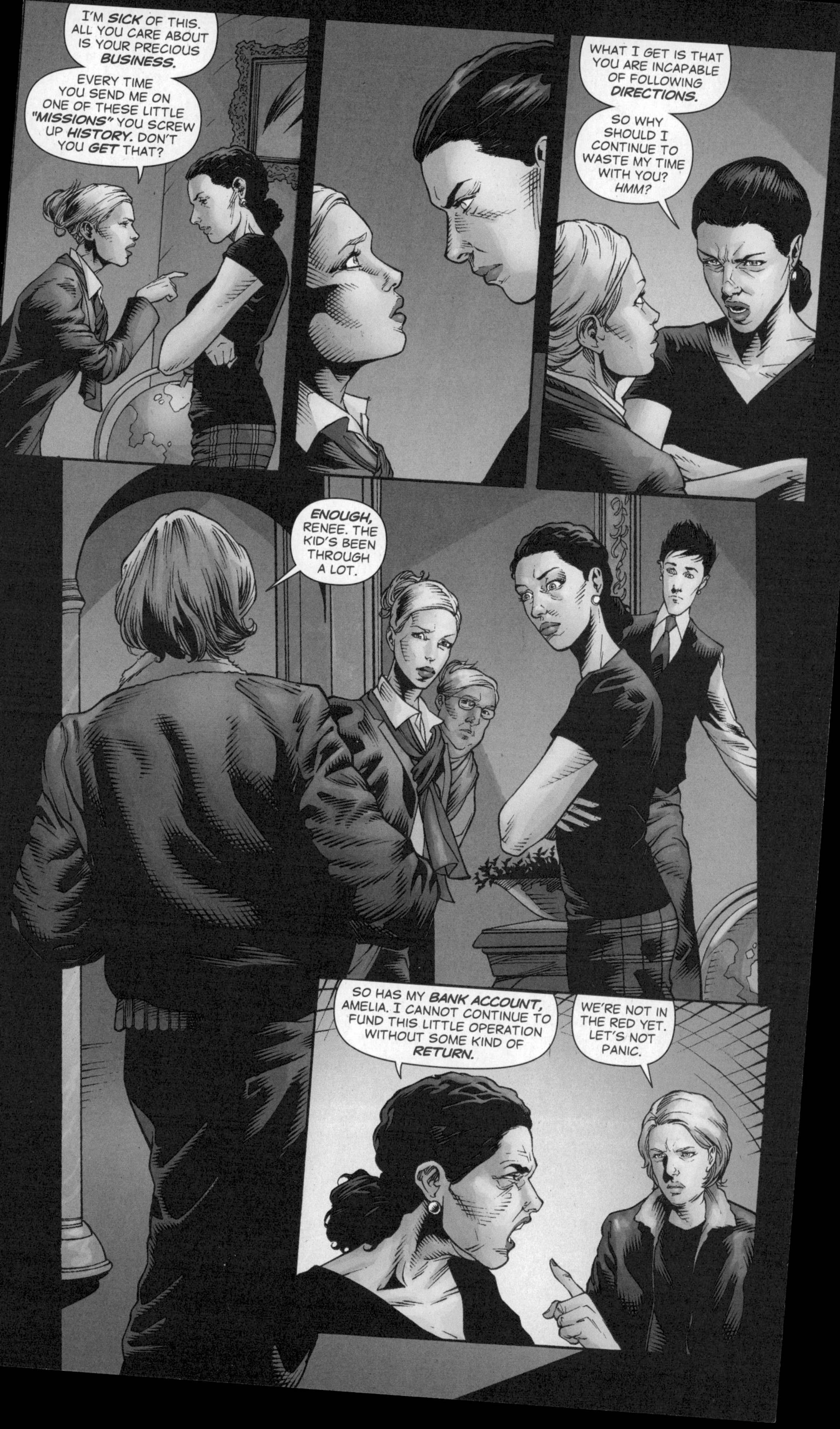
I'M SICK OF THIS. ALL YOU CARE ABOUT IS YOUR PRECIOUS BUSINESS.
EVERY TIME YOU SEND ME ON ONE OF THESE LITTLE "MISSIONS" YOU SCREW UP HISTORY. DON'T YOU GET THAT?
WHAT I GET IS THAT YOU ARE INCAPABLE OF FOLLOWING DIRECTIONS.
SO WHY SHOULD I CONTINUE TO WASTE MY TIME WITH YOU? HMM?
ENOUGH, RENEE. THE KID'S BEEN THROUGH A LOT.
SO HAS MY BANK ACCOUNT, AMELIA. I CANNOT CONTINUE TO FUND THIS LITTLE OPERATION WITHOUT SOME KIND OF RETURN.
WE'RE NOT IN THE RED YET. LET'S NOT PANIC.

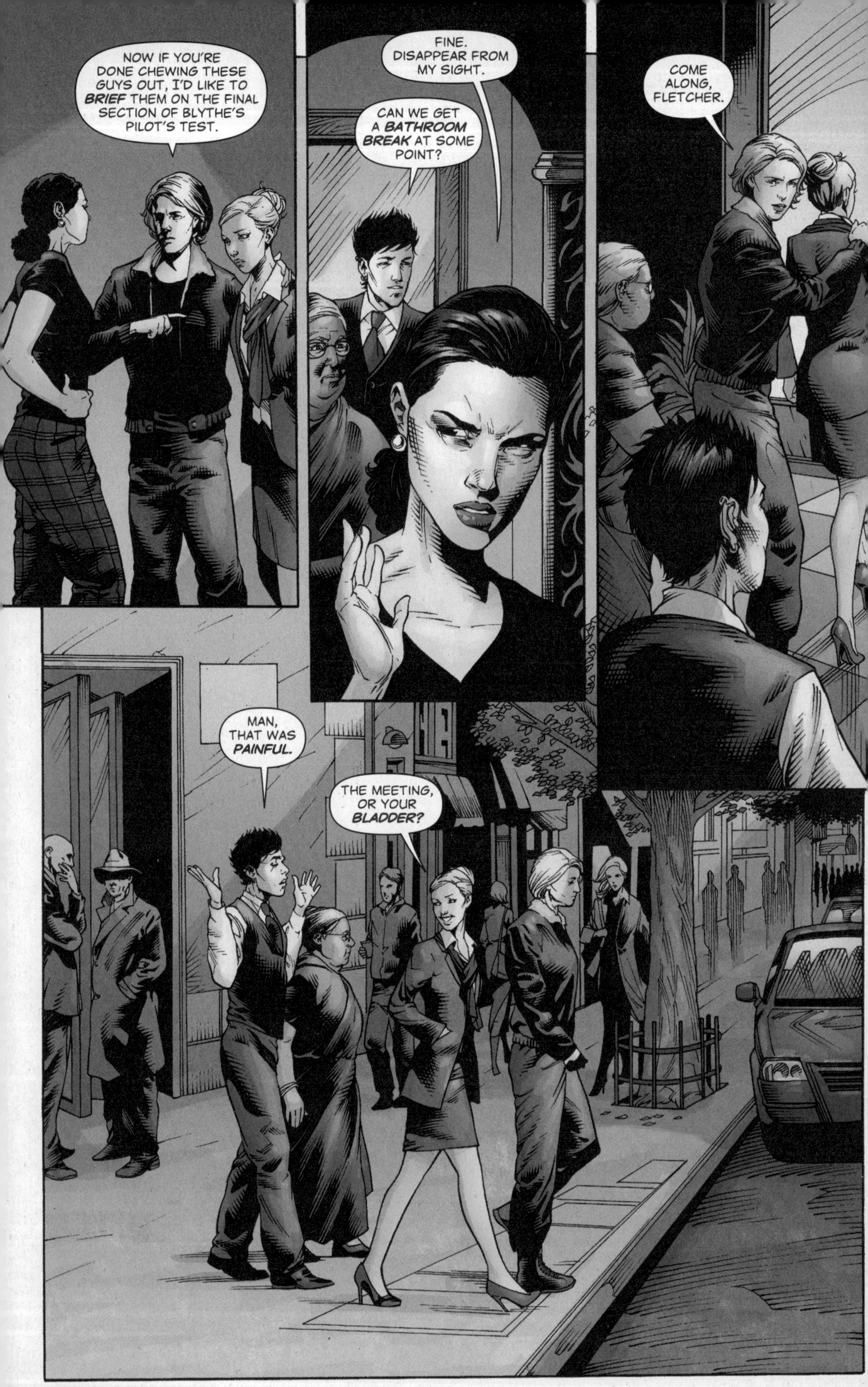
NOW IF YOU'RE DONE CHEWING THESE GUYS OUT, I'D LIKE TO BRIEF THEM ON THE FINAL SECTION OF BLYTHE'S PILOT'S TEST.
FINE. DISAPPEAR FROM MY SIGHT.
CAN WE GET A BATHROOM BREAK AT SOME POINT?
COME ALONG, FLETCHER.
MAN, THAT WAS PAINFUL.
THE MEETING, OR YOUR BLADDER?

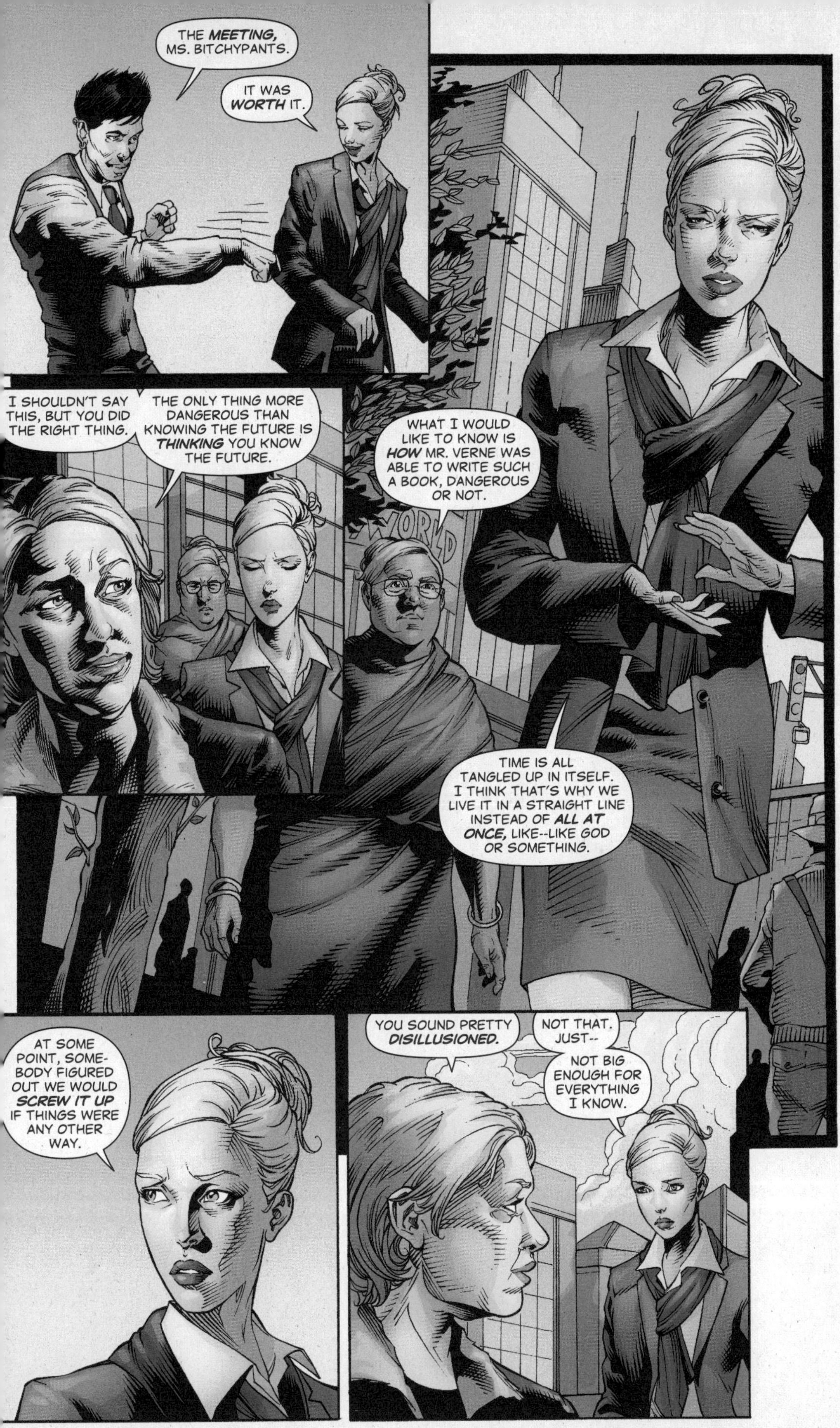
THE MEETING, MS. BITCHYPANTS.
IT WAS WORTH IT.
I SHOULDN'T SAY THIS, BUT YOU DID THE RIGHT THING.
THE ONLY THING MORE DANGEROUS THAN KNOWING THE FUTURE IS THINKING YOU KNOW THE FUTURE.
WHAT I WOULD LIKE TO KNOW IS HOW MR. VERNE WAS ABLE TO WRITE SUCH A BOOK, DANGEROUS OR NOT.
WORLD
TIME IS ALL TANGLED UP IN ITSELF. I THINK THAT'S WHY WE LIVE IT IN A STRAIGHT LINE INSTEAD OF ALL AT ONCE, LIKE--LIKE GOD OR SOMETHING.
AT SOME POINT, SOMEBODY FIGURED OUT WE WOULD SCREW IT UP IF THINGS WERE ANY OTHER WAY.
YOU SOUND PRETTY DISILLUSIONED.
NOT THAT. JUST--
NOT BIG ENOUGH FOR EVERYTHING I KNOW.

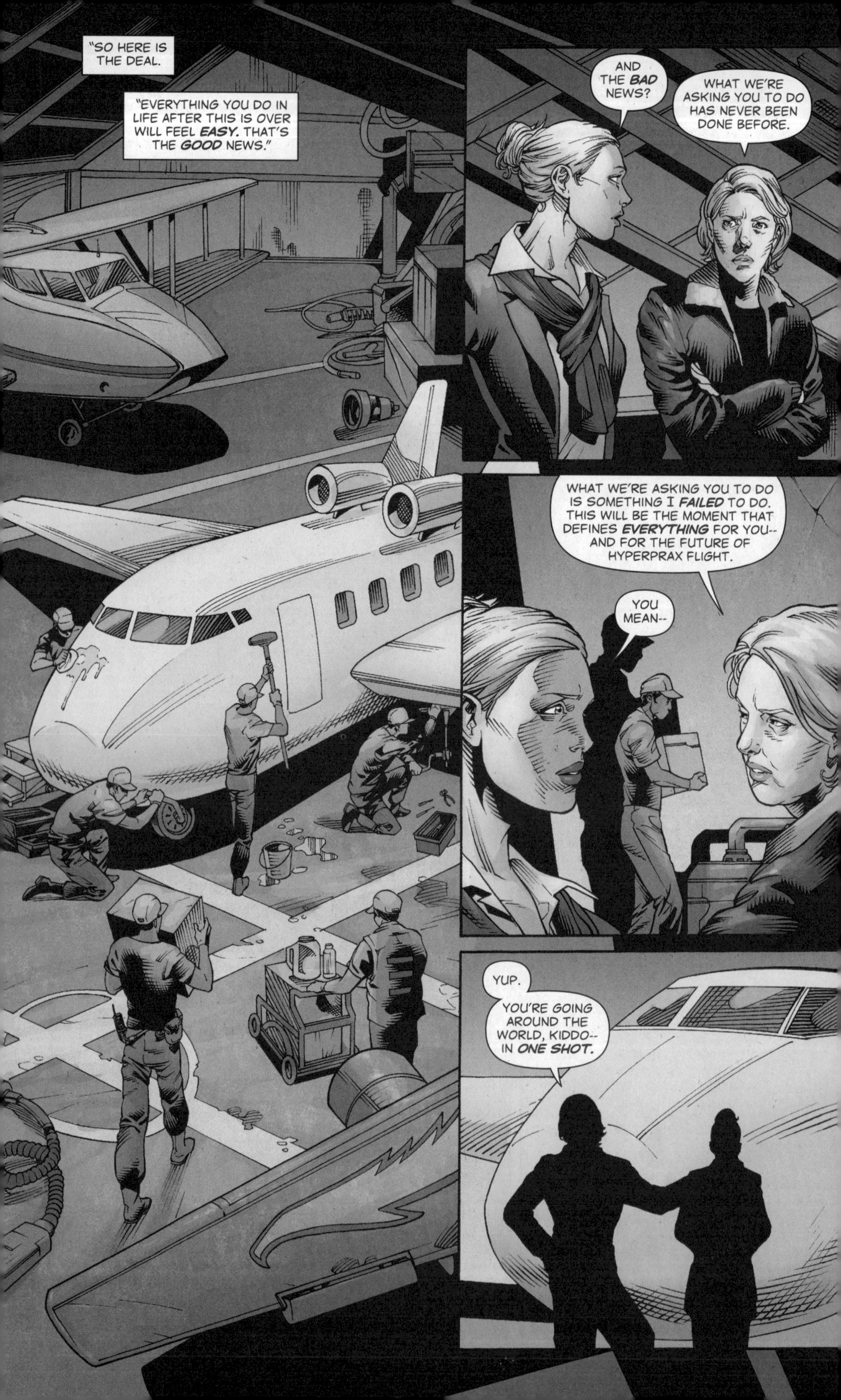

"SO HERE IS THE DEAL.
"EVERYTHING YOU DO IN LIFE AFTER THIS IS OVER WILL FEEL **EASY**. THAT'S THE **GOOD** NEWS."
AND THE **BAD** NEWS?
WHAT WE'RE ASKING YOU TO DO HAS NEVER BEEN DONE BEFORE.
WHAT WE'RE ASKING YOU TO DO IS SOMETHING I **FAILED** TO DO. THIS WILL BE THE MOMENT THAT DEFINES **EVERYTHING** FOR YOU-- AND FOR THE FUTURE OF HYPERPRAX FLIGHT.
YOU MEAN--
YUP.
YOU'RE GOING AROUND THE WORLD, KIDDO-- IN **ONE SHOT**.

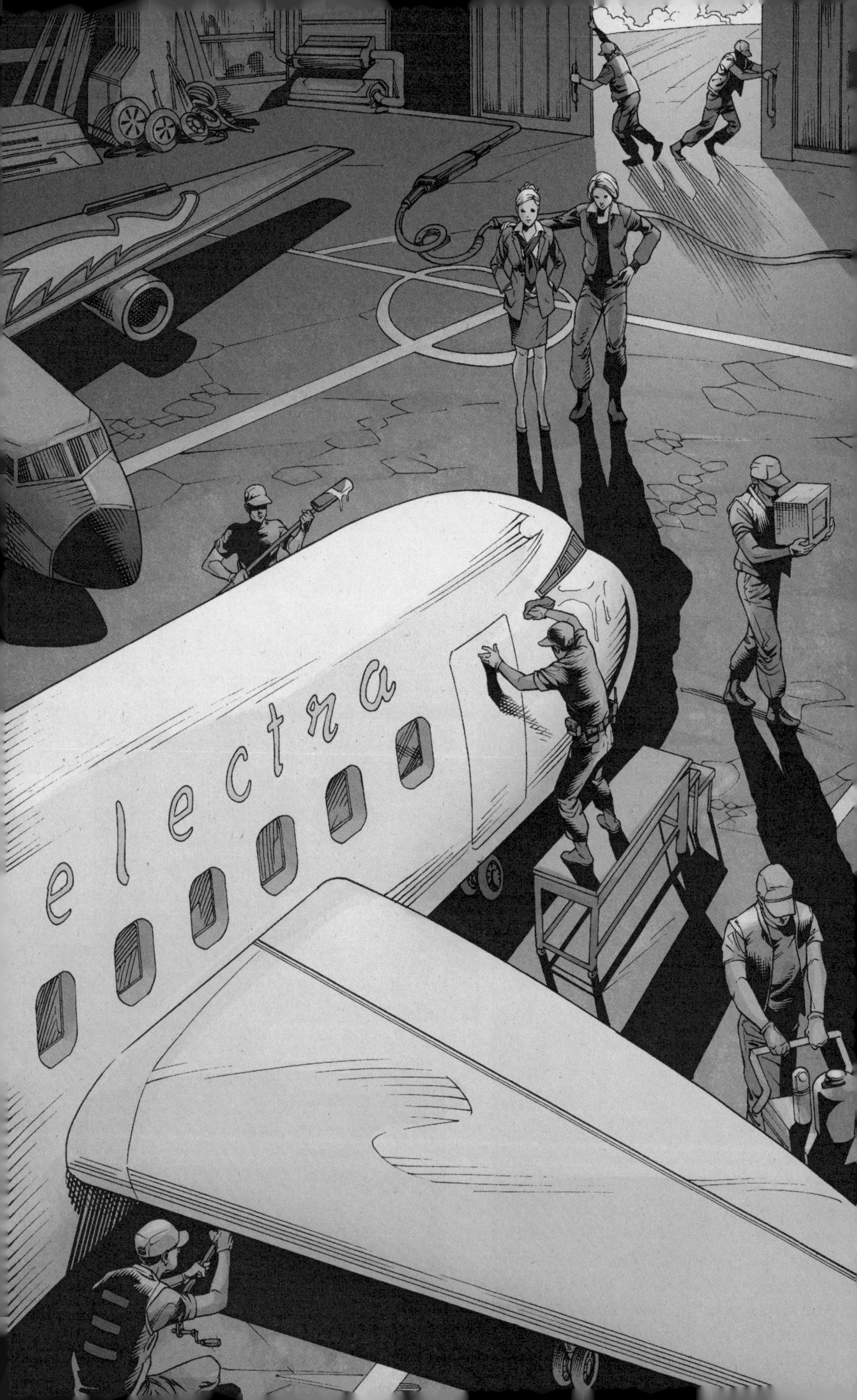
electra

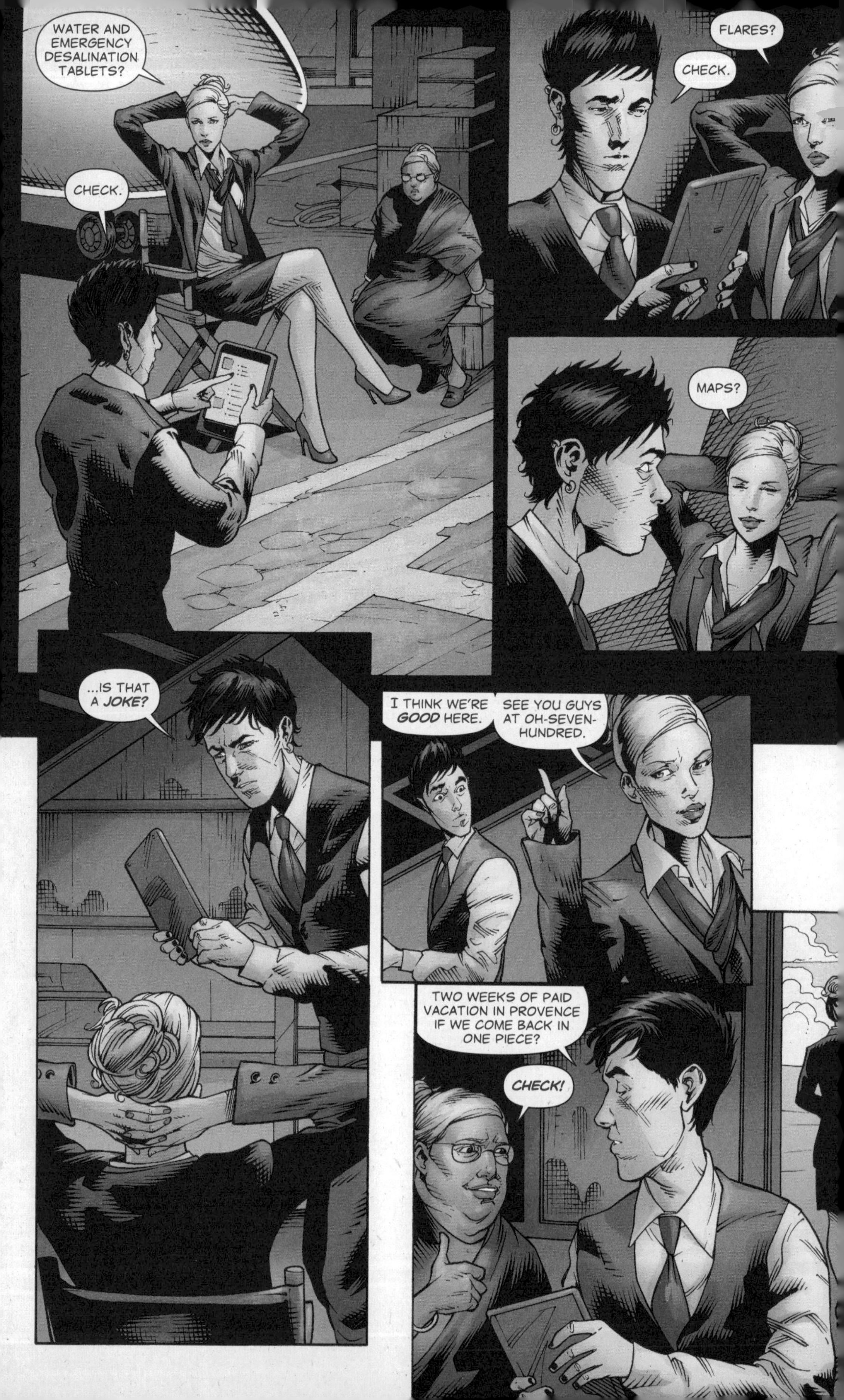

WATER AND EMERGENCY DESALINATION TABLETS?
CHECK.
FLARES?
CHECK.
MAPS?
...IS THAT A *JOKE?*
I THINK WE'RE *GOOD* HERE.
SEE YOU GUYS AT OH-SEVEN-HUNDRED.
TWO WEEKS OF PAID VACATION IN PROVENCE IF WE COME BACK IN ONE PIECE?
CHECK!

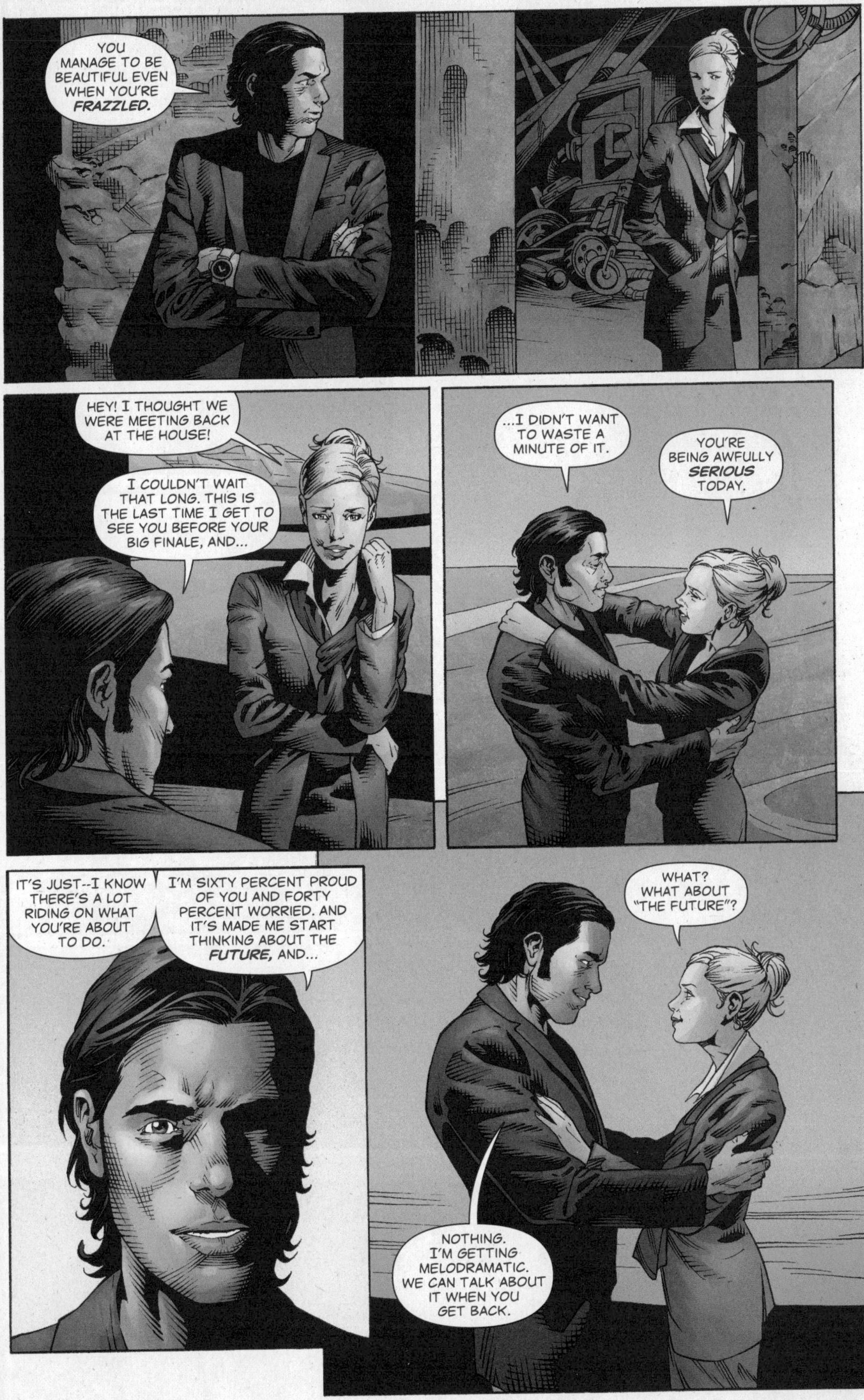
YOU MANAGE TO BE BEAUTIFUL EVEN WHEN YOU'RE FRAZZLED.
HEY! I THOUGHT WE WERE MEETING BACK AT THE HOUSE!
I COULDN'T WAIT THAT LONG. THIS IS THE LAST TIME I GET TO SEE YOU BEFORE YOUR BIG FINALE, AND...
...I DIDN'T WANT TO WASTE A MINUTE OF IT.
YOU'RE BEING AWFULLY SERIOUS TODAY.
IT'S JUST--I KNOW THERE'S A LOT RIDING ON WHAT YOU'RE ABOUT TO DO.
I'M SIXTY PERCENT PROUD OF YOU AND FORTY PERCENT WORRIED. AND IT'S MADE ME START THINKING ABOUT THE FUTURE, AND...
WHAT? WHAT ABOUT "THE FUTURE"?
NOTHING. I'M GETTING MELODRAMATIC. WE CAN TALK ABOUT IT WHEN YOU GET BACK.

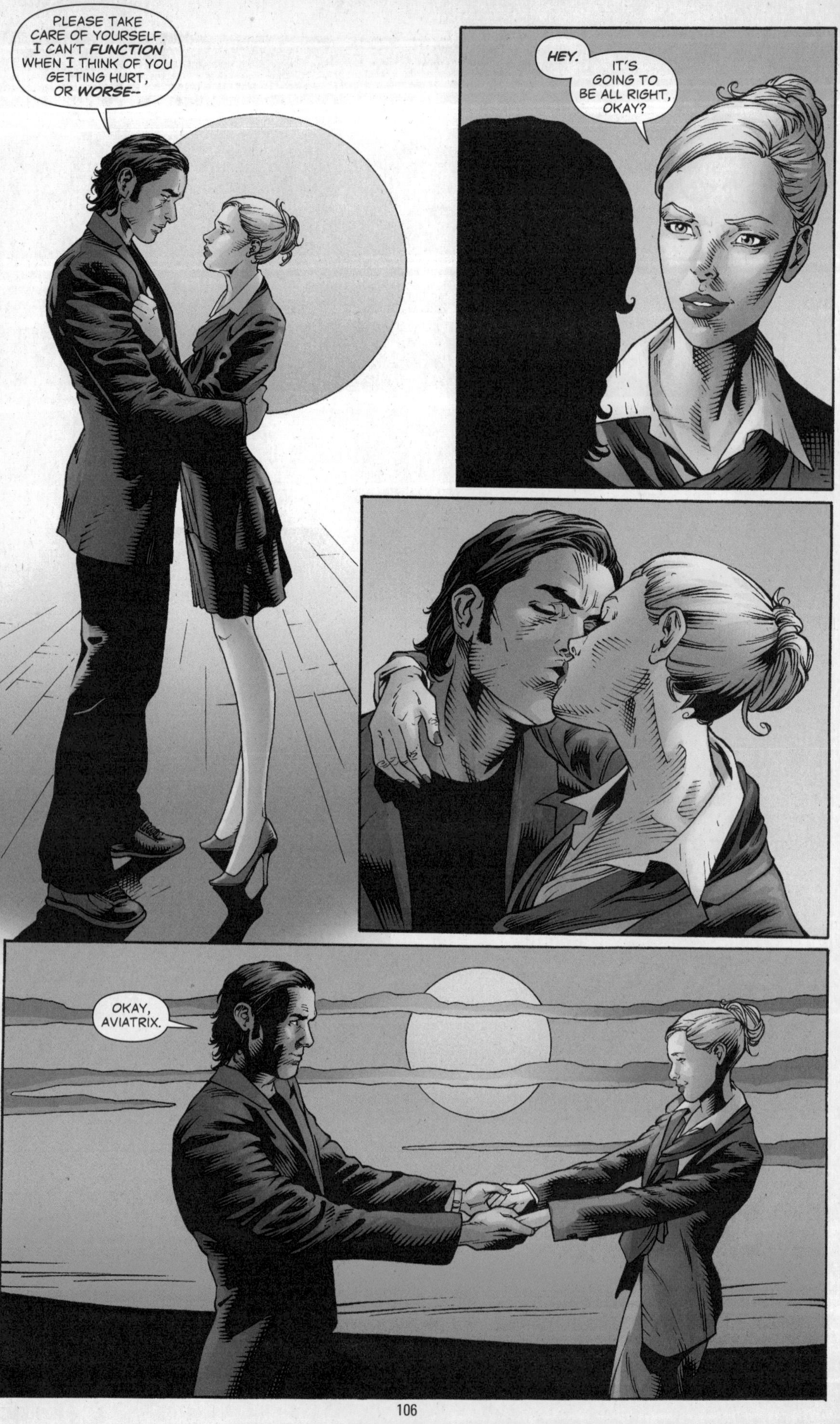
PLEASE TAKE CARE OF YOURSELF. I CAN'T *FUNCTION* WHEN I THINK OF YOU GETTING HURT, OR *WORSE*--
HEY.
IT'S GOING TO BE ALL RIGHT, OKAY?
OKAY, AVIATRIX.

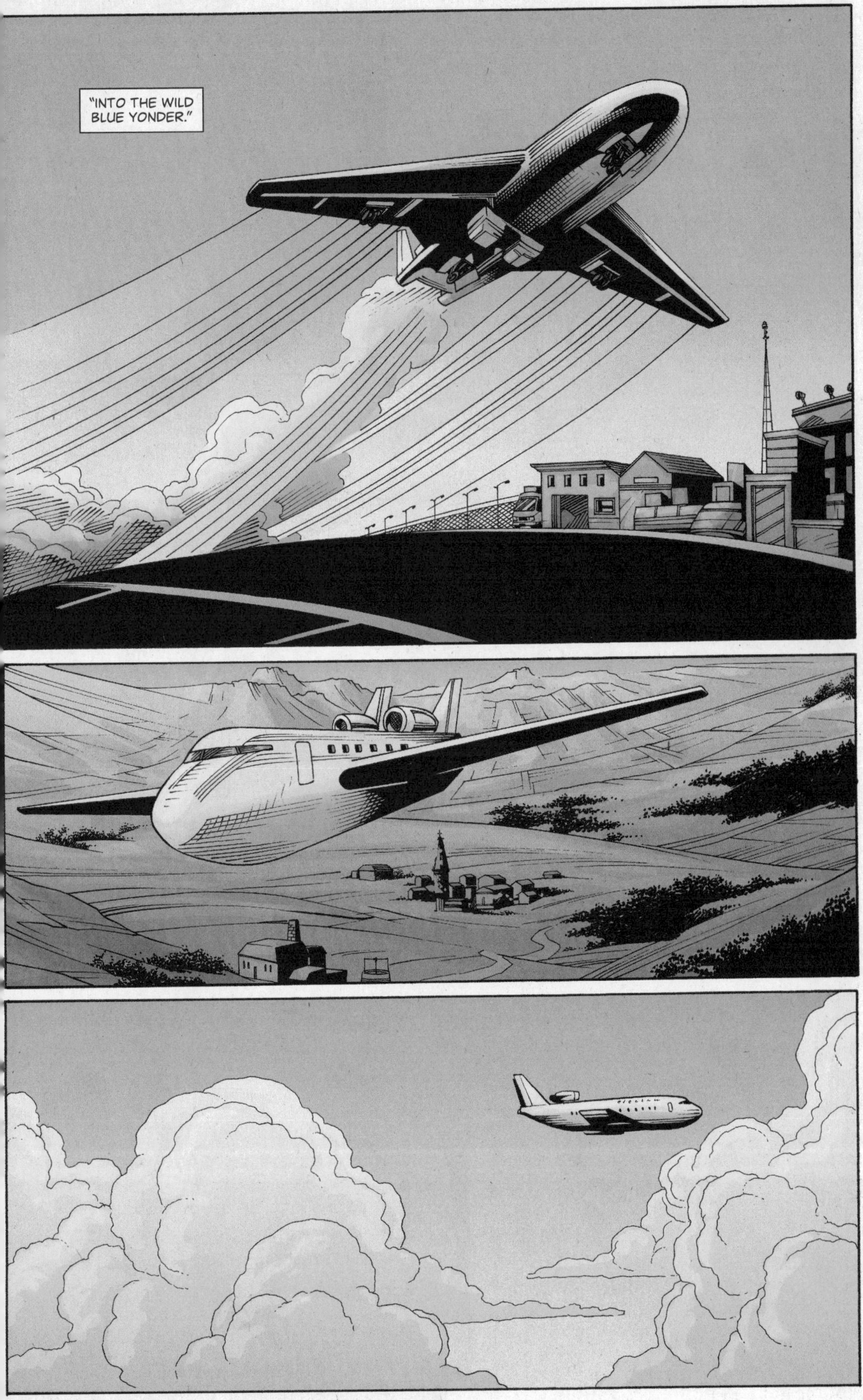
"INTO THE WILD BLUE YONDER."

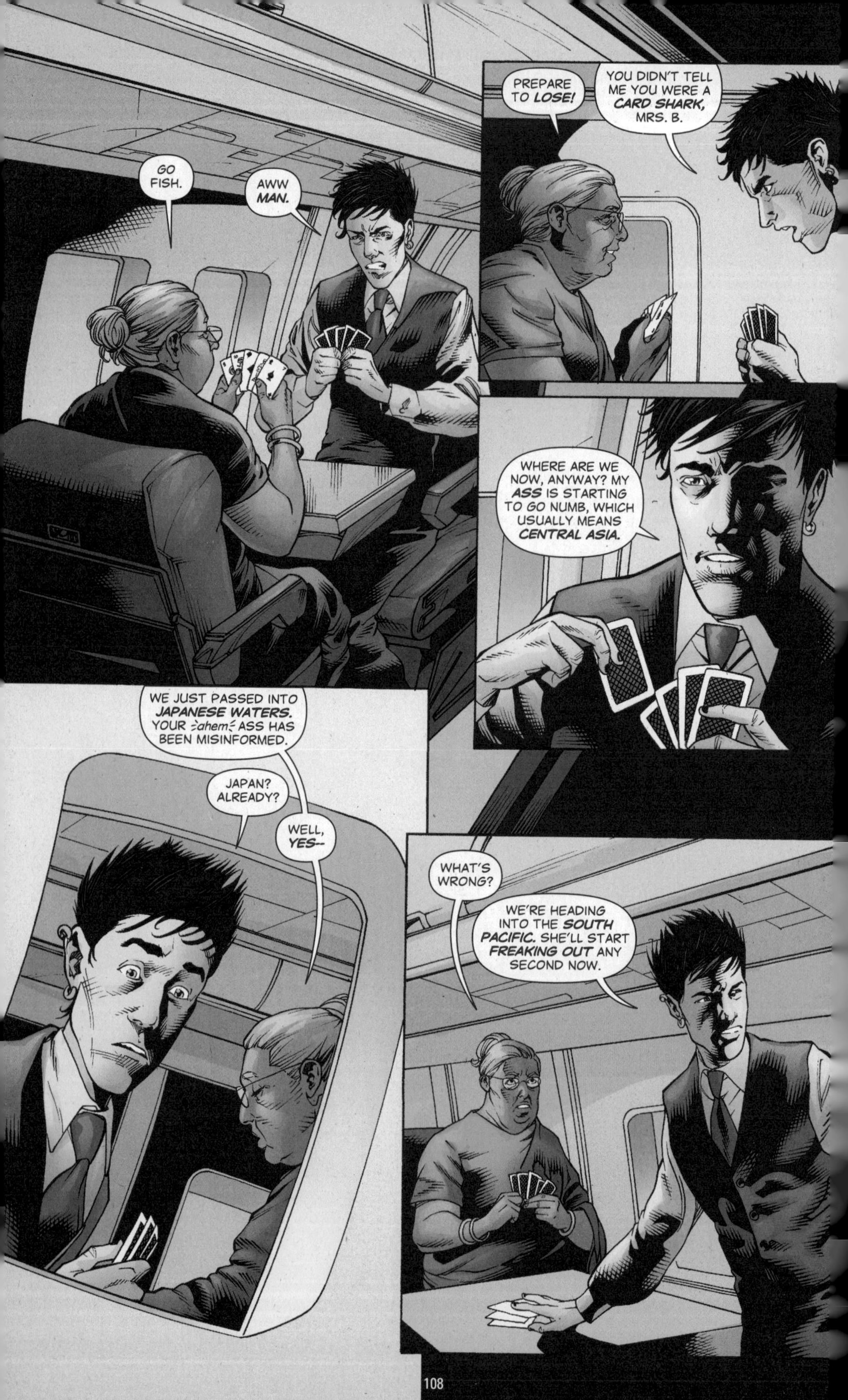

GO FISH.
AWW *MAN.*
PREPARE TO *LOSE!*
YOU DIDN'T TELL ME YOU WERE A *CARD SHARK,* MRS. B.
WHERE ARE WE NOW, ANYWAY? MY *ASS* IS STARTING TO GO NUMB, WHICH USUALLY MEANS *CENTRAL ASIA.*
WE JUST PASSED INTO *JAPANESE WATERS.* YOUR *ahem* ASS HAS BEEN MISINFORMED.
JAPAN? ALREADY?
WELL, *YES--*
WHAT'S WRONG?
WE'RE HEADING INTO THE *SOUTH PACIFIC.* SHE'LL START *FREAKING OUT* ANY SECOND NOW.

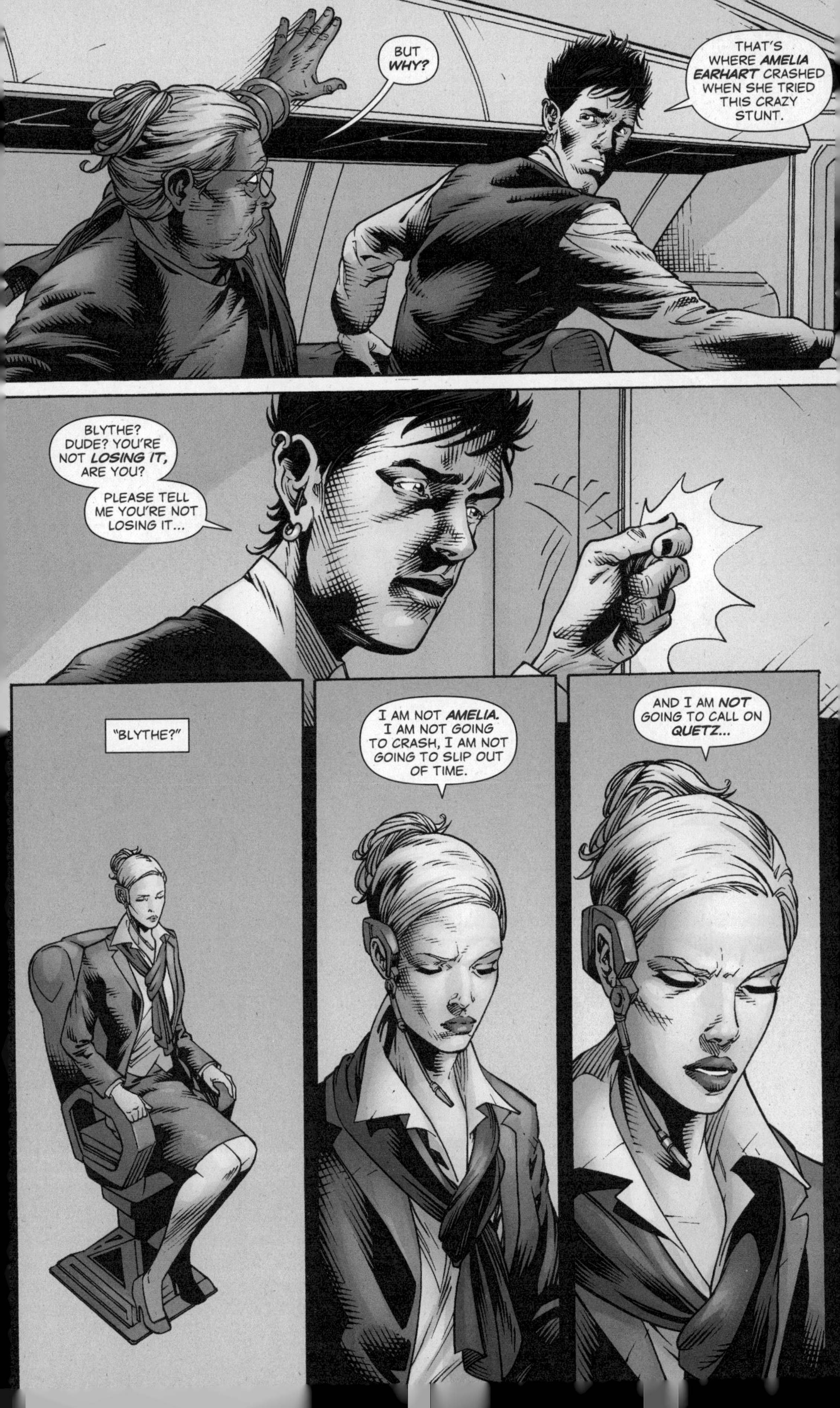
BUT WHY?
THAT'S WHERE AMELIA EARHART CRASHED WHEN SHE TRIED THIS CRAZY STUNT.
BLYTHE? DUDE? YOU'RE NOT LOSING IT, ARE YOU?
PLEASE TELL ME YOU'RE NOT LOSING IT...
"BLYTHE?"
I AM NOT AMELIA. I AM NOT GOING TO CRASH, I AM NOT GOING TO SLIP OUT OF TIME.
AND I AM NOT GOING TO CALL ON QUETZ...

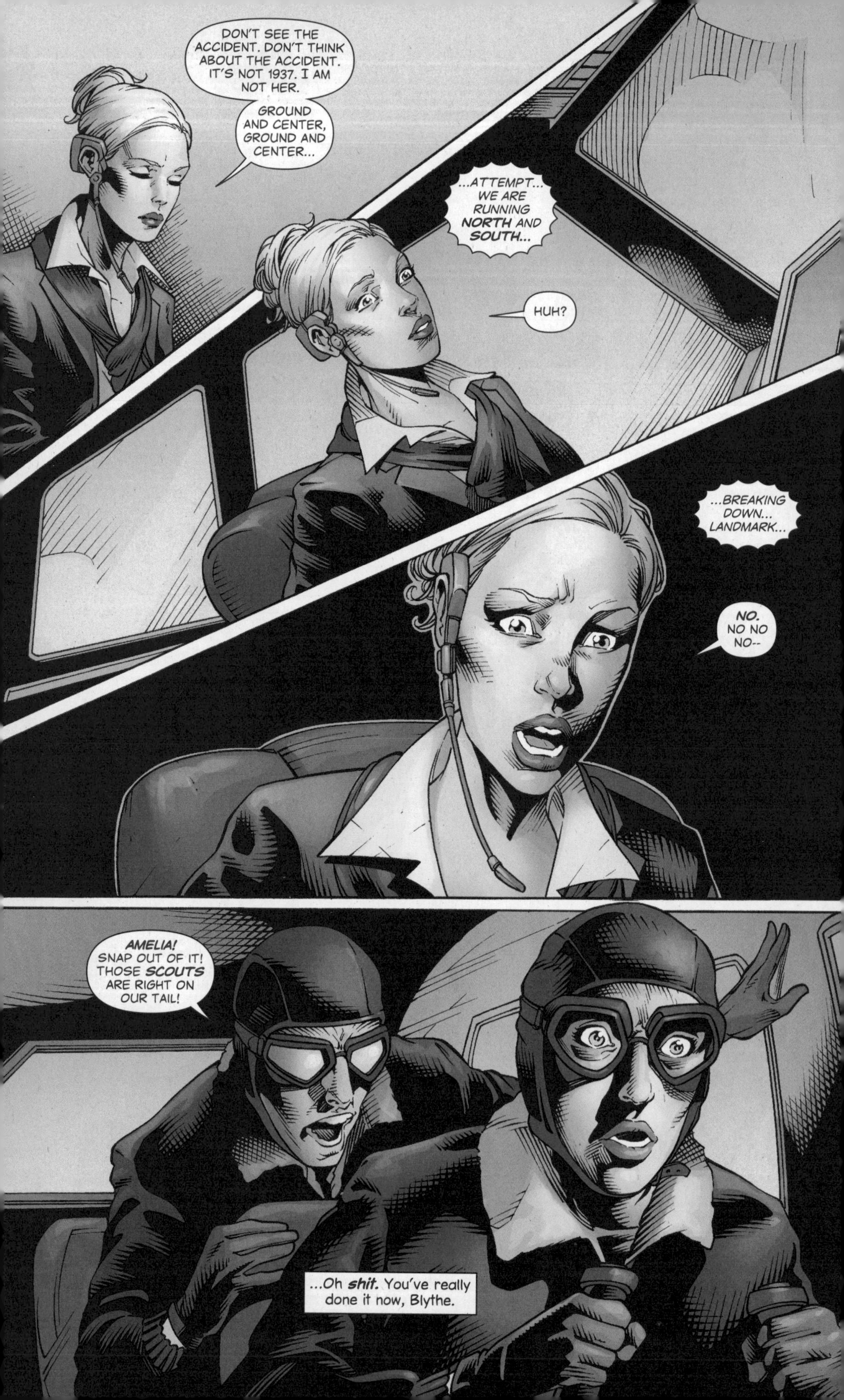
DON'T SEE THE ACCIDENT. DON'T THINK ABOUT THE ACCIDENT. IT'S NOT 1937. I AM NOT HER.
GROUND AND CENTER, GROUND AND CENTER...
...ATTEMPT... WE ARE RUNNING NORTH AND SOUTH...
HUH?
...BREAKING DOWN... LANDMARK...
NO. NO NO NO--
AMELIA! SNAP OUT OF IT! THOSE SCOUTS ARE RIGHT ON OUR TAIL!
...Oh shit. You've really done it now, Blythe.

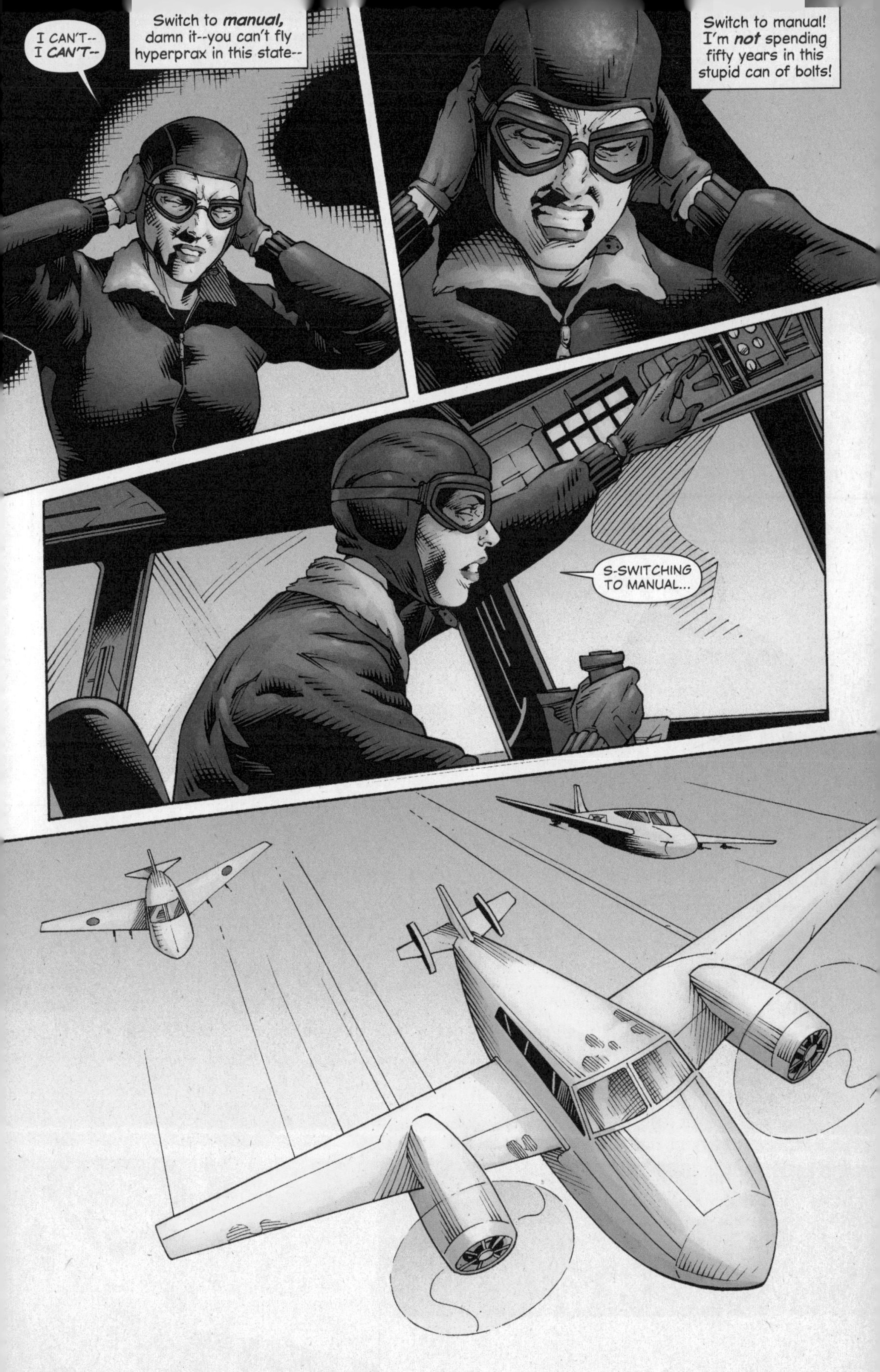
I CAN'T--
I CAN'T--
Switch to manual, damn it--you can't fly hyperprax in this state--
Switch to manual! I'm not spending fifty years in this stupid can of bolts!
S-SWITCHING TO MANUAL...

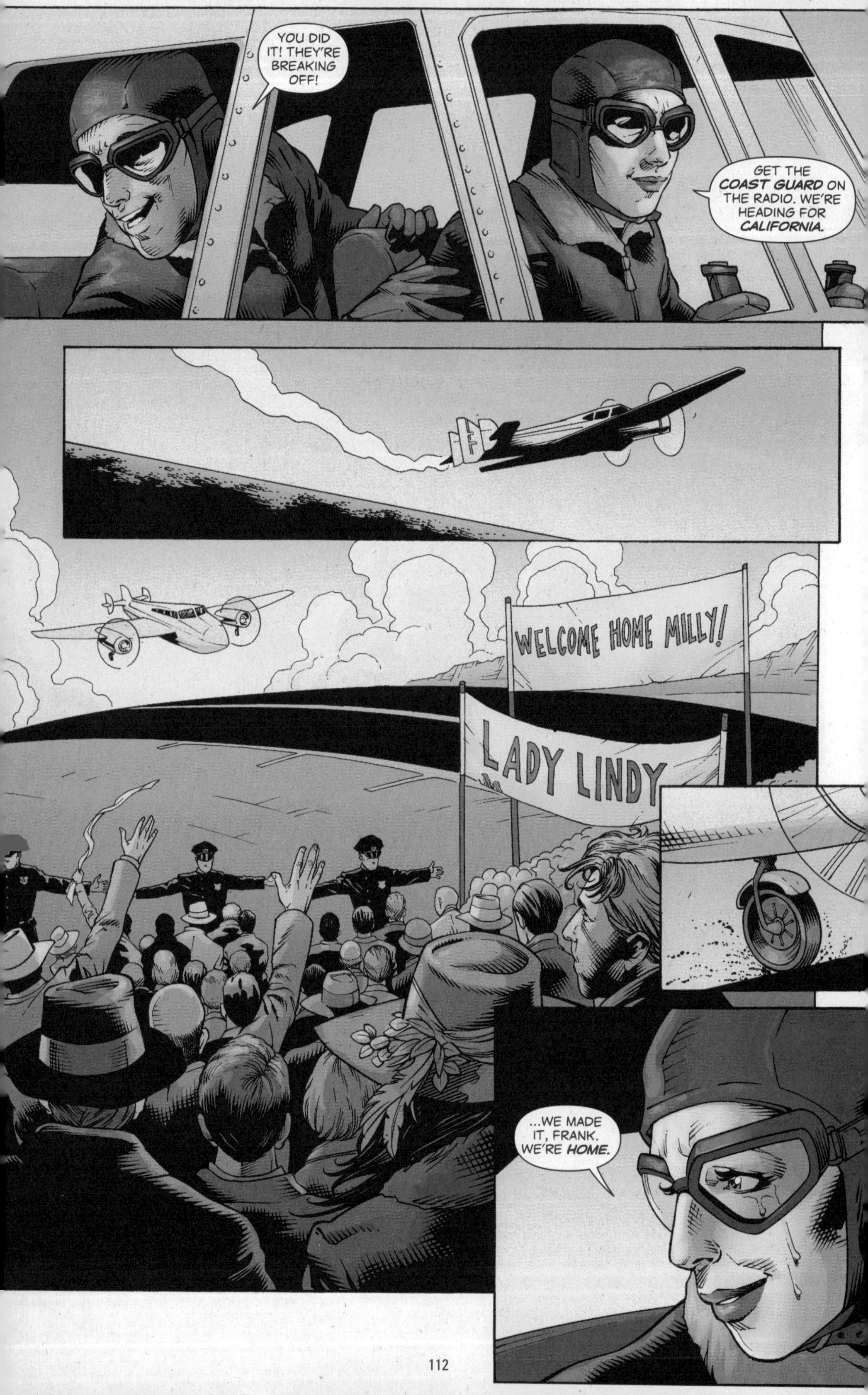
YOU DID IT! THEY'RE BREAKING OFF!
GET THE COAST GUARD ON THE RADIO. WE'RE HEADING FOR CALIFORNIA.
WELCOME HOME MILLY!
LADY LINDY
...WE MADE IT, FRANK. WE'RE HOME.

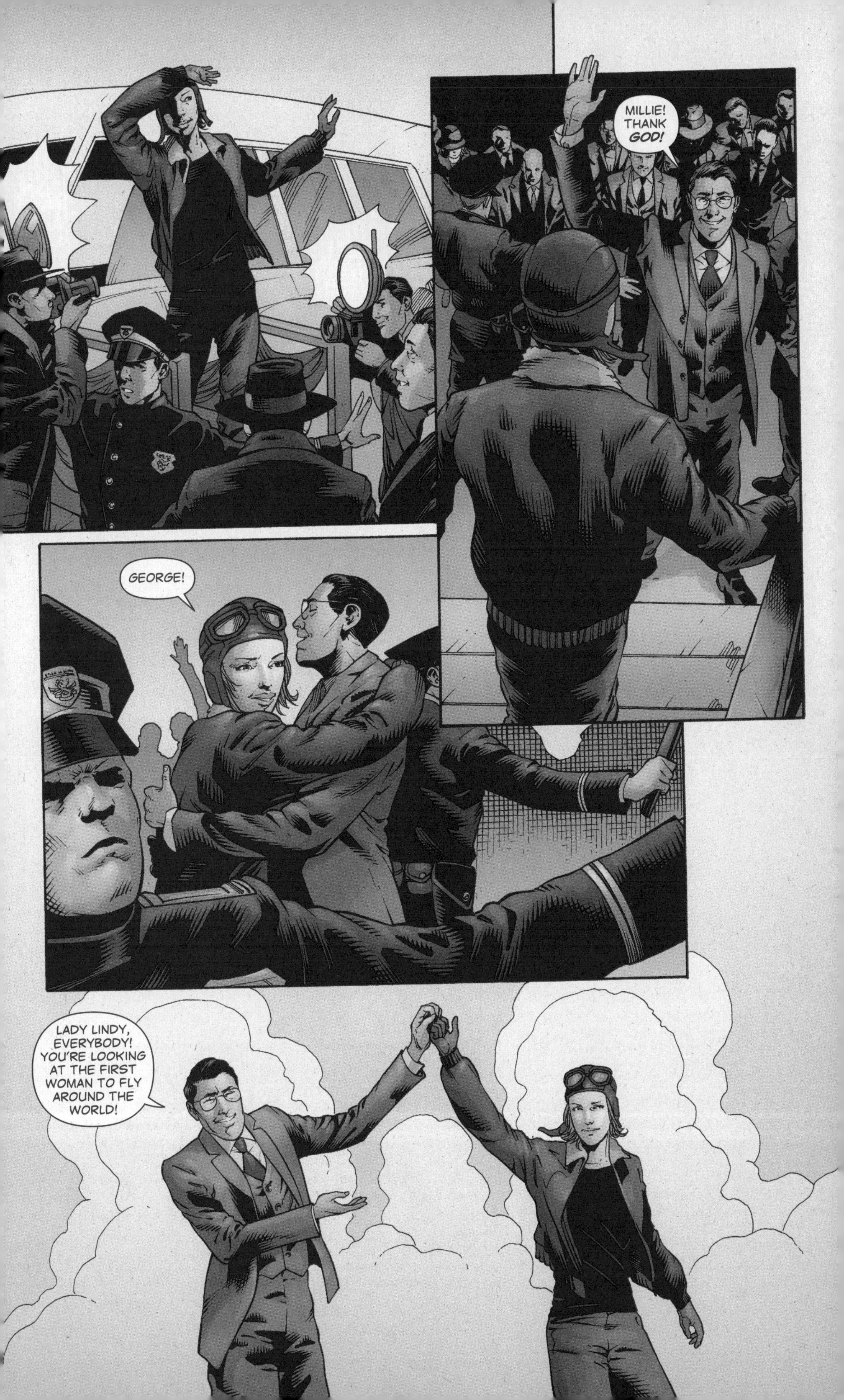
MILLIE! THANK GOD!
GEORGE!
LADY LINDY, EVERYBODY! YOU'RE LOOKING AT THE FIRST WOMAN TO FLY AROUND THE WORLD!

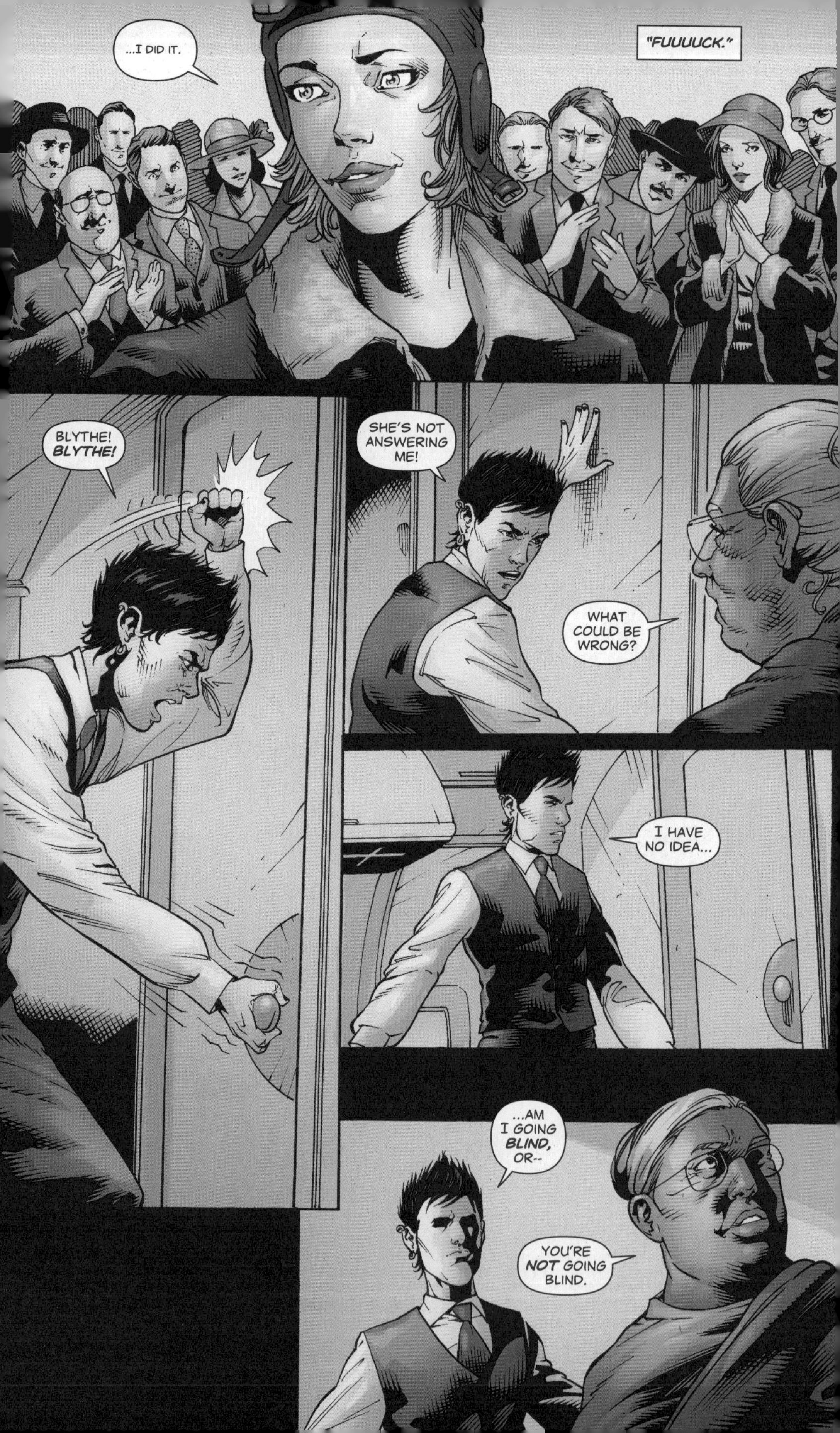

...I DID IT.
"FUUUUCK."
BLYTHE! BLYTHE!
SHE'S NOT ANSWERING ME!
WHAT COULD BE WRONG?
I HAVE NO IDEA...
...AM I GOING BLIND, OR--
YOU'RE NOT GOING BLIND.

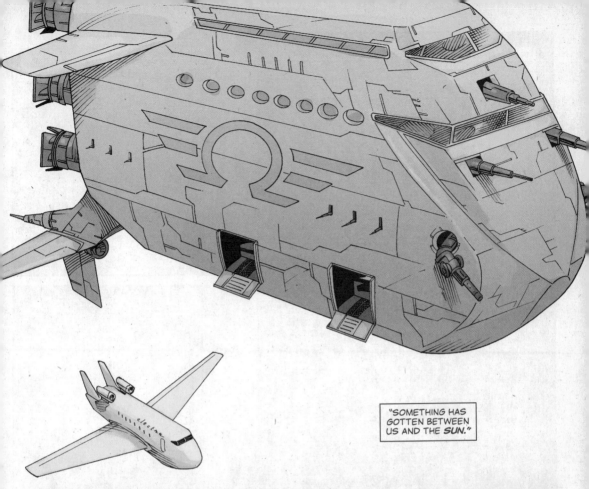

"SOMETHING HAS GOTTEN BETWEEN US AND THE *SUN.*"

COME *ON,* BLYTHE! WE'VE GOT *SERIOUS* TROUBLE OUT HERE!

STUPID *SAFETY* REGULATIONS! IN THE OLD DAYS YOU COULD JUST *BUST IN!*

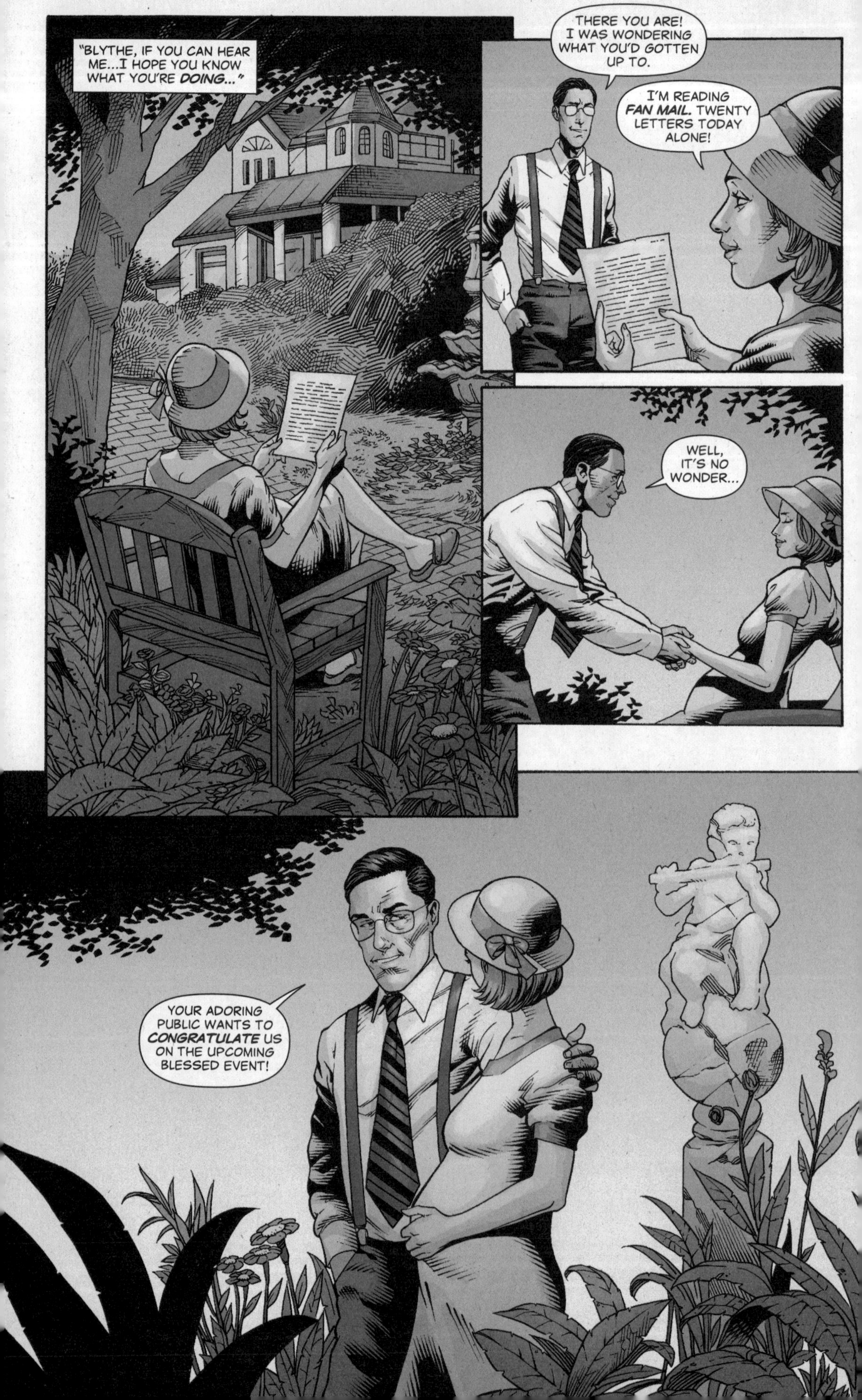
"BLYTHE, IF YOU CAN HEAR ME...I HOPE YOU KNOW WHAT YOU'RE DOING..."
THERE YOU ARE! I WAS WONDERING WHAT YOU'D GOTTEN UP TO.
I'M READING FAN MAIL. TWENTY LETTERS TODAY ALONE!
WELL, IT'S NO WONDER...
YOUR ADORING PUBLIC WANTS TO CONGRATULATE US ON THE UPCOMING BLESSED EVENT!

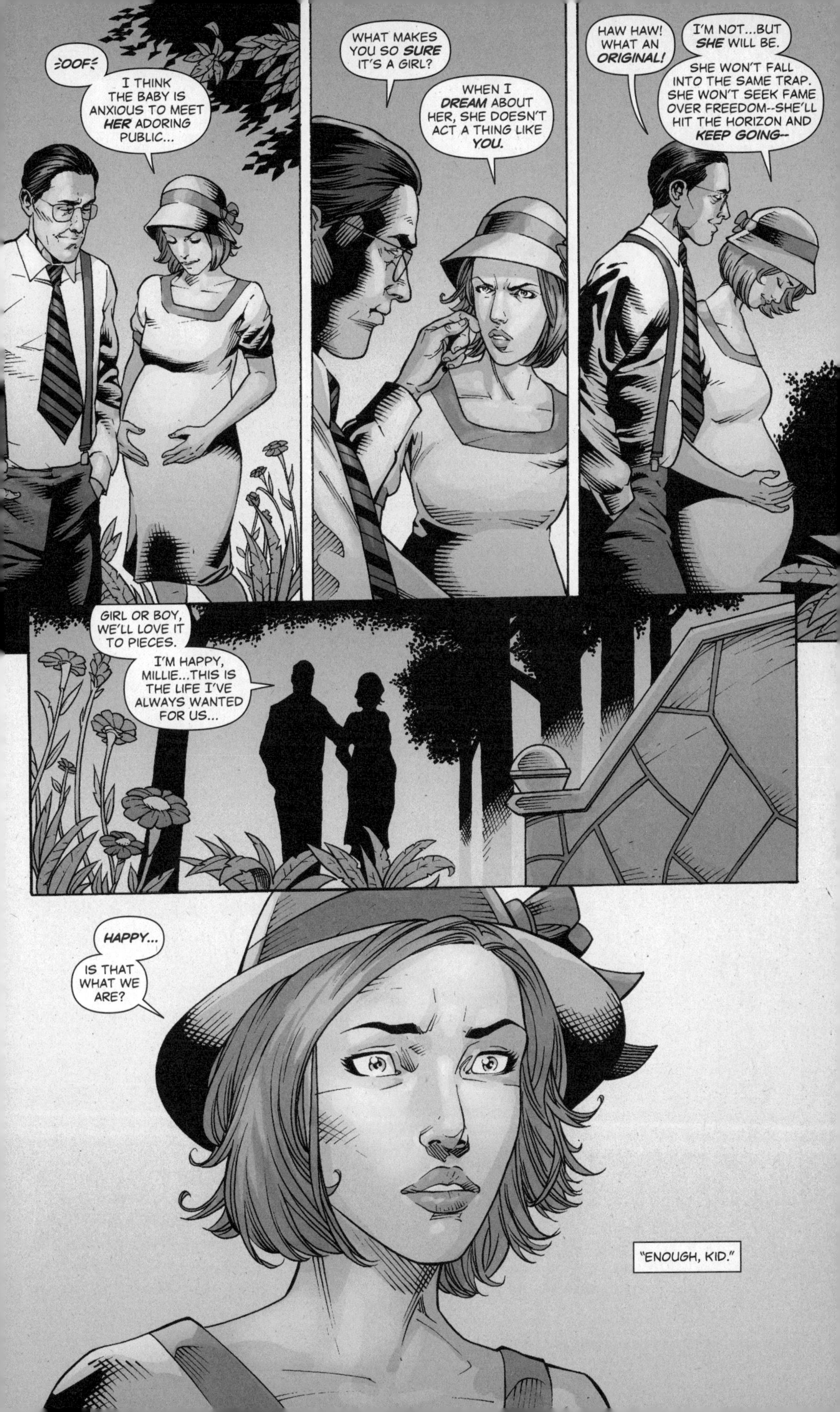
OOF
I THINK THE BABY IS ANXIOUS TO MEET HER ADORING PUBLIC...
WHAT MAKES YOU SO SURE IT'S A GIRL?
WHEN I DREAM ABOUT HER, SHE DOESN'T ACT A THING LIKE YOU.
HAW HAW! WHAT AN ORIGINAL!
I'M NOT...BUT SHE WILL BE.
SHE WON'T FALL INTO THE SAME TRAP. SHE WON'T SEEK FAME OVER FREEDOM--SHE'LL HIT THE HORIZON AND KEEP GOING--
GIRL OR BOY, WE'LL LOVE IT TO PIECES.
I'M HAPPY, MILLIE...THIS IS THE LIFE I'VE ALWAYS WANTED FOR US...
HAPPY...
IS THAT WHAT WE ARE?
"ENOUGH, KID."

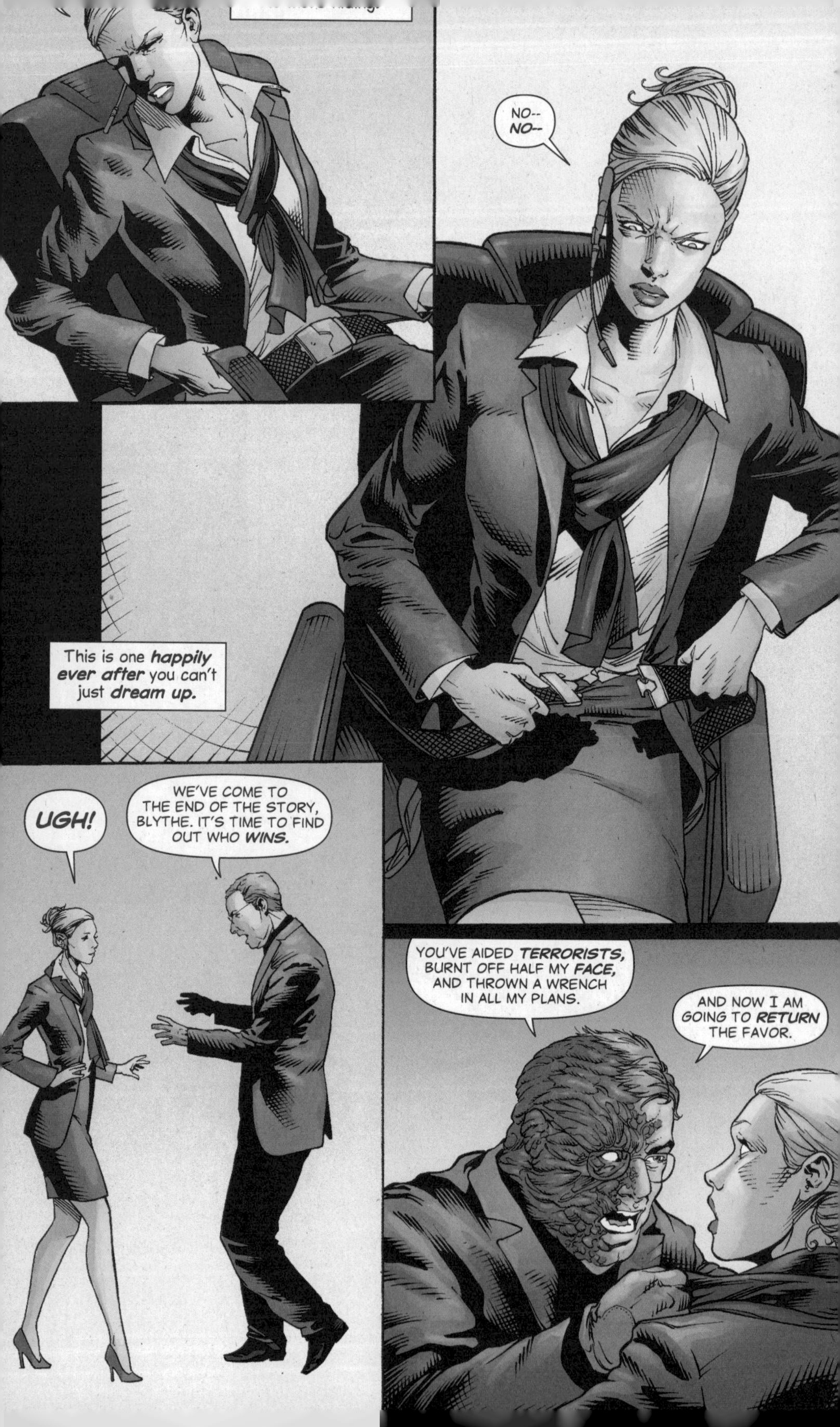
NO--
NO--
This is one happily ever after you can't just dream up.
UGH!
WE'VE COME TO THE END OF THE STORY, BLYTHE. IT'S TIME TO FIND OUT WHO WINS.
YOU'VE AIDED TERRORISTS, BURNT OFF HALF MY FACE, AND THROWN A WRENCH IN ALL MY PLANS.
AND NOW I AM GOING TO RETURN THE FAVOR.

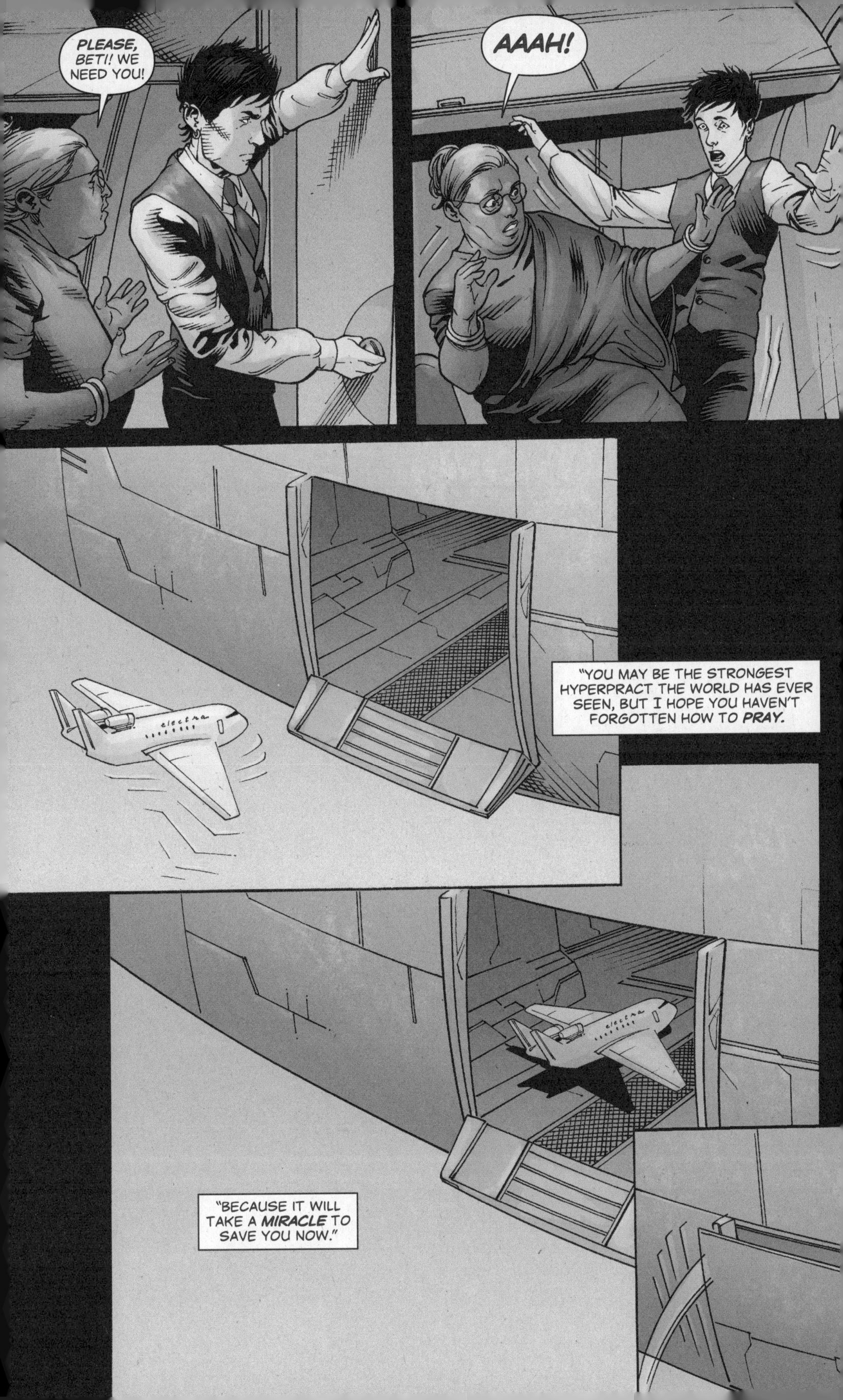
PLEASE, BETI! WE NEED YOU!
AAAH!
"YOU MAY BE THE STRONGEST HYPERPRACT THE WORLD HAS EVER SEEN, BUT I HOPE YOU HAVEN'T FORGOTTEN HOW TO PRAY.
"BECAUSE IT WILL TAKE A MIRACLE TO SAVE YOU NOW."

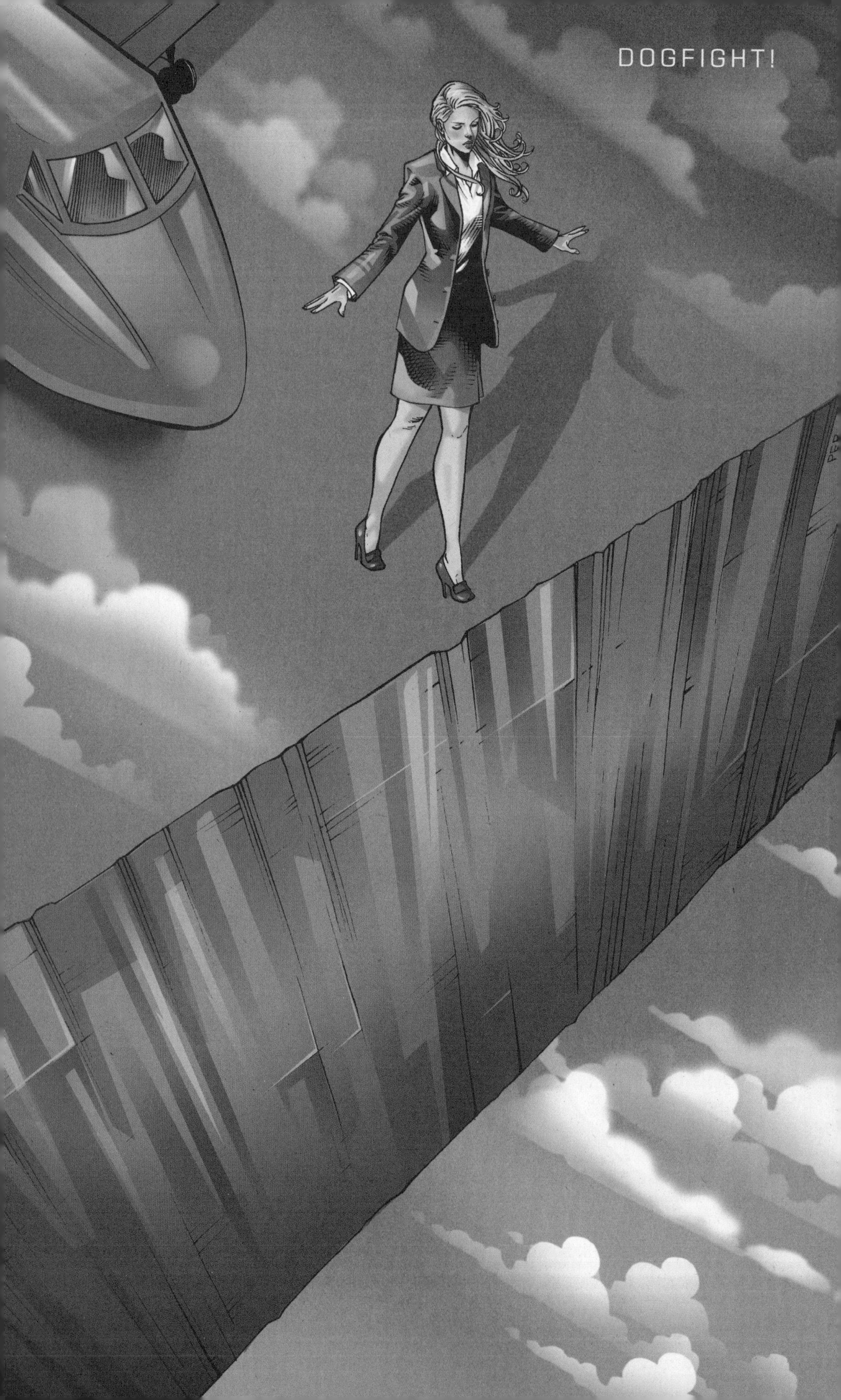

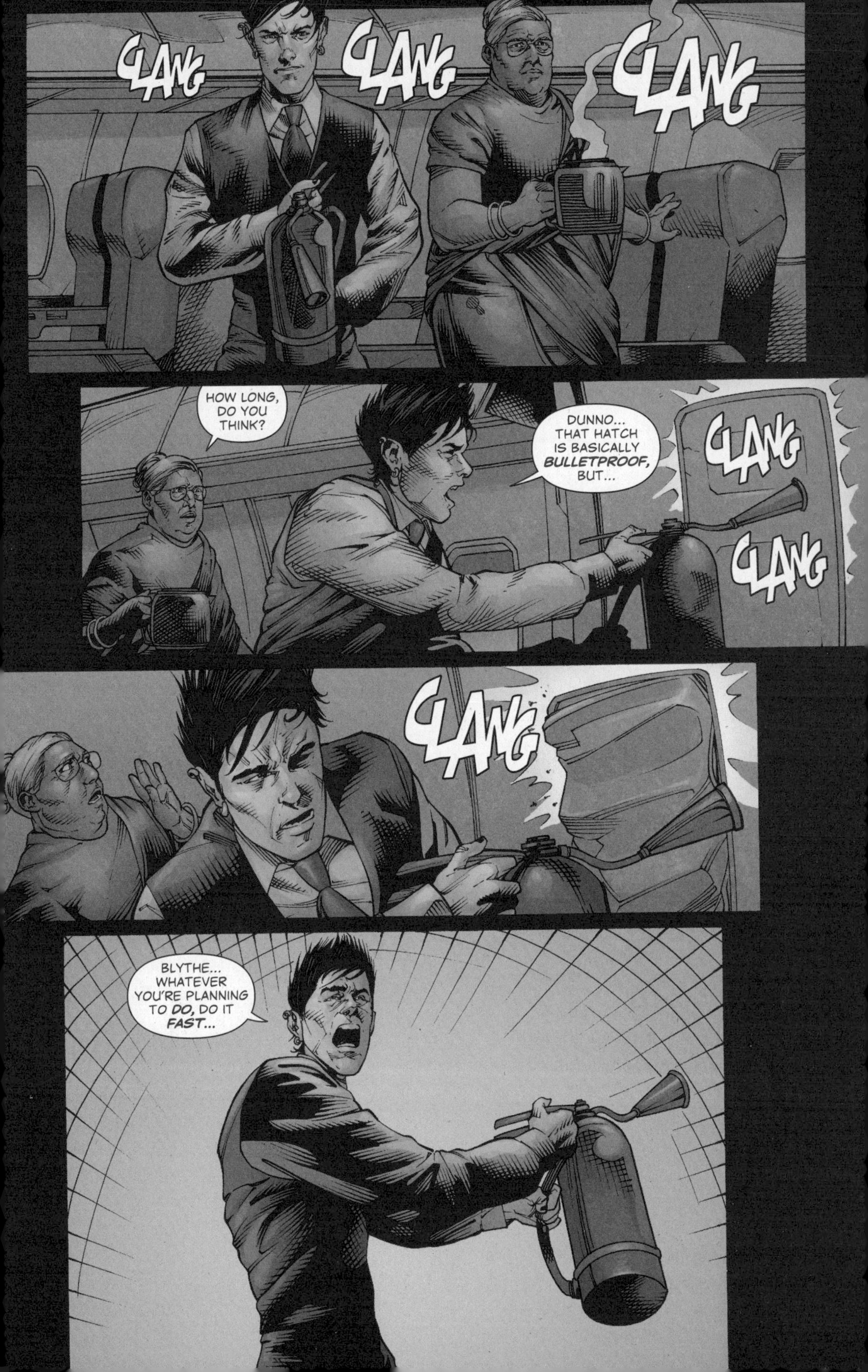
CLANG
CLANG
CLANG
HOW LONG, DO YOU THINK?
DUNNO... THAT HATCH IS BASICALLY BULLETPROOF, BUT...
CLANG
CLANG
CLANG
BLYTHE... WHATEVER YOU'RE PLANNING TO DO, DO IT FAST...

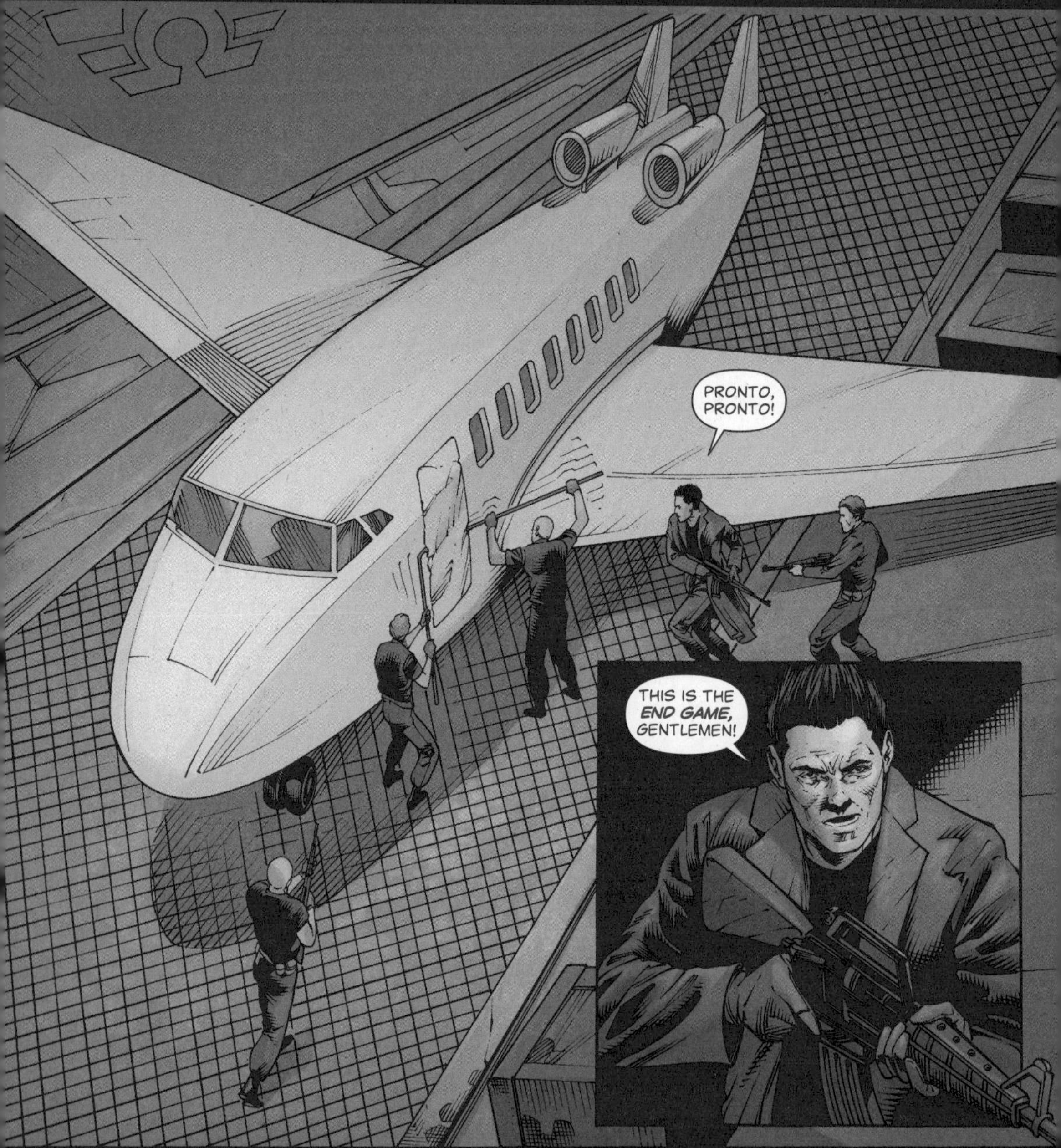
PRONTO, PRONTO!
THIS IS THE END GAME, GENTLEMEN!

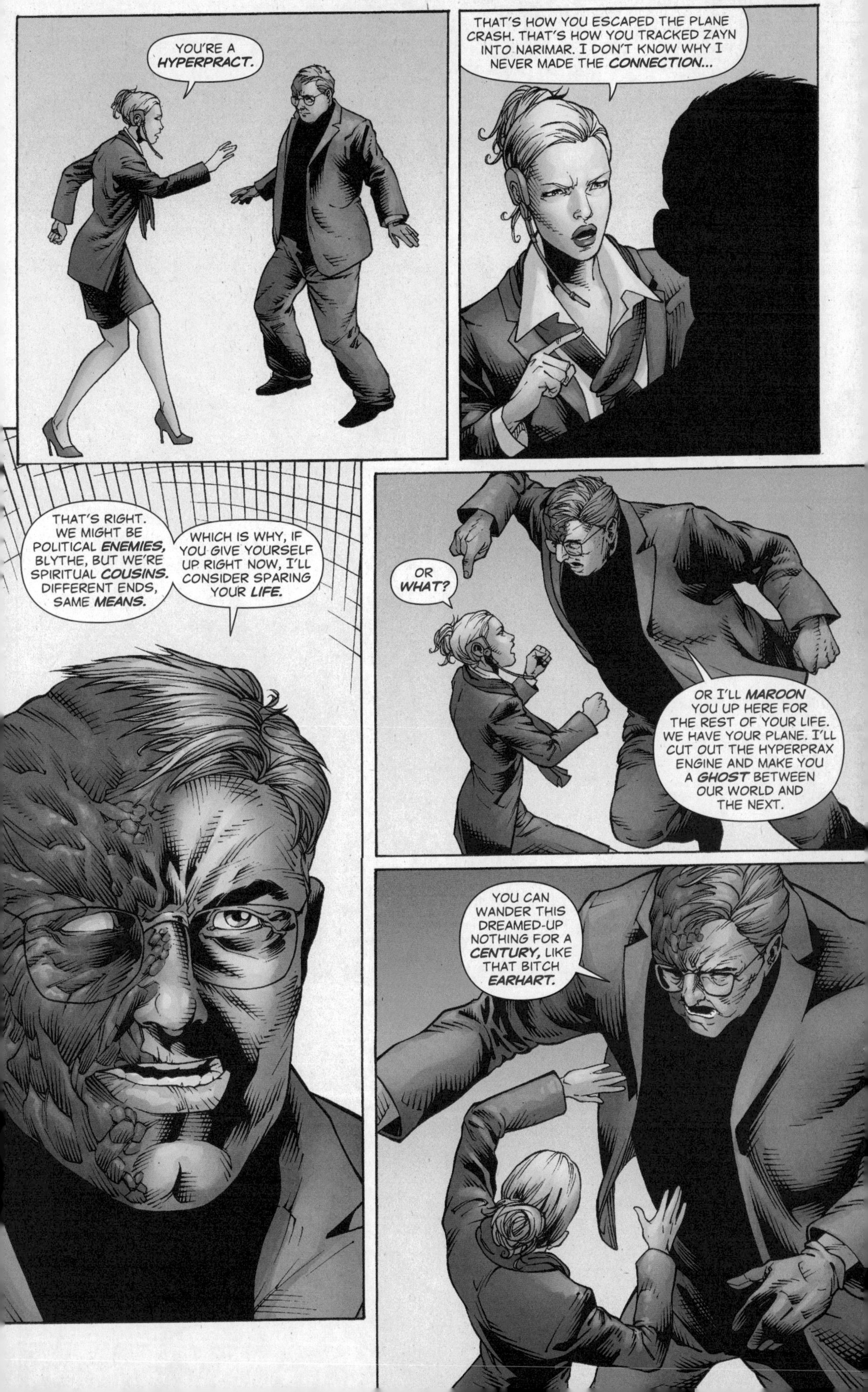
YOU'RE A HYPERPRACT.
THAT'S HOW YOU ESCAPED THE PLANE CRASH. THAT'S HOW YOU TRACKED ZAYN INTO NARIMAR. I DON'T KNOW WHY I NEVER MADE THE CONNECTION...
THAT'S RIGHT. WE MIGHT BE POLITICAL ENEMIES, BLYTHE, BUT WE'RE SPIRITUAL COUSINS. DIFFERENT ENDS, SAME MEANS.
WHICH IS WHY, IF YOU GIVE YOURSELF UP RIGHT NOW, I'LL CONSIDER SPARING YOUR LIFE.
OR WHAT?
OR I'LL MAROON YOU UP HERE FOR THE REST OF YOUR LIFE. WE HAVE YOUR PLANE. I'LL CUT OUT THE HYPERPRAX ENGINE AND MAKE YOU A GHOST BETWEEN OUR WORLD AND THE NEXT.
YOU CAN WANDER THIS DREAMED-UP NOTHING FOR A CENTURY, LIKE THAT BITCH EARHART.

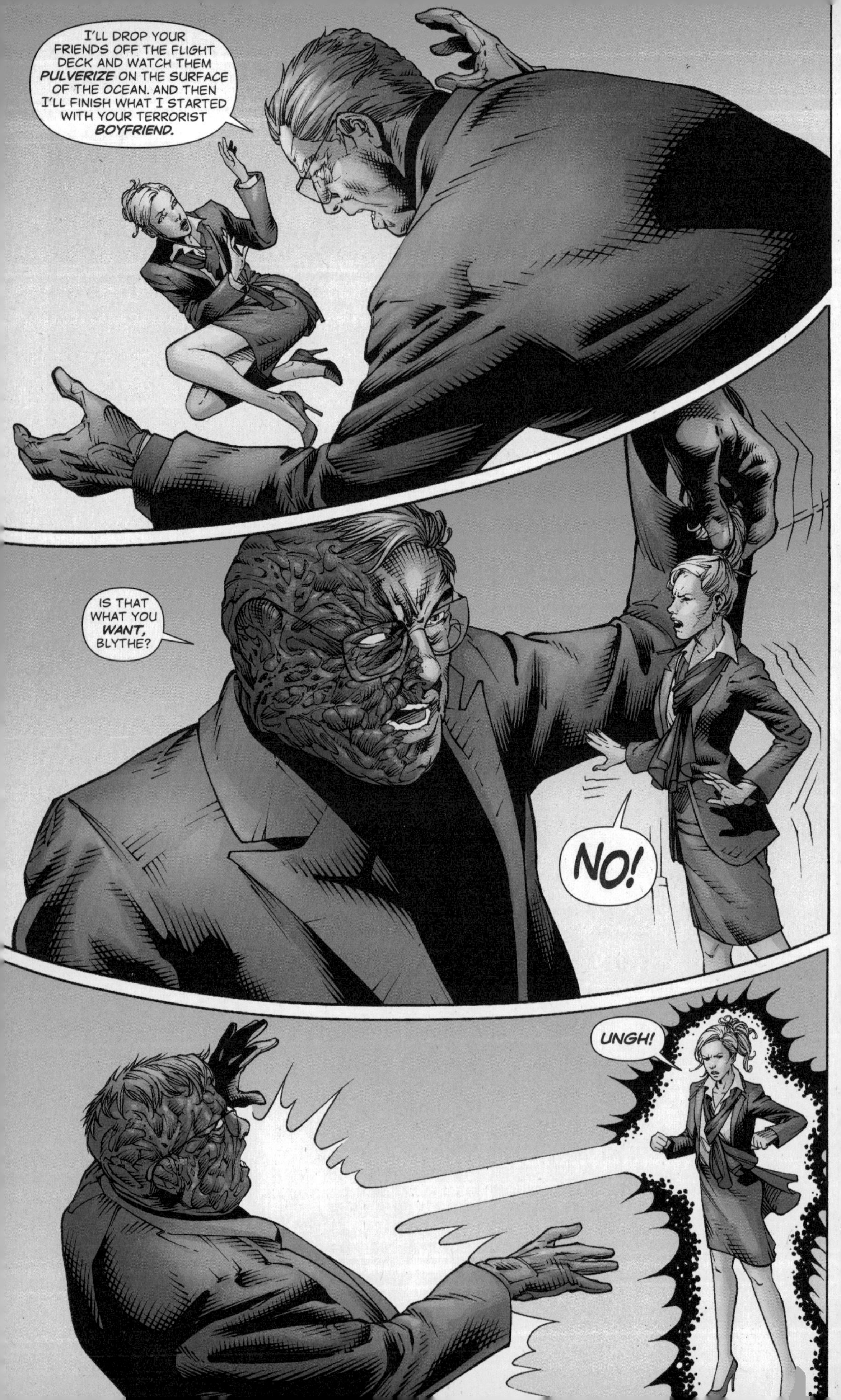
I'LL DROP YOUR FRIENDS OFF THE FLIGHT DECK AND WATCH THEM PULVERIZE ON THE SURFACE OF THE OCEAN. AND THEN I'LL FINISH WHAT I STARTED WITH YOUR TERRORIST BOYFRIEND.
IS THAT WHAT YOU WANT, BLYTHE?
NO!
UNGH!

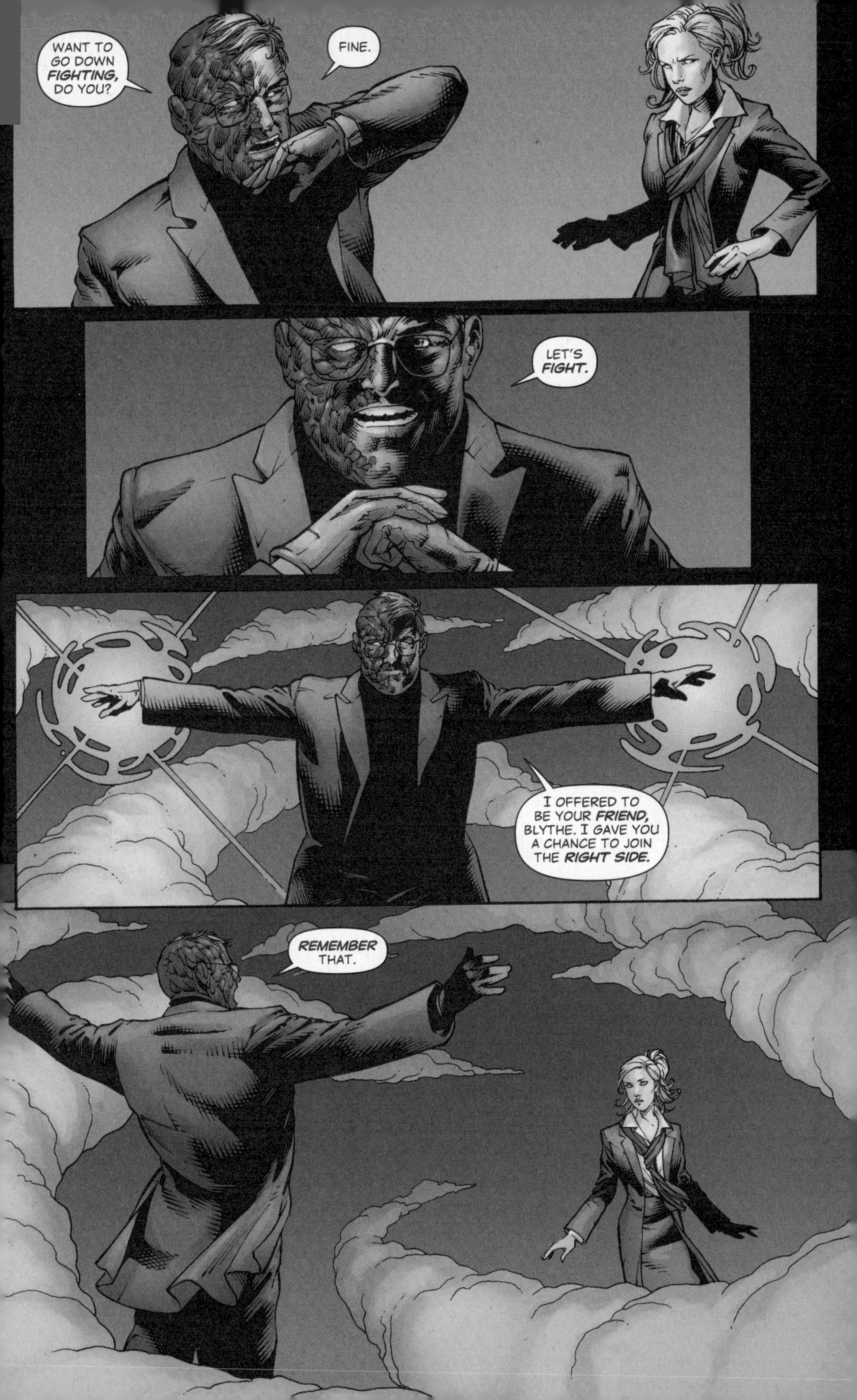
WANT TO GO DOWN FIGHTING, DO YOU?
FINE.
LET'S FIGHT.
I OFFERED TO BE YOUR FRIEND, BLYTHE. I GAVE YOU A CHANCE TO JOIN THE RIGHT SIDE.
REMEMBER THAT.

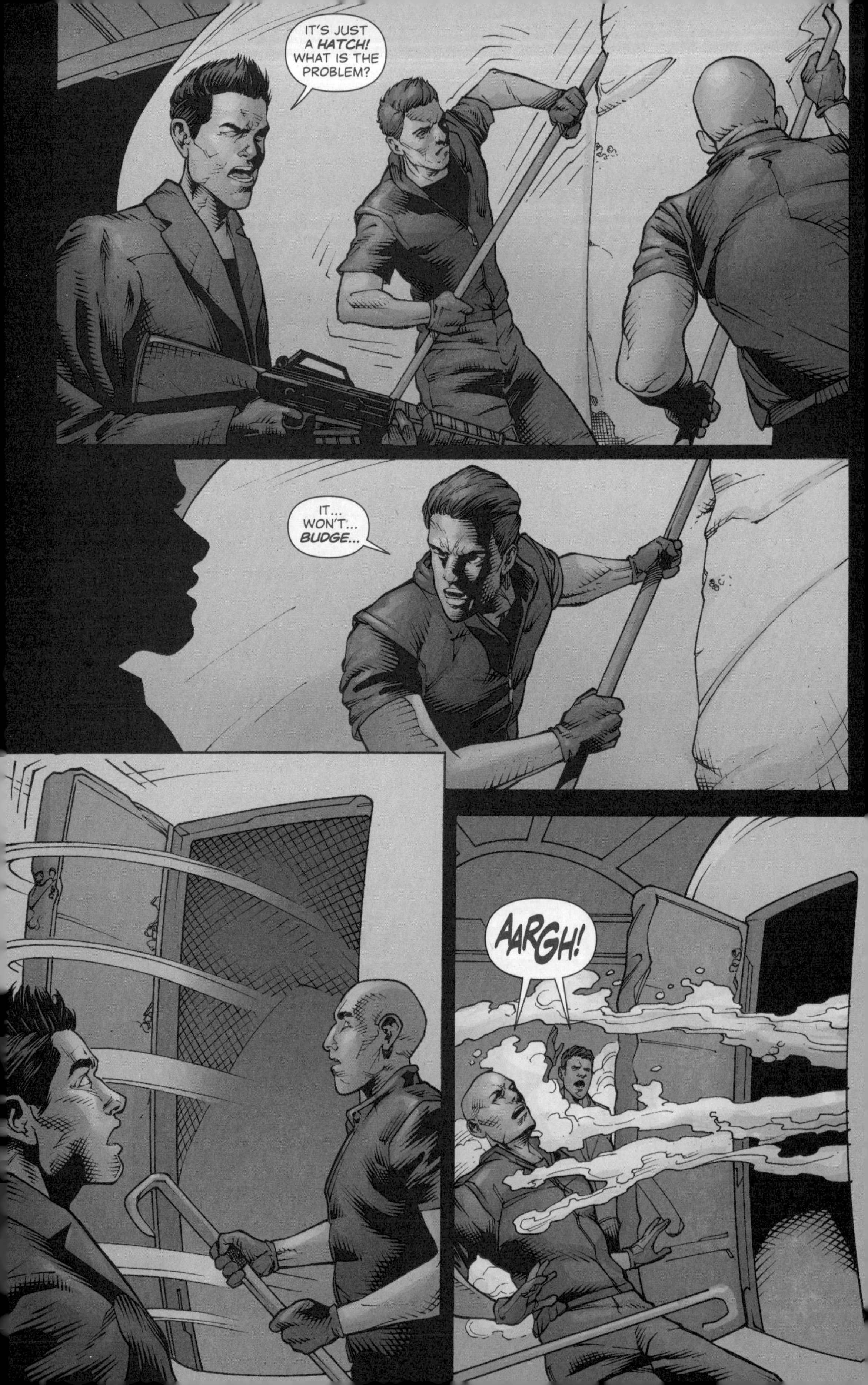
IT'S JUST A HATCH! WHAT IS THE PROBLEM?
IT... WON'T... BUDGE...
AARGH!

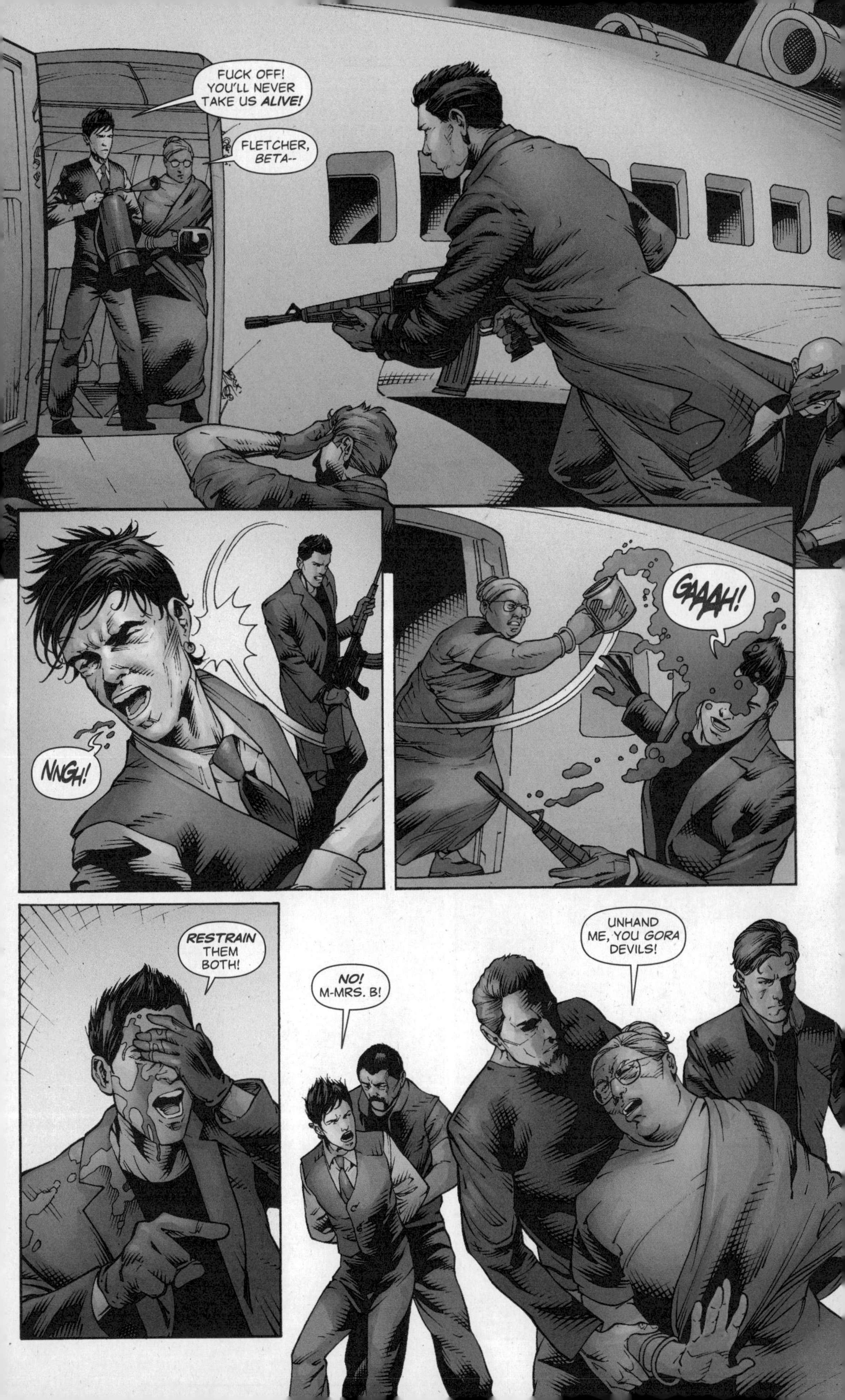
FUCK OFF! YOU'LL NEVER TAKE US ALIVE!
FLETCHER, BETA--
NNGH!
GAAAH!
RESTRAIN THEM BOTH!
NO! M-MRS. B!
UNHAND ME, YOU GORA DEVILS!

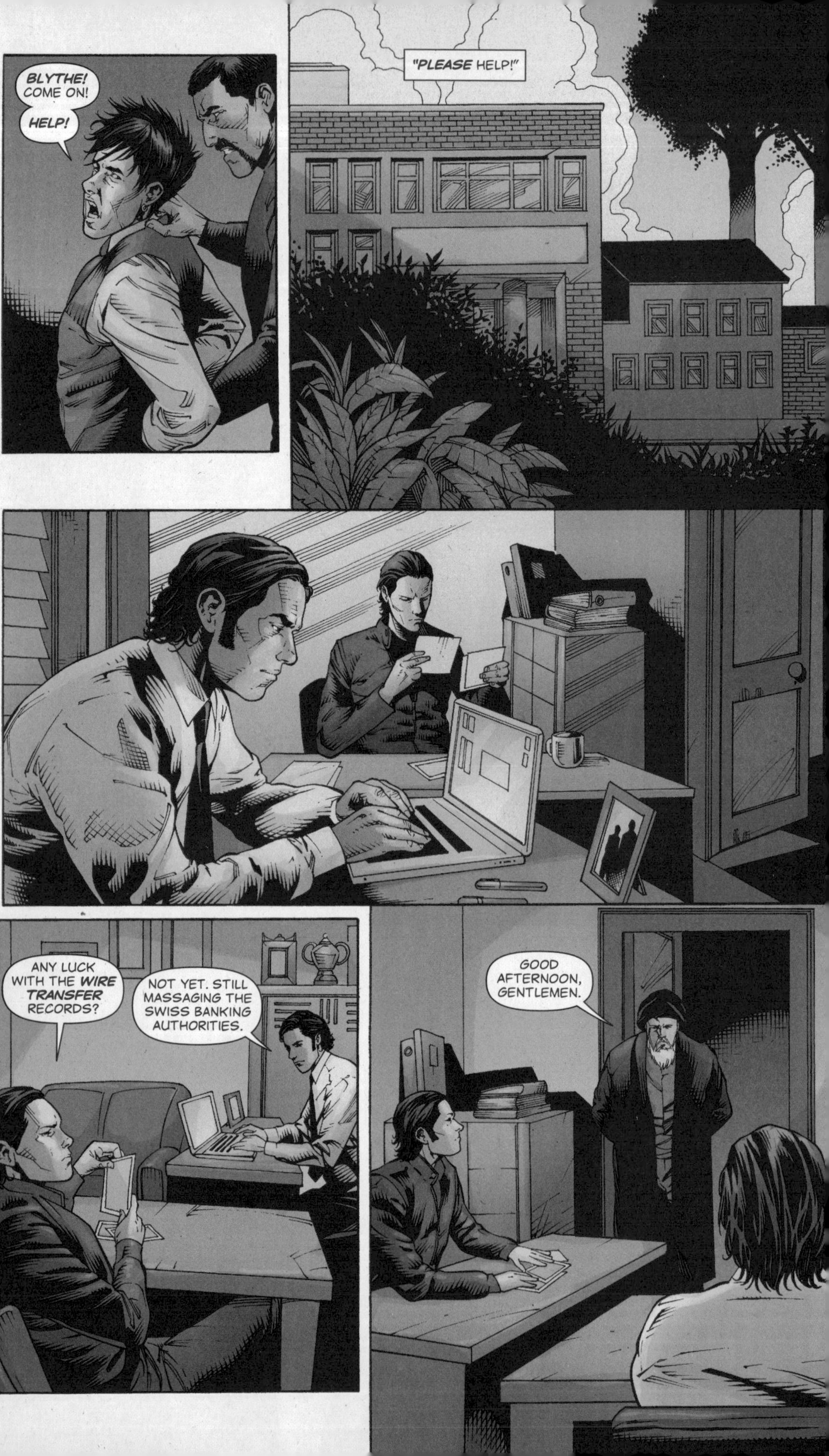
BLYTHE! COME ON!
HELP!
"PLEASE HELP!"
ANY LUCK WITH THE WIRE TRANSFER RECORDS?
NOT YET. STILL MASSAGING THE SWISS BANKING AUTHORITIES.
GOOD AFTERNOON, GENTLEMEN.

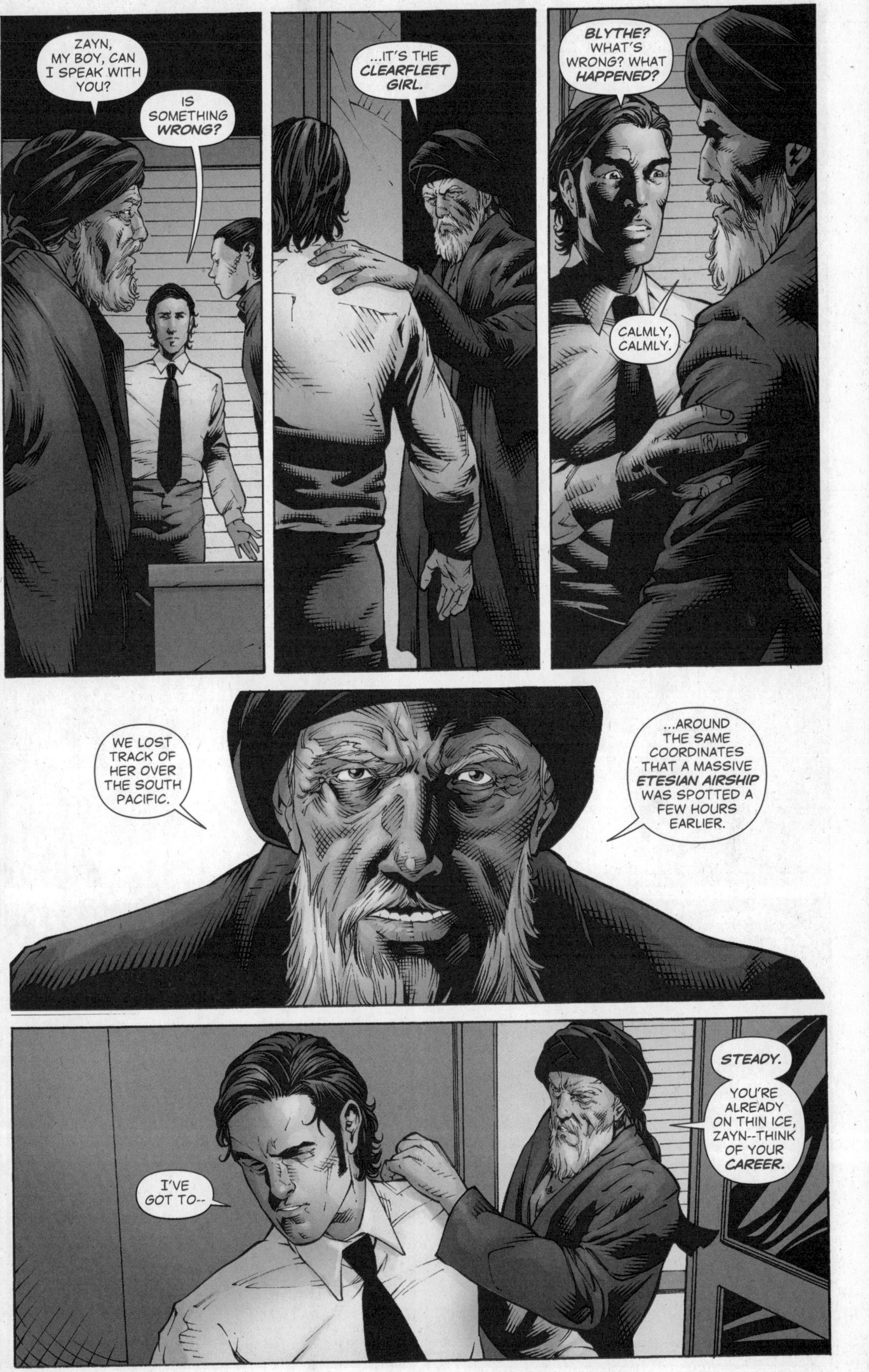
ZAYN, MY BOY, CAN I SPEAK WITH YOU?
IS SOMETHING WRONG?
...IT'S THE CLEARFLEET GIRL.
BLYTHE? WHAT'S WRONG? WHAT HAPPENED?
CALMLY, CALMLY.
WE LOST TRACK OF HER OVER THE SOUTH PACIFIC.
...AROUND THE SAME COORDINATES THAT A MASSIVE ETESIAN AIRSHIP WAS SPOTTED A FEW HOURS EARLIER.
I'VE GOT TO--
STEADY.
YOU'RE ALREADY ON THIN ICE, ZAYN--THINK OF YOUR CAREER.

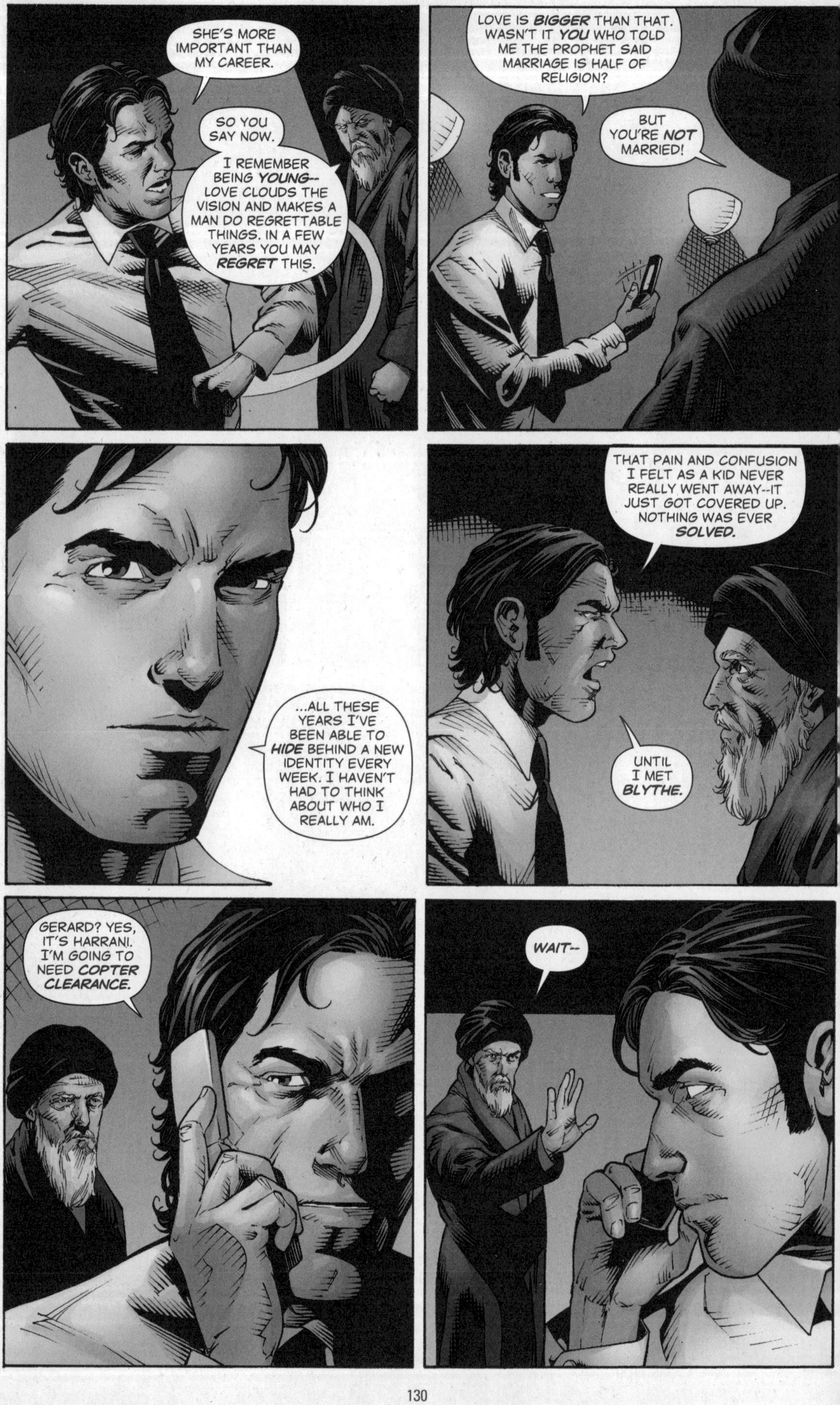
SHE'S MORE IMPORTANT THAN MY CAREER.
SO YOU SAY NOW.
I REMEMBER BEING YOUNG-- LOVE CLOUDS THE VISION AND MAKES A MAN DO REGRETTABLE THINGS. IN A FEW YEARS YOU MAY REGRET THIS.
LOVE IS BIGGER THAN THAT. WASN'T IT YOU WHO TOLD ME THE PROPHET SAID MARRIAGE IS HALF OF RELIGION?
BUT YOU'RE NOT MARRIED!
...ALL THESE YEARS I'VE BEEN ABLE TO HIDE BEHIND A NEW IDENTITY EVERY WEEK. I HAVEN'T HAD TO THINK ABOUT WHO I REALLY AM.
THAT PAIN AND CONFUSION I FELT AS A KID NEVER REALLY WENT AWAY--IT JUST GOT COVERED UP. NOTHING WAS EVER SOLVED.
UNTIL I MET BLYTHE.
GERARD? YES, IT'S HARRANI. I'M GOING TO NEED COPTER CLEARANCE.
WAIT--

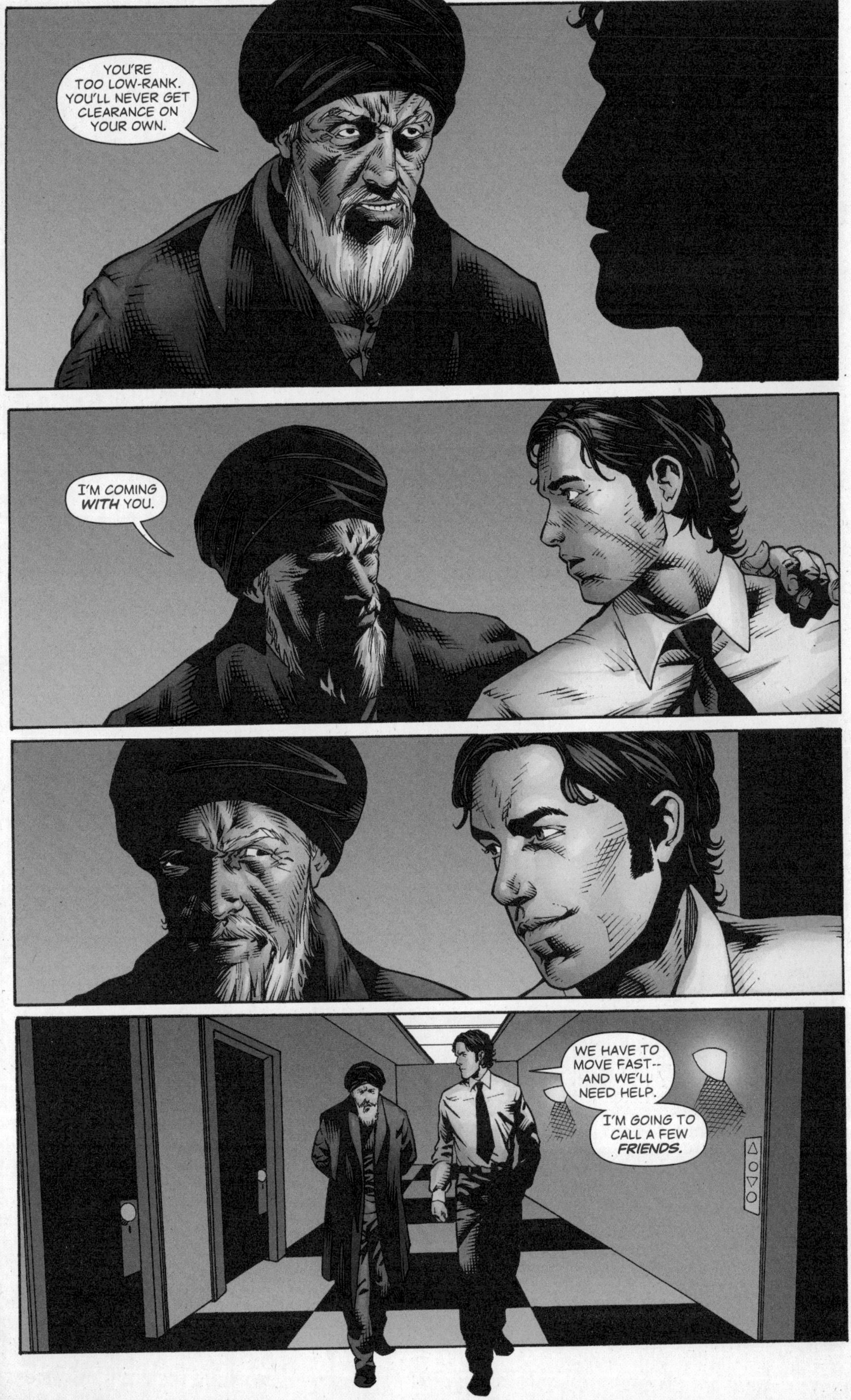
YOU'RE TOO LOW-RANK. YOU'LL NEVER GET CLEARANCE ON YOUR OWN.
I'M COMING WITH YOU.
WE HAVE TO MOVE FAST-- AND WE'LL NEED HELP.
I'M GOING TO CALL A FEW FRIENDS.

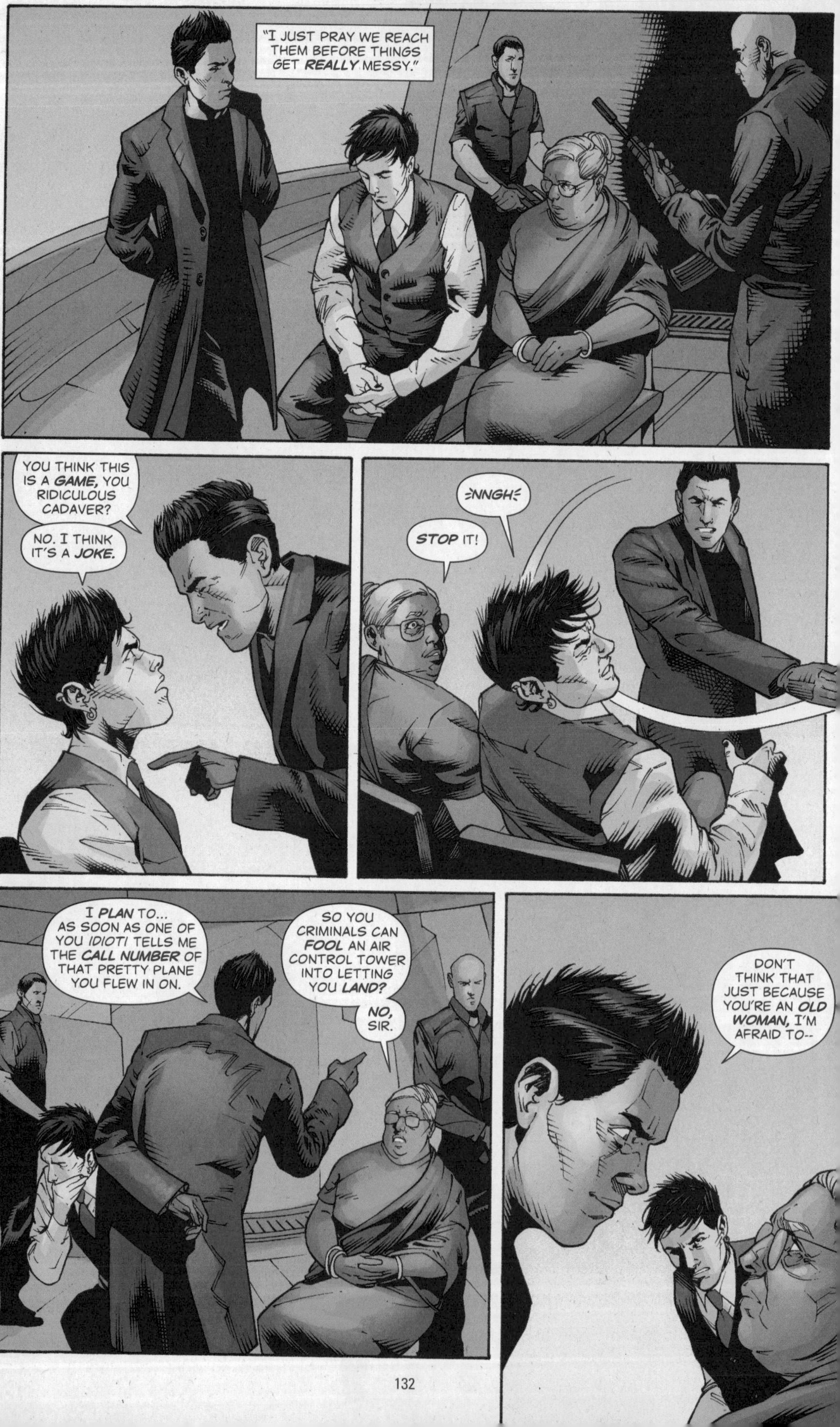
"I JUST PRAY WE REACH THEM BEFORE THINGS GET REALLY MESSY."
YOU THINK THIS IS A GAME, YOU RIDICULOUS CADAVER?
NO. I THINK IT'S A JOKE.
STOP IT!
NNGH
I PLAN TO... AS SOON AS ONE OF YOU IDIOTI TELLS ME THE CALL NUMBER OF THAT PRETTY PLANE YOU FLEW IN ON.
SO YOU CRIMINALS CAN FOOL AN AIR CONTROL TOWER INTO LETTING YOU LAND?
NO, SIR.
DON'T THINK THAT JUST BECAUSE YOU'RE AN OLD WOMAN, I'M AFRAID TO--

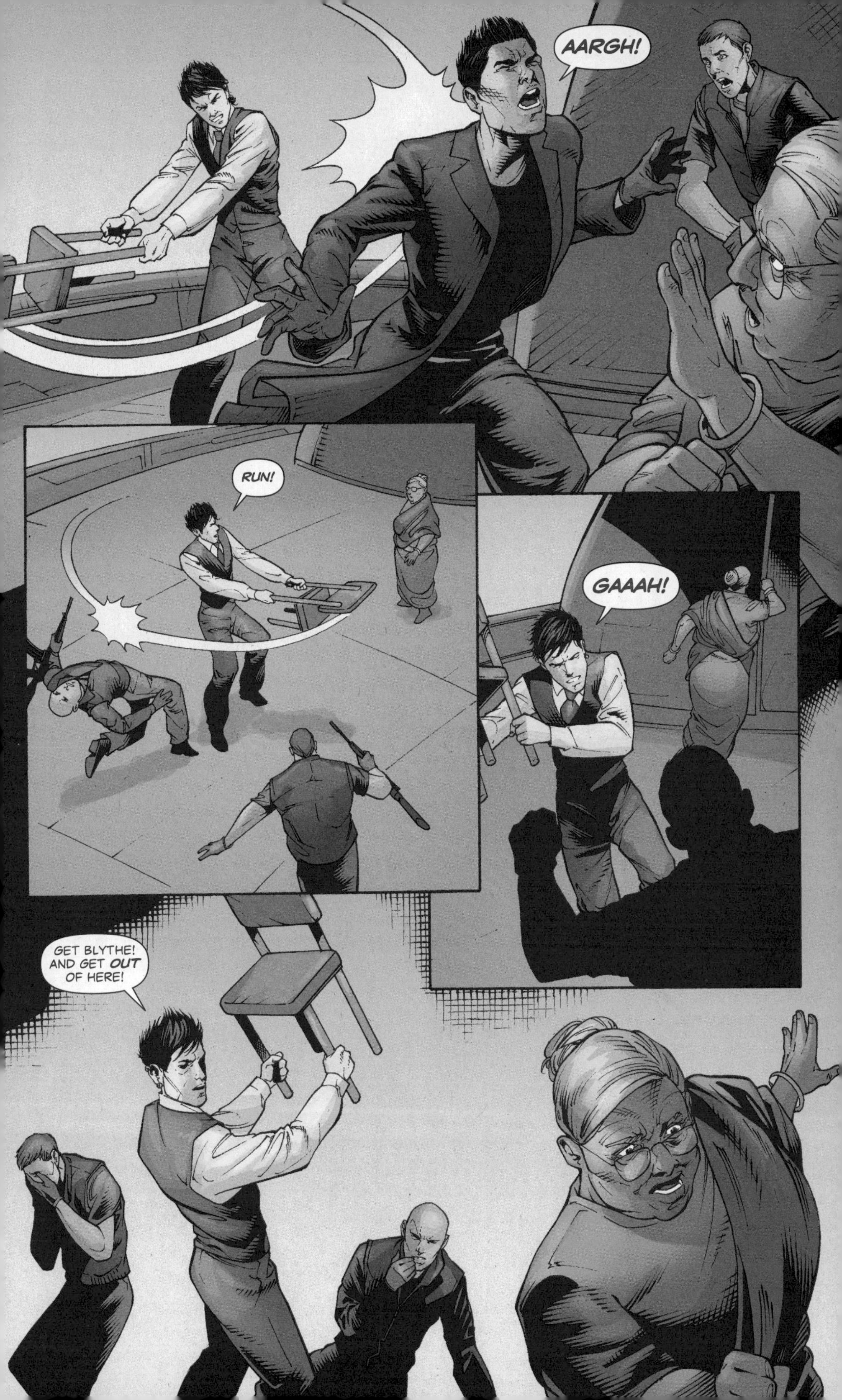
AARGH!
RUN!
GAAAH!
GET BLYTHE! AND GET OUT OF HERE!

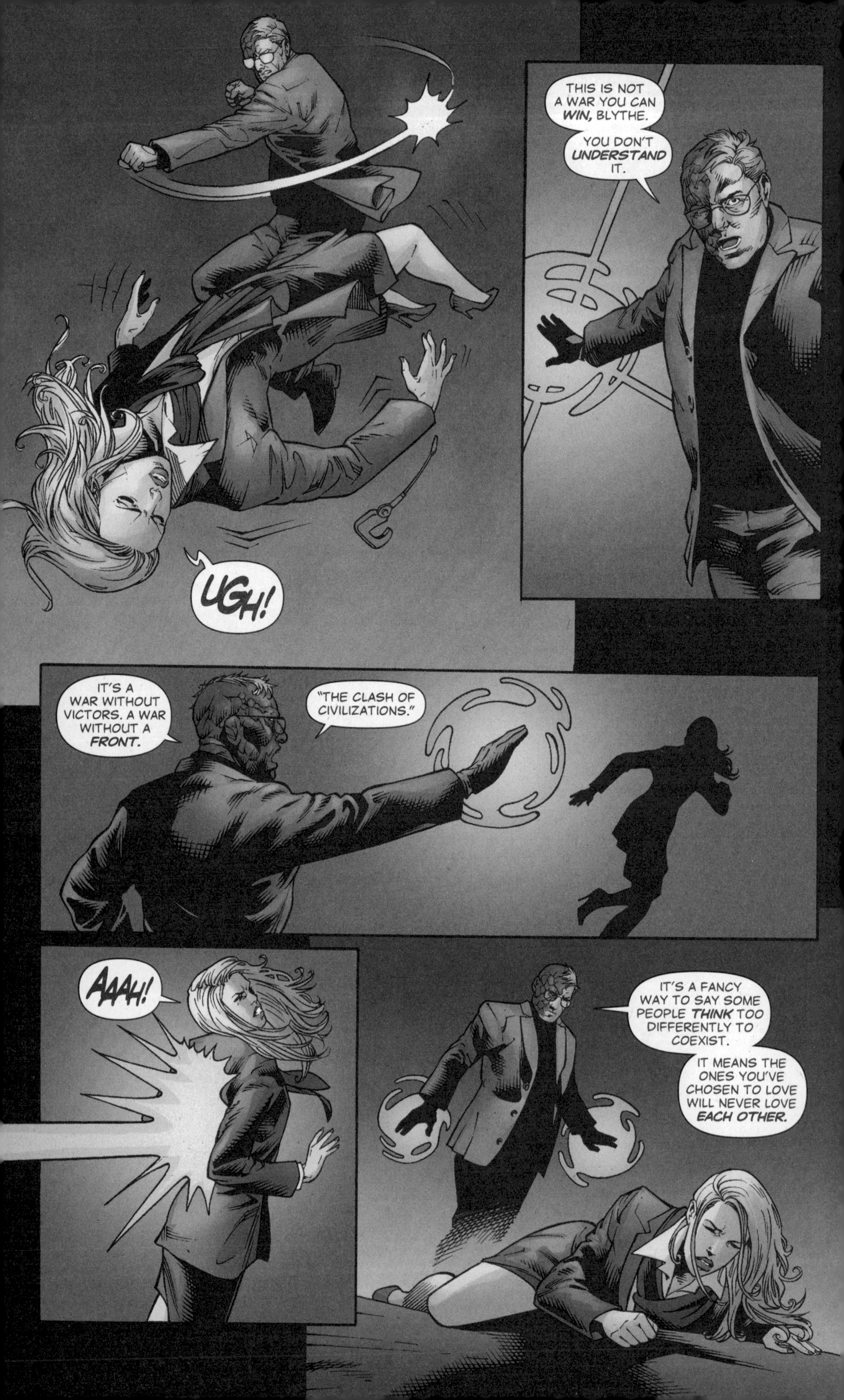
UGH!
THIS IS NOT A WAR YOU CAN WIN, BLYTHE.
YOU DON'T UNDERSTAND IT.
IT'S A WAR WITHOUT VICTORS. A WAR WITHOUT A FRONT.
"THE CLASH OF CIVILIZATIONS."
AAAH!
IT'S A FANCY WAY TO SAY SOME PEOPLE THINK TOO DIFFERENTLY TO COEXIST.
IT MEANS THE ONES YOU'VE CHOSEN TO LOVE WILL NEVER LOVE EACH OTHER.

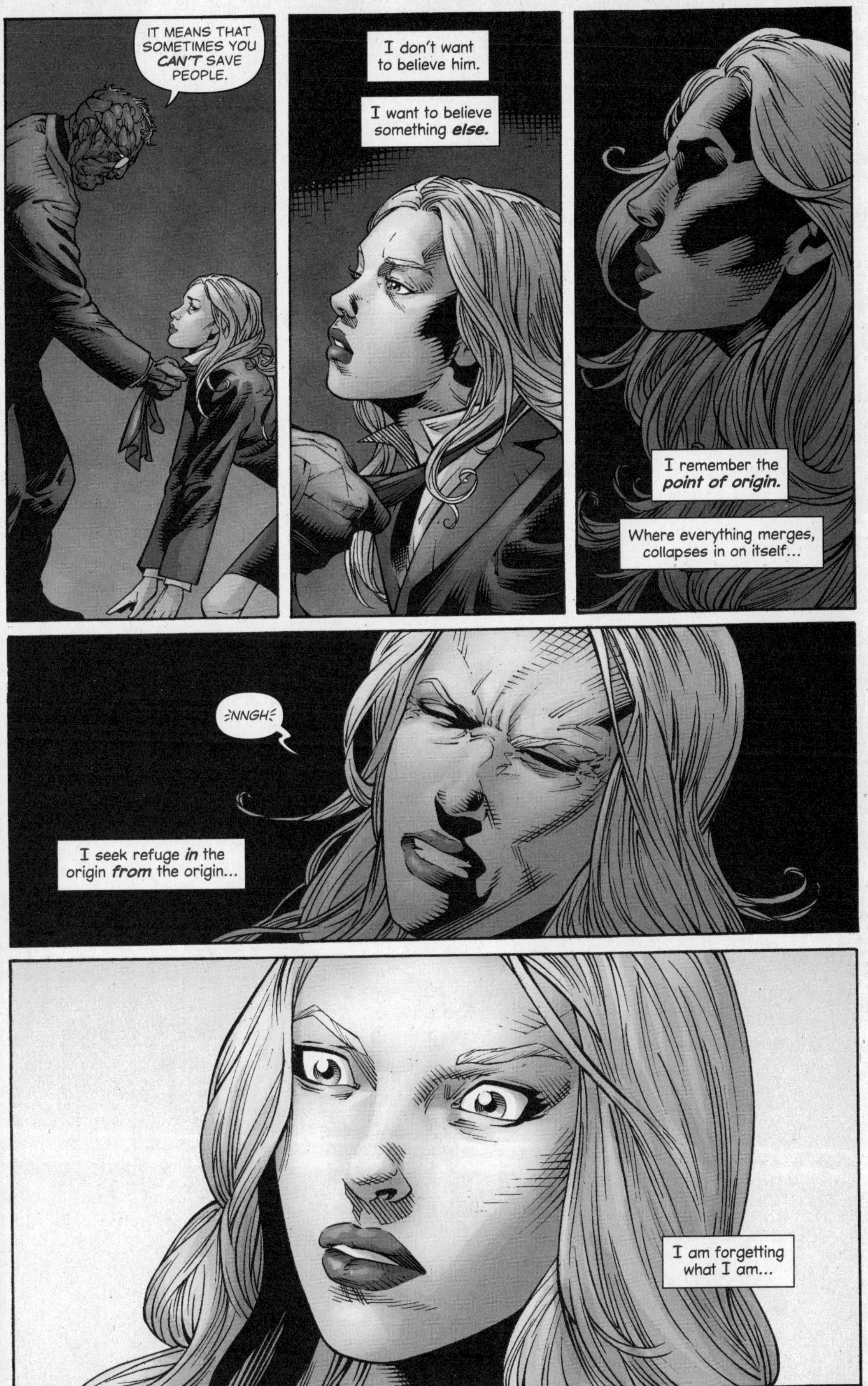
IT MEANS THAT SOMETIMES YOU CAN'T SAVE PEOPLE.
I don't want to believe him.
I want to believe something else.
I remember the point of origin.
Where everything merges, collapses in on itself...
NNGH
I seek refuge in the origin from the origin...
I am forgetting what I am...

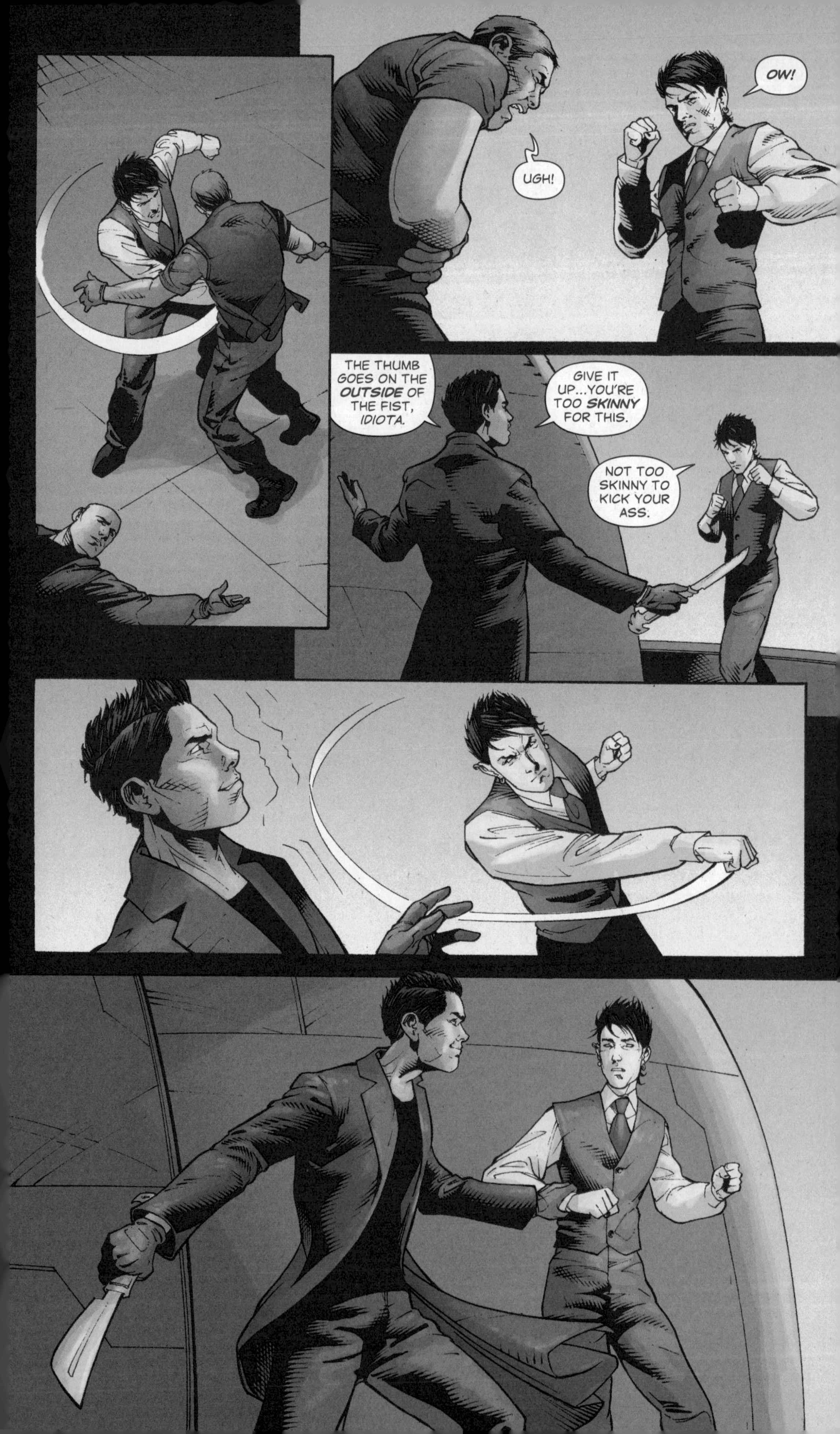

UGH!
OW!
THE THUMB GOES ON THE OUTSIDE OF THE FIST, IDIOTA.
GIVE IT UP...YOU'RE TOO SKINNY FOR THIS.
NOT TOO SKINNY TO KICK YOUR ASS.

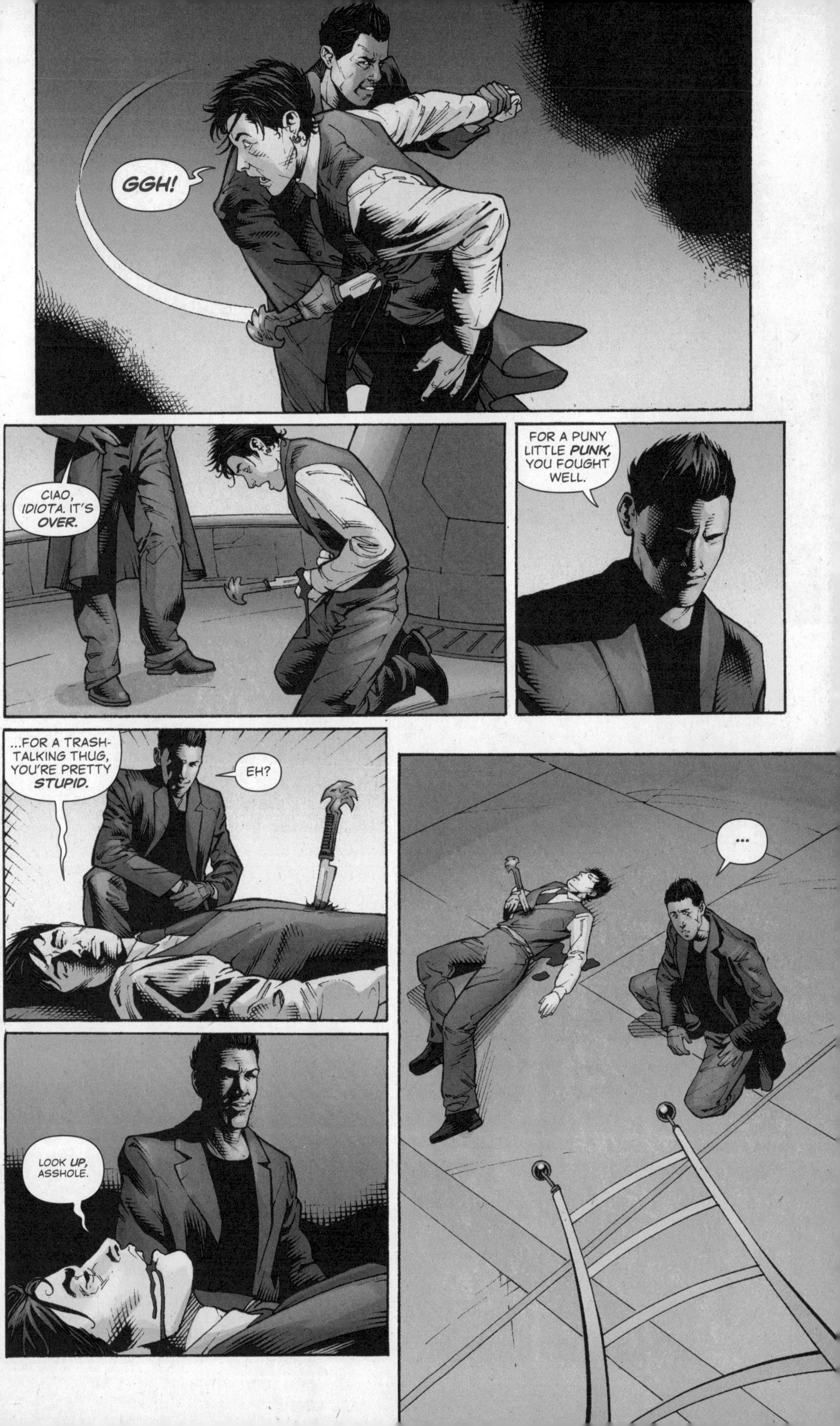
GGH!
CIAO, IDIOTA. IT'S OVER.
FOR A PUNY LITTLE PUNK, YOU FOUGHT WELL.
...FOR A TRASH-TALKING THUG, YOU'RE PRETTY STUPID.
EH?
LOOK UP, ASSHOLE.
...

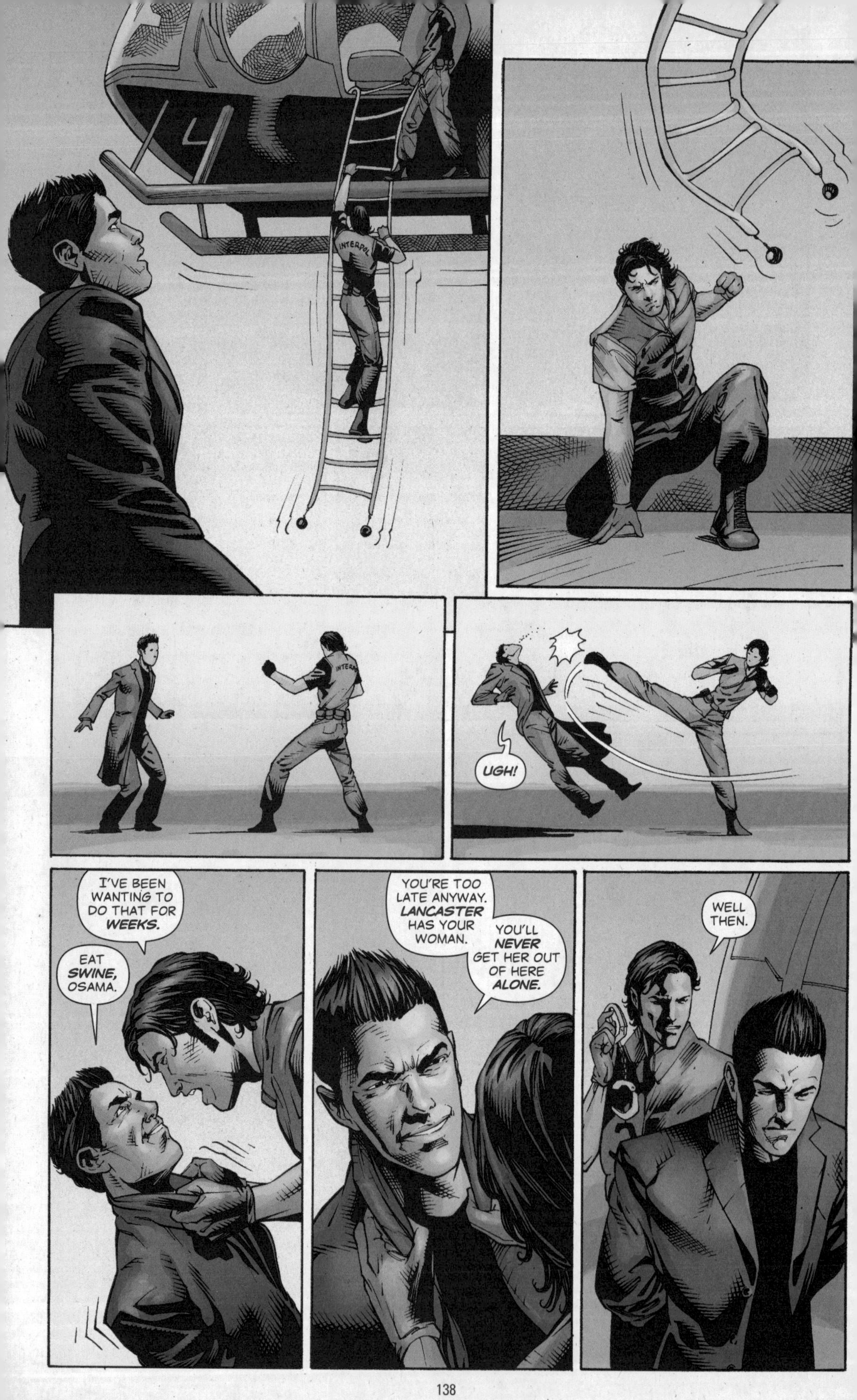
UGH!
I'VE BEEN WANTING TO DO THAT FOR WEEKS.
EAT SWINE, OSAMA.
YOU'RE TOO LATE ANYWAY. LANCASTER HAS YOUR WOMAN.
YOU'LL NEVER GET HER OUT OF HERE ALONE.
WELL THEN.

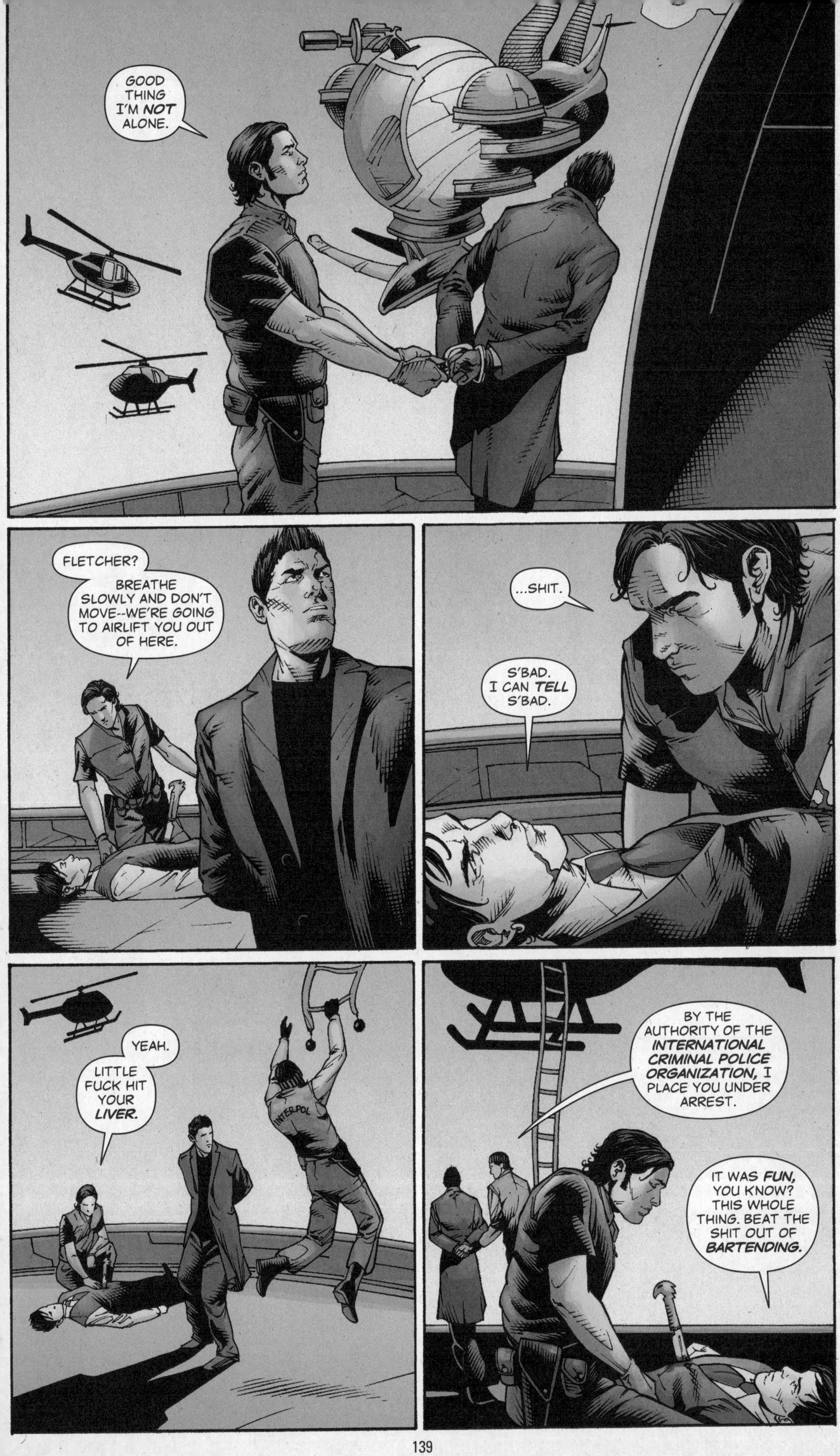
GOOD THING I'M **NOT** ALONE.
FLETCHER?
BREATHE SLOWLY AND DON'T MOVE--WE'RE GOING TO AIRLIFT YOU OUT OF HERE.
...SHIT.
S'BAD. I CAN **TELL** S'BAD.
YEAH.
LITTLE FUCK HIT YOUR **LIVER.**
INTERPOL
BY THE AUTHORITY OF THE **INTERNATIONAL CRIMINAL POLICE ORGANIZATION,** I PLACE YOU UNDER ARREST.
IT WAS **FUN,** YOU KNOW? THIS WHOLE THING. BEAT THE SHIT OUT OF **BARTENDING.**

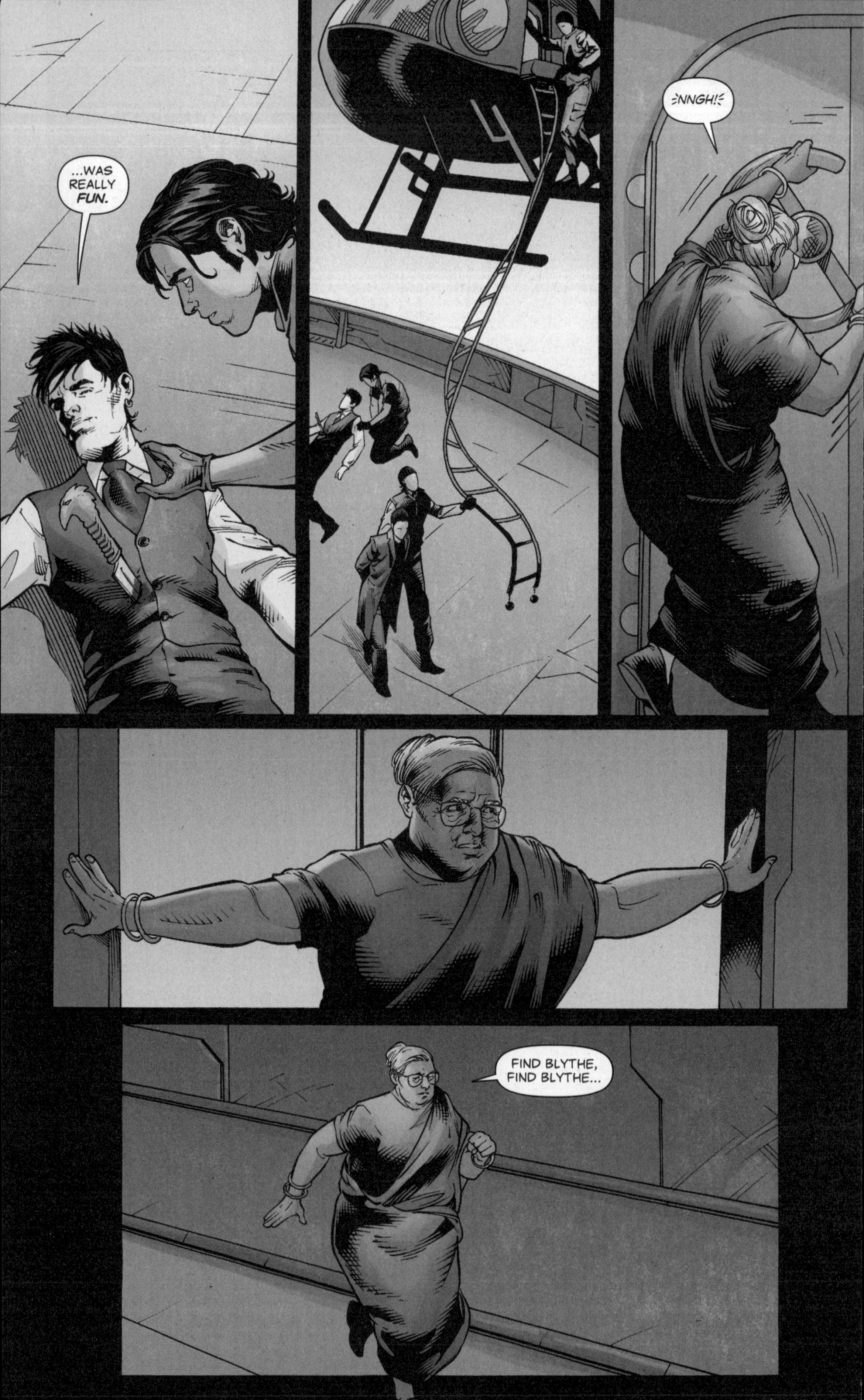
...WAS REALLY FUN.
NNGH!
FIND BLYTHE, FIND BLYTHE...

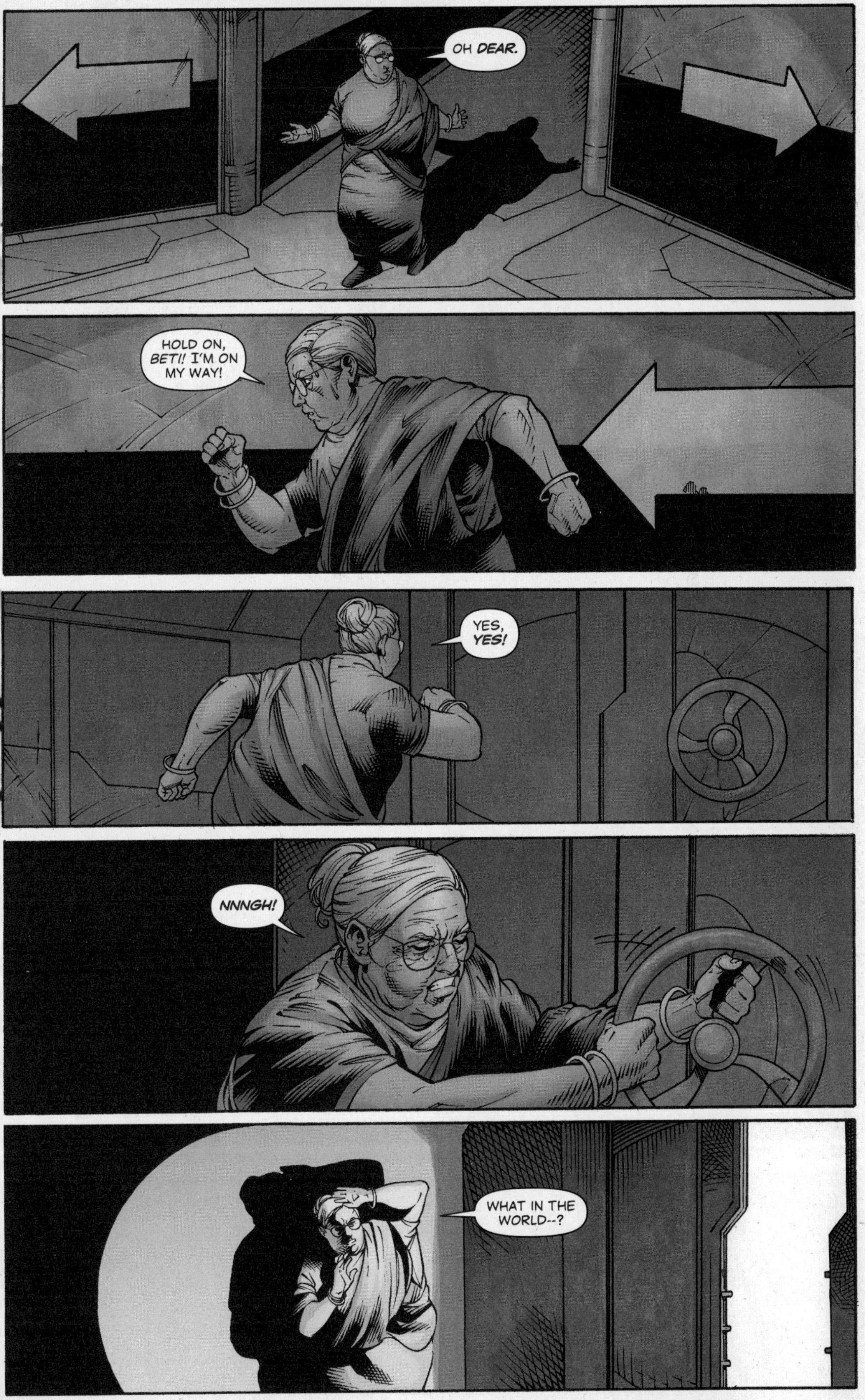
OH DEAR.
HOLD ON, BETI! I'M ON MY WAY!
YES, YES!
NNNGH!
WHAT IN THE WORLD--?

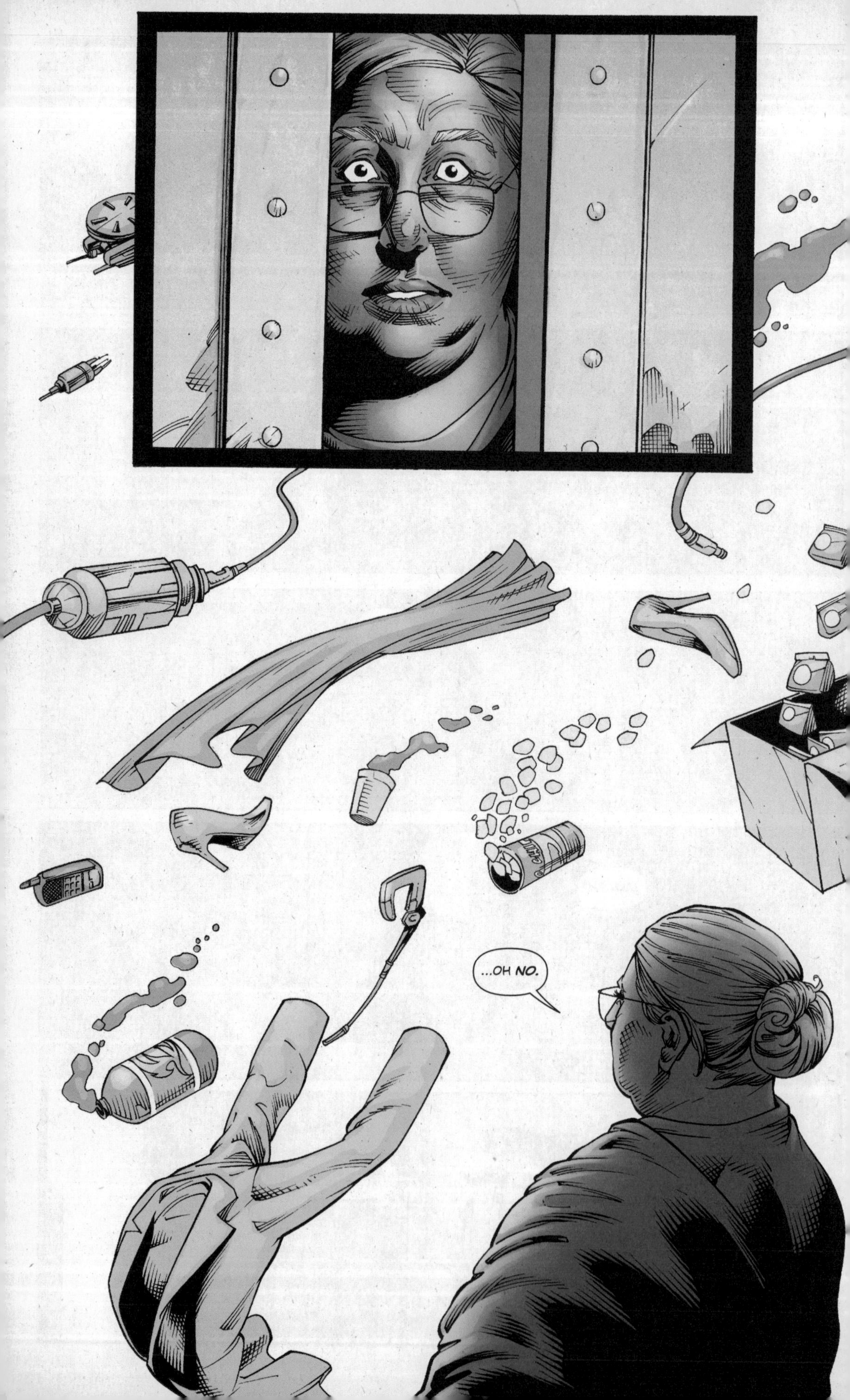
...OH NO.

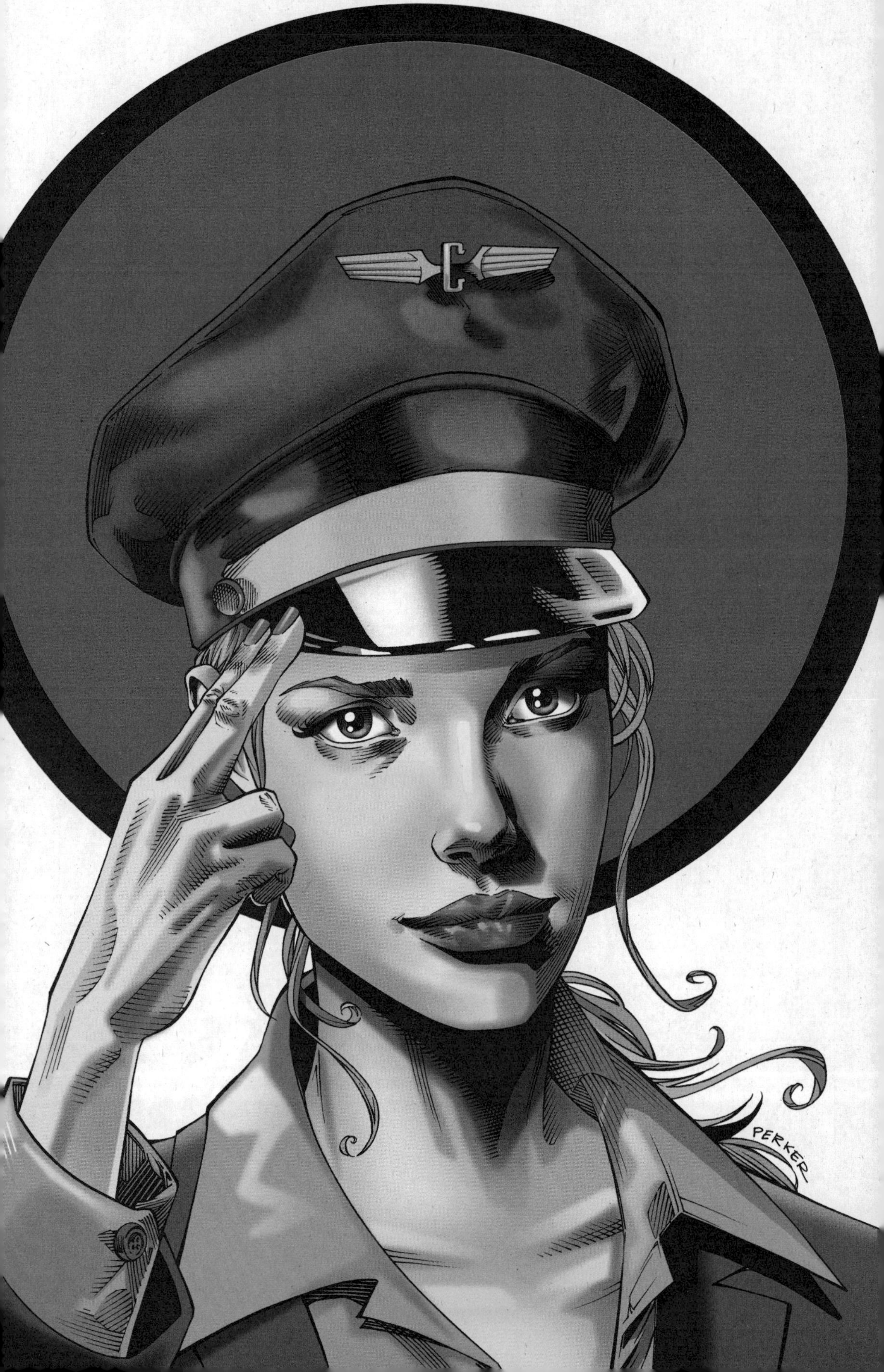
PERKER

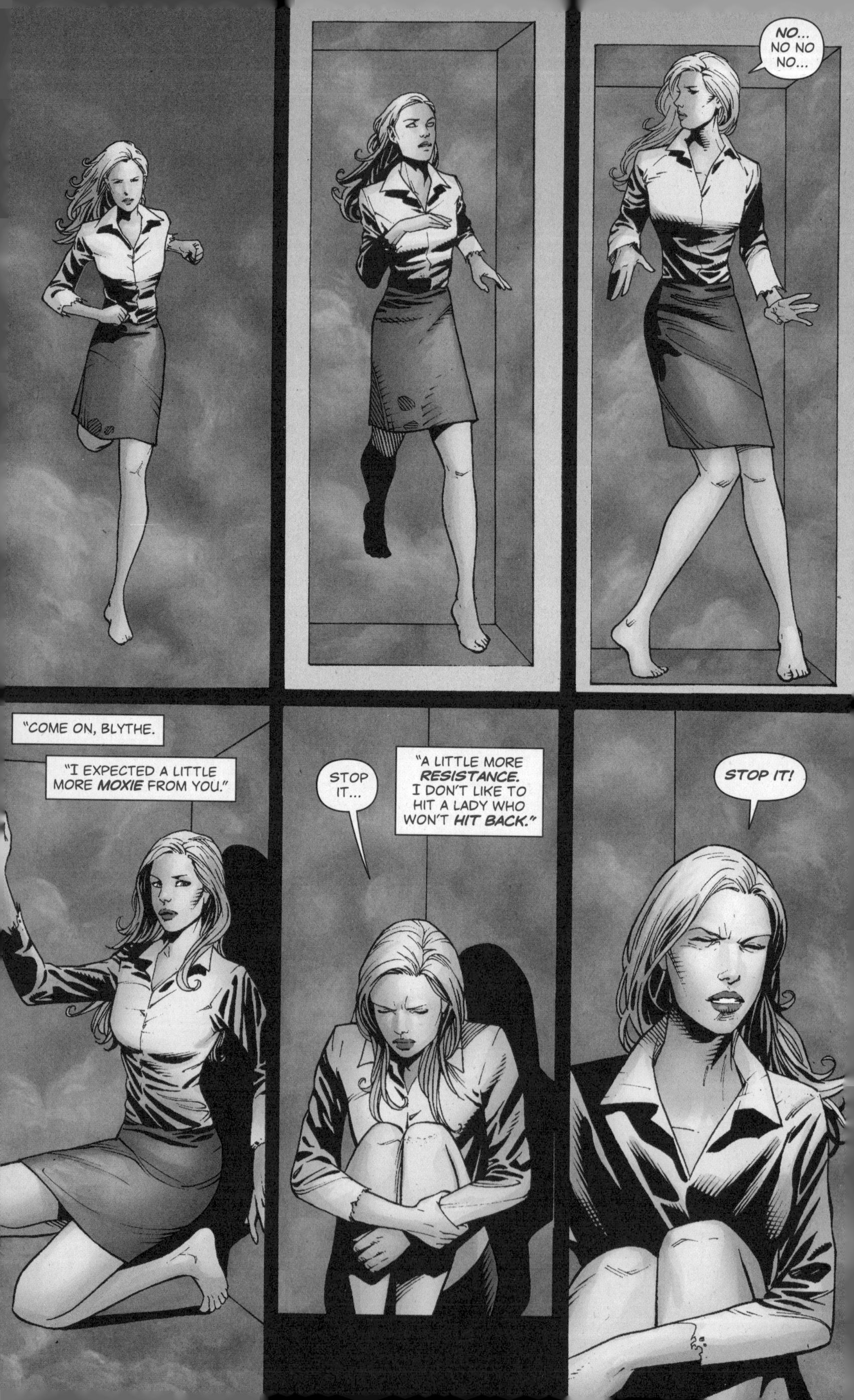
NO... NO NO NO...
"COME ON, BLYTHE.
"I EXPECTED A LITTLE MORE MOXIE FROM YOU."
STOP IT...
"A LITTLE MORE RESISTANCE. I DON'T LIKE TO HIT A LADY WHO WON'T HIT BACK."
STOP IT!

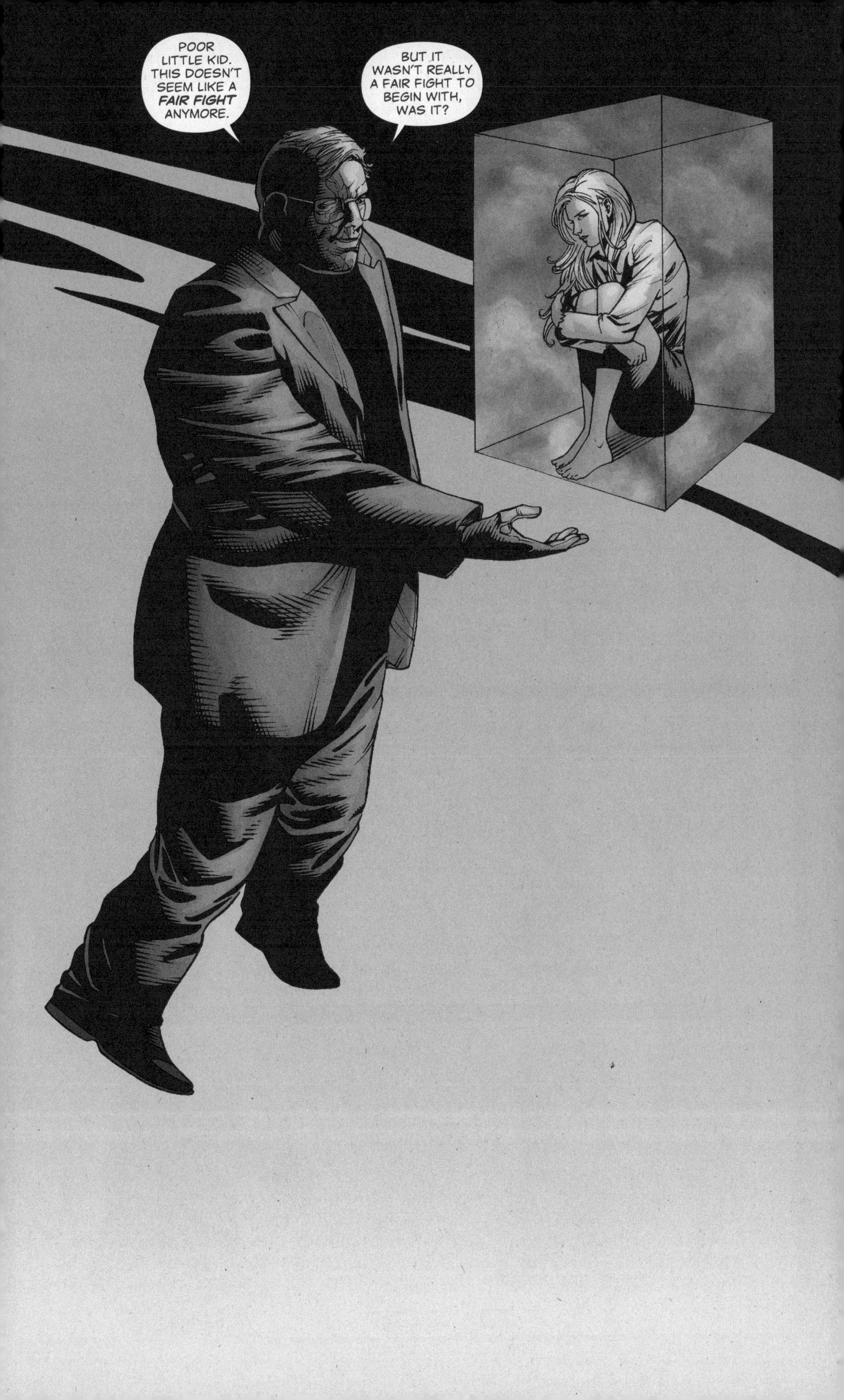
POOR LITTLE KID. THIS DOESN'T SEEM LIKE A **FAIR FIGHT** ANYMORE.
BUT IT WASN'T REALLY A FAIR FIGHT TO BEGIN WITH, WAS IT?

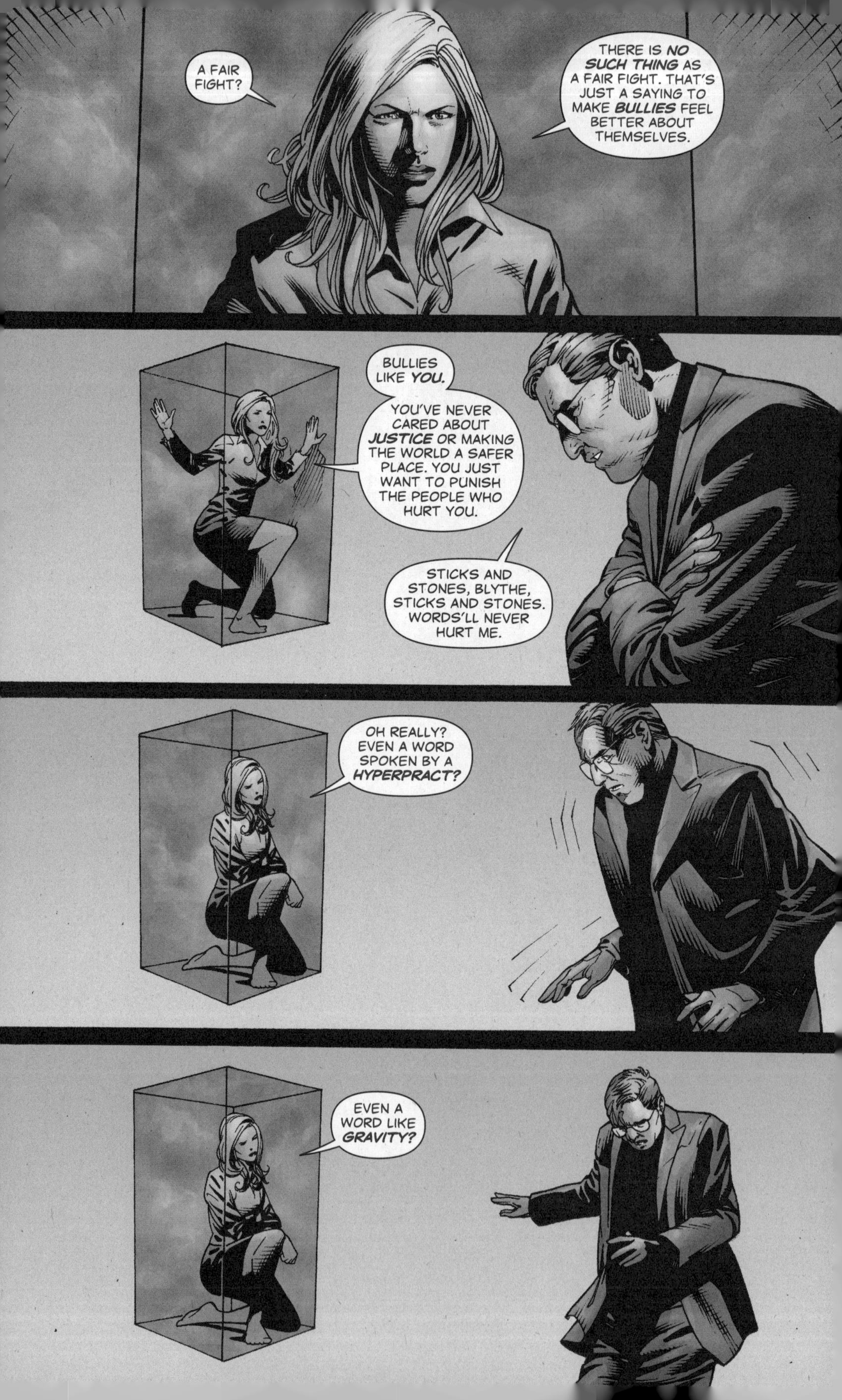
A FAIR FIGHT?
THERE IS NO SUCH THING AS A FAIR FIGHT. THAT'S JUST A SAYING TO MAKE BULLIES FEEL BETTER ABOUT THEMSELVES.
BULLIES LIKE YOU.
YOU'VE NEVER CARED ABOUT JUSTICE OR MAKING THE WORLD A SAFER PLACE. YOU JUST WANT TO PUNISH THE PEOPLE WHO HURT YOU.
STICKS AND STONES, BLYTHE, STICKS AND STONES. WORDS'LL NEVER HURT ME.
OH REALLY? EVEN A WORD SPOKEN BY A HYPERPRACT?
EVEN A WORD LIKE GRAVITY?

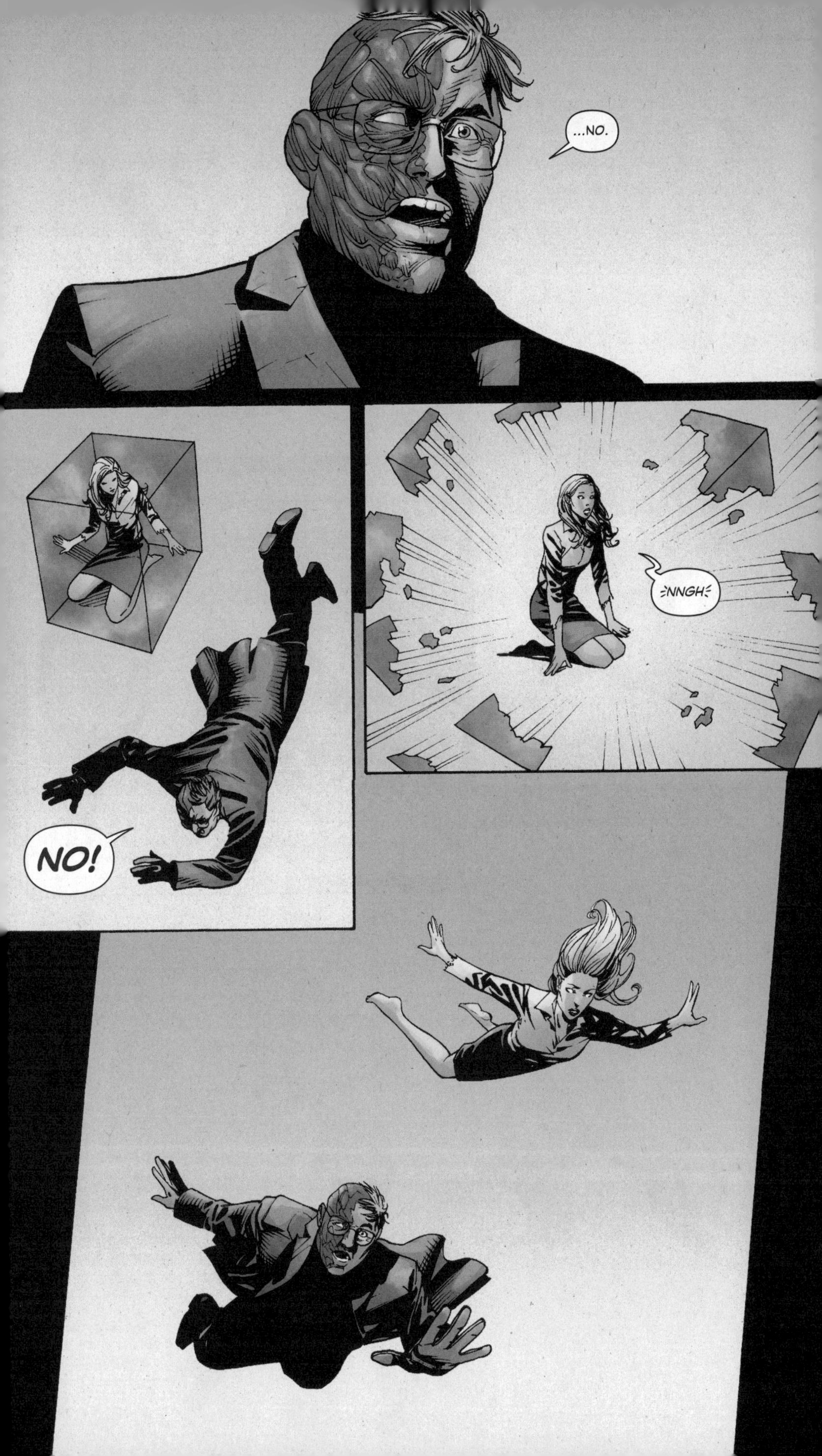
...NO.
NO!
NNGH

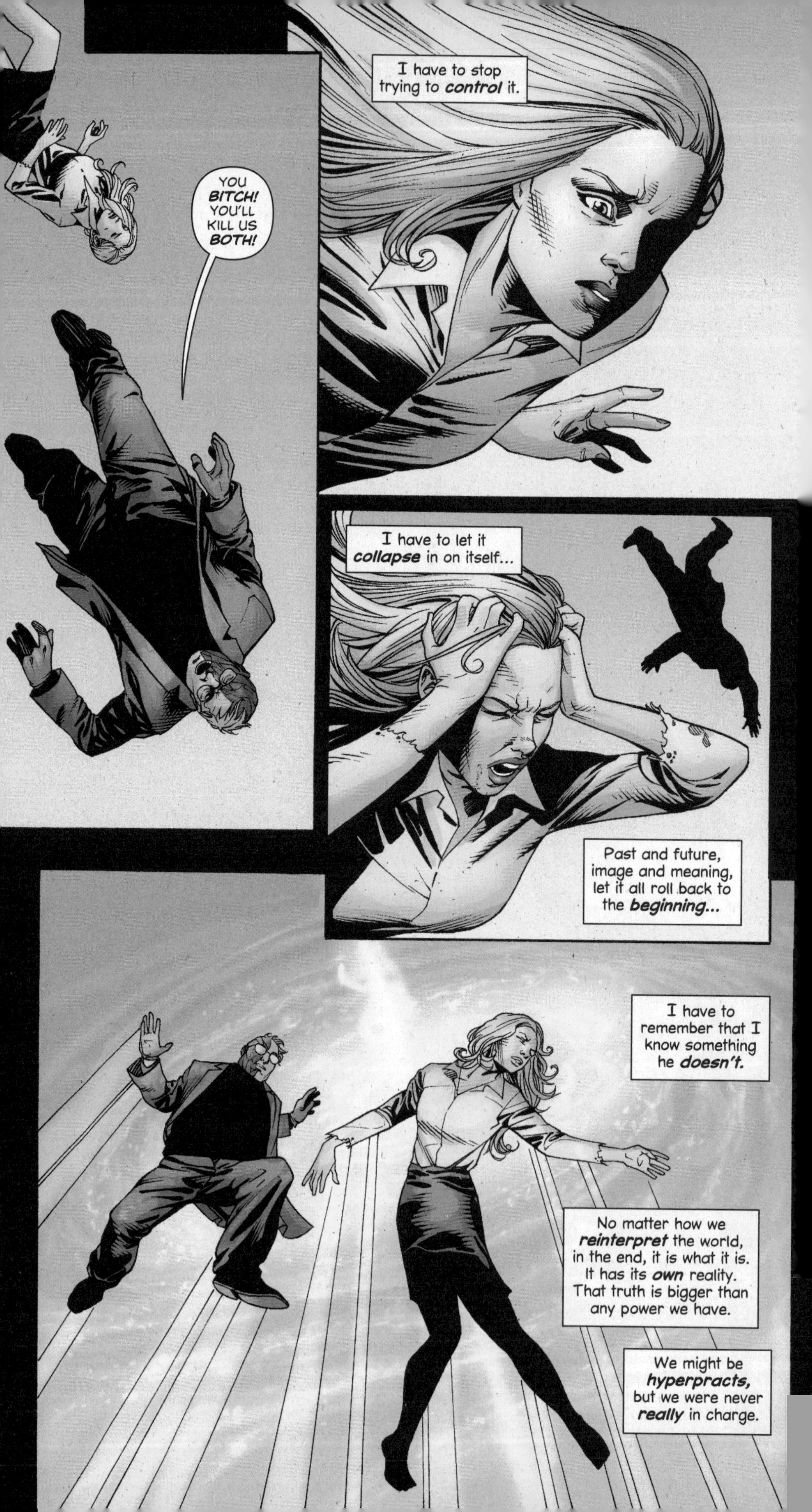
I have to stop trying to *control* it.
YOU *BITCH!* YOU'LL KILL US *BOTH!*
I have to let it *collapse* in on itself...
Past and future, image and meaning, let it all roll back to the *beginning...*
I have to remember that I know something he *doesn't.*
No matter how we *reinterpret* the world, in the end, it is what it is. It has its *own* reality. That truth is bigger than any power we have.
We might be *hyperpracts,* but we were never *really* in charge.

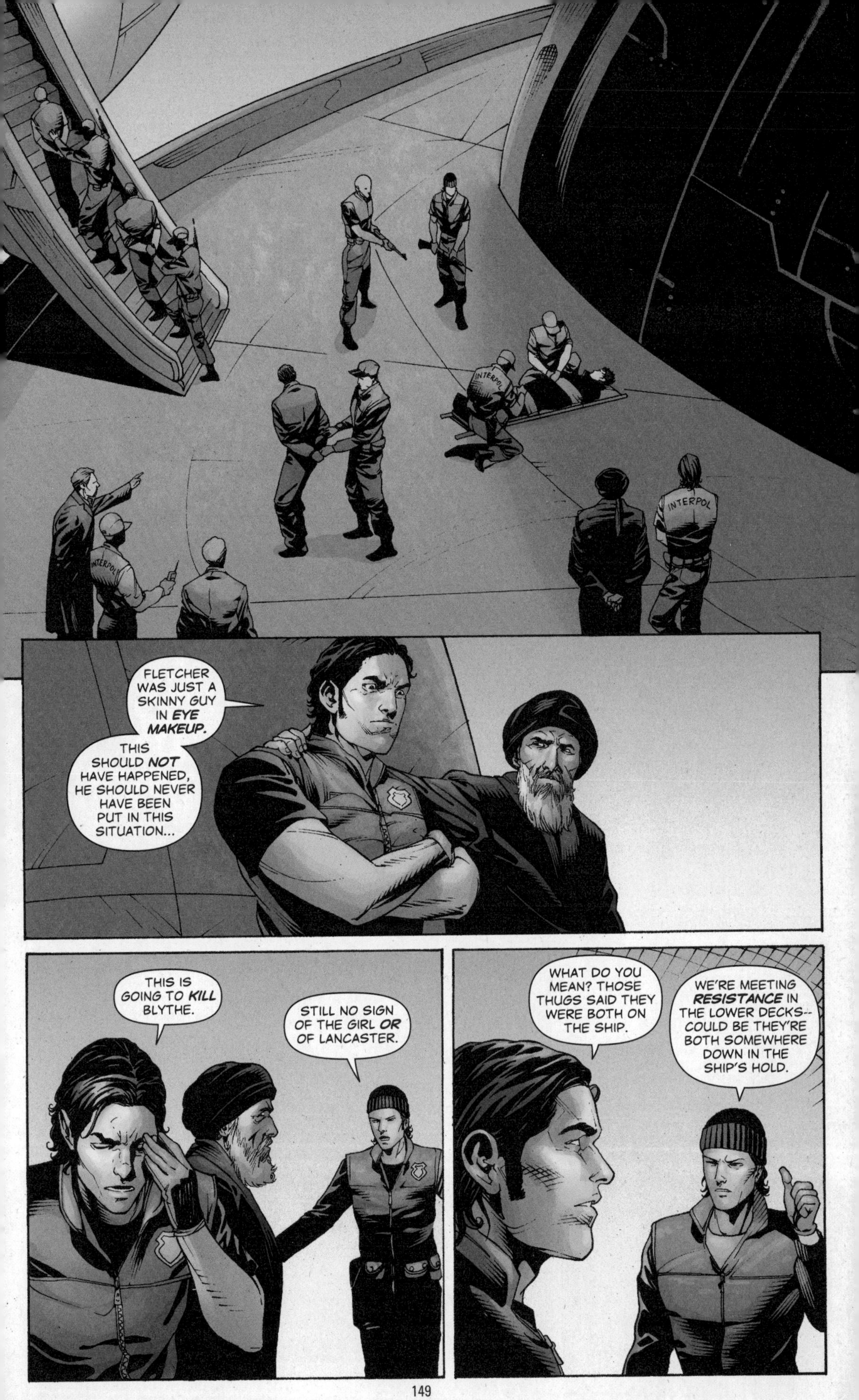
INTERPOL
INTERPOL
INTERPOL
FLETCHER WAS JUST A SKINNY GUY IN **EYE MAKEUP.**
THIS SHOULD **NOT** HAVE HAPPENED, HE SHOULD NEVER HAVE BEEN PUT IN THIS SITUATION...
THIS IS GOING TO **KILL** BLYTHE.
STILL NO SIGN OF THE GIRL **OR** OF LANCASTER.
WHAT DO YOU MEAN? THOSE THUGS SAID THEY WERE BOTH ON THE SHIP.
WE'RE MEETING **RESISTANCE** IN THE LOWER DECKS-- COULD BE THEY'RE BOTH SOMEWHERE DOWN IN THE SHIP'S HOLD.

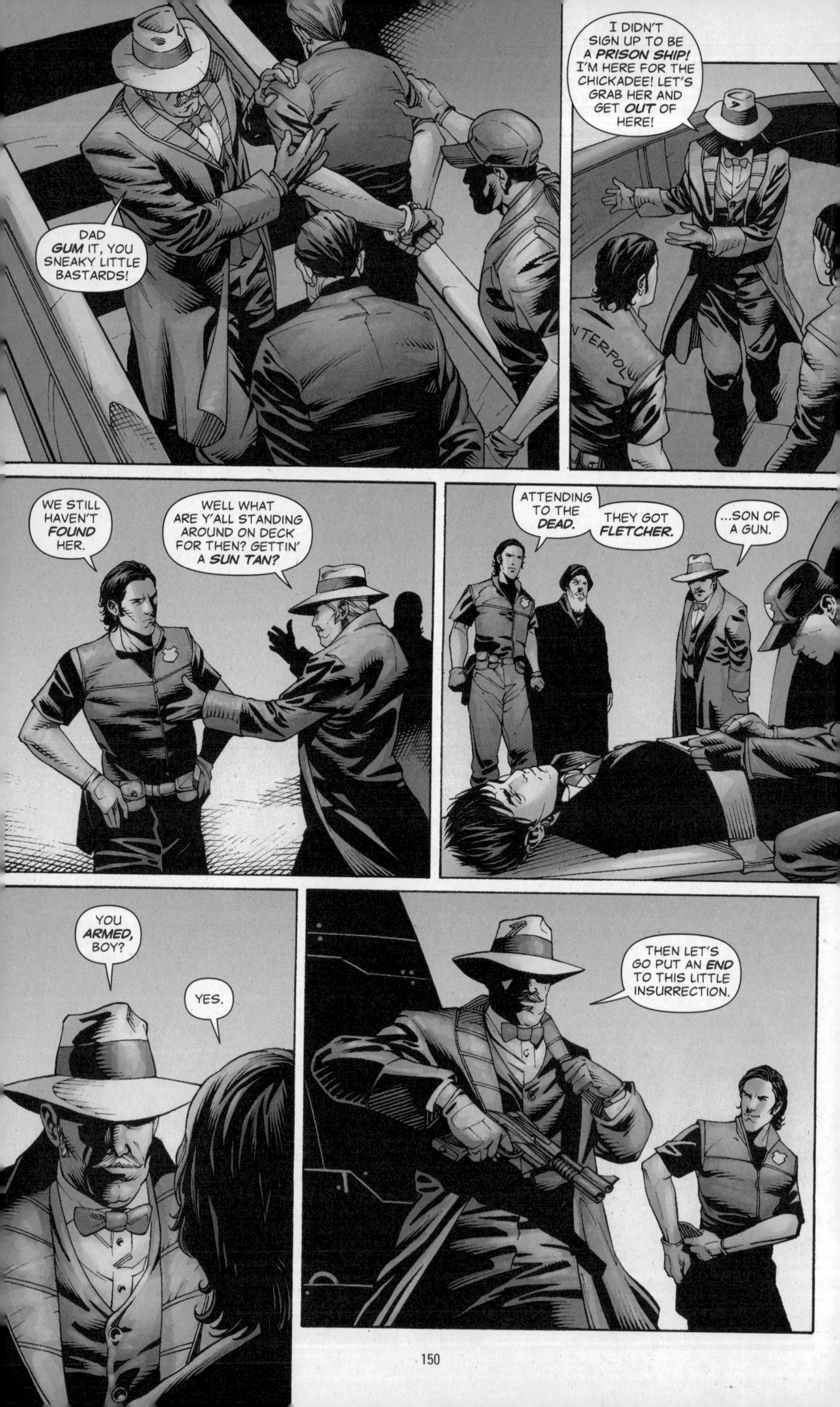
DAD GUM IT, YOU SNEAKY LITTLE BASTARDS!
I DIDN'T SIGN UP TO BE A PRISON SHIP! I'M HERE FOR THE CHICKADEE! LET'S GRAB HER AND GET OUT OF HERE!
INTERPOL
WE STILL HAVEN'T FOUND HER.
WELL WHAT ARE Y'ALL STANDING AROUND ON DECK FOR THEN? GETTIN' A SUN TAN?
ATTENDING TO THE DEAD.
THEY GOT FLETCHER.
...SON OF A GUN.
YOU ARMED, BOY?
YES.
THEN LET'S GO PUT AN END TO THIS LITTLE INSURRECTION.

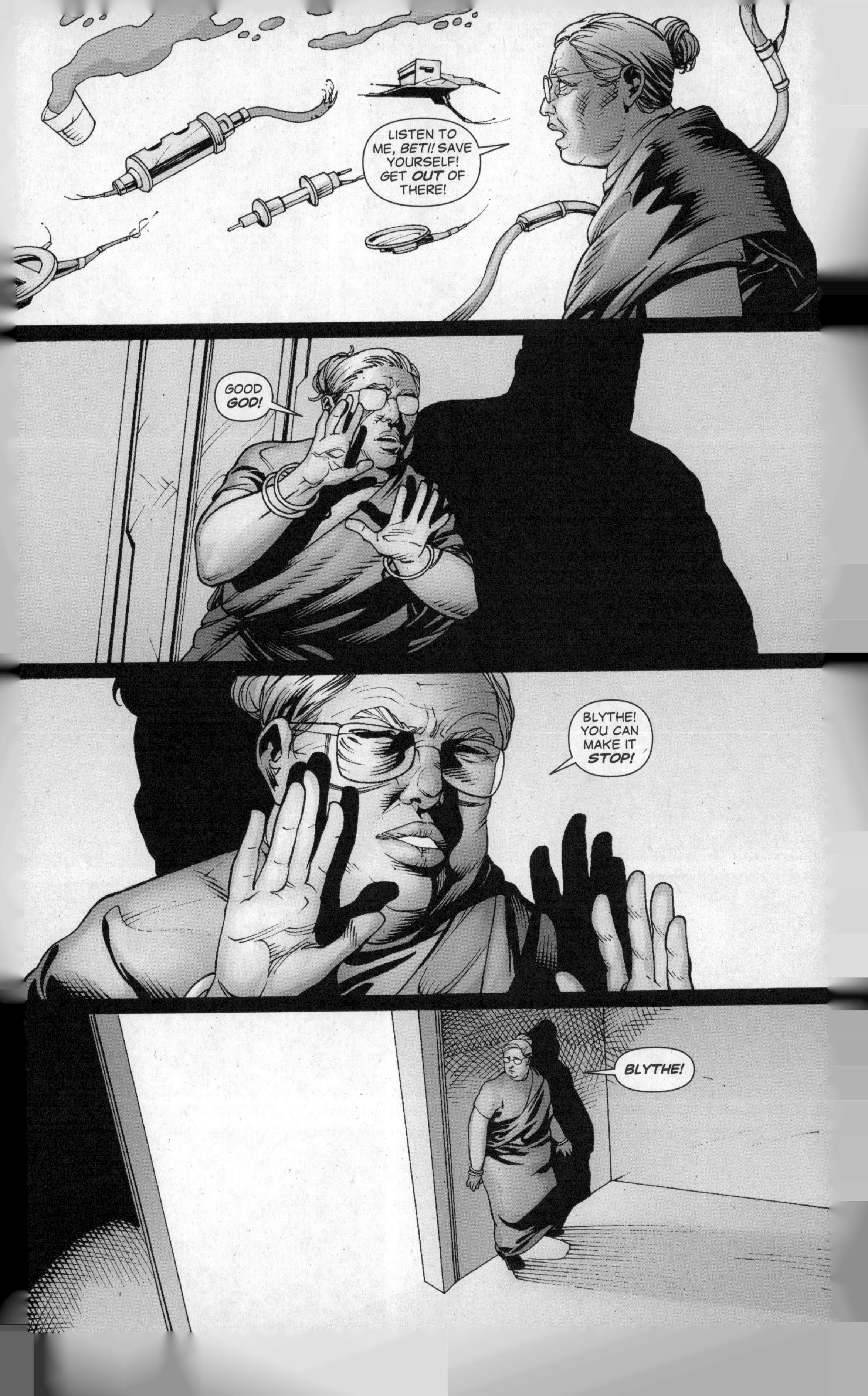
LISTEN TO ME, BETI!! SAVE YOURSELF! GET OUT OF THERE!
GOOD GOD!
BLYTHE! YOU CAN MAKE IT STOP!
BLYTHE!

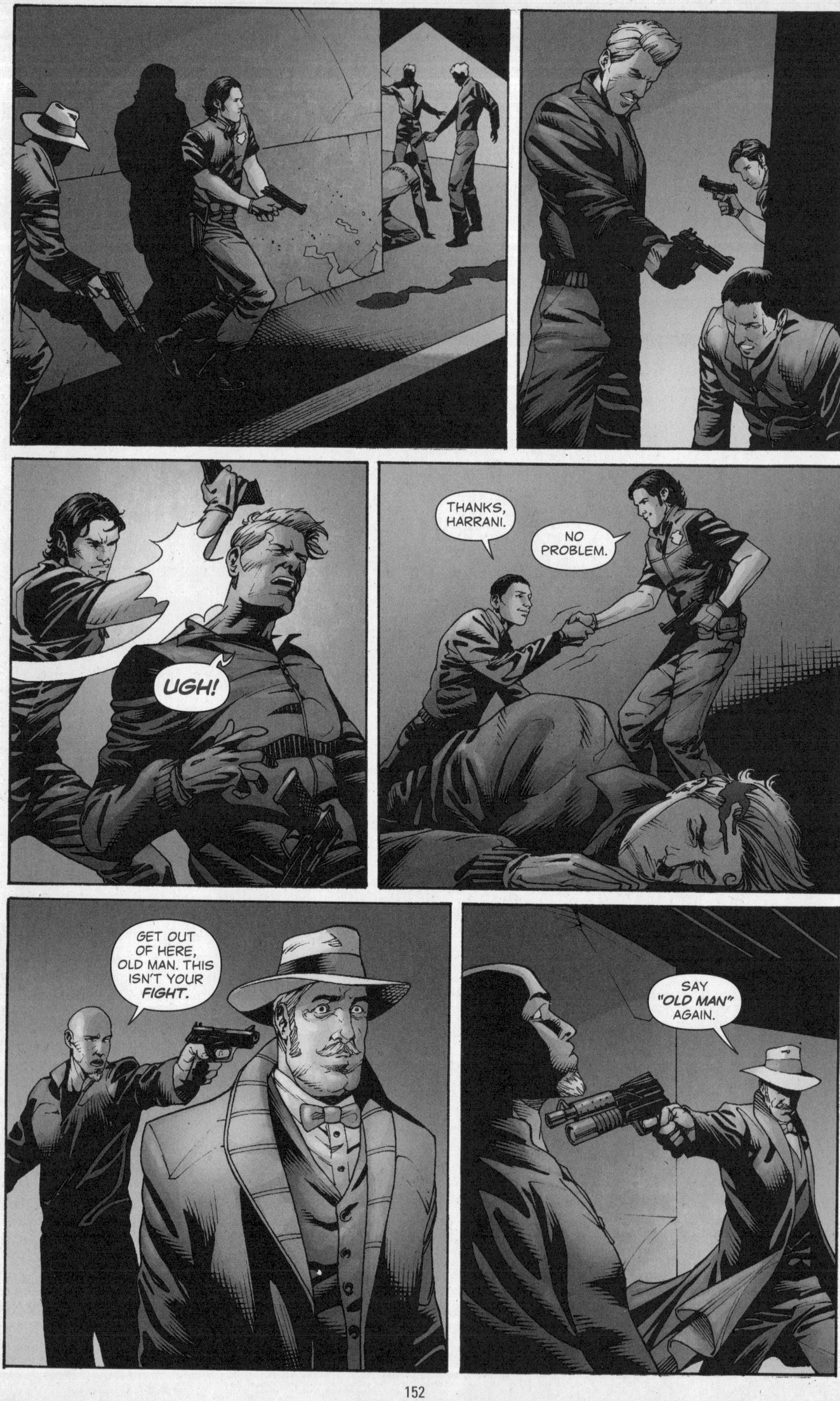

UGH!
THANKS, HARRANI.
NO PROBLEM.
GET OUT OF HERE, OLD MAN. THIS ISN'T YOUR FIGHT.
SAY "OLD MAN" AGAIN.

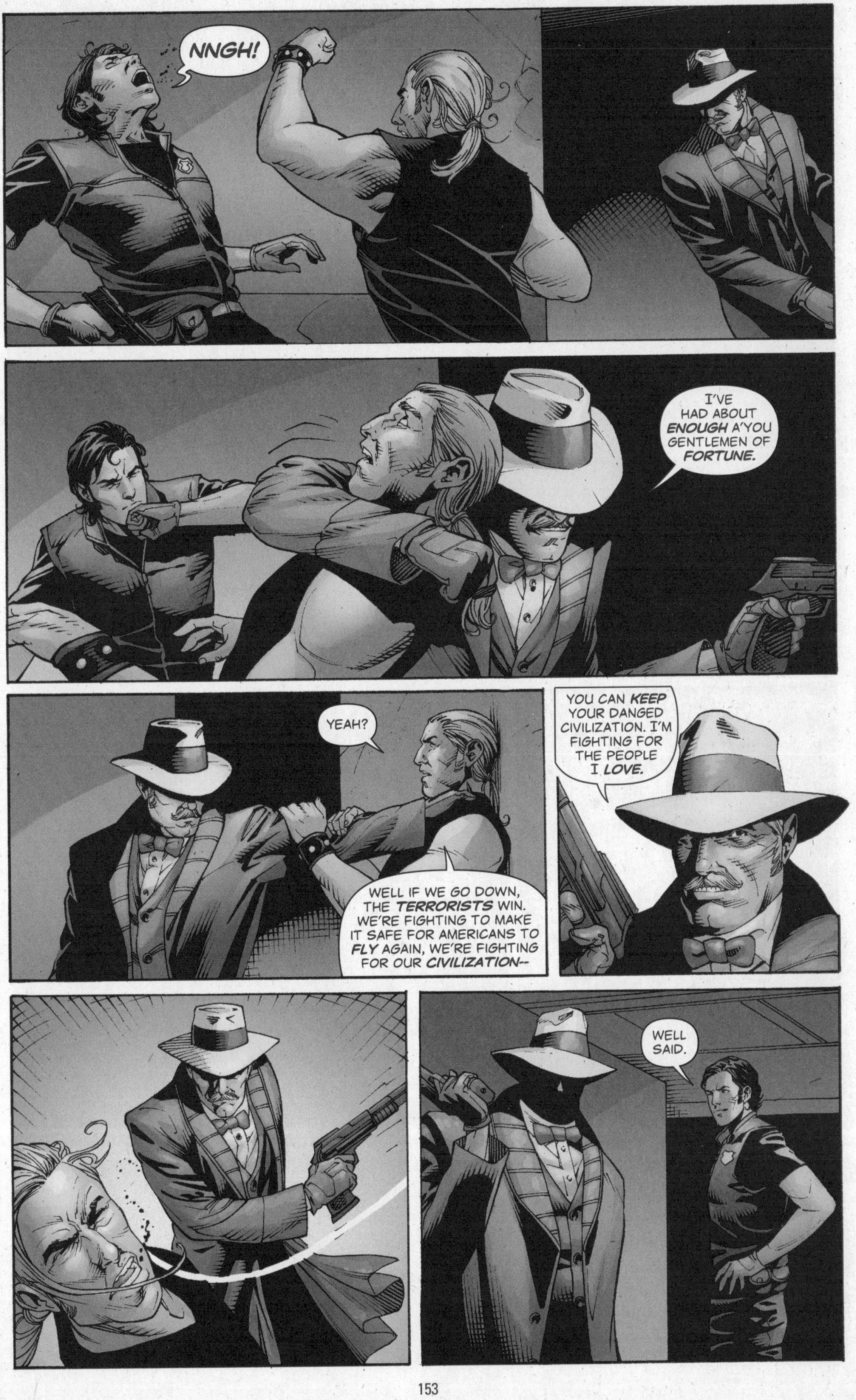
NNGH!
I'VE HAD ABOUT ENOUGH A'YOU GENTLEMEN OF FORTUNE.
YEAH?
WELL IF WE GO DOWN, THE TERRORISTS WIN. WE'RE FIGHTING TO MAKE IT SAFE FOR AMERICANS TO FLY AGAIN, WE'RE FIGHTING FOR OUR CIVILIZATION--
YOU CAN KEEP YOUR DANGED CIVILIZATION. I'M FIGHTING FOR THE PEOPLE I LOVE.
WELL SAID.

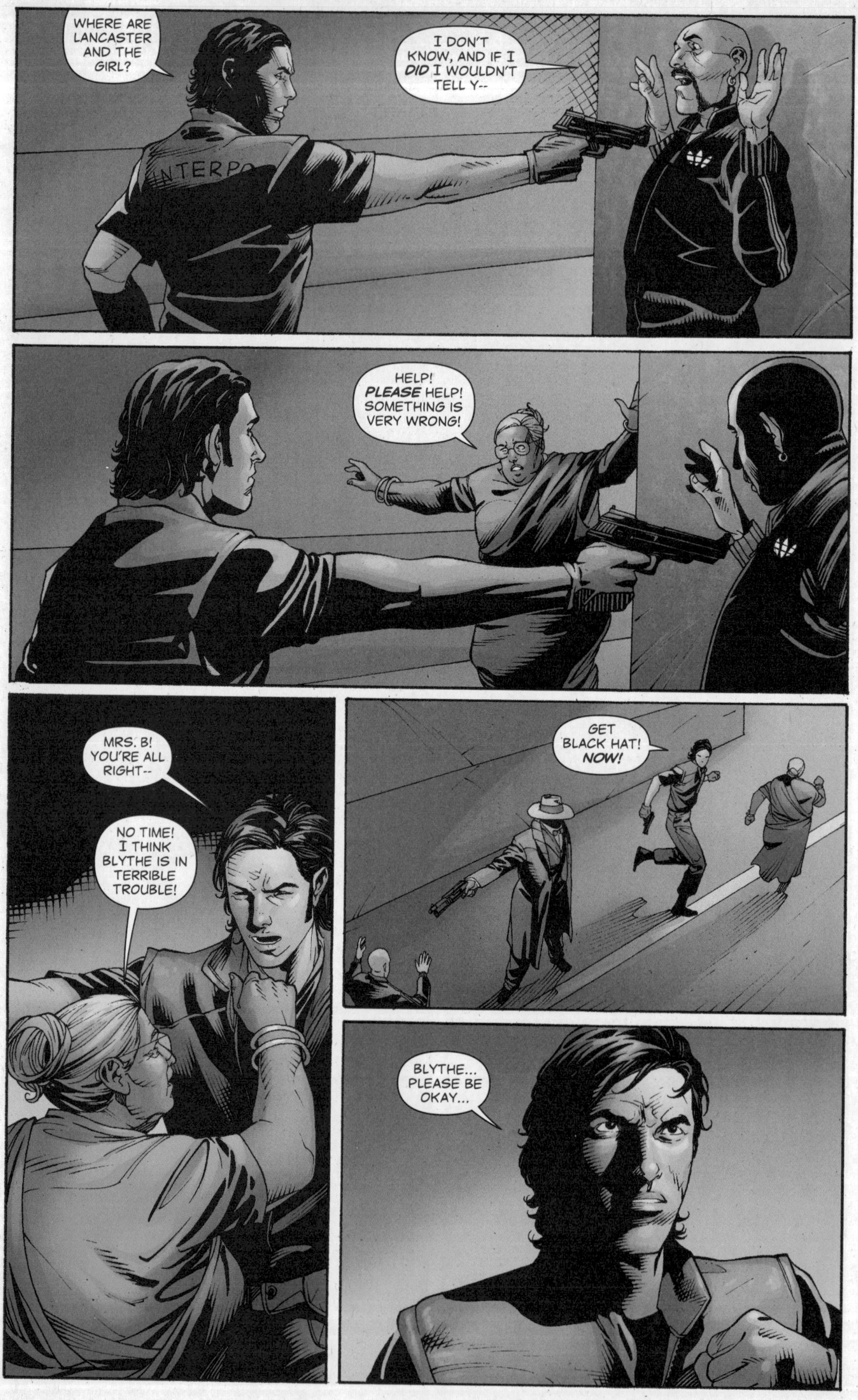
WHERE ARE LANCASTER AND THE GIRL?
I DON'T KNOW, AND IF I *DID* I WOULDN'T TELL Y--
INTERPO
HELP! *PLEASE* HELP! SOMETHING IS VERY WRONG!
MRS. B! YOU'RE ALL RIGHT--
NO TIME! I THINK BLYTHE IS IN TERRIBLE TROUBLE!
GET BLACK HAT! *NOW!*
BLYTHE... PLEASE BE OKAY...

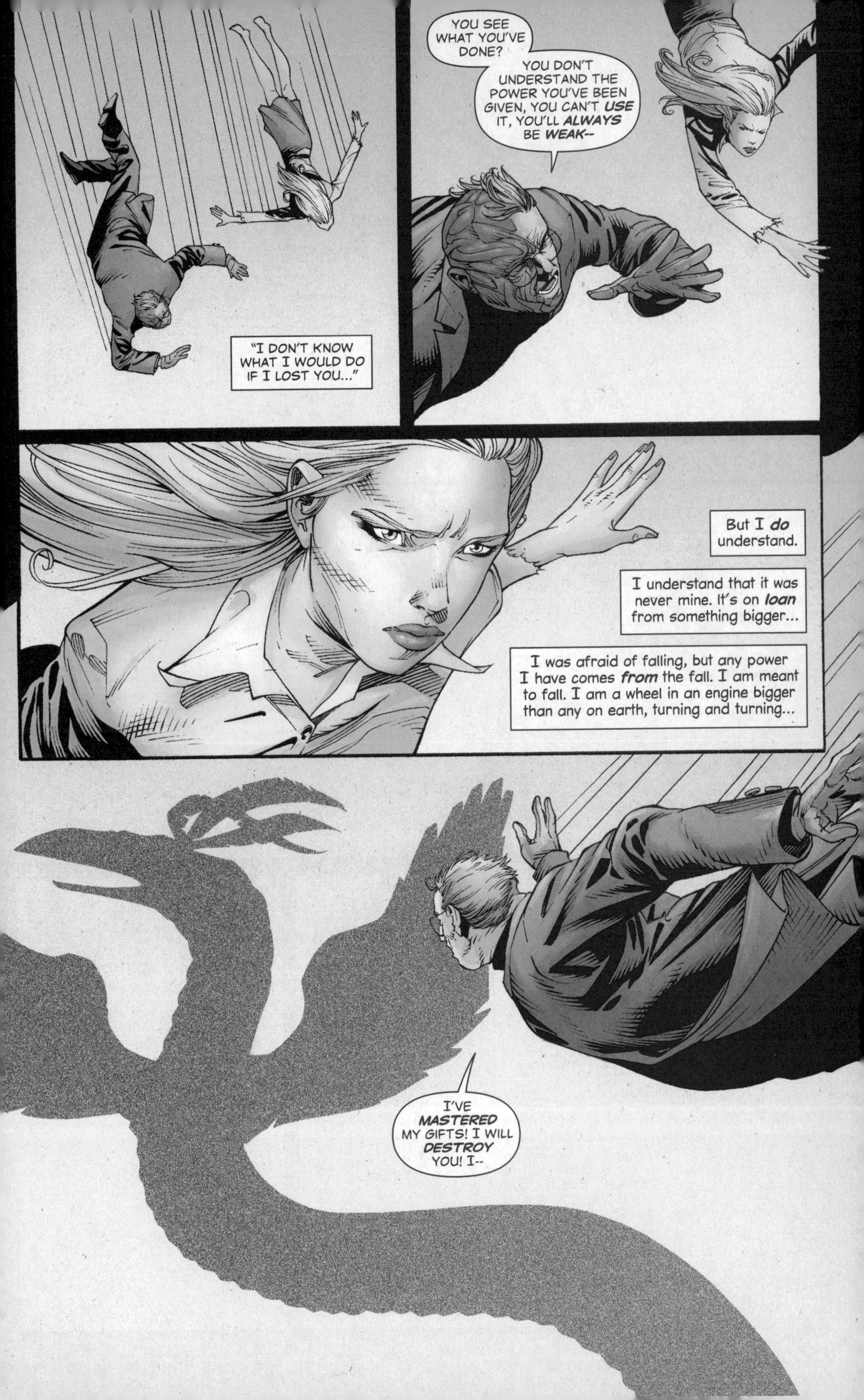

"I DON'T KNOW WHAT I WOULD DO IF I LOST YOU..."
YOU SEE WHAT YOU'VE DONE?
YOU DON'T UNDERSTAND THE POWER YOU'VE BEEN GIVEN, YOU CAN'T USE IT, YOU'LL ALWAYS BE WEAK--
But I do understand.
I understand that it was never mine. It's on loan from something bigger...
I was afraid of falling, but any power I have comes from the fall. I am meant to fall. I am a wheel in an engine bigger than any on earth, turning and turning...
I'VE MASTERED MY GIFTS! I WILL DESTROY YOU! I--

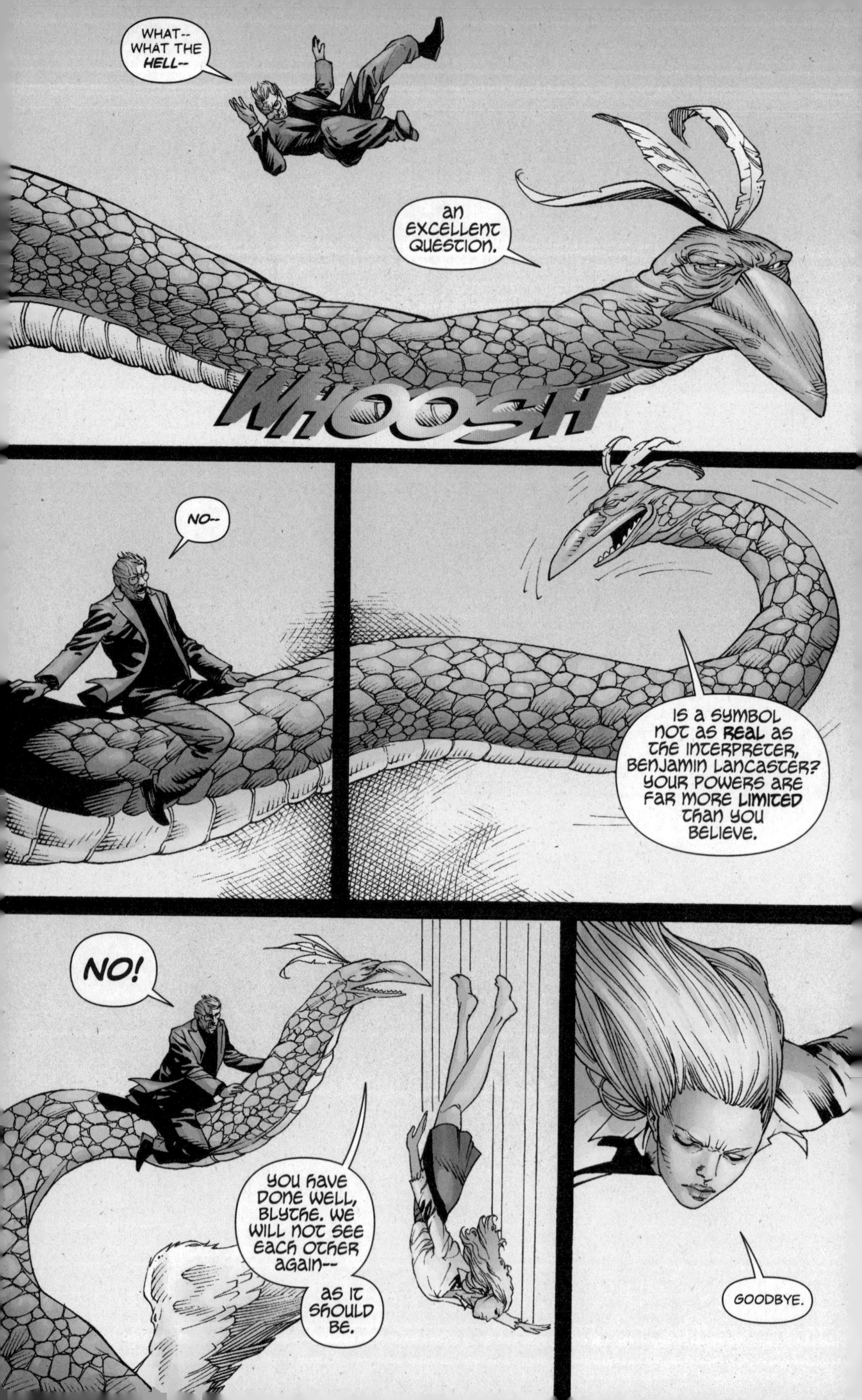
WHAT-- WHAT THE HELL--
an EXCELLENT QUESTION.
WHOOSH
NO--
IS A SYMBOL NOT AS REAL AS THE INTERPRETER, BENJAMIN LANCASTER? YOUR POWERS ARE FAR MORE LIMITED THAN YOU BELIEVE.
NO!
YOU HAVE DONE WELL, BLYTHE. WE WILL NOT SEE EACH OTHER AGAIN--
AS IT SHOULD BE.
GOODBYE.

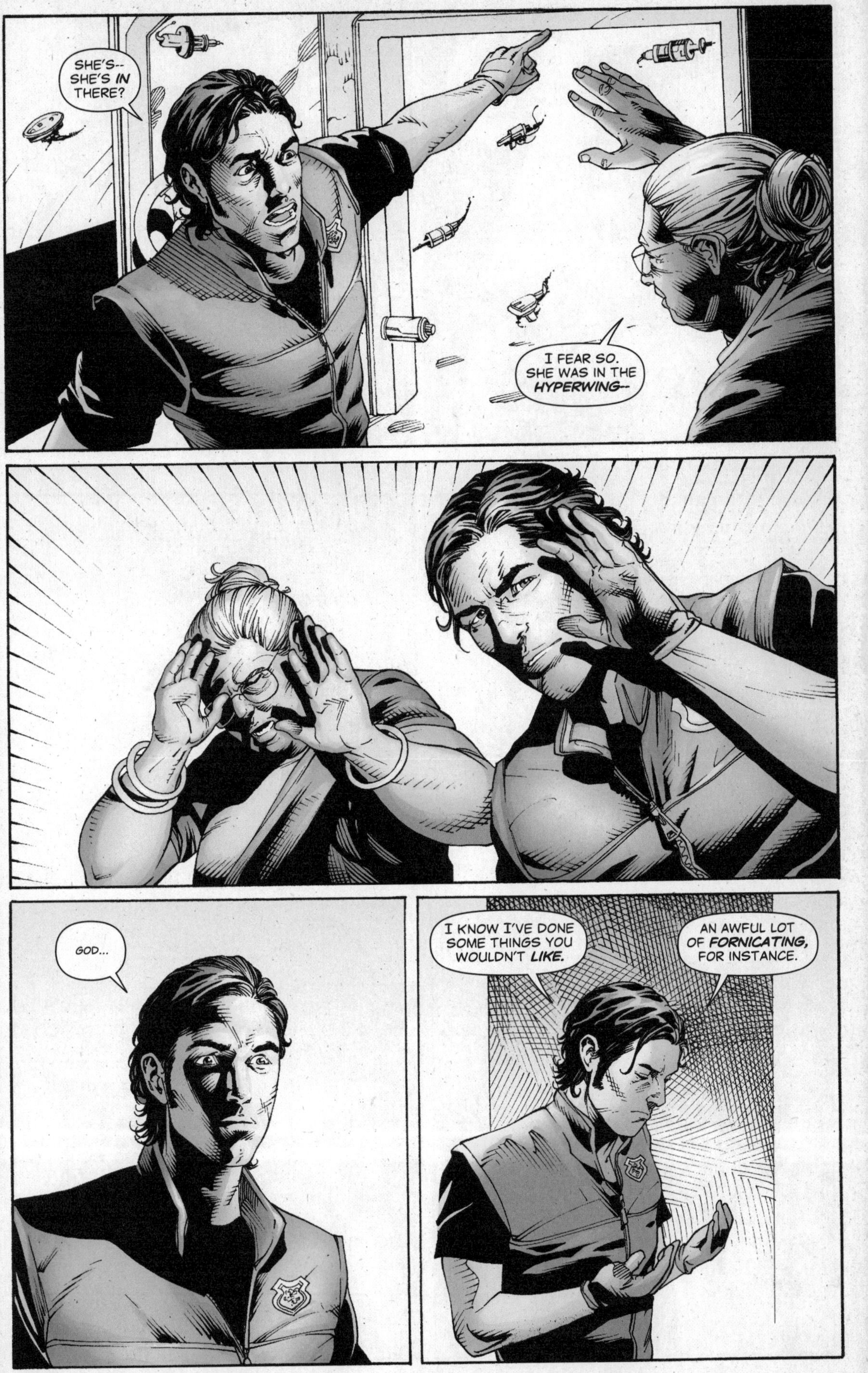
SHE'S-- SHE'S IN THERE?
I FEAR SO. SHE WAS IN THE HYPERWING--
GOD...
I KNOW I'VE DONE SOME THINGS YOU WOULDN'T LIKE.
AN AWFUL LOT OF FORNICATING, FOR INSTANCE.

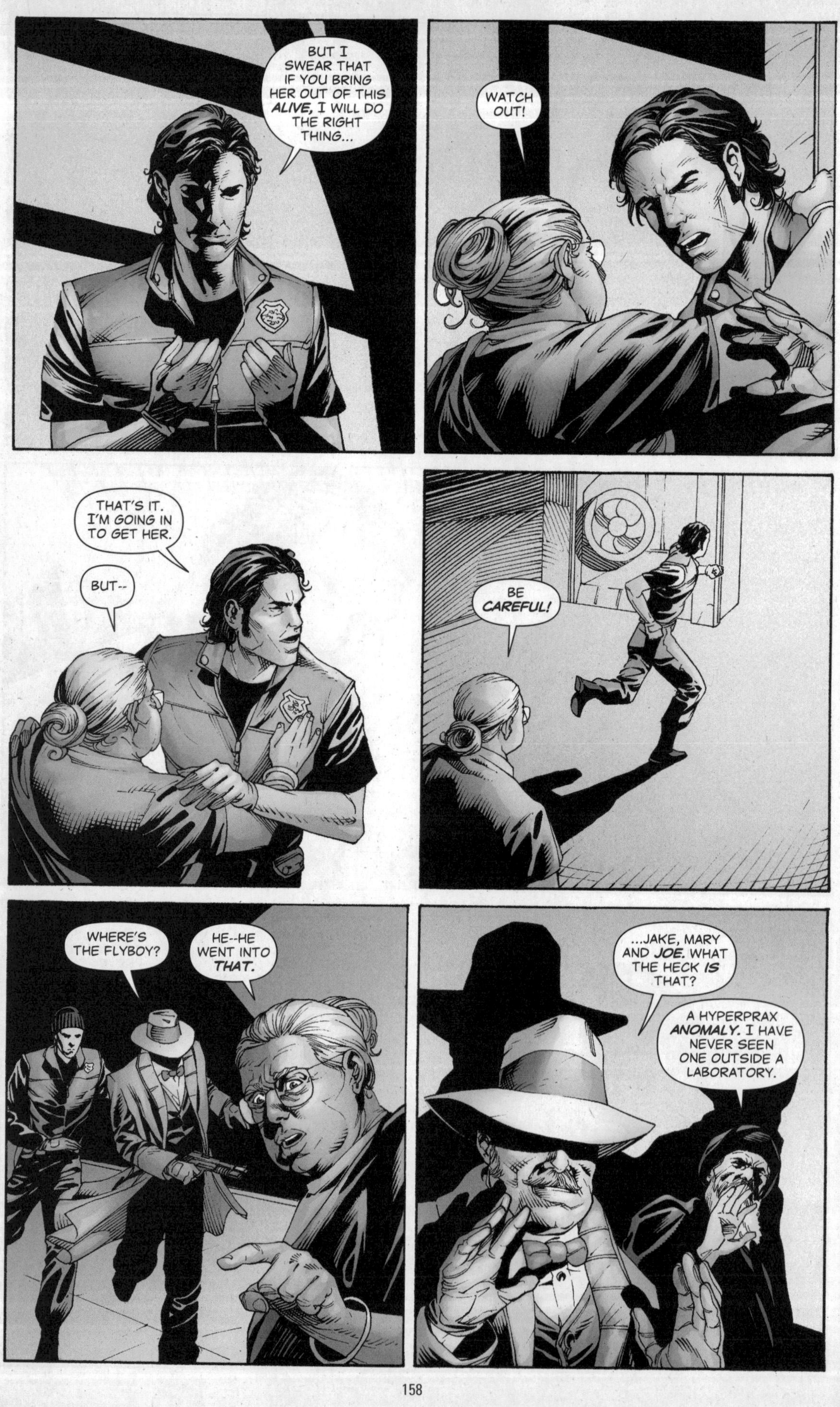
BUT I SWEAR THAT IF YOU BRING HER OUT OF THIS ALIVE, I WILL DO THE RIGHT THING...
WATCH OUT!
THAT'S IT. I'M GOING IN TO GET HER.
BUT--
BE CAREFUL!
WHERE'S THE FLYBOY?
HE--HE WENT INTO THAT.
...JAKE, MARY AND JOE. WHAT THE HECK IS THAT?
A HYPERPRAX ANOMALY. I HAVE NEVER SEEN ONE OUTSIDE A LABORATORY.

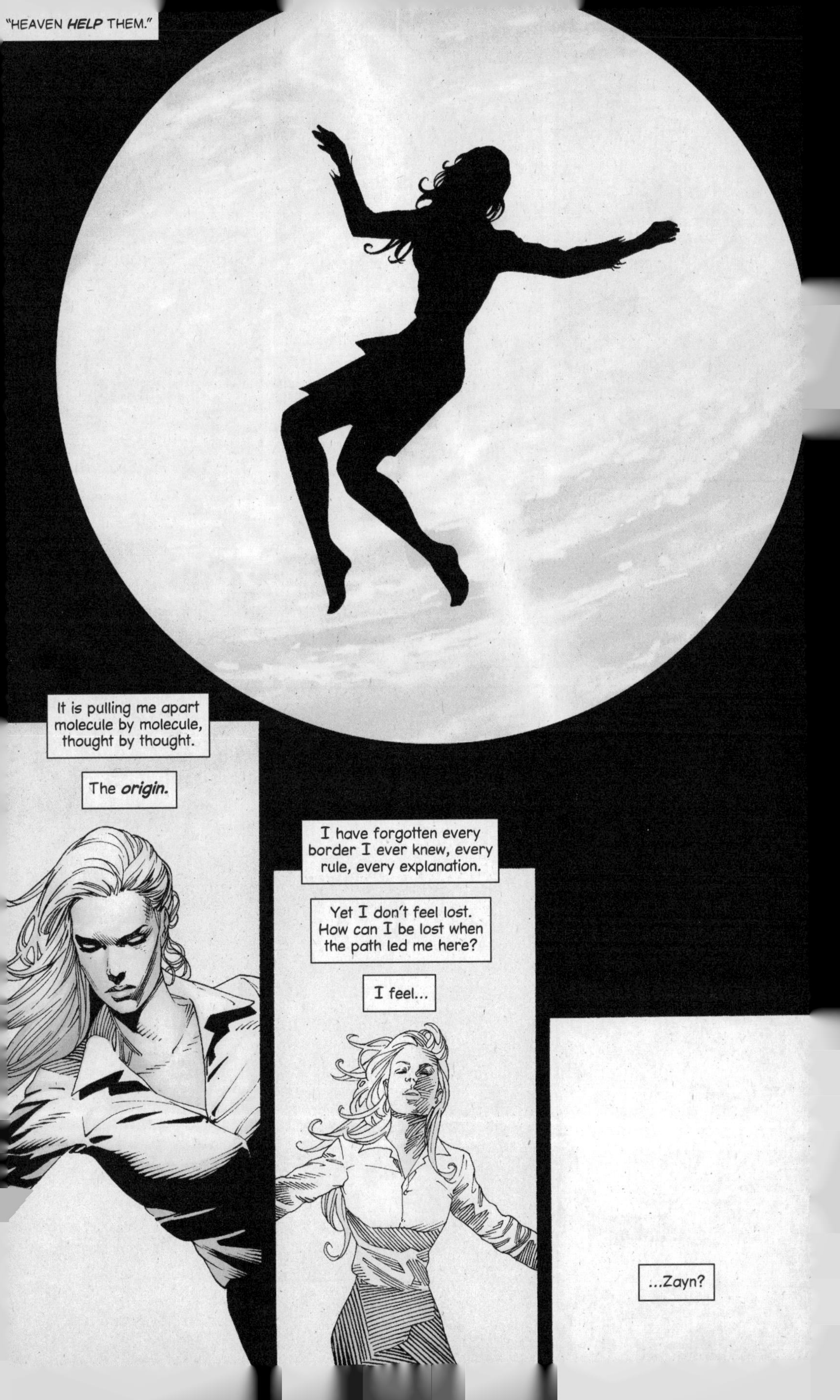
"HEAVEN HELP THEM."
It is pulling me apart molecule by molecule, thought by thought.
The origin.
I have forgotten every border I ever knew, every rule, every explanation.
Yet I don't feel lost. How can I be lost when the path led me here?
I feel...
...Zayn?

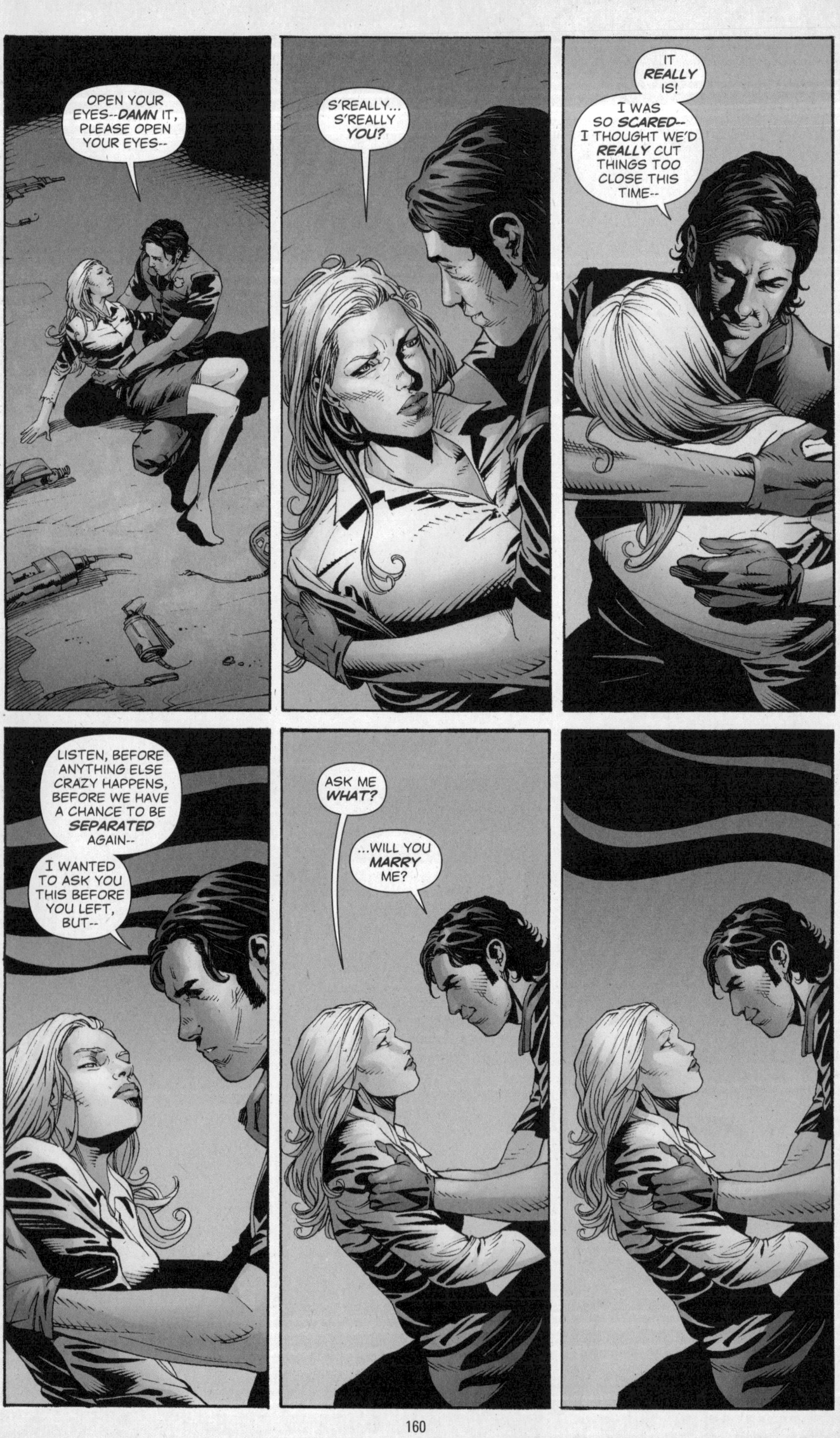
OPEN YOUR EYES--DAMN IT, PLEASE OPEN YOUR EYES--
S'REALLY... S'REALLY YOU?
IT REALLY IS!
I WAS SO SCARED-- I THOUGHT WE'D REALLY CUT THINGS TOO CLOSE THIS TIME--
LISTEN, BEFORE ANYTHING ELSE CRAZY HAPPENS, BEFORE WE HAVE A CHANCE TO BE SEPARATED AGAIN--
I WANTED TO ASK YOU THIS BEFORE YOU LEFT, BUT--
ASK ME WHAT?
...WILL YOU MARRY ME?

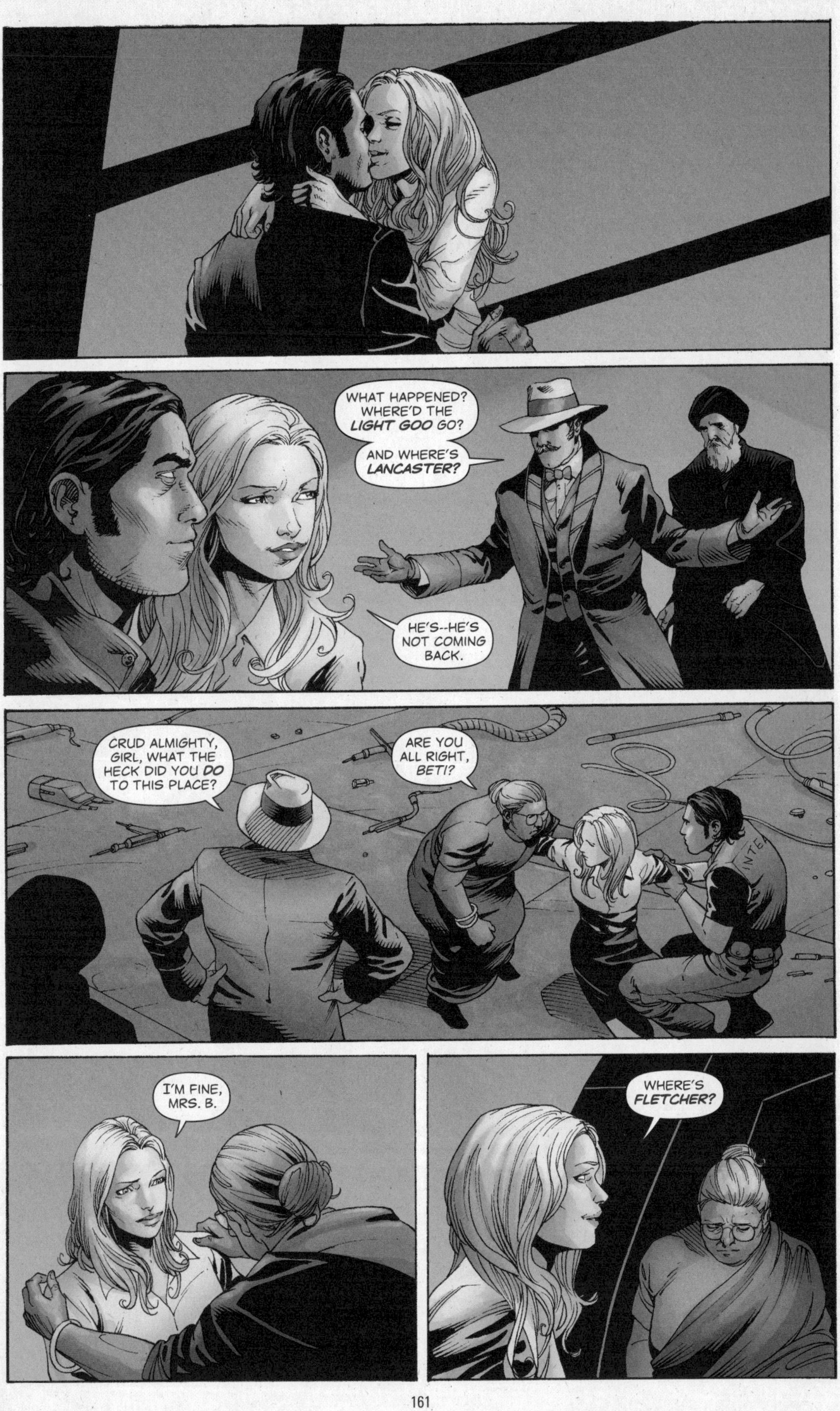
WHAT HAPPENED? WHERE'D THE LIGHT GOO GO?
AND WHERE'S LANCASTER?
HE'S--HE'S NOT COMING BACK.
CRUD ALMIGHTY, GIRL, WHAT THE HECK DID YOU DO TO THIS PLACE?
ARE YOU ALL RIGHT, BETI?
I'M FINE, MRS. B.
WHERE'S FLETCHER?

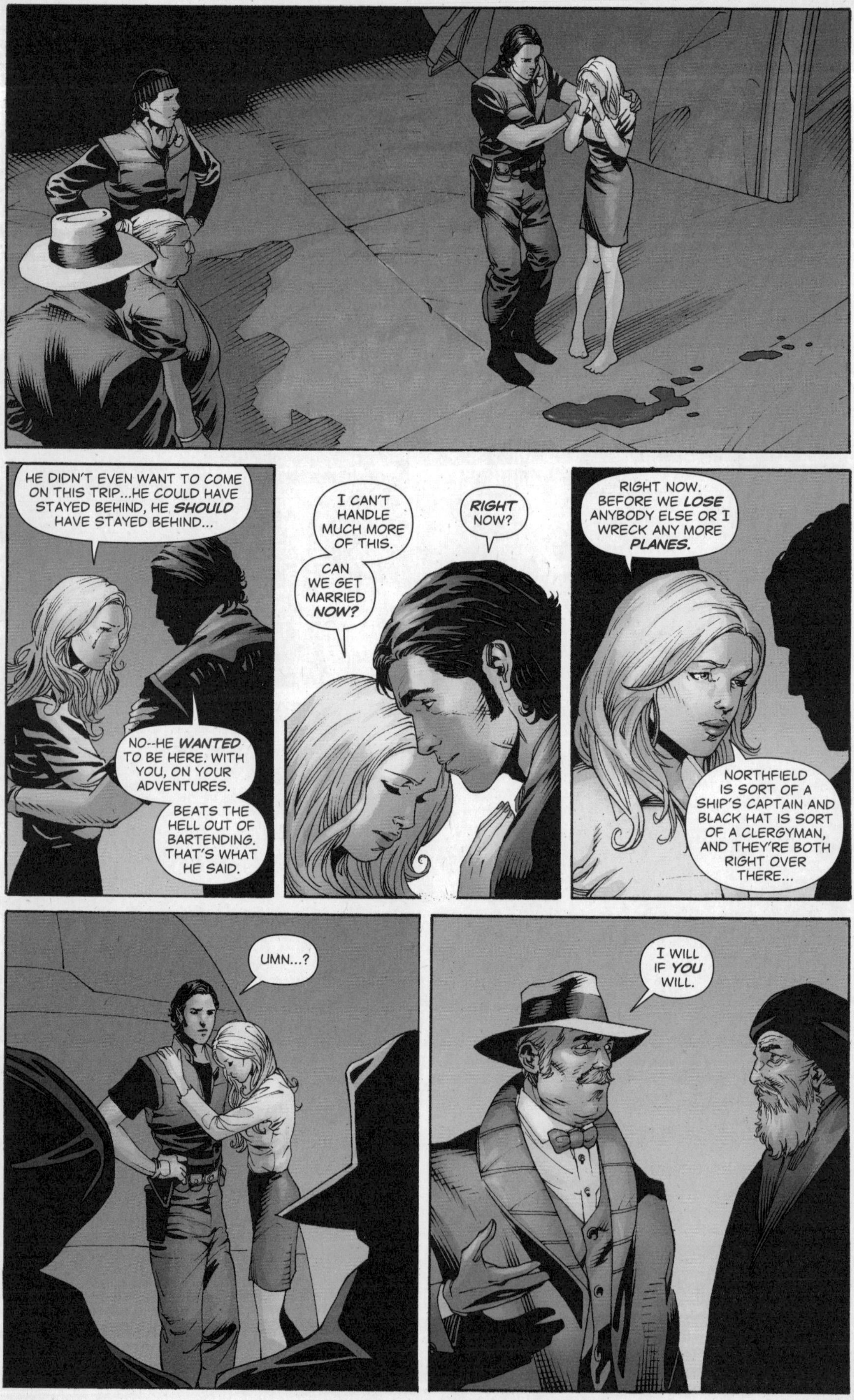
HE DIDN'T EVEN WANT TO COME ON THIS TRIP...HE COULD HAVE STAYED BEHIND, HE SHOULD HAVE STAYED BEHIND...
NO--HE WANTED TO BE HERE. WITH YOU, ON YOUR ADVENTURES.
BEATS THE HELL OUT OF BARTENDING. THAT'S WHAT HE SAID.
I CAN'T HANDLE MUCH MORE OF THIS.
CAN WE GET MARRIED NOW?
RIGHT NOW?
RIGHT NOW. BEFORE WE LOSE ANYBODY ELSE OR I WRECK ANY MORE PLANES.
NORTHFIELD IS SORT OF A SHIP'S CAPTAIN AND BLACK HAT IS SORT OF A CLERGYMAN, AND THEY'RE BOTH RIGHT OVER THERE...
UMN...?
I WILL IF YOU WILL.

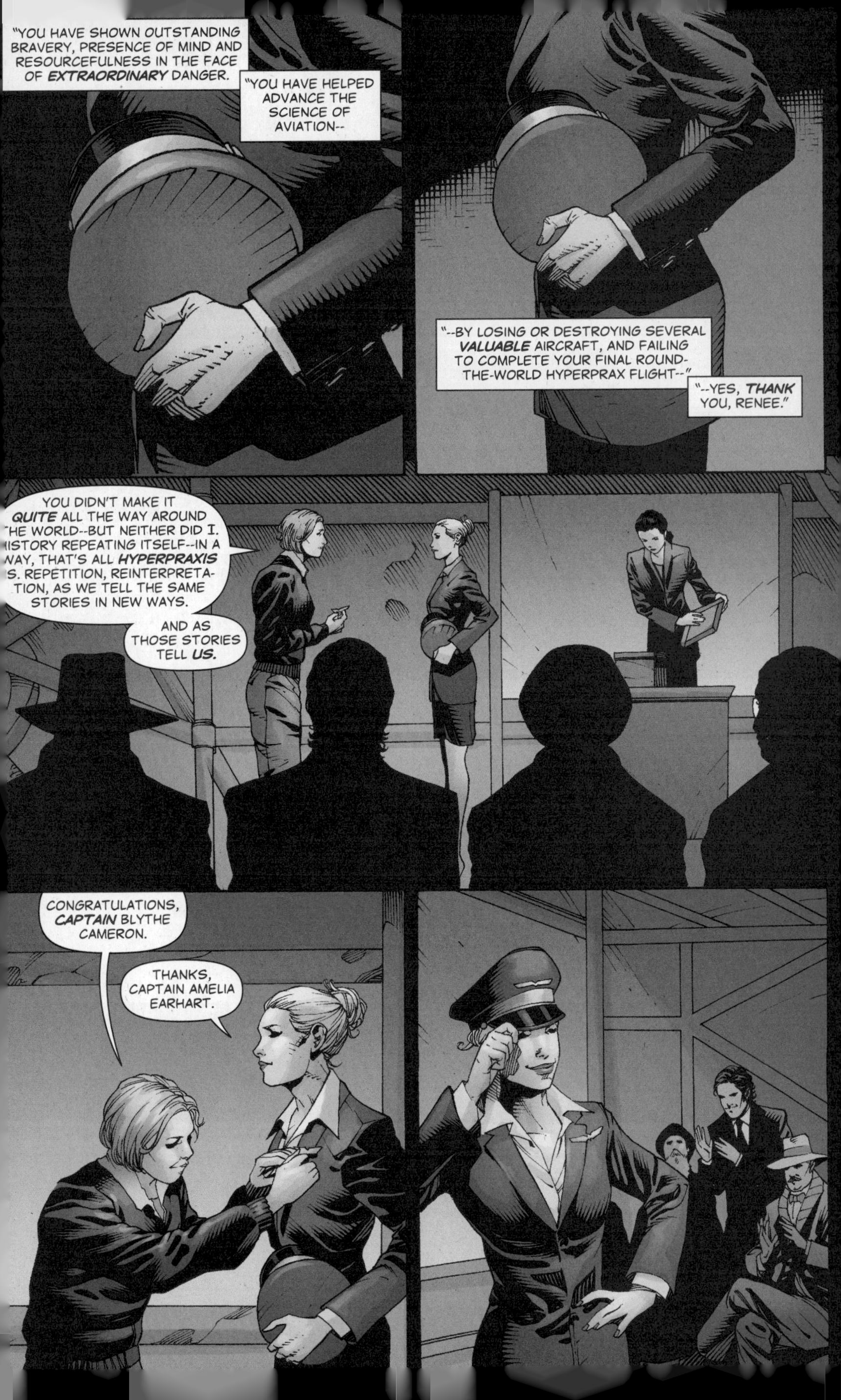
"YOU HAVE SHOWN OUTSTANDING BRAVERY, PRESENCE OF MIND AND RESOURCEFULNESS IN THE FACE OF EXTRAORDINARY DANGER.
"YOU HAVE HELPED ADVANCE THE SCIENCE OF AVIATION--
"--BY LOSING OR DESTROYING SEVERAL VALUABLE AIRCRAFT, AND FAILING TO COMPLETE YOUR FINAL ROUND-THE-WORLD HYPERPRAX FLIGHT--"
"--YES, THANK YOU, RENEE."
YOU DIDN'T MAKE IT QUITE ALL THE WAY AROUND THE WORLD--BUT NEITHER DID I. HISTORY REPEATING ITSELF--IN A WAY, THAT'S ALL HYPERPRAXIS IS. REPETITION, REINTERPRETATION, AS WE TELL THE SAME STORIES IN NEW WAYS.
AND AS THOSE STORIES TELL US.
CONGRATULATIONS, CAPTAIN BLYTHE CAMERON.
THANKS, CAPTAIN AMELIA EARHART.

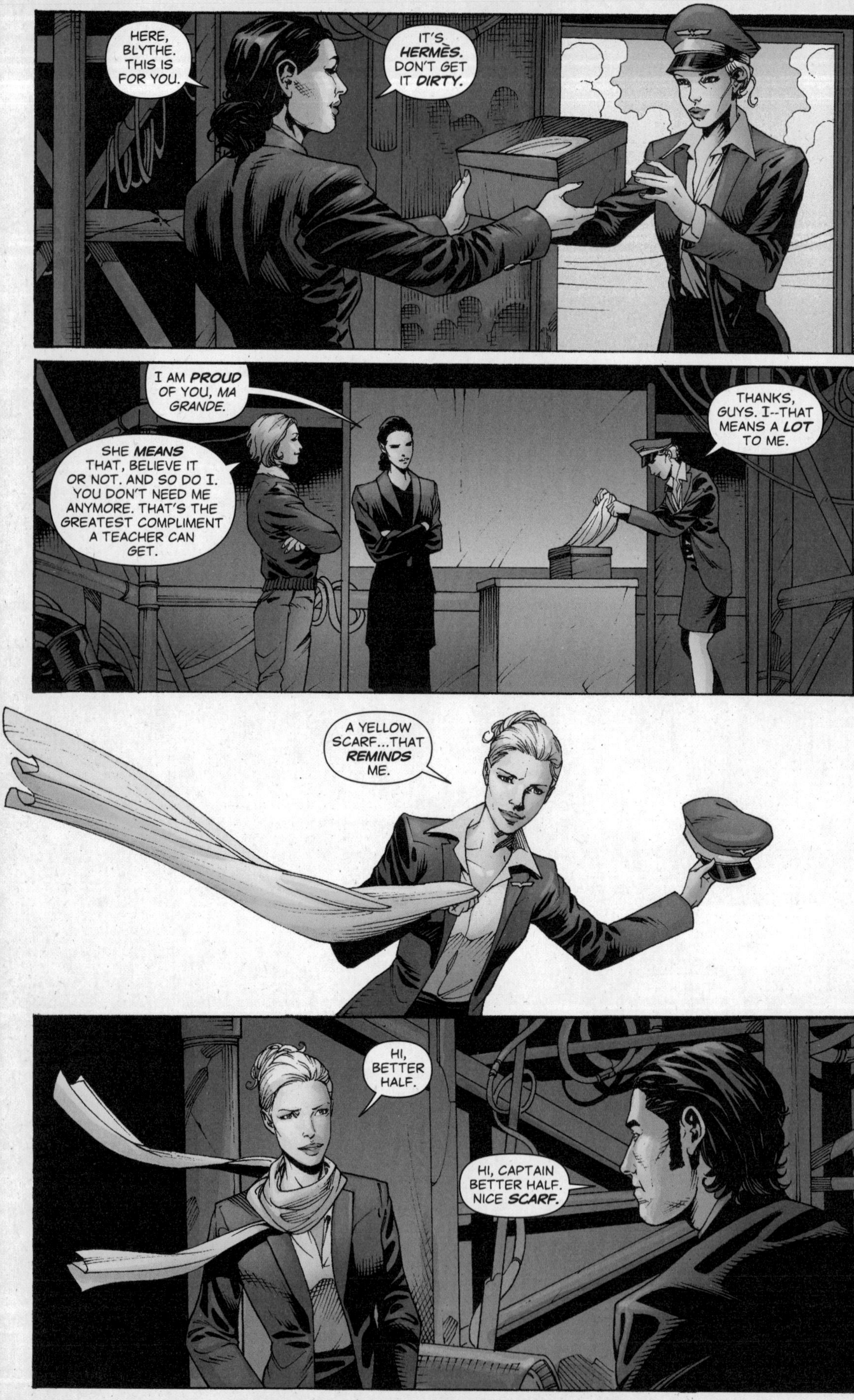
HERE, BLYTHE. THIS IS FOR YOU.
IT'S HERMÈS. DON'T GET IT DIRTY.
I AM PROUD OF YOU, MA GRANDE.
SHE MEANS THAT, BELIEVE IT OR NOT. AND SO DO I. YOU DON'T NEED ME ANYMORE. THAT'S THE GREATEST COMPLIMENT A TEACHER CAN GET.
THANKS, GUYS. I--THAT MEANS A LOT TO ME.
A YELLOW SCARF...THAT REMINDS ME.
HI, BETTER HALF.
HI, CAPTAIN BETTER HALF. NICE SCARF.

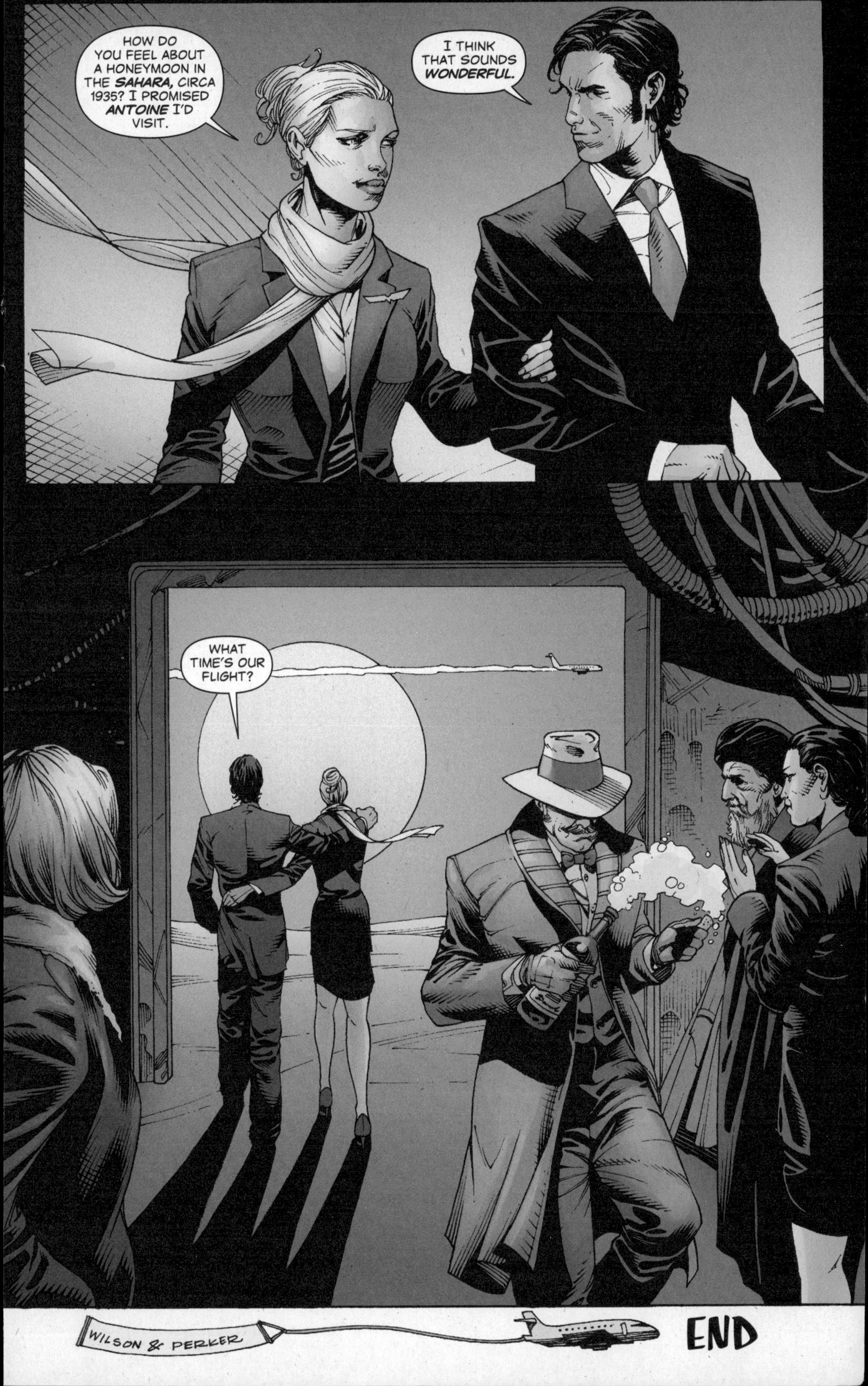
HOW DO YOU FEEL ABOUT A HONEYMOON IN THE SAHARA, CIRCA 1935? I PROMISED ANTOINE I'D VISIT.
I THINK THAT SOUNDS WONDERFUL.
WHAT TIME'S OUR FLIGHT?
WILSON & PERKER
END

air

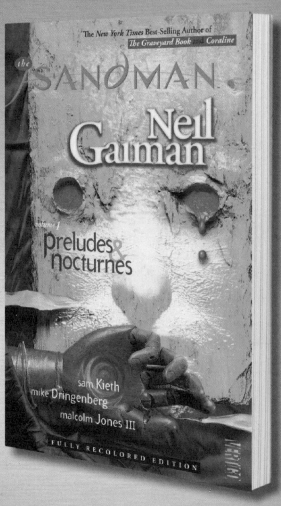
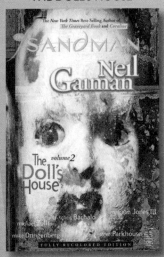
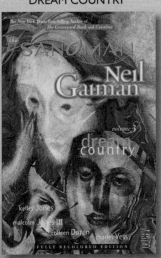
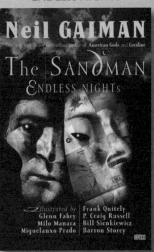